To David
on his 9..
from Hall
29th April 1997.

BELFAST MERCHANT FAMILIES IN
THE SEVENTEENTH CENTURY

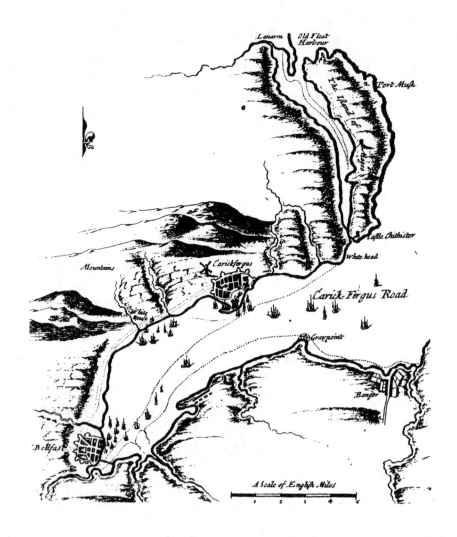

Belfast Lough in 1689

Belfast Merchant Families in the Seventeenth Century

Jean Agnew

FOUR COURTS PRESS

Set on 10.5 on 12 point Ehrhardt by
Verbatim Typesetting & Design for
FOUR COURTS PRESS
Kill Lane, Blackrock, Co. Dublin, Ireland
and in North America for
FOUR COURTS PRESS
c/o ISBS, 5804 N.E. Hassalo Street,
Portland, OR 97213.

A catalogue record for this title
is available from the British Library.

ISBN 1-85182-251-8

This book is printed on acid-free paper.

Printed in Ireland
by βetaprint Ltd, Dublin.

For Kenneth and Giles

Preface

This book is based on a doctoral thesis completed in 1994. It has been published with the help of grants from the Belfast Natural History and Philosophical Society and the late Miss Isobel Thornley's Bequest to the University of London, to both of which bodies I am deeply grateful.

I owe particular thanks to my supervisor, Dr Mary O'Dowd, for her guidance and encouragement, and to my examiners, Dr David Hayton and Dr David Dickson, for much good advice on turning my thesis into a book.

I wish to express my gratitude to the staff of the following institutions who have helped me when I visited them, answered my many queries, or made exhaustive searches in their indexes in response to my letters:

Amsterdam Municipal Archive; Antwerp Municipal Archive; Belfast Central Library; British Library; Carrickfergus Borough Council; Chapter House, Derry; Clwyd Record Office (Ruthin Branch); Corporation of London Records Office; Court of the Lord Lyon, Edinburgh; Cumbria Record Office, Carlisle; Dr Williams's Library, London; Dublin Corporation Archives; Genealogical Office, Dublin; General Register Office for Scotland; Guildhall Library, London; Historical Manuscripts Commission; History of the Irish Parliament, Belfast; Honourable Society of the Inner Temple, London; Honourable Society of the Middle Temple, London; Lancashire Record Office; Linen Hall Library, Belfast; Liverpool Record Office; Manx Museum; Maritime Records Centre, Merseyside; Mitchell Library, Glasgow; National Archives, Dublin; National Library of Ireland; National Library of Scotland; National Maritime Museum; National Trust; Orkney Archives; Presbyterian Historical Society, Belfast; Public Record Office, London; Public Record Office of Northern Ireland; Rotterdam Municipal Archive; Scottish Record Office; Society of Friends' Libraries, Dublin and London; Strathclyde Regional Archives; Suffolk Record Office (Ipswich Branch); Queen's University Library, Belfast; Trinity College, Dublin; Ulster Museum, Belfast; Union Theological College, Belfast; and Whitehaven Museum.

I am also grateful to the following individuals who have, variously, answered my queries, suggested new avenues of research, and generously shar-

ed the results of their own research with me: Sonia Anderson, Elizabeth
Danbury, Peter Francis, Raymond Gillespie, Robert Heslip, Phil Kilroy,
Richard Leathes, Rolf Loeber, George Macartney, Bill Maguire, Henry
Roseveare, Sheela Speers and Julian Walton.

Finally, I wish to thank my friends, who have listened patiently, my
son, who has cheerfully solved many computing problems, and my husband, whose constant support and encouragement have been the most cru-
cial part of the entire undertaking.

J.H.A.

Contents

Illustrations

Frontispiece: Belfast Lough in 1689 (from George Story, *A continuation of the impartial history of the wars of Ireland* [London, 1693]; photograph reproduced with the kind permission of the Trustees of the Ulster Museum, Belfast)

CHARTS AND TABLES

Abbreviations

Anal. Hib.	*Analecta Hibernica*
Benn	George Benn, *A history of the town of Belfast* (2 vols, Belfast, 1877).
B.L.	British Library
B.N.L.	*Belfast Newsletter*
Bodl.	Bodleian Library, Oxford
Butle	Out-letter book of David Butle, 1696–1703 (P.R.O.N.I., Lenox-Conyngham papers, D1449/13/1).
Cal. S.P. col.	*Calendar of state papers, colonial series*
Cal. S.P. dom.	*Calendar of state papers, domestic series*
Cal. S.P. Ire.	*Calendar of the state papers relating to Ireland*
Coleraine minutes	Copy minutes of Coleraine corporation, 1672–1710 (P.R.O.N.I., T3380/1)
Commons' jn. Ire.	*Journals of the house of commons of the kingdom of Ireland* (Dublin, 1763)
D.N.B.	*Dictionary of National Biography*
Donegall minority accounts	Accounts of income and expenditure during the minority of the fourth earl of Donegall, 1706–15 (P.R.O., C107/16).
Econ. Hist. Rev.	*Economic History Review*
E.H.R.	*English Historical Review*
Geneal. Office	Genealogical Office, Dublin
Gen. synod Ulster rec.	*Records of the general synod of Ulster from 1691 to 1820* (vol. i, Belfast, 1890).
G.R.O.S.	General Register Office for Scotland
Hastings MSS	*Report on the manuscripts of the late Reginald Rawdon Hastings, esq.* (4 vols, H.M.C., London, 1930–37).
H.M.C.	Historical Manuscripts Commission
I.E.S.H	*Irish Economic and Social History*
I.H.S.	*Irish Historical Studies*

I.M.C.	Irish Manuscripts Commission
Kirkpatrick	James Kirkpatrick, *An historical essay upon the loyalty of presbyterians in Great Britain and Ireland from the reformation to this present year* (Belfast, 1713).
Londonderry minutes	Copy minutes of Londonderry corporation (P.R.O.N.I., MIC440/1)
Lords' jn. Ire.	*Journals of the Irish house of lords* (Dublin, 1783).
L.H.L.	Linen Hall Library, Belfast
Macartney 1	Out-letter book of George Macartney, 1661–68 (L.H.L.)
Macartney 2	Out-letter book of George Macartney, 1679–81 (L.H.L.)
Macartney 3	Out-letter book of Isaac Macartney, 1704–06 (P.R.O.N.I., D501)
N.A.	National Archives, Dublin
N.L.I.	National Library of Ireland
O.P.R.	Old Parish Register (Scotland)
Ormonde MSS	*Calendar of the manuscripts of the marquess of Ormonde, preserved at Kilkenny Castle*
P.R.O.	Public Record Office
P.R.O.N.I.	Public Record Office of Northern Ireland
R.I.A. Proc.	*Proceedings of the Royal Irish Academy*
Scottish Hist. Rev.	*Scottish Historical Review*
S.R.O.	Scottish Record Office
T.C.D.	Trinity College, Dublin
Tisdall	William Tisdall, *Conduct of the dissenters of Ireland with respect to both church and state* (Dublin, 1712).
Town book	R.M. Young (ed.), *The town book of the corporation of Belfast, 1613–1816* (Belfast, 1892).
U.J.A.	*Ulster Journal of Archaeology*

Notes on Dates, Spelling and Quotations

Until 1752, the new year began officially on 25 March in England. Where documents are dated between 1 January and 24 March, their year has been modernised in the text, but they are cited with both years in footnote references, i.e. 1 January 1677/8. The new year began on 1 January in Scotland so Scottish documents are not affected. R.M. Young, who edited the Belfast town book, assumed mistakenly that it followed Scottish practice and printed the dates as they were written, occasionally re-arranging items which he thought appeared out of sequence. Such dates have been modernised in this book.

Quotations from the letter books of George Macartney appear by kind permission of the Linen Hall Library; those from the letter books of both Isaac Macartney and David Butle appear by kind permission of the Deputy Keeper of Records in Northern Ireland and the National Trust.

In quotations from manuscript sources, spelling has been modernised and, where the text is not readily comprehensible, a minimum of punctuation has been added. The name McCartney was first spelt 'Macartney' by Justice James Macartney because it was mis-spelt in a patent. This form was adopted by Justice Macartney's brothers and their descendants, and by the descendants of Black George McCartney. For the sake of consistency however, the modern form has been used throughout this book.

Introduction

The merchant community of seventeenth-century Belfast was small. Although the Belfast freemen's roll of 1636–82 describes 255 individuals as merchants, this term was used loosely and included dealers and retailers.[1] Only a minority of merchants were involved in overseas trade and there were probably no more than fifty such merchants in Belfast at any one time until the 1690s. Much of this book is based on a study of thirty-two merchant families comprising just over 20% of the surnames of all merchants in the Belfast freemen's roll up to 1682, and at least 50% of the overseas trading community for most of the seventeenth century. Profiles of these families have been assembled, like jigsaws, from a wide range of manuscript and printed sources, and they contain details of each family's place of origin, religion, property and social background, the careers of individual members, their trading activities, their marriage alliances and kinship links with other families. These profiles appear in appendix A.

The thirty-two families are representative of the merchant community as a whole. At least twenty-two were of Scottish origin, including direct immigrants from Scotland and descendants of Scottish families already settled in Ulster. Four families (Leathes, Theaker, Thetford, Waring) were of English origin, one was Old English[2] (Dobbin), and one was from the Low Countries (Thompson). Ten families in the group arrived in Belfast before 1641, eight between 1641 and 1660, and fourteen after the restoration. Four of those arriving before 1641 were Scots, as were all who arrived in the period 1641–60. Some Scots were members of the Church of Ireland and several families included both presbyterians and conformists. The thirty-

1 Freemen's roll printed in R.M. Young, *The town book of the corporation of Belfast* (Belfast, 1892), pp 246–86, hereafter cited as *Town book*; Sir George Rawdon to Lord Conway, 30 Aug. 1680, 'Cornet Rogers, our chief burgess, has bred his son a young merchant, as we call shopkeepers here' (P.R.O., SP.63/339, no.128); earl of Orrery to earl of Essex, 4 June 1672, 'For ye Generality of ye Irish are not very Critticall in their words, but who ever is a Shop-keeper is amongst most of them a Merchant' (*Essex papers 1672–79*, ed. Osmund Airy [vol. i, London, 1890], p.7).

2 That is, descended from an English family which had settled in Ireland in the middle ages.

two families are predominantly Scottish and presbyterian, and thus typical
of the community as a whole, but they also include families from every
identifiable group in seventeenth-century Belfast, categorized by place of
origin, time of immigration and religion.

It has not been possible to represent all the different social and economic strata within the merchant community because families are usually
documented in direct proportion to their economic and social achievements,
and those who remained in the lowest stratum seldom left records. There
is, however, considerable variety among the thirty-two families in the
group. They include the leading families in the community (Anderson,
Chalmers, Eccles, Knox, Macartney, and Smith), but also a number of
families whose success and status were more modest (Biggar, Clugston,
Nevin and Thompson), and only eighteen of the families served on the corporation. However, it has been impossible to reconstruct the history of a
consistently unsuccessful family, so families which actually failed in trade
are not represented, although a few spectacular failures of individual merchants are noted in chapter 6. Since the trade of Belfast expanded to a
remarkable extent in the second half of the seventeenth century, it can be
assumed that the majority of Belfast merchants were successful, even
though the degree of success was variable. The group can therefore be
taken to be representative of the merchant community as a whole, with a
bias towards wealth and success.

The profiles of these thirty-two families have been used to illustrate the
growth of the town and to identify different categories of settlers throughout the century. They provide the raw material for an analysis of the social
and economic composition of the merchant community. They throw light
on the religious division within the town and on corporation politics, and
make it possible to take a fresh look at the crises of 1688–89 and 1704–07.
Finally, they have been used to document the growth of a network of
Belfast merchants at other trading centres.

In addition, a series of merchant letter books provides an abundance of
information, which is unique in Ireland, about the trading methods and
contacts of the Belfast merchant community. The two out-letter books of
George Macartney, 1661–68, and 1679–81,[3] are well known to economic
historians and have been widely used to illustrate economic trends, but a
similar out-letter book of Isaac Macartney, covering the years 1704–06,[4] has
been surprisingly little used. The first two Macartney letter books were
previously thought to have been written by George Macartney of Auchinleck, ancestor of Earl Macartney. However, internal evidence[5] identifies

---

3 Out-letter books of George Macartney, 1661–68, 1679–81 (L.H.L.), hereafter cited
   as Macartney 1 and 2.
4 Out-letter book of Isaac Macartney, 1704–06 (P.R.O.N.I., D501), hereafter cited as
   Macartney 3.
5 See appendix C.

their author as 'Black' George Macartney, the father of Isaac Macartney, which makes it possible to study the trade and business methods of a Belfast merchant family over a period of forty-five years. In addition, these letter books illustrate the pattern of trade from Belfast, merchant life, business practice and commercial morality and document the daily life of the Belfast merchant families.

Belfast: The Growth of the Town and the Community

THE REASONS FOR GROWTH

The rapid growth and prosperity of Belfast in the second half of the seventeenth century was a phenomenon that impressed and excited contemporaries. Claims that Belfast was the second port in Ireland by the end of the century were exaggerated,[1] but the fact that such claims were made at all is a measure of the town's achievement. The rapid growth of a port is a sure indication of the existence of a stable and prosperous merchant community; indeed, the growth of Belfast is largely a reflection of the growth of the community. The origins and increase of this community cannot be studied without first outlining the history of the town and identifying the factors which encouraged merchants to settle there.

Belfast had become a centre for the provisions trade by the 1630s but the history of the town before that date is poorly documented and obscure. It was one of forty towns which received charters in 1613 in order to create protestant members of parliament to sit in the Irish house of commons. Most of the body of twelve burgesses named in the charter of 1613 were local gentry who were unlikely to have been resident in the town.[2] After the deaths of the original burgesses the elections of their replacements were not noted in the town book so it is not possible to compile another full list of burgesses until 1639, or even to list the sovereigns (as the mayors were called) before 1630. Hardly any bye-laws were entered before 1633 and there was no roll of freemen until 1636. The impression given by the town book is that Belfast barely existed before the 1630s and that trade there was small in volume.

The slow growth of the Ulster ports in the early seventeenth century was the result of underpopulation of the countryside and poor inland com-

---

1 William Sacheverall, *An account of the Isle of Man ... with a voyage to I Columb-Kill* (London, 1702), p.125; George Benn, *A history of the town of Belfast* (2 vols, Belfast, 1877), p.327, hereafter cited as Benn; L.M. Cullen, *An economic history of Ireland since 1660* (London, 1972), p.25.
2 *Town book*, p.174.

munications. The agricultural surpluses produced were small and it was difficult to get them to market. In addition, Belfast suffered both from a lack of investment and a lack of revenue, particularly when compared with Londonderry and Coleraine which were generously funded and endowed by the London companies.[3] The town of Belfast was part of the great estate granted to Sir Arthur Chichester, ancestor of the earls of Donegall, but after the initial outlay on building materials the encouragement given to the town by the Chichester family was in the form of favourable leases for settlers rather than cash investment. Indeed, investment on the scale that was needed was beyond most landowners in Ireland at this date. Although the earl of Cork was able to put £14,000 into the development of Bandon, the Chichesters were never in possession of any sizeable financial surplus from their estates.[4]

As immigration from Scotland and England increased both the labour force and the proportion of productive land in Ulster, a rapid rise in the number of inland fairs and markets, coupled with gradual improvements in communications, made this produce easier to market. However, the effect of a series of poor harvests was compounded by political difficulties in Ulster in the late 1630s, leading to a drop in trade. The impact of the wars of the 1640s seems to have been particularly serious in Ulster but the consequences for Belfast are harder to guage. On the one hand, Patrick Adair, the presbyterian minister of Belfast who settled in Ulster in 1646, wrote that much of the country was wholly desolate in 1642 (although the towns of Belfast, Carrickfergus, Lisnegarvey [Lisburn] and Antrim were 'preserved'), and the town book gives an impression of a discouraged and heavily taxed community in Belfast in 1651.[5] On the other hand, a description of the town at the end of the 1640s hardly suggests that trade was at a standstill for long:

> When Carrickfergus was constituted a port in this kingdom there was hardly a house in Belfast except Lord Chichester's castle. Afterwards his lordship coming there to live, several British families did come to settle, upon which, for the good of the English interest his lordship did prevail with James of blessed memory who gave it a charter. It had few or no mer-

---

3 Estimates of the cost of founding these two towns together were in the region of £50,000 (T.H. Mullin, *Coleraine in by-gone centuries* [Belfast, 1976], pp 28, 31).
4 Raymond Gillespie, *The transformation of the Irish economy, 1550–1700* (Dublin, 1991), pp 37–8; R.A. Butlin, 'Irish towns in the sixteenth and seventeenth centuries' in R.A. Butlin (ed.), *The development of the Irish town* (London and New Jersey, 1977), p.82; Peter Roebuck, 'The Donegall family and the development of Belfast, 1600–1850' in Paul Butel and L.M. Cullen (ed.), *Cities and merchants: French and Irish perspectives on urban development, 1500–1900* (Dublin, 1986), p.128.
5 Patrick Adair, *A true narrative of the rise and progress of the presbyterian church in Ireland*, ed. W.D. Killen (Belfast, 1866), p.90, hereafter cited as Adair, *Narrative; Town book*, pp 62–3.

chants trading beyond the seas. Now by the encouragement of the earl of
Donegall ... and the industry with God's blessing, upon the endeavours of
the merchants ... the trade imported and exported at Belfast is at least
seven-eighths part of the whole customs and excise that are taken at the
port of Carrickfergus.[6]

By the end of the 1630s, Scots and English had settled in roughly equal
numbers in Belfast. However, the majority of the leading merchant families
in the latter half of the seventeenth century were descended from immigrants who settled in Belfast in the 1650s and early 1660s, most of whom
came directly from Scotland. In the 1650s, therefore, Belfast must have
appeared sufficiently thriving to attract new settlers or at least to have had
obvious potential as a centre for trade. In particular, there was clearly
money to be made in provisioning the army, and times of scarcity are generally times of opportunity for entrepreneurs. By the late 1650s agriculture
in Ulster had recovered and the volume of exports rose above preceding
levels.

As Belfast grew, the nearby port of Carrickfergus was declining. Indeed
the growth of the former was at the expense of the latter. In the late sixteenth and early seventeenth centuries Carrickfergus had been the leading
town in Ulster, and such places as Newry and Enniskillen were little more
than military outposts. Carrickfergus was both a military stronghold, the
seat of the lord deputy of Ireland, and a centre of 'Englishness' in what
was the most 'Irish' province in Ireland. Counties Antrim and Down were
not part of the official plantation of Ulster but immigrants from Scotland
and England arrived there from the end of the sixteenth century, and by
1641 east Ulster was becoming the most stable area of Ireland outside the
Pale. There continued to be a garrison at Carrickfergus but Belfast was not
even fortified. Belfast Castle had been re-built as a dwelling house by Sir
Arthur Chichester and the town had no walls. In 1642 an earth 'rampier'
was hastily thrown up but its effectiveness as a defence was never put to
the test.

Carrickfergus was a county corporate, distinct from the County of
Antrim, and remained the administrative centre for the southern part of the
county, and the location of the assizes. These activities provided a considerable local market for food and drink but overseas trade declined. Richard
Dobbs, several times mayor and a local landowner, wrote in 1683 that the
town's greatest trade was then in taverns and alehouses, and he attributed
the decline of the port to the loss of the revenue from the customs.[7] The

6 Petition for removal of customhouse to Belfast, n.d. [but post–1647] (*Cal. S.P. Ire.,
  1647–60*, p.336); in 1651, County Antrim, which included Belfast, was charged with
  a larger monthly assessment to maintain the army than any other Ulster county
  (Benn, p.152).
7 Richard Dobbs's account of County Antrim, 1683 (P.R.O.N.I., Dobbs papers,

town had enjoyed a third part of the customs received there, with the exception of the customs of Olderfleet (Larne), Bangor and Belfast. This brought in an annual income of about £300 which had been surrendered to the crown in 1637 in return for the sum of £3,000 which was to be used for the purchase of lands for the corporation. Although this loss of revenue may well have contributed to the decline of the town (and the compensatory sum was mishandled and never brought in any revenue to the corporation), this is not in itself sufficient to account for this decline, particularly since the corporation of Belfast never had any significant revenue from any source. Other explanations, therefore, must be sought for the reduction in the trade of Carrickfergus and the prosperity of Belfast.

Carrickfergus was originally built as a military stronghold on Belfast Lough. It stands on a narrow coastal strip backed by mountains. Belfast was better situated to receive the agricultural produce of the Lagan valley. Its position at the lowest fordable point of the river Lagan at the head of Belfast Lough had been recognised as 'a place meet for a corporate town, armed with all commodities' as early as 1573, although the motives of the earl of Essex who recommended it were political rather than mercantile.[8] Although the lough itself was easy of access, neither Belfast nor Carrickfergus had a good harbour. Few Irish ports, however, had that advantage; even shipping for Dublin had to cross the sandbar at Ringsend. The oldest part of Belfast town was built on a narrow strip of sandy land between the mouths of the Farset and Owynvarra rivers, small tributaries of the Lagan, which itself dwindled to a stream at low tide. The mouth of the Farset was deep enough to provide a dock for small ships but larger vessels had to lie three miles away in the pool of Garmoyle and be unloaded by gabarts which brought their cargoes up to the town quay, on the Farset, at high tide.[9]

As Belfast prospered and Carrickfergus declined, two more factors made the former pre-eminent among the ports of Ulster and thus attractive to merchants. The first was the town's position as the nearest of the major Ulster ports to Dublin. In the middle of the seventeenth century the provisions trade was dominated by Dublin merchants who employed the Ulster merchants as factors, so the relative ease of communication with Dublin, both by land and sea, gave Belfast an advantage over Londonderry and Coleraine. The second factor was that from the time of the navigation acts the port's closeness to the English mainland became additionally important.

D162/6), printed in George Hill, *An historical account of the Macdonnells of Antrim* (Belfast, 1873), pp 387–9.

8 *Calendar of the Carew manuscripts preserved in the archiepiscopal library at Lambeth, 1515–1624* (6 vols, London, 1867–73), 1st series, p.448.

9 There was eight or nine feet of water at 'full sea' (John Dubourdieu, *Statistical survey of the county of Antrim* [Dublin, 1812], p.501); Molyneux's account of his journey to the north (T.C.D., MS 883/2, ff 136–8).

As incoming cargoes from the colonies had to be entered and unloaded in England, generally at Bristol or Liverpool, far less time was wasted by Belfast ships than those from the ports of the north coast where all the advantage of being able to sail 'northabout' direct to the colonies was lost on the return journey.

Other factors combined to make Belfast particularly attractive to settlers. The first of these is implicit in the terms of the charter of 1613 which instituted an extremely narrow form of town government. The ancient Irish towns had enjoyed a considerable measure of self-government and although loyal to the crown had not been co-operative when their rights and privileges were in question.[10] The new towns which received borough status in 1613 (some of which were little more than settlements) were intended to elect protestant members of parliament, and to ensure that they continued to do so they were given small corporations which made them easy to control. Their charters named a small body of burgesses, generally not more than twelve or fourteen, and only they, and the mayor, provost or sovereign, could vote in parliamentary elections. In fact it was not just boroughs that were created in 1613, but pocket boroughs.

In many of the older ports of Ireland, the body of freemen had some share in municipal affairs; in Dublin they voted in both municipal and parliamentary elections, in Carrickfergus they took part in the election of the mayor.[11] In Belfast, a preponderance of non-resident burgesses in the mid-1630s led to the formation of an unofficial body known as the 'grand jury representative of the commonalty', which included freemen, to deal with day-to-day problems in the town, but this experiment seems to have been short-lived.[12] The Belfast freemen petitioned, unsuccessfully, in 1644 for the right to vote in the election of burgesses, claiming that this had been granted them in the charter of 1613, and also that the burgesses should be residents of the town, freemen, and have taken the covenant.[13] The 1613 charter was in fact imprecise about election procedure, but it certainly did not give voting rights to freemen, and like most corporations that of Belfast was self-perpetuating. After the 1640s, the freemen of Belfast played little part in the running of the town, apart from some say in the assessing and collecting of local rates. The fact that they had so little influence on municipal affairs meant that there was no reason to limit their numbers. In

---

10 Anthony Sheehan, 'Irish towns in a period of change 1558–1625' in Ciaran Brady and Raymond Gillespie (ed.), *Natives and newcomers, essays on the making of Irish colonial society, 1534–1641* (Dublin, 1986), pp 113–14.

11 Samuel M'Skimin, *The history and antiquities of the town of Carrickfergus* (3rd edn, Belfast, 1832), p.183.

12 *Town Book*, p.178; Raymond Gillespie, *Colonial Ulster, the settlement of east Ulster 1600–41* (Cork, 1985), pp 185–6.

13 *Examination of Thomas Theaker*, 16 July 1644 (T.C.D., MS 838, ff 7–8).

Carrickfergus, Coleraine and Londonderry, the admission of freemen was strictly controlled, being limited to sons of freemen, to those who had served an apprenticeship with a freeman, or had married a freeman's daughter, and to a few who were admitted 'by special grace', the latter paying a fine on admission. All three towns made enactments against non-resident freemen at various dates, which suggests that this was seen as an undesirable development, and that they were resisting pressure to accept them.

By contrast, Belfast appears to have been ready to admit all comers. A bye-law of 1666 refers to the number of free commoners 'dayly increasing rather to the hurt and detriment of this Corporacon than to the creditt or advantage thereof' but deals rather with the better collection of fines on admission than with any change of policy. Between 1636 and the beginning of 1682 no less than 1,225 freemen were admitted, about 14% of whom were non-resident. The freedom of the town was frequently granted to local gentry and to army officers commanding troops in the vicinity. Twelve per cent of the total admissions were of this kind and, from the evidence of the hearth money roll of 1669, the majority of these were non-resident. They may be considered as 'honorary' freemen (although this term was not used) because they paid no fee on admission and derived no financial advantage from their freedom. A bye-law of 1671 forbade non-resident freemen from claiming any reduction on the duty payable on goods brought in to the town and this may have been aimed at local gentry who sent their agricultural surpluses to market there.[14]

Merchants were normally admitted as 'merchants of the staple' rather than free commoners, although this style was an anachronism. James I had attempted to revive the staple system in Ireland in order to restrict the export of wool by confining the trade to designated towns. Belfast appears to have been named as a staple town by 1610 but the title was meaningless because there was little wool produced locally, and its export was forbidden in 1614. A new staple organisation was set up in 1616, including Carrickfergus but not Belfast.[15] The continued use of the style 'merchant of the staple' at Belfast may indicate that the staple became a kind of merchant guild. Merchants of the staple seem to have been regarded as superior to ordinary free commoners as virtually all 'honorary' freemen were made merchants of the staple. However, there is no indication in the town book of any special rights or privileges enjoyed by merchant staplers and there is no mention of any separate organisation, officials or meeting place. No reference can be found to guild organisation of any kind at Belfast

14 *Town book*, pp 105, 115, 246–8; S.T. Carleton (ed.), *Heads and hearths, the hearth money rolls and poll tax returns for Co. Antrim, 1660–69* (Belfast, 1991), p.36; Gillespie, *Colonial Ulster*, p.176.

15 George O'Brien, 'The Irish staple organization in the reign of James I' in *Economic History*, i (1926), pp 44, 55.

before the eighteenth century. Whatever guild structure existed was informal, and this lack of rigid guild organisation may have been an additional attraction for some settlers.

It was important for any merchant, artisan or retailer, who was in business on his own account, to be a freeman in order to be excused, or to pay at a lower rate, a series of customs, tolls, fines and court fees. It is probable therefore that the majority of such persons became freemen and comparison between the freemen's roll and the hearth money roll of 1669 shows that just under half of the householders in the latter can be identified as freemen and a further quarter bore the same surname as a freeman. Since the fines paid on admission were an important source of revenue for the town it is unlikely that many applicants who were able to pay the fine were turned away. As in other towns, apprentices of freemen normally received their own freedom without a fee although it was enacted in 1666 that they had to apply for their freedom within three months of completing their apprenticeship.[16] This was amazingly fast compared with practice in the royal burghs of Scotland. In Glasgow, for example, it usually took thirteen years for a merchant to become a burgess (i.e. freeman) from the start of his apprenticeship, although the sons of burgesses could qualify sooner.[17] After 1660, the Belfast freemen's roll generally lists those who qualified through apprenticeship but hereditary freemen are harder to identify. Occasionally the roll states that someone was son of a freeman, but they were not always admitted *gratis*, and there is no indication that it was ever possible to become an hereditary freeman through marriage, although this was so in Londonderry, Coleraine and Dublin. Between 1682 and 1721 no roll has survived. By the 1720s the hereditary principle had clearly become established, although judging by the reduced numbers of those listed, the commercial privileges to which freemen were entitled had become meaningless.

As far as can be ascertained, there was no property qualification for prospective freemen in the Ulster ports as there was in Scotland, but the fines payable on admission varied considerably. In 1657 the corporation of Carrickfergus fixed a fine of £10 for all who did not qualify to become freemen by birth or apprenticeship, presumably as an attempt by the Church of Ireland aldermen to discourage settlers from Scotland. The rates in Coleraine and Londonderry were variable but, in addition, new freemen normally purchased silver spoons for the corporation. By contrast, the stan-

---

16 *Town book*, p.105; in Londonderry the corporation found that masters were antedating their apprentices' indentures so that they could become freemen sooner, 23 Feb. 1676/7 (P.R.O.N.I., minutes of Londonderry corporation, MIC440/1, hereafter cited as Londonderry minutes).

17 T.C. Smout, 'The Glasgow merchant community in the seventeenth century' in *Scottish Hist. Rev.*, xlvii (1968), pp 58–60.

dard fine in Belfast after the restoration was 10s.[18] Merchants and the wealthier tradesmen paid more, but they were few in number. Only sixty of the freemen or merchant staplers admitted between 1636 and 1682 are stated to have paid 20s or more, although others whose fine is not specified may belong to this group. The highest fine was 60s paid by the merchant George Martin in 1639, followed by 50s paid by William Taylor in 1656. Even the fairly modest sum of 40s was only paid by six merchants who include Hugh Eccles, William Smith and the two George Macartneys.

All corporations administered a corporate oath to new freemen – generally to uphold and defend the constitution of the town – and a similar oath was taken by mayors, aldermen and burgesses. In addition, until 1691, the latter group was legally required in most towns to take the oath of supremacy, which effectively disbarred presbyterians from holding municipal office. The law with respect to freemen seems to have been open to different interpretations. In Coleraine, freemen were obliged to take the oath and there was considerable harassment of presbyterians who refused, although there was some relaxation in the 1680s.[19] In Londonderry, there is no trace of harassment of freemen in the corporation minutes and the few dissenters who served as aldermen or burgesses are said to have taken the oath and attended church occasionally.[20] In Belfast, where the Chichester family had strong puritan sympathies, neither freemen nor burgesses were required to take the oath. Coupled with the ease and moderate cost of becoming a freeman, this would have been a powerful factor in attracting potential settlers from Scotland.

A second factor which attracted settlers to Belfast in the 1650s and 1660s was the availability of premises and building sites. Belfast was a pocket borough controlled by one great landowner. The earl of Donegall owned the entire town and most of surrounding townlands on the County Antrim side of the river Lagan. From the evidence of the town book, Belfast was slow to develop. In 1630 rents and other revenue from the town probably only amounted to about £80 per annum, and the effect of the war years was to impoverish and discourage many of the early settlers. Not only was trade impeded in the 1640s, but the presence of a garrison made it necessary to levy rates with unprecedented frequency. Many townspeople, including some of the burgesses, may have moved away. In

---

18 Dean Dobbs's book of Carrickfergus, 19 Nov. 1657 (P.R.O.N.I., T707); the entry fine was fixed at 20s in Dublin in 1651 (J.T. Gilbert, *Calendar of ancient records of Dublin* [i–vi, Dublin and London, 1889–96], iv, p.5); £67 (about £5 sterling) was the fine fixed for unapprenticed strangers in Edinburgh in 1654 (T.C. Smout, *A history of the Scottish people*, 1560–1830 [Glasgow and London, 1970], p.159).

19 William Tisdall, *Conduct of the dissenters of Ireland with respect to both church and state* (Dublin, 1712), p.54, hereafter cited as Tisdall; copy minutes of Coleraine corporation, 17 and 24 Apr. 1673 (P.R.O.N.I., T3380/1, hereafter cited as Coleraine minutes).

20 Bishop King to bishop of Killaloe, 30 Oct. 1706 (T.C.D., MS 750/3/2/62–3).

the 1650s there were properties on prime sites available in the town, even parts of the original burgage shares which included land in the town fields, and there is every indication that Lord Donegall, who had lost control of his estates between 1644 and 1656 and was consequently heavily in debt, was happy to let them to the new wave of settlers regardless of nationality or religious denomination.[21]

In 1659 it was possible for a newcomer like George Macartney of Auchinleck to become tenant for three lives, or 99 years, of a half burgage share in Belfast High Street. In the 1660s his kinsman Black George Macartney was able to build one of the largest houses in the town, also in the High Street on the quay. Many of the Donegall leases were building leases specifying good English-like houses in brick or stone. Property for development on the outskirts of the town was leased to those with capital to invest. In the 1670s–80s, William Waring received a lease of a substantial holding, including six half burgage shares, to enable him to expand his tanning business and to erect new houses, and Macartney of Auchinleck became the tenant of four water corn mills, a tuck mill, and half the sugar refinery, and was able to grant building leases to his undertenants. Lord Donegall and his successors, whose income generally failed to meet their needs, were eager to develop the town, thereby increasing the revenue which it produced.[22]

This was in contrast to the situation in Coleraine and Londonderry. Although property was also available there, the policy of the London companies, expressed in leases from the late 1650s to the 1670s, was to forbid their tenants to sub-let to Scots, if they were recent immigrants.[23] The situation regarding property in Carrickfergus was unique, because the corporation was the sole owner of the lands of both town and county; but by the 1650s these lands had long since been divided and leased and the most important families had contrived to increase and consolidate their shares. This had resulted in the town's being controlled by an oligarchy. Most of the leading families of Carrickfergus had originated in England and were members of the established church.[24] The division of the town lands led to

21 Roebuck, 'Donegall family', p.128; *Town book*, pp 62–3, 83; Benn, p.90; Gillespie, *Colonial Ulster*, p.175; Peter Roebuck, 'Landlord indebtedness in Ulster in the seventeenth and eighteenth centuries' in J.M. Goldstrom and L.A. Clarkson (ed.), *Irish population, economy and society* (Oxford, 1981), p.142.

22 Carleton, *Heads and hearths*, p.36; Macartney to George Martin and John Viccar, Jan. 1665/6, and to Thomas Moore, 30 May 1666 (Macartney 1, pp 318, 365); memorials of leases, 1659–86 (N.A., Lodge's records of the rolls, vii, pp 429, 452, 555, viii, pp 207, 208, 219); Donegall to John Drenan, lease, 1670 (P.R.O.N.I., Donegall leases, D509/25); Macartney to Alex. Arthur, lease, 2 Mar. 1685/6 (P.R.O.N.I., Brett papers, D271/2).

23 Mullin, *Coleraine*, p.114.

24 I am indebted to Sheela Speers for much valuable information about Carrickfergus corporation and the town lands.

a decline in trading activity. In 1683, Richard Dobbs wrote that 'people for the most part are little given to industry or labour, many of them having little estates since the dividing of the Town Lands'.[25] Lack of encouragement did not actually deter Scots from settling in Coleraine, Londonderry and Carrickfergus, and all three had large Scots presbyterian populations. Nevertheless, although the proportion of Scots in these towns was high, actual numbers were small, and the relatively large influx of Scots into Belfast, leading to the rapid growth of the town's population, confirms that Belfast had the most to offer to prospective settlers.

SETTLEMENT AND POPULATION

Belfast did not exist as a town before the seventeenth century. A medieval keep was added to by Sir Arthur Chichester, but whatever dwellings had grown up around it were probably obliterated when the town was 'plotted out in a good forme' prior to 1611.[26] Certainly there is no trace in any source of an indigenous urban population. The town attracted settlers throughout the seventeenth century and these fall into four main categories. The first category is that of the earliest settlers. Although the town was said in 1611 to have been settled by English, Scots and Manxmen, only the English can be reliably documented and in the earliest corporation records it is they who predominate. The group of thirty-two merchant families contains three families of English origin (Leathes, Theaker and Thetford) which were in Belfast from the beginning of the seventeenth century. All held land in the vicinity of Belfast as well as in the town and were normally described as gentry. Their trading activities, therefore, may never have been their main source of income. The most important of these, the Leathes family, were minor gentry and yeoman farmers in Cumberland. By the 1660s there were branches of this family in Belfast, Carrickfergus, and Lisburn. No specific place of origin has been found for the Thetford and Theaker families but since both held land in the vicinity of Belfast as Donegall tenants-in-chief they may have been among the families from the West Country encouraged to settle by Sir Arthur Chichester.

The second category of immigrants consisted of Scots who had settled in Belfast by the time of the Irish rebellion in 1641. Most of those who can be identified appear to have arrived in Belfast in the early 1630s when there was a marked increase in the migration of Scots to Ulster. From 1634

25 Hill, *Macdonnells of Antrim*, p.388.
26 Transcript of part of Carew MS 630 (S. Shannon Millin, *Additional sidelights on Belfast history* [Belfast and London, 1938], pp 2–3); there must have been a tavern or alehouse there as it was possible to obtain wine from Belfast in 1603 (George Hill (ed.), *The Montgomery manuscripts 1608–1706: compiled from the family papers by William Montgomery of Rosemount esquire* [Belfast, 1869], p.21).

an Irish Act made naturalization unnecessary for Scots settling in Ireland but, judging by the few Scottish naturalizations or denizations recorded before that date, most of the Scots who arrived after the original plantation period in the early seventeenth century ignored these formalities.[27] Those who settled in Belfast included Robert Barr, Robert Nevin, the Clugstons, Lockharts and Doakes. Some like George Martin and Gilbert Eccles operated first from Lisburn or Carrickfergus and may not have settled in Belfast before the end of the decade. All appear to have belonged to merchant families in the south-west of Scotland, particularly in Ayr and Irvine, and all were presbyterians. Several fled back to Scotland in 1638 to avoid anti-presbyterian measures in Ulster, but they seem to have returned soon afterwards.[28]

The third category of immigrants arrived from Scotland in the 1650s–60s. They are distinguished from the previous group not only by date of arrival, but also because they were a far less homogenous group. Firstly, they were not all presbyterians. Three of the most notable merchants in this group (the two George Macartneys and Thomas Knox) became members of the established church. Secondly, although most were from south-west Scotland, their places of origin ranged from Glasgow to Wigtown and Kirkcudbright, and a few were from further afield. For example, strong circumstantial evidence suggests that the Pottingers were from the Orkneys.[29] Judging by their rapid success as merchants in Belfast, all had some experience, capital, and trading contacts. Many came from burgess families in the Scottish royal burghs[30] and emigrated because prospects for the trade in provisions were better in Ulster than in Scotland where agriculture was depressed by plague and civil war.[31] To this group

27 Philip S. Robinson, *The plantation of Ulster, British settlement in an Irish landscape* (Dublin, 1984), p.106; W.A. Shaw, *Letters of denization and acts of naturalization for aliens in England and Ireland 1603–1700* (Lymington, 1911), p.xxii; David Stewart, *The Scots in Ulster, their denization and naturalization, 1605–34* (2 vols, Belfast, 1952, 1954).

28 Barr and his sons-in-law were partners in the earliest Belfast iron works; Barr, Nevin and Martin were among those named by Bishop Leslie in 1638 as having 'fled to Scotland for fear of the High Commission, but have left their land behind them' (*The earl of Strafforde's letters and dispatches*, ed. William Knowler [2 vols, Dublin, 1740], ii, p.227); the property of Martin and of Robert Clugston was the subject of exchequer inquisitions in their absence in 1639 (N.A., record commissioners, RC9/1, pp 39–41).

29 Appendix A.23.

30 The Andersons, Smiths and Knoxes were burgess families of Glasgow, Macartney of Auchinleck was a burgess of Kirkcudbright and James Chalmers became, through marriage, a burgess of Edinburgh (appendix A.1, 7, 14, 18, 26); Raymond Gillespie noted that most Scots settlers in towns before 1641 can be traced back to urban backgrounds (*Colonial Ulster*, p.171).

31 This was not the case in Glasgow, the development of which parallels that of Belfast, but motives for emigration are always a combination of economic and

belong many of the most successful Belfast families such as the Macartneys, Chalmerses, Smiths, and Andersons. Belfast continued to attract immigrants from Scotland during the second half of the seventeenth century, particularly kinsmen of those already settled there, but the most notable of the settlers after the 1660s belong to the next category.

As trade in Belfast expanded, the town exerted the normal attraction of an urban centre to settlers from the surrounding countryside. The fourth and last category is composed of second or third generation immigrants, members of families already living in Ulster, most of whom moved to Belfast between the late 1670s and the early 1690s. This group includes David Butle, Edward Brice and James Stewart from County Antrim, William Sloane from County Down, and Robert Lennox from Londonderry, all of whom were from gentry or merchant families of Scottish origin.[32] However, if all second generation immigrants are to be considered as part of this group, it must also include Thomas Waring, who was of English origin and a member of the established church, who settled in Belfast in the early 1640s, operating first as a tanner, and then as a merchant and shipowner.[33] Moreover, a number of Carrickfergus merchants are said to have transferred their operations to Belfast as their own town declined.[34] It is not possible to identify this group from the freemen's roll as so many freemen were non-resident, but it is represented among the thirty-two families in appendix A by the Dobbin brothers, who came from an Old English family of Carrickfergus and Duneane in County Antrim.[35] In the Williamite wars of 1689–91, conditions once again favoured entrepreneurs, and a number of minor traders, already settled in Ulster, made enough capital to set themselves up as merchants. Although some contemporary sources referred to such traders with contempt, and established merchants attempted to close ranks against them,[36] they nevertheless became assimilated into the merchant communities of the Ulster towns. Because they themselves left no records at this date they have not been included among the thirty-two families.

personal factors; T.C. Smout, 'The development and enterprise of Glasgow, 1556 –1707' in *Scottish Journal of Political Economy*, vii, p.198, and 'Glasgow merchant community', pp 53–5.

32 Appendix A.4, 5, 16, 25; for James Stewart, see deed, 2 Aug. 1682 (P.R.O.N.I., Lenox-Conyngham papers, T420, p.97), and abstract of will, 1693 (P.R.O.N.I., Stewart transcripts, D1759/3B/1, p.71).

33 Appendix A.30.

34 M'Skimin, *Carrickfergus*, p.122.

35 The Dobbin brothers were never active in trade in Carrickfergus but their uncle was an alderman there (appendix A.11).

36 *A discourse concerning Ireland and the different interests thereof in answer to the Exon and Barnstable petitions* (London, 1698), pp 36–7; James Kirkpatrick, *An historical essay upon the loyalty of presbyterians in Great Britain and Ireland from the reformation to this present year* (Belfast, 1713), pp 434, 436, hereafter cited as Kirkpatrick; *Town book*, pp 171, 186; Londonderry minutes, 10 Oct. 1693, 22 Mar. 1696/7.

Inevitably there were some families which do not belong to any of these four categories. Lewis Thompson, for example, who was active as a merchant in the second half of the seventeenth century and who appears at first sight to belong to the group of English-origin Church of Ireland families who settled in Belfast in or before the 1620s, was actually the grandson of another Lewis Thompson, a native of 'Lower Germany', who was granted letters of naturalization in 1624 and who was trading from Belfast with Holland in the 1620s–30s.[37] Other foreign nationals are known to have lived at Belfast from time to time, but no other family of foreign origin became completely integrated into the merchant community.

The merchant community of Belfast was therefore composed of families from a variety of social, religious, economic and geographical backgrounds, but from the 1650s virtually all of the newcomers were Scots, and by the late 1670s the Belfast merchant community was perceived by contemporaries as Scottish. In 1679 a merchant from the nearby town of Lisburn, where the majority of settlers were of English origin, complained about loss of trade to his town and wrote of the Belfast merchants as though they were all Scots: '... those Scotch have got all the general commissions from the London merchants for the trade into their hands and not one Englishman in these parts is so employed ...'.[38] There is no indication that any English merchants settled in Belfast after the 1640s and a breakdown of admissions of freemen shows the rapid growth of the Scottish community after 1660.

Table 1: Belfast freemen, 1640–79

	new freemen	*merchants*	*merchant apprentices*
1640–49	112	28	—
1650–59	111	29	—
1660–69	346	59	19
1670–79	481	106	24

Table 1 shows that there was a great increase in the number of freemen admitted in the 1660s and that numbers continued to rise in the next decade. The numbers of merchants admitted also rose, and these figures are minimums as the roll does not always give the occupation of the freemen. Of the merchants admitted in the 1650s, many can be identified as new immigrants from Scotland and they include six out of the total of eight freemen who paid the highest fees for admission for the whole of the period covered by the roll. These six, Hugh Eccles, the two George

37 Appendix A.29.
38 Thomas Taylor to Lord Conway, 3 Dec. 1679 (*Cal. S.P. dom., 1679–80*, p.298).

Macartneys, John Corry, William Smith and William Taylor,[39] were to become extremely prosperous and it is perhaps a measure of their acumen that they were quick to realise the town's potential and move in ahead of most of their contemporaries. The percentage of merchants who had served as apprentices appears to have been 32% in the 1660s and 22.6% in the 1670s. The latter is virtually the same as the rate for the whole body of freemen between 1660 and 1681.[40] It would be unwise to rely on the consistency of the freemen's roll, as some of those freemen who were admitted *gratis* may have been apprentices, but the low proportion of townsmen qualifying for freedom through apprenticeship suggests that many newcomers were settling in the town who had served their apprenticeships elsewhere.

Although it is demonstrable that the merchant community and the population as a whole grew rapidly after 1660, it is by no means easy to make any estimates of actual population size. Previous estimates have erred heavily on the side of caution and it has been generally accepted that Belfast's population was in the region of 1,000 in the middle of the century and reached 2,000 in the reign of James II. Since, within a few years, the town was to rank fourth in trade in the whole of Ireland, the figure of 2,000 must be a serious under-estimate. Estimates of population have generally followed those made by Benn for the 1660s, and by actually counting the number of houses shown on Thomas Phillips's map of 1685.[41] Since Benn's figures are based on a misinterpretation of the poll tax returns of 1660 and on the notoriously defective hearth money roll of 1666, and since Phillips's map cannot seriously be considered an adequate basis for estimating population, a reassessment of the available data is long overdue.[42]

The earliest source for the town's population is a series of cess lists contained in the town book showing contributions for the support of the garrison between 1640 and 1645. The figure of 1,076, in the table below,

39 Appendix A.12, 18, 19, 26; Macartney of Auchinleck was the earliest settler in 1649; John Corry purchased land in County Fermanagh and was the ancestor of the earls of Belmore; William Taylor was one of the small group of Belfast merchants who appear in the subsidy rolls of 1661 and 1666 (Benn, pp 314–15).

40 No record was kept of freemen who qualified through apprenticeship before 1660; the percentage of apprentices in the whole group (22.5%) has been calculated after subtracting the non-resident gentry.

41 See page 19.

42 Benn, pp 296–300; J.C. Beckett, 'The seventeenth century' in Beckett and Glasscock, *Belfast: origin and growth*, pp 33–4; I. Budge and C. O'Leary, *Belfast: approach to crisis: a study of Belfast politics 1613–1970* (London, 1973), p.3; Roebuck, 'Donegall family', p.125; L M. Cullen, 'Economic trends, 1660–91' in T.W. Moody, F.X. Martin, F.J. Byrne (ed.) *A new history of Ireland, iii, Early modern Ireland 1534–1761* (Oxford, 1978), p.391; J.W. Nelson estimates a population of about 2,500 by 1694 ('The Belfast presbyterians 1670–1830, an analysis of their political and social interests' [PhD thesis, Q.U.B., 1985], p.28); Norman E. Gamble, 'The business community and trade of Belfast 1767–1800' (PhD thesis, T.C.D., 1978), p.10.

has been reached by multiplying the total number of surnames in the lists for the period 1643–45 by 5.25, as the average number in each household.[43] Because this tax was assessed and collected locally it can be assumed that evasion was difficult, but the total population figure reached must nevertheless be an underestimate because some households may have been too poor to pay anything and, more significantly, because there was certainly more than one household for many surnames.[44]

Table 2: The population of Belfast

date	estimate	source
1643–45	1,076	cess lists (205 surnames x 5.25)
1660	1,914	poll tax returns (589 individuals x 2.5 + 30%)
(1666)	(1,197)	(hearth money roll [228 individuals x 5.25 + 15%])
1669	3,200	hearth money roll (530 individuals x 5.25 + 15%)
1706	5,000	presbyterian congregation was 3,000

The poll tax returns of 1660 give a total of 589 individuals, which has been multiplied by 2.5.[45] It is generally agreed that poll tax returns were low throughout Ireland so 30% has been added to the total.[46] Since the level of evasion was probably higher than this, even in towns, it is safe to assume that the population of Belfast was over 2,000 in 1660. The hearth money roll of 1666 was seriously defective but has been included above because Benn based his population figures on it.[47] The total of households listed in this, and in the more accurate return of 1669, has been increased by 15% to allow for households which were exempt, and for a measure of evasion.[48] For consistency, a figure of 5.25 individuals per household has been used

43 David Dickson, C. Ó Grada, S. Daultrey, 'Hearth tax, household size and Irish population change 1672–1821', in *R.I.A. Proc.*, lxxxii, sect. C., no.6 (1982), pp 128–81.

44 For example, 13 Thompsons are listed after 1640.

45 Seamus Pender (ed.), *A census of Ireland circa 1659, with supplementary material from the poll money ordinances* (I.M.C., Dublin, 1939), p.8; for a summary of the evidence that the 'census of Ireland' was a statistical abstract of the poll tax returns for 1660, see Carleton, *Heads and hearths*, xi; L.M. Cullen suggests a multiplier of 3 which may have been less in towns ('Population trends in seventeenth century Ireland' in *Economic and Social Review*, vi, no. 2 [1975], p.153).

46 W.J. Smyth believes poll tax returns were underestimated by about a third in Ulster ('Society and settlement in seventeenth century Ireland: the evidence of the 1659 Census' in W.J. Smyth and Kevin Whelan (ed.), *The common ground, essays on the historical geography of Ireland, presented to T. Jones Hughes* [Cork, 1988], p.56; S.T. Carleton claims a deficiency of at least 50% [*Heads and hearths*, p.177], and see also review of *Heads and hearths* by W.J. Smyth in *I.E.S.H.*, xx [1993], pp 111–13).

47 Benn, pp 299–300.

48 Carleton, *Heads and hearths*, pp 36–9; the figure of 10% for exemptions is suggested by Dickson, Ó Grada and Daultry, op. cit., p.159; it was easier to misrepresent the number of hearths than to be omitted altogether in a town; Carleton states that comparison of names in the hearth money rolls of 1666 and 1669 with those in the

in all the above calculations. A national average (excluding Dublin) of 4.3 to 5 is suggested by contemporary sources but urban households often included apprentices, servants and lodgers. D.J. Dickson based population figures for Cork in 1659–64 on a household size of 8.5, and Arthur Dobbs considered that 10 per house was a 'low enough computation' for Dublin in 1729, although Dublin households were large by contemporary standards.[49] Belfast, however, contained very few large houses in the 1660s and, since many householders there at that date were immigrants, their households are unlikely to have included members of their parents' generation, and so the average would have been lower than in Dublin or Cork.

No figures are available for the rest of the century. There was high mortality in the town in 1689–90 when Schomberg's 'Great Hospital' was at Belfast,[50] but losses were rapidly made up in the 1690s, and the new meeting house, built *circa* 1694, was too small for the the congregation by 1706. In that year, the congregation reached 3,000 and a second meeting house was built.[51] A high proportion of the townspeople were presbyterians. If the proportion were 'upwards of 70%',[52] this suggests a total population of 4,285. However since there is no way of establishing the exact proportion of church-going presbyterians to anglicans, conformists and backsliders of all denominations, it is likely that 4,285 is an underestimate and that it would be safe to assume that the population of Belfast in 1706 totalled at least 5,000.

Although these calculations suggest that Belfast was larger than has previously been supposed, it was still a very small town. No Irish town, of course, had anything approaching the population of Dublin, which was about 62,000 in 1706, but even when contrasted with other Irish provincial ports, Belfast was extremely small (Cork, for example, had a population of over 17,500 in 1706) and this makes the town's emergence as the fourth port of Ireland by the end of the seventeenth century all the more remarkable.[53]

freemen's roll shows that substantial numbers evaded the tax (*Heads and hearths*, p.182); however, since it was usual to become a freeman within three months of completing an apprenticeship, many of those admitted in 1665–69 (39% of whom are not included in the hearth money roll of 1669) would have been young unmarried men who had not yet formed independent households, and this would also apply to many admitted in 1670–72 (91% of whom do not appear in the roll of 1669).

49 David Dickson, 'The place of Dublin in the eighteenth century Irish economy', in T.M. Devine and David Dickson, *Ireland and Scotland 1600–1850: parallels and contrasts in economic and social development*, p.178; David J. Dickson, 'An economic history of the Cork region in the eighteenth century' (PhD thesis, T.C.D., 1977), appendix xxii; Arthur Dobbs, *An essay on the trade and improvement of Ireland* (Dublin, 1729), p.10.

50 George Story, *An impartial history of the wars of Ireland* (London, 1693), p.50.

51 120 heads of families were unable to worship in the meeting house (*Records of the general synod of Ulster from 1691–1820*, i, 1691–1720 [Belfast, 1890], p.146).

52 Nelson, 'Belfast presbyterians, p.49.

53 L.M. Cullen, 'Economic trends, 1660–91', pp 390–1; J.G. Simms, *War and politics*

THE DEVELOPMENT OF THE TOWN

Even by the late 1660s, the customs figures do not indicate that Belfast was the leading port in Ulster, let alone of national importance. No separate figures were issued for Belfast, as the customs were administered from Carrickfergus. In 1669 Carrickfergus (including Belfast) was ranked only seventh in Ireland for imports and ninth for exports, the volume of trade being more or less the same as at Londonderry which was ranked eighth for both exports and imports.[54] However, the figures for the 1660s under-represent Belfast's trade since some of the goods loaded for Dublin merchants were sent to them in small craft and reloaded for export from Dublin. Most of the trade recorded at the Carrickfergus customhouse was from Belfast. Even in the late 1640s seven-eighths of Carrickfergus's trade was said to be through Belfast, and the port books for Glasgow show a further decline of Carrickfergus in the 1660s–70s. In 1665–67 more ships arrived there from Carrickfergus than Belfast but the principal commodity carried by the ships from the former was timber and Glasgow's export trade was primarily with Belfast. In 1671–72, the number of ships from Belfast exceeded those from Carrickfergus, and the latter port did not receive any of Glasgow's exports.[55]

The full impact of merchant immigration into Belfast in the 1650s and early 1660s is first visible in the unique set of detailed trade figures for 1683–86, which reveal that Belfast was, with Youghal, the exporter of about 47% of Irish butter by 1683 and was a leading exporter of linen.[56] Since Belfast is named in these figures rather than Carrickfergus, it can be assumed that the town's customhouse had been built by 1682. Previously, all goods had had to be entered in or out at Carrickfergus causing delays of two to three days. Agitation for a resident collector of customs at Belfast had begun by the late 1640s and there was a customs storehouse in Belfast from about 1663. This became 'too small for the receipt of merchants goods in regard of the great increase of trade at that port' and a second larger storehouse was built in the 1670s.[57] Nevertheless the merchants found this arrangement unsatisfactory and the need for a separate customhouse at Belfast was sufficiently obvious in the 1660s for a country gentleman like William Montgomery of Rosemount to be aware of it. He

in Ireland 1649–1730, ed. D.W. Hayton and Gerald O'Brien (London, 1986), p.49; Gillespie, *Transformation of the Irish economy*, p.28; Dickson, 'An economic history of the Cork region', p.420.

54 *Cal. S.P. Ire., 1666–69*, pp 672–73.

55 Glasgow port books 1665–67, 1669–70, 1671–72 (S.R.O., E72/10/1–3).

56 Exports and imports of Irish ports, Dec. 1682–Dec. 1686 (B.L., Add. MS 4759).

57 Its dimensions are not known but it cost £442 11s 6d which suggests a large building (Benn, p.329, and Pinkerton transcript [P.R.O.N.I., Young MSS, D2930 (addnl), MS9/17]).

brought it up in a conversation with the duke of Ormond at Carrickfergus in 1666:

> I bringing in a discourse of the encouragement the only trading merchants (who lived in Belfast) had, and also of the advantage it was to the King that the custom house were settled in that town, and a bridge built to join the two counties.[58]

In 1673, Black George Macartney, as sovereign, with other leading merchants, petitioned Lord Conway for the removal of the customhouse to Belfast, although Carrickfergus was to retain its own collector.[59] Since this petition was not repeated it was presumably successful, although the exact date of the building of the Belfast customhouse is not known. Macartney also petitioned in 1680 for Conway's support for the building of a bridge over the river Lagan at Belfast, pointing out 'If our town prosper, your town of Lisburn certainly must, for one depends on the welfare of the other.'[60] Building was started in 1682 but the bridge was unfinished (although in use) in 1689 when the passage of Schomberg's artillery is said to have weakened the structure and to have led to its partial collapse in 1693.[61] The Long Bridge, as it was called, brought directly into the town traffic which had previously crossed a few miles higher up the river at Shaw's Bridge. Belfast, at this date, lay entirely on the County Antrim side of the river Lagan and the Long Bridge opened up direct communications with suppliers and consumers in County Down.

The town itself grew rapidly. The 'rampier' of 1642 enclosed an area of eighty–six acres including the castle gardens. Building proceeded apace and three story houses were being erected in 1670.[62] Phillips's map of Belfast in 1685 shows development outside the 'rampier' of 1642, part of which had been demolished.[63] The corporation met in the town house opposite the castle gates in the centre of the town, and George Macartney of Auchinleck's mansion is to the far right of the map, above the mill pond. Thomas Phillips, who made this map, described Belfast as 'the third place of trade in this kingdom ... having never less than forty or fifty sail of ships always before it, the place very rich and numerous' and recommended that

58 Hill, *The Montgomery manuscripts*, p.425.
59 Petition, 19 Feb. 1672/3 (P.R.O., SP.63/333, no.82).
60 *Cal. S.P. dom., 1679–80*, pp 455–6.
61 Extracts from journal of Robert Leathes (L.H.L., Joy MSS, 7; the original does not appear to have survived); journal of Gideon Bonnivert, June–July 1689 (B.L., Sloane MS 1033); Story, *Impartial history*, p.38; James Duchal (ed.), *Sermons of the Reverend John Abernethy* (London, 1762), preface; Charles Smith and Walter Harris, *Ancient and present state of the county of Down* (Dublin, 1744), p.129.
62 *Cal. S.P. Ire., 1669–70*, p.140.
63 Reproduced from the map in Benn, opposite p.282; south is at the top.

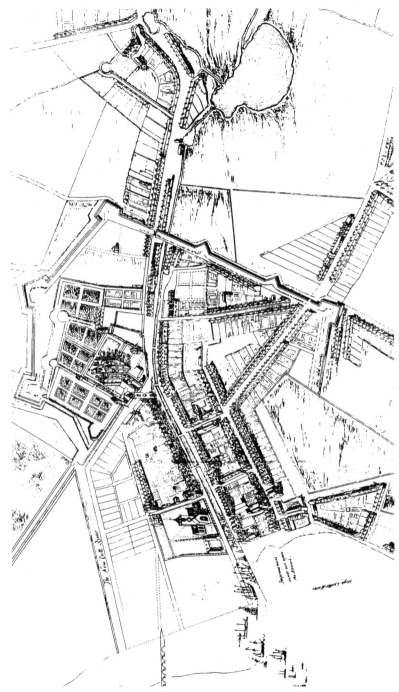

1 Belfast in 1685, by Thomas Phillips

Carrickfergus castle be demolished and the material used towards the building of a citadel and port at Belfast.[64]

Growth, however, came to a halt in the period of the Jacobite wars for, as in the 1640s, much of the fighting took place in Ulster. Even before the war began, cattle disease had caused a slump in trade. From the beginning of 1689 many merchants fled with their cash and trade was at a standstill.[65] Economic dislocation was severe as livestock losses meant that levels of exports were low long after peace was made in 1691, but Belfast itself was undamaged by the war, unlike Londonderry which took years to recover, and some at least of the merchants had made profits provisioning the Williamite armies. The rapid recovery of trade in the north was assisted by good harvests and by the influx of a wave of Scottish settlers attracted by favourable leases in Ulster. In the 1690s, Belfast was called 'a very large town, and the greatest for Trade in the North of Ireland',[66] and 'the second town in Ireland, well built, full of people, and of great Trade'.[67] This was untrue, but by 1709 Belfast was the fourth port in Ireland, after Dublin, Cork and Waterford, and was soon to overtake the latter.[68]

Not only was Belfast the economic and commercial centre of the north, it was also an important social centre. The earls of Donegall were both proprietors and patrons of the town. Since, through a series of extravagant wills, settlements and lawsuits, they were perpetually in debt, they were unable to invest much capital in the development of the town, although they made donations from time to time for specific purposes.[69] However, in spite of the indebtedness of the Chichester family, they made a significant contribution to the town's status and growth by actually residing there. After the death of Sir Arthur Chichester in 1625, and until the destruction of Belfast Castle by fire in 1708, the Chichester family lived at Belfast rather than at Carrickfergus where they also had a mansion house.[70] Belfast Castle and the town became the focus for the Donegall tenants in County Antrim and to some extent for the whole region, particularly because the other great landlord of the Lagan valley, Lord Conway, spent much of his time in England. Even during the Commonwealth period, when the Chichester family had lost control of the town, it was referred to as 'the

64 *Ormonde MSS*, ii, p.319.
65 Sir Arthur Rawdon to Hans Sloane, 10 May 1688 (B.L., Sloane MS 4036, f.35); John Johnston, Lisburn, to Richard Crumpe, 15 Jan. to 17 Feb. 1688/9, 'Many thousands are fled, hundreds are daily fleeing, the country is laid waste, all husbandry neglected' (Bodl., Carte MSS 40, f.522).
66 Story, *Impartial history*, p.38.
67 Sacheverall, *Account of the Isle of Man*, p.125.
68 Benn, p.327.
69 Roebuck, 'Landlord indebtedness', pp 140–47; Benn, pp 447–8; *Town book*, pp 130, 151.
70 This was 'making haste to fall to the ground' in 1708 (T.C.D., Molyneux's journey to the north, MS 883/2, f.138).

place where country gentlemen and officers then most haunted', and although the Commonwealth commissioners were based at Carrickfergus, much of their correspondence was addressed to and from Belfast.[71] The large numbers of gentry who were made freemen *gratis* has been noted previously. The town book has nothing to say about these non-resident freemen other than to ensure that their freedom did not benefit them financially. However, the fact that 'honorary' freemen were made at all indicates that freedom conferred some sort of status on the recipient and confirms that the town was seen as a focal point for the gentry of the region.

Some gentlemen, many of them Donegall satellites, actually had houses in Belfast. The hearth money roll of 1669 includes the names of gentry such as Captain Thomas Beverley, Michael Harrison, Sir Hercules Langford, Edward Reynells, and John Tooley.[72] The marquess of Antrim was resident in the town in 1660–61.[73] The town had an excellent school, built and endowed by the first earl of Donegall. It was sometimes referred to as a 'latin school' but the exercise book of Thomas Agnew, who appears to have attended the school in 1686, suggests that it also offered a good grounding in mathematics, trigonometry, astronomy, navigation and surveying.[74] The sons of the local gentry attended Lord Donegall's school in the seventeenth century, together with the sons of most Belfast merchants. Apart from the school, however, the town's amenities were limited. The castle had beautiful gardens which William III described as a 'little Whitehall' in 1690, and there was a racecourse of sorts and a bowling green, but although there were a large number of inns and alehouses, drinking and gaming were forbidden after nine o'clock, except for lodgers.[75]

From the 1630s, there was a considerable clothing industry in Belfast, involving large numbers of tailors, shoemakers, glovers and hatters. The export figures for 1683–86 show that the town was exporting substantial quantities of shoes, stockings and hats to the colonies in the years when the navigation acts were suspended. Even though it is probable that such goods continued to find their way there illegally, the fact that almost 11% of freemen were involved in the clothing industry suggests that there was a considerable home market. The freemen's roll also shows that, in the latter half of the century, the town had stationers, a bookbinder, a cutler, several

71 Adair, *Narrative*, p.168; Benn, p.134.
72 The three latter were burgesses; for Harrison see appendix B.4.
73 Pender, *Census Ire.*, p.8; *Town book*, p.241; Jane H. Ohlmeyer, *Civil war and restoration in the three Stuart kingdoms, the career of Randal MacDonnell, marquis of Antrim, 1609–1683* (Cambridge, 1993), pp 250, 273.
74 Benn, pp 448–9; *Essex papers*, i, p.116; exercise book of Thomas Agnew, 1686 (S.R.O., Agnew of Lochnaw, D154/935); the 'patriot parliament' of 1689 made provision for setting up of schools of mathematics and navigation in ports including Belfast (Simms, *War and politics in Ireland*, pp 78–9).
75 *Town book*, pp 105, 243; *Cal. S.P. Ire., 1666–69*, p.584.

goldsmiths, a watchmaker, a clockmaker, a bowmaker, two gunsmiths and a confectioner, and there is evidence for the manufacture of furniture,[76] all of which indicate the existence of a local market for luxury goods. By the beginning of the eighteenth century, there were two sugar refineries, a pottery and a printing press. In 1708, Molyneux wrote 'Belfast is a very handsome, thriving, well-peopled town; a great many new houses and good shops in it'.[77]

Much of the credit for this must go to the Belfast corporation which was composed of merchants, a few local tradesmen, and members of the gentry, generally in the employ of the Donegall family.[78] Although the deficiencies of the town book make it impossible to analyse membership from 1613, table 3 shows that, at least from the middle of the century, a high proportion of burgesses and sovereigns were members of merchant families, and that the merchants who were sovereigns served more terms than the gentry. Therefore, the day-to-day running of the town was in the hands of the leading merchant families.[79]

Table 3: Percentages of burgesses and sovereigns from merchant families, 1650–1706

	merchant families	others
new burgesses elected from 1650	67%	33%
sovereigns	75%	25%
total sovereign years served	83%	17%

Not only was it easy for the Scottish newcomers to become freemen, several were elected burgesses within a short time of their arrival. Continuity with the earlier period was maintained by the presence within the corporation of members of the Leathes, Thetford, Theaker and Thompson families, but most of the outstanding sovereigns after 1660 came from families which had only settled in Belfast in the late 1640s–50s. The most notable among these were the two George Macartneys. George Macartney of Auchinleck settled in Belfast in 1649 and, in addition to his trading activities, invested in commercial undertakings such as milling, sugar refining and iron founding. He was the leading member of the Belfast corporation for about thirty years and served as sovereign nine times. George Macartney of Blacket was known as 'Black George' to distin-

76 Liverpool port book, 1695–96 (P.R.O., E190/1355/5, f.30); Macartney to Abraham Mayo, 17 July 1706 (Macartney 3, p.334).
77 Molyneux's journey to the north (T.C.D., MS 883/2, f.136).
78 For a complete list of the corporation from 1660–1707 see appendix D.
79 This is in contrast to Coleraine where the election of 'those who live by their rents and not by their trade' was seen as the cause of a lawsuit between corporation members, 1678 (Coleraine minutes).

guish him from Macartney of Auchinleck,[80] and this may refer to his colouring, or be a play on his place of origin. He became one of the most successful merchants of his day, was a burgess of Belfast for almost forty years and four times sovereign. Both men served as high sheriff of County Antrim.

Macartney of Auchinleck was the first of the Scots who settled in Belfast in the late 1640s–50s to become a burgess. Although this was a period of growth, both in population and trade, it was also a period of disorganisation in the government of the town. There were several absentee burgesses and there was nowhere for the corporation to meet because the garrison had taken over all public buildings such as the market house and the church. In 1659, the year of Macartney's election as burgess, the sovereign, William Leathes, was endeavouring to build up funds for the corporation by collecting arrears of admission fees owed by freemen. Since the corporation was totally lacking in endowments and the profits of the market courts went to the Chichester family,[81] these admission fees were a major source of income. Leathes's death in 1660 was a great loss to the town for he seems to have been a man of great ability and prestige,[82] and the lack of a successor of his calibre from among the older families of the town may have led to the election of Macartney as sovereign in June 1662. Over the next two years (he served a second term) he enacted a series of bye-laws regulating such basic matters as the hygienic disposal of rubbish by butchers, the clearing of garbage from the streets, the sweeping of the streets, the embanking of the river Farset and the building of bridges over it. He concluded his term of office by providing the corporation with a new market house or town house, over his premises in High Street, building a staircase to it, providing it with seats and adorning it with the royal coat of arms, at his own expense.[83] This first term of office established Macartney as the natural leader of the corporation. The re-organisation continued under other sovereigns. There were bye-laws about street lighting, fire precautions, the admission of freemen, enrolment of apprentices, and use of standard weights and measures. Sovereigns were required to account for money received in their term of office, and there were improvements in the management of charitable donations for the town's poor. The town dock was enlarged and a covered market was provided for the retailing of meat.

80 Sir George Rawdon states in 1670 that Macartney of Auchinleck was known as 'White George' but no other reference has been found to him under this name (*Cal. S.P. Ire., 1669–70*, p.300); another George Macartney who was active as a Belfast merchant from the 1680s was known as 'Brown George' (appendix B.5).
81 Gillespie, *Colonial Ulster*, p.188.
82 *Town book*, p.241.
83 The town house, with its tower, is shown in the illustration overleaf, but the surrounding buildings date from the mid-eighteenth century; by then, the river Farset ran beneath High Street into the town dock which is visible in the distance.

2 High Street, Belfast, in 1786

In 1678 Black George Macartney and Robert Leathes submitted a proposal for piping the town's water supply from the tuck mill dam, to the west of the town, for £175 and the work was completed by 1680.[84]

The burgesses in the second half of the century were a group of men who had travelled widely. References can be found to most of them visiting Dublin, London, Scotland or Europe. They were aware of standards in other trading centres and their bye-laws reflect a determined effort to improve the standing, organisation and cleanliness of the town. Since almost 11% of the freemen between 1636 and 1682 were butchers, tanners and tallow chandlers, this was no easy task. As the funds available never allowed outlay on any but the most basic amenities, it is a measure of their success that contemporary visitors spoke highly of the town. De Rocheford, who visited the town in 1672, wrote 'Here is a very fine Castle, and two or three large streets as in a new built town', and Bonnivert went so far as to call Belfast a 'large and pretty town' in 1690.[85] The prestige of the sovereign and burgesses also rose within this period. It is clear from the town book that in the 1640s–50s the political climate had led to disobedience to the sovereign, quarrels within the corporation, and even brawling in the street. In his first period of office, George Macartney took a firm line with unruly freemen who challenged the authority of the sovereign and his officers and thereafter the corporation was treated with respect. Moreover the burgesses behaved themselves decorously and any private disagreements never became public scandals.

As the status of the town grew, so did that of the sovereign, and the office was held by a number of particularly able men whose activities were not confined to Belfast. All sovereigns were *ex officio* magistrates within Belfast, but from the 1660s they were also justices of the peace for County Antrim. Four were high sheriffs of County Antrim and one of County Down, and Macartney of Auchinleck was surveyor-general of the customs of Ulster. After the Jacobite wars, the sovereign was also *ex officio* captain of the Belfast militia, and several served as commissioners of array and had military experience. The choice of the town's representatives in parliament is an indication of the improved status of the corporation and of the merchant community. In 1661 the town was represented by Colonel William Knight, a lawyer, and by one of the sons of John Davies of Carrickfergus, merchant and member of parliament for County Antrim, who although a burgess of Belfast was never a member of the town's merchant community. In 1692 the corporation elected James and George Macartney, sons of George Macartney of Auchinleck. James Macartney was re-elected in 1695 and, although not a merchant himself, he looked after the interests of the community. For example, in 1697 he introduced the heads of a bill for the

84 *Town book*, pp 97–105, 107, 110–11, 116–17, 133–4, 136–9, 146–7, 149–52, 154–6.
85 Benn, p.288; Bonnivert's journal (B.L., Sloane MS 1033).

reforming of abuses in making butter casks and packing butter which became law in the following year. In 1703, the town was represented by William Craford, a Belfast merchant and burgess, and William Cairnes, banker and merchant of Dublin. Belfast burgesses were also elected to other constituencies. In the period 1660–1707 ten Belfast burgesses were members of the Irish house of commons and many served on parliamentary committees concerned with trade. The growth in status of the corporation reflects the growth of the town but was also the result of the personal standing of many of the burgesses.

The Belfast merchant community was made up of immigrants with different places of origin and different religious affiliations. Although differences of religion remained distinct and intermarriage between the English and Scottish families was uncommon, it will be shown that there was considerable goodwill between these sections of the community and that their aims and interests coincided. Belfast was seen as a largely Scots town but Bonnivert noted in 1690 that 'the inhabitants speak very good english'.[86] Although this remark is difficult to interpret, it must at least mean that he was able to understand them and that regional accents and dialects, particularly lowland Scots, had become less pronounced. The Scottish immigrants' perception of their own nationality and identity was also modified. Some indication of this is visible in the Macartney letter books. In 1665 in a letter to James Cunningham, a Scottish factor at Cadiz, Black George subscribed himself as his 'friend and countryman'.[87] Forty years later, Macartney's son Isaac displayed faint stirrings of colonial nationalism when he wrote to a correspondent in Devon offering to supply him with linen 'when the Parliament of England is pleased to let poor Ireland export directly linen to the English plantation'.[88] These forty years had seen the transformation of a heterogeneous group of settlers into a community with a sense of its own identity and a measure of civic pride. Since 1660, both the population and the town had grown rapidly and the presence of a stable and successful merchant class contributed to the spectacular increase in the volume of trade. The availability of data on thirty-two of these merchant families makes it possible, next, to reveal the close-knit structure of this community, and to determine status within the community in terms of wealth, office and land.

86 Bonnivert's journal (B.L., Sloane MS. 1033).
87 Macartney to Cunningham, 6 Oct. 1663 (Macartney 1, p.73).
88 Macartney to John Buck, 12 Mar. 1704/5 (Macartney 3, p.68).

2

The Merchant Community

KINSHIP, AND OTHER RELATIONSHIPS WITHIN THE COMMUNITY

The rapid success of many of the merchants who came from Scotland to Belfast in the 1650s and 1660s suggests that they arrived with some capital and trading experience. However, they had left behind them that network of kinsmen and trading partners which was equally essential to the success of any seventeenth-century merchant. Every merchant developed around himself a group which contemporaries called his 'friends', consisting of older relatives by blood and marriage, godparents, boyhood friends, the merchant to whom he was apprenticed, his fellow apprentices, business partners and members of his church. They would help him to start up in business, advise him on a suitable marriage, stand as godparents to his children, play a part in arranging their apprenticeships and marriages, and act as trustees in marriage settlements and sureties for debts. Finally, they would be executors or administrators of his will, give advice to his widow, and be trustees for any children who were minors. Such friends expected to be consulted when major decisions were to be taken or when crises threatened which could be averted by sound advice or financial assistance. Studies of seventeenth- and eighteenth-century merchant communities on both sides of the Atlantic show that these overlapping networks of kinsmen and friends were common to all such communities and provided the framework within which most business transactions took place.[1]

Many of the Scots who settled in Belfast appear to have emigrated in family groups or induced other family members to follow them. For

---

1 Peter Earle, *The making of the English middle class 1660–1730* (London, 1991), pp 91–2; Bernard Bailyn, *The New England merchants in the seventeenth century* (Cambridge, Mass., 1955), pp 87, 135–7; Paul Butel, *Les negotiants bordelais, l'Europe et les îles au xviiie siècle* (Paris, 1974), p.154; T.M. Devine, 'The Scottish merchant community, 1680–1740' in R.H. Campbell and A. Skinner (ed.), *The origins and nature of the Scottish enlightenment* (Edinburgh, 1982), p.29; L.M. Cullen, 'The Dublin merchant community in the eighteenth century' in Butel and Cullen, *Cities and merchants*, p.195; Gamble, 'Business community and trade of Belfast', p.25.

example, there were three Clugston brothers active in trade in Belfast in the 1630s–40s, and in the next decade there were four Biggars who were probably brothers. Other pairs of brothers such as the Pottingers, Knoxes and Smiths can be identified in the 1660s, and there were other family groups containing several adult males whose relationships are difficult to determine, such as the Chalmerses, Doakes and Lockharts. The majority of the Scottish immigrants appear to have been young unmarried men who set about creating new kinship networks in Ulster. For example, within a year of his arrival in Belfast in 1649, George Macartney of Auchinleck married the daughter of a Scots presbyterian merchant who had been settled there at least since the 1630s, and through this marriage became kin to several other Belfast families.[2]

Merchants normally married into other merchant families, thereby establishing kinship links and adding to the circle of friends who might assist them at various stages of their careers. The relationship was of course reciprocal and the merchant was expected to further the careers of members of his wife's family. These kinsmen by marriage occasionally proved to be more of a liability than an asset. Black George Macartney's son Isaac married the daughter of William Haltridge, a wealthy Dromore merchant, and was gradually drawn into the financial affairs of her brother, which eventually ruined him.[3] This however is an extreme case, and is not representative because Macartney's brother-in-law was a landowner not a merchant. In general, the merchant who married into a merchant family not only established useful kinship links but, in addition, usually acquired a wife who would be capable of managing her husband's business in his absence. Very little source material relates directly to the Belfast merchants' wives, who generally remain little more than names, but two examples can be found of wives acting for their husbands in their absence. In 1677 Jane Pottinger wrote to her husband, Edward, who was in France, reporting on the progress of some of his concerns. As she had been unable to get freight as he wished, she proposed to lay out what money she had by her 'for our best advantage'.[4] In 1693, Jane Leathes wrote to Black George Macartney's wife, Martha, to inform her of the death at Whitehaven of her husband, Ensign John Leathes, a burgess of Belfast, and to ask her to send five dozen clift boards 'for here we shall want to clear us'. Leathes's illness and death had probably used up the money the couple had with them; Jane needed goods to sell in Whitehaven, in order to raise cash, and expected Martha, whose husband was in Dublin, to be able to supply them.[5]

2 Appendix A.18.
3 Appendix A.19 and B.3.
4 Jane to Edward Pottinger, 27 Nov. and 10 Dec. 1677 (N.A., Sarsfield–Vesey letters, 42–43).
5 Young, *Town book*, pp 170, 327; clift boards were thin planks; Young, writing in 1892, was unable to take this letter at face value and suggested that they were some kind of code for money.

All evidence points to frequent intermarriage between the Belfast merchant families. Of the thirty-two families, twenty had intermarried with one or more of the others, and seven more were kin with one or more in the group through marriage. Of the remaining five families, one was connected with another merchant family outside the thirty-two, and only four families cannot be proved to have been related by blood or marriage to other Belfast merchant families. Three of these latter families were members of the Church of Ireland (Theaker, Thetford, Thompson) and very little intermarriage between this group and the presbyterians has been found. However there is so little information about the marriages of the English-origin group that they cannot even be proved to have intermarried among themselves. Most of the information about marriages comes from the latter part of the seventeenth century. By then, it is likely that many families were already related by marriages which took place between the 1640s and 1670s, but which are not documented. Furthermore, relationships may have existed between merchant families from the same region in Scotland, such as the Doake, Eccles and Chalmers families from Ayrshire. This makes it likely that the relationships between the leading merchant families were even more complex than the surviving evidence suggests.

Relationships were further complicated by the high incidence of re-marriage among both widows and widowers. Most settler societies contain more men than women so widows are likely to remarry. In the hearth money roll of 1669 for Belfast only twenty-six women, twenty-two of whom are named as widows, are listed as householders.[6] This is about 4.9% of the total which suggests that remarriage of widows was common throughout the community, although there may have been more widows who were exempt through poverty from paying the tax. Of those listed, only five had more than one hearth. Merchant widows however were often wealthy. For example, Ellinor Chalmers's portion of her husband's estate amounted to about £1,000, 'full of all jointure, dower or other demands', and she remarried soon after his death in 1681.[7] Similarly Grissell Clugston's second husband left her £1,200 in 1684 'in consideration of a contract made with her before marriage in 1674'. Grissell also had property in and around Belfast and in her will of 1701 she referred to sums totalling over £800 which she had lent to her sons-in-law and to other Belfast merchants.[8] Wealthy widowers also often remarried; Grissell Clugston was William Smith's second wife, and George Macartney of Auchinleck, Hugh Eccles, Thomas Pottinger, John Hamilton and Francis Thetford all married twice or more, and these later marriages were not necessarily to produce heirs. Macartney and Smith, for example, both had two sons by their first marriages.

6 Carleton, *Heads and hearths*, p.36.
7 Appendix A.7.
8 Appendix A.8, 26.

Second marriages could lead to lawsuits in which it was claimed that the widow, or her new husband, had taken property which rightfully belonged to the children of her first marriage. Since a widow's property became, during her lifetime, her husband's on remarriage, it was not difficult for a second husband to enrich himself at the expense of his stepchildren. Because of the destruction of most seventeenth-century legal records, few examples relating to Belfast survive of lawsuits arising from remarriage. However a transcript of a chancery bill of 1677 alleged that Anne, widow of Robert Foster (or Forster), a former sovereign of Belfast, had seized property which Foster had intended for his son, and had subsequently married the merchant Francis Thetford.[9] Even where there were no children by an earlier marriage, there was sometimes a member of the first husband's family who claimed to have been defrauded. For example, Hugh Eccles of Belfast's first wife, Janet, was the widow of the merchant Archibald Moore of Lisnegarvey (i.e. Lisburn). Eccles obtained Moore's property through the agency of his friend John Corry and his wife, who were probably related to the widow, and who took possession of 'all his said goods, chattels, merchandize, bonds, bills, shop books and other commodities' after Moore's death. In 1656, Moore's mother, Jennett Petilla als M'Culy (who herself sounds like a much-married widow), alleged in a chancery bill that Moore had intended to leave his widow only £30–£40 out of an estate which she valued at £1,000, and that she herself had lent her son at least £500 between 1625 and 1651. This had entitled her to a half share of the profits and she now claimed the bulk of Moore's goods.[10]

Frequent intermarriage between merchant families and remarriage of widows and widowers led, within two generations, to complex ties of kinship. In 1705, William Rainey the younger, a Belfast merchant, entered in his journal 'Brother John married to Aunt Elinor Galt of Coleraine'.[11] Elinor Galt was in fact the sister of William's first wife's mother (and so his aunt by marriage) and, as far as is known, was not related by blood to John Rainey. The Rainey brothers' marriages into the Galt family brought them kinship ties with the Chalmers and Smith families of Belfast, the Martins of Belfast and Dublin, and the Brookes, Lennoxes and Vances of Londonderry. Similarly, the marriage of Grissell Clugston's daughter with her second husband William Smith's eldest son by his first wife brought the Smiths kinship ties with the Clugstons, Crafords and Youngs, in addition to those they already had with the inter-related White and Martin families. Table 4 shows a series of alliances which connected twenty-seven

9 Transcript of chancery bill, 23 June 1677 (P.R.O.N.I., Society of Genealogists abstracts, T581/1, p.424).
10 Earl of Belmore, *The history of the Corry family of Castlecoole* (London and Dublin, 1891), pp 10–11.
11 Extracts from Rainey's journal (L.H.L., Joy MSS, 10); the original journal was destroyed.

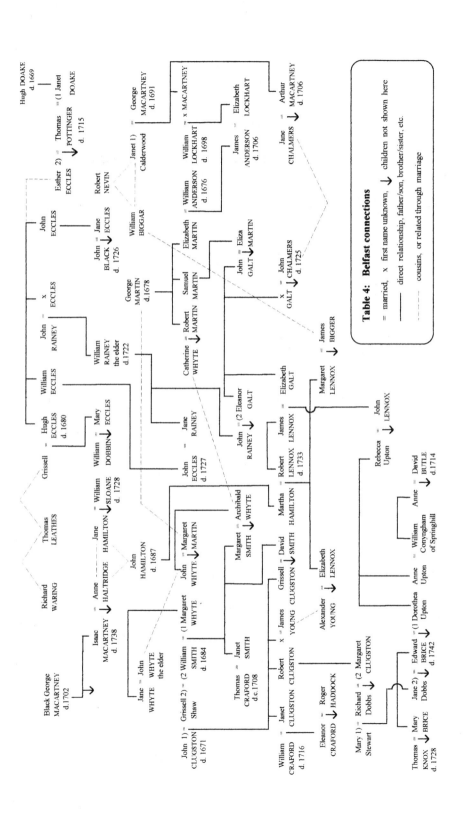

Table 4: Belfast connections

= married, x first name unknown, → children not shown here

—— direct relationship, father/son, brother/sister, etc.

-·-·- cousins, or related through marriage

of the thirty-two families, and the family profiles in appendix A not only note the marriages of each family but their alliances through marriage (for example, the husbands of wives' sisters), to show the extended kinship network of each family.

Godparents also counted as kin. They were frequently of superior social or economic rank and their offering or consenting to stand as sponsors was seen as an undertaking to promote the welfare and career of their godchild. Presbyterianism, as practiced in England and Scotland, forbade sponsors at baptism but Ulster presbyterians did not adhere to this rule, so it seems probable that children in presbyterian merchant families had godparents.[12] However, because there are no surviving church registers for Belfast for the seventeenth century, there is virtually no information about godparents at that date apart from a reference in the will of the first earl of Donegall to one of the sons of Macartney of Auchinleck as his godson.[13] Macartney of Auchinleck was a member of the established church. However, in the early eighteenth century, Isaac Macartney, a presbyterian elder, who refused to take the sacramental test, was the godfather to a daughter of Lord Conway's agent, and his own son William was godson of William Sloane of London.[14] If sponsorship was normal in the Macartney family, it may be assumed that it was widespread in the community, and that godparents and their children were included among each merchant's 'friends'.

To such complex bonds of kinship and marriage must be added the ties of apprenticeship and employment. No seventeenth-century merchant apprenticeship indentures have survived for Belfast, but apprentices normally served seven years and towards the end of this period would have acted as 'supercargoes', i.e. factors on trading voyages. Some continued to be employed by their master until they had amassed enough capital to set up on their own. The freemen's roll seldom gives the names of apprentices' masters but a few groups can be reconstructed around leading merchants. John Hamilton and James Young were both apprentices of Black George Macartney in the 1660s, and Thomas Pottinger and William Biggar were both employed by him in the same period. Hamilton continued to be closely associated with him in later years. In the 1670s, Black George was employing William Sloane and George Anderson, who had probably both been his apprentices, and who became personal friends of his son. Similarly, four apprentices can be identified of Hugh Eccles, including two from the thirty-two families, George Theaker and William Dobbin. Links creat-

---

12 Raymond Gillespie, 'The presbyterian revolution in Ulster, 1660–1690' in W.J. Sheils and Diana Wood (ed.), *The churches, Ireland and the Irish* (Oxford 1989), p.162.

13 *Town book*, p.131.

14 Macartney to Nathaniel Hornby, 22 June 1706 (Macartney 3, p.327); abstract of will of Isaac Macartney, 30 Jan. 1736 (P.R.O.N.I., Stewart abstracts, D1759/3B/1, p.59).

ed by apprenticeship were often reinforced by marriage. For example, William Dobbin married Eccles's eldest daughter and was executor to his will. Francis Cromie, who married Black George's elder daughter, had probably also been his apprentice. John Black was Thomas Pottinger's apprentice and both his wife and Pottinger's were members of the Eccles family.

The freemen's roll shows that lads were apprenticed to masters across the religious and ethnic groups. For example, George Theaker, who belonged to one of the English-origin Church of Ireland families, served his apprenticeship with Hugh Eccles, a presbyterian Scot, and James Buller, who was one of the presbyterians elected to the corporation after the Williamite wars, was apprenticed to Thomas Waring. In the early eighteenth century, presbyterian merchants were accused of refusing to take apprentices from Church of Ireland families and of trading only among themselves thus ruining Church of Ireland merchants. The reply of the presbyterians was that although they preferred their apprentices to accompany them to the meeting house where they could keep an eye on them, rather than leave them to get up to mischief unsupervised, they would never refuse to take apprentices from Church of Ireland families which could afford the premiums.[15] However, the implication was that many Church of Ireland families could not afford the premiums and, by the early 1700s, the wealthiest merchants were presbyterians.

Trading partnerships also created links between merchants. Any merchant operating on a large scale had shares in several ships and freighted others in a number of simultaneous short-term partnerships. A few semi-permanent partnerships can be identified, but because there were probably never more than forty to fifty merchants engaged in overseas trade from Belfast at any one time during this period, each would at some time have been in partnership with most of the others. Religious differences did not prevent co-operation between merchants. The Macartneys and Thomas Knox, who were all conformists, were frequently in partnership with William Smith, Hugh Eccles and William Craford, who were presbyterians. Similarly, presbyterians and conformists were co-owners of many of the town's ships. There is less evidence of partnerships between the older English-origin families and the presbyterians, but this can be attributed to the diminishing trading activities of many of the former. The most active merchant in this group was Lewis Thompson,[16] who owned shares in ships, including a gabart in partnership with George Macartney. By contrast, by the 1670s, neither the Leathes, Theaker nor Thetford families owned

---

15 Gillespie, 'Presbyterian revolution', pp 162–3; Tisdall, pp 60–1; Kirkpatrick, pp 438–9; Thomas Witherow, *Historical and literary memorials of presbyterianism in Ireland (1623–1731)* (London and Belfast, 1879), p.15.

16 Although the Thompsons were of Dutch origin they belonged to this group (appendix A.29).

shares in any Belfast ships, and by the beginning of the next century only Lewis Thompson and the Thetfords appear to have been actively involved in trade. They were not concerned in any trading ventures with Isaac Macartney in the years 1704–06, but the few references to them in his letter book suggest friendly co-operation.

The Belfast merchants were born into a world where kinsmen and god-parents would help them to get started in business. When they married, their wives' kinsmen and connections would promote their business careers. They would trade in partnership with men who were personally known to them, many of whom attended their church. However, at no stage in their lives were their friends more important to them than when they were on their deathbeds. Most merchants appointed their widows and/or their eldest sons as executors but to these was often added the name of a family friend, and other family friends, relations or close associates were appointed administrators. Although it was normal to appoint between one and three executors and two administrators there appears to have been no recognised upper limit. John Galt the younger, a presbyterian merchant of Coleraine, whose will was written in 1715, named six executors, six administrators, and four guardians for his children from two marriages. Although none of these men were Galts, they can almost all be shown to have been related in some way to the Galt family. Galt went on to add codicils over the next twelve years naming another four executors including his headstrong eldest son, once the latter had redeemed himself by marrying into 'a sober family'. Galt's will shows not only a wish to provide for his family but a determination to continue to control them from beyond the grave.[17] To a lesser extent, this is true of the will of George Macartney of Auchinleck, in which he attempted to enforce co-operation and goodwill between the sons of his first marriage and his second wife and her children.[18] Other merchant wills are simpler, merely showing a concern to protect the interests of young children. An examination of the surviving wills of the thirty-two merchant families shows that twenty-four, including two of English origin, were linked by ties of executorship or administratorship, with the services of individuals such as Samuel Martin, an attorney, and Thomas Craford, a notary public, being in great demand.

It has been possible to uncover links by blood, marriage, trade and reli-gion between most of the thirty-two families. Many were connected in a number of different ways. For example, John Hamilton was first an apprentice, then an employee of Black George Macartney. In his will, made during or after his first marriage which was childless, he named Black George's four young children as beneficiaries, so he may have been related to Black George or Martha, his wife. After Hamilton's death in 1687, Black

17 Appendix B.1.
18 Appendix A.20.

George was one of a group of merchants who took out letters of administration. Two of Hamilton's children by his second marriage were named George and Martha, which suggests that they were godchildren of Black George and his wife. Martha Hamilton, his last surviving child and heiress, married Robert Lennox who was a close friend and business associate of Black George's son Isaac, and they were both elders of the Belfast presbyterian church. Similarly William Sloane was employed by Black George, having probably been his apprentice. Sloane and Isaac Macartney married cousins, they were partners in trading voyages, and Isaac acted as Sloane's factor in Belfast after he moved to England. Finally Sloane was godfather to Isaac's second son William Macartney, and Sloane's son offered financial help to William Macartney when he visited London after the collapse of Isaac's business in the 1730s. Other families were clearly interrelated by equally complex ties although they are less well documented.[19] Merchants with different places of origin and different religions established links of kinship, employment or business with each other and by the end of the century they formed a close-knit community.

WEALTH

Since so many contemporaries remarked on the growth and prosperity of the town in the latter half of the seventeenth century, it follows that the merchant community was also considered prosperous and that the most successful merchants were rich. Unfortunately there are few sources relating to merchant income in Belfast. However, even where account books have survived, merchant finances are notoriously difficult to unravel because in the seventeenth century men were more interested in their rate of accumulation than in profit and loss.[20] Just as Samuel Pepys recorded what he was worth at the end of each year, so merchants charted the increase in their personal fortunes. Before studying the available evidence for the personal fortunes of Belfast merchants however, it must first be ascertained how much money a merchant needed to accumulate before he was considered rich.

Richard Lawrence, a member of the council of trade, suggested that successful merchants in Ireland could amass £9,000–£10,000 and bemoaned the fact that most of them then quit trade and laid out their money in land, the implication being that they would have been able to make larger fortunes had they continued in trade.[21] Although £10,000 would have been

---

19 In particular, the Martins, Whytes and Smiths intermarried several times.
20 Richard Grassby, 'The rate of profit in the seventeenth century' in *E.H.R.*, lxxxiv (1969), pp 722–3, 749.
21 Richard Lawrence, *The interest of Ireland in its trade and wealth stated* (Dublin, 1682), pt 1, p.7.

a moderate fortune for a successful London merchant, as he might expect to achieve at least twice that sum, a man worth £10,000 was still counted as a wealthy man in London and everywhere else in the British Isles.[22] At least two unnamed Belfast merchants were alleged to be worth £10,000. George Macartney of Auchinleck gave their names as bondsmen or sureties when he became collector at Belfast in 1688. When the commissioners of the revenue queried these names he wrote:

> it's true they are both merchants but their credit is good for ten thousand pounds not only in trade but in rent charges and judgments but if it be contrary to [the commissioners'] method pray let me know by a line and I shall provide other country gentlemen as soon as I get time to speak to them.[23]

Information about the wealth of individual Belfast merchants is contained in their wills although the figures given must be treated with caution because seventeenth-century merchants generally counted debts, even bad debts, as assets. Moreover, most of the Belfast wills have only survived in the form of abstracts which may be incomplete, and there are few for the first half of the century. They do not have inventories of possessions or debts, and property bequeathed is seldom valued. Nevertheless, these wills do at least give some idea of the hierarchy of wealth in Belfast. In 1661, Robert Nevin, a fairly minor merchant, reckoned that his assets amounted to £1,599 which sum he broke down thus: £1,000 owing to him, £315 in wares and merchandise in his shop, cellar and warehouse, £54 in cattle and horses, £150 in ready cash, and land to the value of £80 in County Armagh. Thus almost two-thirds of his fortune consisted of debts, although there is no reason to suppose that they were bad debts. However, he himself owed £1,092 which reduced his accumulated wealth at the time of his death to about £500. Nevin may have died young, as his children were all minors, and it was unusual for a merchant to be rich and young. Three richer (and probably older) merchants died in the early 1680s. Hugh Eccles who wrote his will in 1680 valued his cash and stock, excluding land, at £4,500 and left cash bequests of over £3,600. In 1681, James Chalmers reckoned that his worldly substance would amount to about £3,000, after payment of his debts and funeral expenses, and in 1684 William Smith left £3,800.

Average merchant fortunes may have risen slightly in the next generation. Hugh Rainey, brother of William Rainey of Belfast, left property worth £4,650 in 1708, and James Anderson of Belfast who died in 1706

22 Earle, *English middle class*, p.14; Richard Grassby, 'The personal wealth of the business community in seventeenth-century England' in *Econ. Hist. Rev.*, 2nd series xxiii (1970), pp 228, 231; Devine, 'Scottish merchant community', p.33.
23 Macartney to John Ellis, 2 Apr. 1688 (B.L., Ellis papers, Add. MS 28,876, f.87).

leaving cash bequests of just under £1,000, also had considerable estates in Counties Antrim, Down, Kilkenny and Kildare. However, the picture of merchant wealth derived from wills is incomplete because, in addition to the children named as beneficiaries, there may have been other older children who had already been provided for, and because even the beneficiaries may already have received part of their inheritance. For example, George Macartney of Auchinleck's will of 1691 states that God had blessed him with 'a considerable clear personal estate' but the size of his fortune cannot even be guessed at. His cash bequests totalled less than £1,000 but he stated that his son Arthur had already had £800 and that unspecified sums had been paid 'to and for' his son James. Moreover he had paid for an expensive education at the Inns of Court for two of his sons, and his daughter had been married for some years so presumably her dowry had been paid long since. Furthermore in most wills, including Macartney's, assets were not valued so many merchants may have left far more than their cash bequests suggest and the figures derived from wills are generally underestimates.

Information from other sources suggests that very large fortunes could be made by merchants. For example, in a letter to William Sloane who was living in England to escape his creditors, Isaac Macartney mentioned a Dublin merchant who had been forced to live abroad for twelve years but had eventually been able to repay his debts and died worth £20,000 and, perhaps inspired by this 'turn again Whittington' advice, Sloane cleared his debts in Ireland and is said to have been worth £100,000 at his death in 1726.[24] Sloane, however, had spent the last twenty years of his life in London, and lived until his mid-seventies, two factors which helped him to accumulate such a fortune. Although it was possible for Dublin merchants to amass similar, or even larger, fortunes[25] there is no evidence to suggest that even the richest Belfast merchant was worth such a sum at the same date. At the other end of the scale there were merchant families who only succeeded in making a living rather than a fortune. Bearing in mind the incomplete nature of the evidence, the most that can be said about merchant wealth in Belfast is that the rising volume of trade indicates a prosperous merchant class, and that a few individuals were very wealthy by provincial standards.

Certainly some merchant families had as much disposable income as the local gentry. For example, an examination of merchant dowries shows that they were similar in size to gentry dowries, although in each case there was a considerable range. Anna Upton, daughter of Arthur Upton of Castle Upton, who married William Conyngham of Springhill in 1680, had a

24 Macartney to Sloane, 17 Oct. 1705 (Macartney 3, pp 211–12); appendix A.25.
25 Joseph Damer, banker and usurer of Dublin, left £400, 000 in 1720 (C.M. Tenison 'The old Dublin bankers' in *Cork Historical and Archaeological Society Journal*, series 1, iii (1894), pp 104–5).

dowry of £300, as did the younger daughters of the merchants James Chalmers and William Smith of Belfast.[26] Mary Vernon, daughter of James Vernon, secretary of state, had a dowry of £1,500 in 1700 when she married Michael Harrison, the son of a Belfast burgess, but so did Dorothea Brice, the daughter of the merchant Edward Brice, who married Henry Maxwell of Finebroague in 1713. Isaac Macartney's daughter Grace, who married Robert Blackwood of Ballyleidy in 1729, had a dowry of £2,000, although this was still unpaid several years later.

It is possible to build up a picture of the economic hierarchy in the merchant community of Belfast in the second half of the seventeenth century. Among the fifteen Belfast townsmen whose names were extracted by Sir William Petty from the poll tax returns of 1659 as 'tituladoes', or property owners, are seven merchants, namely John Leathes, George Martin, Thomas and William Waring, Hugh Doake, George Macartney [of Auchinleck] and John Clugston, all of whom belong to the group of thirty-two families. William Waring, Doake, Macartney and Clugston also appear in the subsidy rolls of 1661 and 1666, with a total of eighteen other men, including fifteen merchants.[27] Of these latter, a further six appear in the profiles in appendix A, namely William Anderson, Hugh Eccles, Black George Macartney, William Moore, William Smith, and Lewis Thompson. In the eyes of the assessors, these were the richest Belfast merchants in the 1660s. The most heavily assessed in 1661 was William Waring (£8), then Hugh Eccles (£6), followed by Macartney of Auchinleck (£5) and William Smith (£4). In 1666 Waring was again the most heavily assessed at £5, followed by the two George Macartneys and John Clugston, all at £3.

Over the next twenty years there were few changes. By the time of the Jacobite wars the richest men were probably George Macartney of Auchinleck and Thomas Knox, followed closely by Black George, William Smith, Hugh Eccles and James Chalmers. It is not possible to arrange the rest in any kind of league table. Some of those who slid to the bottom of the scale, or who started there and never rose, will be considered in chapter 6, and even successful families usually had poor relations who are mentioned in wills, but seldom appear in other records. For example, in 1706, James Anderson mentioned in his will a cousin who was a carpenter in Dublin, and he left £30 to be distributed among the poor relations of his father-in-law William Lockhart, implying that they were too numerous to list by name.

The limited source material makes it impossible to give a detailed picture of the lifestyle of the community but is sufficient for an outline sketch. Forty-three Belfast merchants can be identified from the hearth money roll of 1669 with a total of 124 hearths, or just under three hearths

26 Marriage settlement of William Conyngham, 1680 (P.R.O.N.I., Lenox-Conyngham papers, D1449/1/11); appendix A.7, 26.
27 Pender, *Census Ire.*, p.8; Benn, pp 314–15.

per man. The two largest houses, with nine hearths apiece, were owned by Black George and William Smith. George Macartney of Auchinleck's was one of the two next largest with six hearths. Over half of the merchants appear to have lived in houses with two hearths or less, but under-stating the number of hearths was a common form of tax evasion. In view of the building going on in Belfast throughout the period many of the merchants may subsequently have moved to larger houses. Macartney of Auchinleck, for example, had built a substantial mansion house near his mills to the west of the town by 1685.

Since merchants could acquire luxury goods at wholesale prices it can be assumed that those with the taste and inclination lived well, dressed well and ate well. The source material provides occasional snapshots rather than a panorama. Thomas Waring had a silver cup and silver spoons; Black George ordered a silver salt for his table from Dublin in 1667; Hugh Eccles left his watch to his nephew, William Rainey; Jane Pottinger instructed her husband to buy her an ermine scarf and some scarlet satin ribbons to trim gloves; John Moore had an extensive wardrobe including a waistcoat with silver buttons; David Butle ordered a bible covered with russet leather, 180 black and white tiles for a chimney, and some of the best quality 'hair plush' for breeches from Holland in 1698; in 1705, Isaac Macartney ordered a wig and stockings from Dublin together with two dozen of the best wine glasses, although these were probably for the corporation's 'treat' or reception for the duke of Ormond; Robert Lennox had a wainscotted dining room; James Anderson left books, linen and a new wig to his cousin Dr George Martin of Dublin; and money was frequently left to buy mourning rings. The overall impression is one of comfort, and that some of the merchants (or their wives) aspired to style.[28]

One of the charges against the presbyterian merchants in the early eighteenth century was that they 'underlived' the conformist merchants, and were thus able to undersell them.[29] There must have been some element of truth in this accusation for it to have been brought at all, but it is more likely to relate to the peculiarities of a few individuals rather than the lifestyle of the whole community. For example, James Anderson, who was extremely wealthy, had a reputation for meanness. When Isaac Macartney refused an offer by William Cairnes, Belfast's M.P., to contribute to the 'treat' for the duke of Ormond in 1705, he warned him that

28 Copy will of Thomas Waring, 1665 (N.A., prerogative will book, 1664–84, ff 59–60); Macartney to William Rowe, 12 Mar. 1666/7 (Macartney 1, p.506); abstract of will of Hugh Eccles, 1680 (P.R.O.N.I., Society of Genealogists, T581/2, p.24); Jane to Edward Pottinger, 10 Dec. 1677 (N.A., Sarsfield-Vesey letters, 43); abstract of will of John Moore 1694 (P.R.O.N.I., Stewart abstracts, D1759/3B/1, p.85); Butle to Alex. Adare, 31 Jan. 1697/8 (Butle, p.53); Macartney to Cromie & Stevenson, 24 Mar. 1704/5, to James Lennox, 19 May 1705 (Macartney 3, pp 74, 108); copy will of James Anderson, 1706 (N.A., prerogative will book 1706–08, ff 24–25).

29 Tisdall, p.60.

'Mr James Anderson is to pay a part with us therefore pray do not let him know what is about for if he knew of any offer excused he would not pay one penny'.[30] However, cheese-paring was not confined to the presbyterians. William Waring, a wealthy merchant and a member of the established church, left instructions in 1676 for a frugal funeral 'for wine and tobacco giving to strangers I think it needless'.[31] By contrast, the presbyterian Isaac Macartney was described as 'opulent' which suggests visible wealth and a luxurious lifestyle.[32] These are extreme examples but, in general, both presbyterian and conformist merchants can be assumed to have lived well for a merchant's credit depended on outward appearances as well as reputation. To attract credit, his lifestyle had to reassure those who were preparing to entrust him with their money.

Having established that the Belfast merchants were prosperous, and that some were wealthy, it must next be determined where their money came from. Profits from trade were, of course, the foundation of merchant fortunes. The rate of profit which could be expected from trading ventures, and income from working on commission and handling bills of exchange, will be discussed in detail in chapters 6–7. However the speed of accrual and the size of the final accumulation were directly related to the amount of stock which a young merchant had at his disposal. Stock was 'start-up' money, generally provided by a merchant's parents. Lawrence's successful merchants who achieved fortunes of £9,000–£10,000 were assumed to have started with stock of £1,000, and this was a normal start-up sum in England. This was a large sum by Belfast standards and few merchant families could have afforded it. Evidence suggests that the sons of Macartney of Auchinleck, Black George and Hugh Eccles were given or bequeathed such sums, but the Smith and Chalmers sons only inherited £700–£800 and most young merchants had far less than that. Although Lawrence considered that even a stock of £500 would lead a young merchant into debt and restrict his trade, the sons of poorer Belfast merchant families would have been happy with such a sum. John Black of Bordeaux, for example, never got from his 'pious and worthy parents above £50 sterling stock but thanks be to God excellent good precepts, proper education, and above all their pious good example'.[33]

A small stock could be augmented. Many young merchants travelled as

---

30 Macartney to Cairnes, 5 May 1705 (Macartney 3, pp 101–2).
31 Benn, p.250.
32 Case papers, mid-eighteenth century (P.R.O.N.I., Ellison-Macartney papers, D3649/5).
33 Lawrence, *Interest of Ireland*, pt 1, pp 7, 10; Richard Grassby, 'Social mobility and business enterprise in seventeenth century England' in Donald Pennington and Keith Thomas (ed.), *Puritans and revolutionaries, essays in seventeenth century history presented to Christopher Hill* (Oxford 1978), p.366; John Black's journal, Apr. 1754 (P.R.O.N.I., T1073/7); transcript of letter from John Black the elder to son, 8 Sept. 1698 (P.R.O.N.I., Clarke papers, MIC92).

supercargoes, in charge of selling the cargo on an outwards voyage and buying goods to ship home, and were quite well paid. For example, Alexander Hillhouse was to be paid £16 for a voyage to the West Indies in 1667 (although the arrangement fell through) and would have had the opportunity to ship some goods of his own.[34] However a faster way of accumulating trading capital was through marriage. As shown above, many daughters of merchants brought sizeable dowries and useful connections. For example, after Thomas Pottinger's first marriage he traded in partnership with his father-in-law, Hugh Doake, and Janet Doake inherited property in her father's will. Hugh Eccles's first marriage with the widow Janet Moore has been noted above. It was early in his career as a merchant and her first husband's capital probably laid the foundations of Eccles's own trading fortune. For those who were not fortunate enough to marry heiresses (and unequal marriages were unusual), stock could only be augmented by years of hard work. John Black, for example, had insufficient stock to be taken into partnership by his master in Bordeaux and worked as a clerk in his counting house for about fourteen years before accumulating sufficient capital to be able to set up in business on his own and to marry a wife without a portion.[35]

Once a merchant was established and enjoying visible success he would be asked to take apprentices. Merchant apprenticeship premiums in London between 1650–80 ranged from £100 to £860 (for a Levant merchant) and they rose after this period.[36] Although Belfast rates doubtless started lower than London rates, it seems reasonable to assume that top Belfast merchants such as George Macartney, Black George, Thomas Knox and Hugh Eccles would have been able to charge at least £200. However, there is very little information about apprenticeship premiums paid in Ulster at this date. Arthur Upton of Castle Upton, a country gentleman who was the father-in-law of Edward Brice of Belfast, spent £100 on 'breeding my son Hercules for calling of a merchant' and left him £400 as stock. This latter sum was small compared with the 'start-up' sums inherited by some Belfast merchants and it has been observed that the gentry were frequently unable to raise adequate stock after the apprenticeship had been paid for. It was possible to be apprenticed very cheaply. For example, in 1659, the son of a deceased presbyterian minister was apprenticed to a merchant for two years at £20 16s per annum, but this must be considered as the bottom of the range because it was paid for by a charitable grant, and it is probable that most premiums were higher. Apart from the premium, apprentices were profitable to masters because of the work which they could do. Since they served from their mid-teens for seven years,

34 Macartney to Thomas Hackett, 16 and 23 Mar. 1666/7 (Macartney 1, pp 509, 513).
35 His father-in-law was 'in low circumstances by his attachment to the Jacobite party' (Black's journal, 23 May 1763 [P.R.O.N.I., T1073/16]).
36 Earle, *English middle class*, p.94.

apprentices acted as unpaid assistants in the counting house in their final years. For example, Macartney of Auchinleck's servant in 1689, James Smith, who was probably the clerk whom he described in the previous year as 'of my own education and bringing up', had still not completed his apprenticeship in 1691.[37]

Apart from the profits of trade, or trade-related activities, most merchants also derived an income from investments of various kinds such as ships, urban property, land, commercial undertakings and loans.[38] Most of the thirty-two merchant families studied can be proved to have been ship-owners and this will be discussed in detail in chapter 6. Similarly, virtually all of the thirty-two families owned property in Belfast. Urban property was in many ways like stock – it could be inherited and it could be augmented. The twelve 'tituladoes' of Belfast town must all have been major Donegall tenants, and it has been seen above that they included seven merchants from the group of thirty-two families. Two more of the thirty-two (Sampson Theaker and Francis Thetford) appear in the subsidy roll of 1666 paying £2 each on land in the barony of Belfast.[39] There are no surviving seventeenth-century estate records for Belfast. The earliest Belfast rental dates from 1719, although it lists people who had died some years previously.[40] Twenty of the thirty-two families appear in this rental as Donegall tenants. Bearing in mind that by 1719 seven of the thirty-two had either died out in the main branch, or left Belfast, it is likely that almost all of the group of were at some stage tenants-in-chief of the Donegall family. Moreover, thirteen of these twenty tenants listed in the rental still had land in the town fields which indicates that they were holding parts of the original burgage shares. Thirteen also held more than one house so were able to make money from letting their property, and such property was also useful as collateral for loans.

By far the largest tenant in 1719 was George Macartney, son of Macartney of Auchinleck, whose property included five mills and over one hundred acres of land on the outskirts of Belfast, as well as a number of houses, for which he paid a total annual rent of £173 8s 6d. Only eight other tenants paid more than £16 in rent. These included Michael

---

37 Twelve of Upton's eighteen children lived to adulthood, which must have strained his resources, see copy will (N.A., prerogative will book, 1706–08, ff 27–9); Grassby, 'Social mobility and business enterprise', pp 367, 376; extract from Commonwealth order book, 27 Apr. 1659 (P.R.O.N.I., Tenison Groves abstracts, T808/4038); petition of George Macartney, 27 Sept. 1689 (P.R.O., treasury book, T1/5, p.105); Macartney to Ellis, 13 Aug. 1688 (B.L., Add. MS 28,876, f.141); will of George Macartney, 27 Apr. 1691 (P.R.O.N.I., D1184).

38 Richard Grassby, 'English merchant capitalism in the late seventeenth century, the composition of business fortunes' in *Past and Present*, xlvi (1970), pp 104, 107.

39 Benn, pp 314–5.

40 Rental for town and manor of Belfast for the year ending 1 Nov. 1719 (P.R.O.N.I., D2249/61).

Harrison (£32 10s), Nicholas Thetford (£30 14s), Isaac Macartney (£21 9s 6d), William Bigger (£20 4s) and Westenra Waring (£17 17s 9d). Some idea can be gained of the kind of income which these properties generated. George Macartney of Auchinleck and Black George both appear in the list of protestant refugees who fled from the Jacobites in 1689 and made claims for compensation. The yearly value of their estates is listed as £400 and £300 respectively. Letters from Edward Harrison to James Vernon, secretary of state, about a proposed marriage between his son Michael and Vernon's daughter, reveal that in 1699 he derived about £330, or one third of his income, from his Belfast property, excluding his own house and demesnes.[41] However, Like Macartney of Auchinleck, he owned substantial property outside the town, the income of which is included in this sum. In the 1720s Isaac Macartney was clearing £400 p.a. from leasehold property in Belfast; apart from about twenty-seven acres in the town fields, this was all urban and included land he had reclaimed from the foreshore on which he had built a number of fashionable houses.[42] Even though no figures can be arrived at for the income of other merchant families derived from property within Belfast it can be assumed that, for some, it was a significant percentage of their total income. The Donegall rental underlines the pre-eminent position of George Macartney who was paying a rent almost six times as large as that of any other tenant and was presumably enjoying an income in the same proportion. Nevertheless, this picture of property holding and income in Belfast is over-simplified because the rental reveals that there were only ninety-five tenants in the town and manor of Belfast holding directly from Lord Donegall, and many merchant families held, and sub-let, other properties as Donegall under-tenants.

The Donegall rental of 1719 also shows that a number of families were deriving part of their income from commercial undertakings. George Macartney had inherited his father's four corn mills and tuck mill. Members of the Martin family, then living in Dublin, had a brew house and tan pits, Westenra Waring had a tan pit, and Nicholas Thetford had a malt kiln. Of these, only Nicholas Thetford was still actively involved in trade in 1719. Investment by Belfast merchants in commercial property and undertakings can be documented from the 1660s. In 1665, Macartney of Auchinleck was a partner with William Smith in an ironworks in or near Belfast using imported ore. As nothing further is heard of it, the venture may have been unsuccessful. Certainly over-production made other iron works unprofitable at this date. Macartney and Smith also appear to have been partners in the first Belfast sugar refinery, and a second one was set up by the early eighteenth century. The pottery, which was set up in 1698,

---

41 Claims of protestant refugees (T.C.D., MS 847, f.6); *Cal. S.P. dom., 1699*, p.185.
42 Case papers, mid-eighteenth century (P.R.O.N.I., Ellison-Macartney papers, D3649/21).

was owned by William Smith's sons, David and Patrick, their brother-in-law Thomas Craford, and Henry Chads. Several merchant families had actively combined trade and trade-related processes. The Warings started as tanners and invested their profits in trade. A branch of the Leathes family were tanners. The Thetfords were both merchants and chandlers. However, with the exception of the Thetfords, and the Smiths who were still running the sugar refinery, most merchants were no longer actively participating in such commercial undertakings by the beginning of the eighteenth century although they continued to enjoy the profits from their investments.[43]

In addition to investment in urban and commercial property, loans were seen as a very profitable way of laying out spare cash. Short term loans to remedy the deficiencies of seventeenth-century cash flow were negotiated between merchants at low interest, but the normal rate of interest in Ireland throughout most of the period was 10%. By the 1680s, such numbers of merchants were investing in loans that it was possible to borrow at 8% upon good security,[44] but at the same time many loan agreements, where the risk was greater, carried a penalty clause doubling the debt. Long term loans, which were generally to the gentry, are discussed in chapter seven, which deals in detail with the whole question of credit. It is not possible to estimate the proportion of merchant income that came from investment rather than trade. It has been shown that the London merchants generally accumulated sufficient capital to invest by the time they reached their forties and that investments brought in an increasing percentage of their income from then on.[45] In all probability merchant investment followed the same pattern in Belfast.

LAND

Although urban property, commercial undertakings and loans were all profitable investments, the most reliable investment throughout the seventeenth century was land. Like urban property it brought in an income and could be used as collateral for loans. However, ownership[46] of land could have far-reaching effects on merchant families as, apart from providing a source of income which was unrelated to merchant activities, it also enhanced the

43 Macartney to Thomas Wakefield, 4 Nov. 1665, and to Elizabeth Brittan, 7 Aug. 1666 (Macartney 1, pp 260, 402); *Cal. S.P. Ire., 1662–65*, p.602; extract from Rainey's journal, Nov. 1704 (L.H.L., Joy MSS, 10); Registry of Deeds, Dublin, 26 89 14738; Peter Francis, 'The Belfast potthouse, Carrickfergus clay and the spread of the delftware industry' in *Transactions of the English Ceramic Circle*, xv, pt 2 (1994), pp 267–282.
44 Gillespie, *Transformation of the Irish economy*, pp 56–7.
45 Earle, *English middle class*, p.144.
46 The term ownership is used here loosely; much land was held by leases for lives which were renewable and which conferred the status of freeholder on tenants.

status of those who acquired it and could lead to residence in the country and the abandonment of trade. Most Belfast merchants who reached that period in their lives when they had cash available for investment purposes acquired land, but their motives for acquiring it appear to have been mixed. The traditional view was that the ambition of every merchant was to make enough money to acquire an estate and to join the ranks of the gentry. Lawrence stated that the cheapness of land in Ireland was actually an impediment to trade because it encouraged merchants to purchase estates and retire from trade and 'of a rich Merchant become a Country Gentleman: and then parting with a few Guineys to procure a Dub, or Patent, the Knight's Son will blush if you tell him his Father got his Estate by conversing with Tarpolins'.[47] This may have been true in Dublin where a number of wealthy merchants received knighthoods, but only a few examples can be found before the eighteenth century of Belfast merchants retiring from trade to live on their estates.

In the Commonwealth period land was readily available to protestant purchasers. John Corry, a Scottish merchant who became a freeman of Belfast in 1654, had made enough money by 1656 to buy the manor of Coole in County Fermanagh, and he left Belfast to live there. Similarly, the merchant Gilbert Eccles, a freeman of Belfast in 1647, also acquired land in Counties Fermanagh and Westmeath in this period, and also retired from trade. William Waring, who like his brother Thomas Waring of Belfast made money in the tanning trade, purchased the Clanconnell estate in County Down. Ensign John Leathes, a son of William Leathes, the sovereign who died in 1660, was a royalist army officer, but he also appears to have held office under the Commonwealth when he obtained the townland of Rathnugent in County Westmeath. However, it is not clear whether he retained it after the 1660s, and he continued to be resident in Belfast and involved in trade. The small number of identifiable merchants who acquired estates in the 1650s is an indication that trade from Belfast before that date was on a limited scale and that profits were modest.[48]

The Belfast merchant community prospered in the period 1660–90, but none of the thirty-two families appear to have acquired land in order to live on it and, although there is evidence of some major purchases of land from the 1690s, most of these families remained resident in Belfast. One notable exception was Thomas Knox who purchased the Dungannon estate from Lord Donegall in 1692 and went to live there, resigning as a burgess in 1697. Similarly, Captain Hugh Eccles, eldest son of the burgess Hugh Eccles, married a wealthy widow and acquired an estate in County Wicklow, and so ceased to live in Belfast, although other Eccles cousins

47 Lawrence, *Interest of Ireland*, pt 1, p.7.
48 R.M. Young (ed.), *Historical notices of old Belfast and its vicinity* (Belfast, 1896), pp 110–11; appendix A.12, 15; E.D. Atkinson, *An Ulster parish, being a history of Donaghcloney* (Dublin, 1898), p.24.

remained active in trade in Belfast, Dublin and Waterford. Edward Brice and David Butle, younger sons of two gentry families in County Antrim, ultimately acquired the family estates. Butle inherited property in Glenarm from his brother, and Brice purchased the Kilroot estate from his nephew in order to settle it on the children of his second marriage. There is insufficient evidence to show whether Brice and Butle continued in trade but other merchants who acquired estates do not appear to have lived on them or to have ceased trading. For example, William Craford bought the manor of Florida in County Down in 1692 but continued to live in Belfast, as did the merchant John Young who bought property in County Down from the trustees for the sale of the estates of Sir Hans Hamilton in 1706–09.[49]

Although land was available throughout the seventeenth century for those who could afford it, confiscation of land after the Jacobite wars put whole estates on the market in the 1690s and 1700s. Rather surprisingly there is little evidence that the Belfast merchants took advantage of this opportunity, and none of them made purchases on the same scale as, for example, the Belfast member of parliament, William Cairnes, who acquired extensive estates in County Monaghan.[50] Factors against investment in the forfeited estates may have been that some merchants had made serious losses during the war period[51] and that full economic recovery was not achieved until the mid-1690s and this was short-lived. By the early 1700s when the forfeiture commission put a large number of estates on the market, many merchants were feeling the effects of economic recession and stagnation in trade resulting from the war of the Spanish Succession. Certainly the sales of forfeited estates failed to make as much as had been anticipated.[52] A further factor which may have discouraged investment by Belfast merchants was that comparatively little land was actually available in Ulster, most of the forfeited estates being in the south and west of Ireland. Only one member of a Belfast family can be identified as a direct purchaser of land from the commission. This was James Anderson, the son of a Glasgow merchant who settled in Belfast in the 1650s.[53] Having amassed a considerable fortune Anderson purchased a total of 1,583 acres in Counties Antrim, Down, Kildare and Kilkenny, in 1703. In his purchase of land in the barony of Lecale in County Down, he was acting for a partnership consisting of himself, Edward Brice, and Richard Cadell, a merchant of Downpatrick. The land, which had been part of the private estate of James II, cost the partners £1,715 and was immediately divided between

---

49 Appendix A.4, 5, 9, 32.
50 H.C. Lawlor, *A history of the family of Cairnes* (London, 1906), p.83.
51 For example, Robert Martin was given government debentures for advances of money to Williamite forces which were never paid (L.H.L., Joy MSS, 6).
52 J.G. Simms, *The Williamite confiscation in Ireland 1690–1703* (London, 1956, repr. Connecticut, 1976), pp 149–51.
53 Appendix A.1.

them by lot. Similarly, Anderson sold leases of property in and near Newry for £1,050 within a few days of his purchase being enrolled by the forfeiture commissioners. His purchase of lands in the south of Ireland appears to have been unique among the Belfast merchant families at this date although, by contrast, Dublin merchants were ready to invest in Ulster.[54] Anderson still owned the estates in Counties Kildare and Kilkenny at the time of his death but, since this occurred only three years after their purchase, it is unclear whether he bought them in order to live on them or purely as an investment.

Although, in the second half of the seventeenth century, few Belfast merchants acquired estates in order to settle on them, there were many who purchased land as an investment and it is possible to adduce plenty of examples from the thirty-two families. For example, Thomas Pottinger and John Hamilton acquired the townlands of Ballymacarrett and Cottown, respectively, in County Down from Lord Clanbrassil in 1672.[55] In 1680, Black George Macartney was negotiating with a correspondent on the Isle of Man for half a townland near Belfast held from Lord Donegall and authorised a mutual friend to spend up to twenty shillings on wine 'so to close with him for me getting me a firm deed out of the grand lease he hath'. In 1705, his son Isaac wrote to Lord Conway's agent offering to lay out £1,200–£1,500 for 'a lease or two', and enquired about a number of specified farms for a friend with £500–£700 to lay out, and in 1706 he bought a 2,000 year lease of several townlands in County Down.[56]

Possession of land conferred status, and landowners were automatically numbered among the gentry, although their exact status was determined by their ancestry, income and family affiliations. Three-quarters of the thirty-two families held some land outside Belfast by the early 1700s, but most of these properties were small. For example, only four of the merchant families (Brice, Craford, both Macartneys) appear in a list of gentry with £100 p.a. and upwards, made in the late 1720s.[57] It appears therefore that although many merchants acquired land when the opportunity presented itself, the acquisition of a landed estate was not the prime objective of the Belfast merchants in this period. Furthermore, the possession of land was only one of the factors which determined the status of Belfast merchants both within and outside the community.

54 Hill, *Macdonnells of Antrim*, p.466.
55 Appendix A.13, 23.
56 Macartney to David Murray, 17 Nov. 1680 (Macartney 2, p.392); Macartney to Charles Herron, 3 Nov. 1705 (Macartney 3, pp 220–1); copy lease, 1 Feb. 1705(/6) (P.R.O.N.I., land purchase commission deeds, T810/180); his niece Molly Cromie married his principal tenant there (appendix A.19); Macartney later acquired property in Counties Down and Armagh which had been bought by his father-in-law, William Haltridge of Dromore (appendix B.3).
57 List of the nobility and gentry ... divided into churchmen, dissenters and papists (Lambeth Palace Lib., Gibson letters, MS 1742, ff 49–56).

STATUS

Little information has survived about Belfast townsmen who were not merchants although there are indications in the subsidy, hearth money and freemen's rolls that some tradesmen were wealthy. It is clear however that the merchants were leaders within the town both in terms of wealth and status, the latter being recognised by election to office. Membership of, and office-holding within, craft guilds generally bestowed status in urban communities and was seen as a preliminary to participation in town government. However, there is no evidence to suggest the existence of a guild merchant, such as the Trinity guild in Dublin, or of any craft guilds at Belfast in the seventeenth century. All Belfast freemen, including presbyterians, were eligible to become burgesses without any qualifying period of time, provided they met with the approval of the earls of Donegall. William Waring, for example, was made freeman and burgess on the same day. Moreover, there was no formal property qualification.[58] Since the corporation was self-perpetuating, however, there was a tendency to elect from a small group of families. Eight families each produced more than one burgess (Harrison, Leathes, both Macartneys, Theaker, Thetford, Thompson, Waring) and, of these, five (Leathes, Macartney of Auchinleck, Thetford, Thompson, Waring) produced more than one sovereign. Nevertheless, the composition of the corporation was not unduly narrow. Of the thirty-two families, eighteen produced at least one burgess. These families tended to be the richest within the group but the corporation should not be seen purely as an oligarchy. These families were rich because they were successful, and successful because they were capable, so their election to burgess rank was a reflection both of their wealth and their ability.

Similarly, the leading merchants were also leaders within the church. Although it is not known who were members of the parish vestry, rather more is known of the organisation of the presbyterian congregation. Of the twenty-two families in the group known to be presbyterian, at least twelve produced either elders of, or commissioners from, the Belfast congregation between 1660 and 1707. After the abrogation of the oath of supremacy in 1691, the number of presbyterian burgesses increased and, between 1701 and 1705, six men (Edward Brice, David Butle, John Chalmers, William Craford, Isaac Macartney, and David Smith) were simultaneously burgesses and elders (or commissioners), making them the most powerful group in the community.

Wealth and success contributed to status outside the community. Equally important, however, were such factors as social origins, the education and occupations of sons who did not become merchants, and relationships by blood or marriage with the local gentry. Using the profiles in appendix A it

---

58 There was a property qualification of £500 p.a. for aldermen in Dublin (Sheehan, 'Irish towns in a period of change', p.104).

is possible to determine the social standing of the thirty-two families at civic, local and national levels and to draw more general conclusions about the standing of merchants in this period. Since much of the documentation for their social standing involves their relationships with the gentry, it is necessary first to give a brief account of the gentry of Counties Antrim and Down, and to examine contemporary gentry attitudes towards trade.

Like the merchant community, the gentry of Counties Antrim and Down in the seventeenth century was largely immigrant, from different places of origin and with different religious affiliations. All immigrants, however, were protestants who replaced Roman catholics as landowners. With the notable exception of the earls of Antrim, who were of Scottish origin, few Roman catholics had large estates after 1660 and fewer still managed to retain them after the Jacobite wars. Most of the land was held by protestants. English officers from Essex's army settled in County Antrim in the late sixteenth century, and Scots settled in both counties from the beginning of the seventeenth century. Of the nobility, the Donegall, Conway and Downshire families were English, and the Clanbrassils and Mountalexanders were Scots. Each brought over, or encouraged, settlers from their own native region. The majority of both minor gentry and tenant farmers were Scots but the Lagan valley, in particular the Conway estate around Lisburn, was predominantly English. However, the divide between the gentry was not primarily one of nationality but of religion. Most of the Scots were presbyterian but so too were many gentry families of English origin such as the Clotworthys, Skeffingtons, Dallways and Uptons. The list of 'Scots' whom it was proposed to transport out of Ulster in 1653 is in fact a roll-call of the presbyterian gentry, both Scots and English.[59] Many of these gentry families conformed to the established church in the early eighteenth century, but until then the gentry of Counties Antrim and Down was predominantly presbyterian.

Although, after the restoration, government policy was to exclude presbyterians from local office, members of presbyterian families served as justices and high sheriffs in Ulster, principally because the pool of gentry families from which such appointments could be made was small, even when the presbyterians were included. They were generally regarded with a certain amount of suspicion by the Dublin government and this fluctuated with events in Ulster and Scotland. For example, after Blood's Plot in 1663, a number of County Antrim justices were removed, including Sir John Skeffington, Sir Hercules Langford and Arthur Upton.[60] Even though such English presbyterians were hardly likely to make common cause with the covenanters in Scotland, they were active in supporting their co-religionists against the religious courts.

59 Young, *Historical notices*, pp 80–3.
60 List of County Antrim justices, 1663 (Bodl., Carte MSS 32, ff 448–9).

Although gentry wealth and status were based on land, trade was seen as an excellent investment. For example, when Godert de Ginkel, commander-in-chief of the Williamite army, offered Patrick Sarsfield a reward for his part in the successful peace negotiations of 1691, he asked for the privilege of sending back some cargoes of wine and other goods on the ships which were to transport the Irish soldiers to France. Investment in trade was attractive to all ranks of nobility and gentry and often took the form of direct export of agricultural produce. The duke of Ormond, for example, wrote in 1666 that he and Lord Conway 'had a mind to truck some of the commodities of this country against French wines', and in 1668, Conway's agent, a member of the Leathes family, was getting together butter, salmon and tallow to send to Bordeaux on a ship belonging to Black George Macartney.[61]

Letters to Conway from his brother-in-law, Sir George Rawdon, show that professional advice was recognised as being necessary for success in trade. Rawdon had a high opinion of Black George as 'the only man to advise with in these parts both for honesty and ability to deal with', and in his turn, Rawdon was quick to pass on advice to the merchants about the state of markets abroad. He was on friendly terms with the Dublin merchant Humphrey Jervis and sometimes stayed at his house.[62] Black George also had dealings with Sir Humphrey Langford who was involved with the shipping of beef in the 1660s.[63] David Butle's letter book reveals that in 1701 Lord Donegall was taking two-fifths of a cargo of wines with Butle and other Belfast merchants, and the letters suggest involvement in other cargoes.[64] Minor gentry too were involved in trade and knowledgeable about trading practice. For example, Richard Dobbs of Castle Dobbs, near Carrickfergus, had a 'little boat' and wrote 'If the Commodity she brings be either too much for the market or not vendible, take no more than is fit to go off, leave the rest in pledge for the Duty', and a country gentleman like William Montgomery of Rosemount was sufficiently knowledgeable about trade to be aware that the Belfast merchants needed a customhouse of their own. Gentry were also involved in commercial undertakings, generally to exploit some asset on their own estates. Rawdon, for example, had an ironworks in the 1660s and was quick to advise Conway of other commercial opportunities which seemed viable.[65]

Not only did the gentry invest; active gentry participation in trade makes this period unique in British history. The increasing rigidity of primogeniture, coupled with lower infant mortality, led to a larger sub-class

61 Simms, *War and politics in Ireland*, p.199; *Cal. S.P. Ire.*, *1666–69*, pp 49, 630.
62 Rawdon to Conway, 31 Mar. 1668, 28 Mar. 1674 (P.R.O., SP.63/324, no.49, SP.63/335, no.54); Macartney to Edward Yeard, 15 Nov. 1667 (Macartney 1, p.622); *Cal. S.P. Ire.*, *1666–69*, p.575; *Cal. S.P. dom.*, *1673–75*, p.48.
63 Macartney to [Langford], 28 Feb. 1664/5 (Macartney 1, p.162).
64 Butle to [Donegall], 12 July 1701, to Alex. Cairnes, 1701 (Butle, pp 63–4).
65 Hill, *Macdonnells of Antrim*, p.376; Hill, *Montgomery manuscripts*, p.425; *Cal. S.P.*

of gentry younger sons. As it would have been beyond the resources of most landed families to support them, they were customarily given or bequeathed a sum of money, first to train and then to launch them in some profession which would enable them to live as gentlemen. Their options were narrower than they would be in the following century when both the army and the navy had evolved so that they could absorb vast numbers of younger sons. However, this process had already begun in the late seventeenth century, and in the same period the status of physicians and solicitors improved because of recruitment from the gentry, and the profession of land steward emerged. Trade was widely seen as both respectable and profitable. Increasing numbers of gentry younger sons were apprenticed to merchants and 'merchandizing' became a recognised gentry profession with a potential for profit which made it extremely popular with those who could afford the high apprenticeship premiums and the necessary stock. Rather than trade defiling gentlemen, the result of extensive gentry participation seems to have been a raising of the status of trade. Gentry participation in trade became common in both England and Scotland, and there is sufficient evidence to show that this was this also true in Ireland.[66]

The Irish custom of calling every small retailer a merchant was claimed to have deterred the the Irish gentry from choosing trade as a career for their younger sons:

> But from this degrading of the reputation of Merchants, that Honourable Calling is of so low repute that few Gentlemen, much less Noblemen, will put their Sons Apprentice to a Merchant, but rather breed them for Divines, Souldiers, Lawyers, Physicians, &c[67]

A few affected to despise merchants. Jonathan Swift wrote in a letter to Varina (a grand-daughter of Thomas Waring of Belfast) 'If you like such company and conduct, much good do you with them! My education has been otherwise.'[68] However, this letter was couched in deliberately offensive terms, and Swift chose to ignore the fact that his own family had been involved in trade. There is in fact plenty of evidence that gentry participa-

Ire., 1662–65, p.602; the same gentry awareness of trade and commerce has been observed in Scotland in this period (T.C. Smout, *Scottish trade on the eve of union, 1660–1707* [Edinburgh and London, 1963], pp 73–5).

66 Earle, *English middle class*, p.7 et seq.; Richard Grassby, 'Social mobility and business enterprise', pp 356–60; Joan Thirsk, 'Younger sons in the seventeenth century' in *History*, liv (1968–9), pp 358–77; Edward Hughes, 'The eighteenth–century estate agent' in H.A. Cronne, T.W. Moody, D.B. Quinn (ed.), *Essays in British and Irish history* (London, 1949), pp 188, 192, 195; Lawrence Stone, 'Social mobility in England, 1500–1700' in *Past and Present*, xxxiii (1966), pp 18–19, 27; Devine, 'Scottish merchant community', pp 36–7; Smout, 'Glasgow merchant community', p.67.

67 Lawrence, *Interest of Ireland*, pt 1, p.8.

68 Harold Williams (ed.), *The correspondence of Jonathan Swift* (vol. i, Oxford, 1963), p.35.

tion in trade was widespread in Ireland, and that trade and commerce were acceptable professions in most gentry families. Many instances can be found of the younger sons of Ulster gentry families becoming merchants. Hercules Upton of Castle Upton in County Antrim has been noted above. Of the sons of Hugh Montgomery of Ballymagoun in County Down:

> Samuel, the fifth son hath been kept severall years abroad in the Latin School, he may be a merchant, to which mistery having prepared himself by learning Arithmetick (as he has done a fair hand in writing) he is now entered an apprentice, and if he chance to be unfortunate in those arts he will make a stout Soldier ... to which he is more inclined than to study for a Bishopric.[69]

Eventually both Hercules Upton and Samuel Montgomery went into the army but other gentry merchants were more tenacious or better suited to their profession. The emerging profession of banker also drew recruits from gentry families. The Cairnes brothers who were bankers in London and Dublin at the end of the seventeenth century came from a gentry family of Scottish origin with property in Counties Donegal, Londonderry and Tyrone. Francis Harrison, who became a banker in Dublin at the end of the 1690s, was a younger son of Edward Harrison, burgess of Belfast, who had property in four Ulster counties.[70]

Turning to the thirty-two Belfast families in appendix A, a number clearly belonged to this social class. David Butle, Edward Brice, John Hamilton and William Sloane all came from landed families in Counties Antrim and Down, and had near relatives with substantial estates. In fact, most of the second generation immigrants who settled in Belfast from the surrounding counties and set up in overseas trade probably came from this class because, before the Jacobite wars gave minor traders the opportunity to make fortunes, it was only the gentry who could afford the necessary 'start-up' sums. Similarly, although it has not been possible to prove specific relationships with gentry families in England, there is is no doubt that, among the earliest English settlers, such families as the Leatheses, Theakers and Thetfords, had gentry origins and ranked as gentry in Ulster. For example, William Leathes, sovereign of Belfast, who died in office in 1660, had a full heraldic funeral with painted escutcheons, which was attended by the earl of Donegall and the marquess of Antrim;[71] while Thomas Theaker, another Belfast burgess who died in the same year, had had his arms confirmed in 1644 and, on his death, a funeral entry was made at the office of the Ulster king of arms in Dublin.

---

69 Hill, *Montgomery manuscripts*, p.376.
70 Tenison, 'Old Dublin bankers', pp 36–38, 120–23; L.M. Cullen, 'Landlords, bankers and merchants: the early Irish banking world, 1700–1820' in A.E. Murphy (ed.), *Economists and the Irish economy from the eighteenth century to the present day* (Dublin, 1984), p.32; and see appendix B.4.
71 *Town book*, p.241.

It is harder to determine the social origins of those immigrants who settled in Belfast between the late 1640s and the 1660s. Even those families which were later included in such works as Burke's *Peerage* and *Landed gentry* could seldom name an ancestor prior to the first member of the family to settle in Ireland, and although they frequently claimed kinship with landed families in Scotland or England, this sometimes appears to have been based on the coincidence of surnames rather than any actual proof. The scantiness of the immigrant population in Ulster probably made any settlers of respectable appearance and adequate means welcome in both urban and rural communities, and the accounts of their origins which were handed down to their descendants were vague. But although some settlers may have been what Andrew Stewart, presbyterian minister of Donaghadee, called 'the scum of both nations who for debt, or breaking and fleeing from justice, or seeking shelter, came hither',[72] most of the merchants who settled in Belfast appear to have had some capital, education and trading contacts. Consequently their claims to have come from landed families were probably true, bearing in mind the vast kinship networks of many such families, particularly in Scotland, where some branches were 'upwardly mobile' while others were sinking without trace. Many of the leading Scottish merchants who settled in Belfast can be proved to have come from the royal burghs of Scotland, and this supports their claims to descent from gentry families since many Scottish merchants came from landed stock. For example, Thomas Knox, though from an urban background, had a distinguished ancestry and connections, and the two Macartneys were from minor landed families. A number in this group claimed to be armigerous; James Chalmers and Hugh Eccles both put a coat of arms on the tokens which they issued in the 1650s, and others used heraldic devices.

The seventeenth century was something of an heraldic free-for-all in Ulster. Very few coats of arms were formally registered, and no registers of arms were kept by the Ulster Office until 1698. Families claiming to be armigerous had their arms confirmed, which avoided undermining their social pretensions and gave them the right to the style 'esquire'.[73] Evidence can be found that eleven of the thirty-two merchant families were, or claimed to be, armigerous, although the total was probably far greater as it would have included most of those who came from Ulster gentry backgrounds. A growing social awareness is visible among Belfast merchant families towards the end of the seventeenth century when a number registered their arms, for example George Macartney of Auchinleck in Dublin in 1680, Robert Leathes in London, Edward Brice and Thomas Knox in Edinburgh in 1693, and Westenra Waring (grandson of Thomas Waring) in Dublin in 1706. These registrations were all in the form of confirmations

72 John Stevenson, *Two centuries of life in Down, 1600–1800* (Belfast, 1920), p.45.
73 T.F. McCarthy, 'Ulster Office 1552–1800' (M.A. thesis, Q.U.B., 1983), p.57.

of arms, which also confirmed the ancient gentry status of these families. However, not all merchants had social pretensions. In 1680 Black George Macartney declined to call himself 'esquire' during his term of office as sovereign of Belfast, but still styled himself 'George Macartney merchant', writing 'I intend to continue as I was and will be after'.[74] His motive was to avoid increasing the confusion between himself and George Macartney of Auchinleck but, since he had just been appointed high sheriff of County Antrim, he probably felt that his social standing was unambiguous.

Similarly, increasing social awareness is suggested by the efforts of two Belfast men to discover more about their ancestry. In 1670, Robert Leathes, son of the sovereign William Leathes, wrote to a distant cousin in Cumberland, introducing himself as a kinsman 'who by providence has sprung up in a strange kingdom', and asking for an account of their mutual ancestors. In 1725, John Black the elder, whose father was a 'trooper against Cromwell', was encouraged by his son, the British consul at Cadiz, to write to the laird of Lamont in Scotland. After describing the success and respectability of his own family, Black asked 'to know the origin that the name Black hath in the ancient family of Lamont, and likewise your Coat of Arms'. However, the interest of many Belfast merchants in heraldry and ancestry should not be seen as pretentious. In the seventeenth century, not only did a significant number of merchants come from landed families, but it will be seen by their marriage alliances, the professions of their sons, and by the offices that they held outside the community, that they continued to function as part of that class.[75]

Traditionally, it was the wealthy merchant's heiress who married into the gentry or nobility. In Belfast, the reverse was more common. Indeed, the pattern for most merchant/gentry alliances was the marriage of a well-to-do merchant, or merchant's son, with the daughter of a landed family. For example, John Hamilton, sovereign of Belfast from 1683–85, married a daughter of Colonel Tobias Norris who had an estate at Newcastle. William Sloane married Jane Hamilton of Killyleagh. Edward Brice married first Dorothea Upton, then Jane Dobbs, both from gentry families of County Antrim, and David Butle married Anne, sister of William Conyngham of Springhill in County Londonderry. But although these bridegrooms were merchants, all of them came of landed families in Ulster so they were in fact marrying within their own class. A number of the Scots who arrived in the 1650s–60s also made marriages with the gentry. James Chalmers married a cousin of the Kennedys of Cultra in County Down, Thomas Knox married Mary Brice, and William Anderson's son, George, married Grissell Maxwell of Rubane, also in County Down.

74 Macartney to Humphrey Jervis, 18 Dec. 1680 (Macartney 2, p.405).
75 Copy letter from Robert Leathes to Thomas Laythes, 5 Oct. 1670 (Society of Friends' Library, London, Thomas Laythes's book of letters 1659–80, p.280); Benn, p.523.

The size of the dowries of the daughters of merchant families has already been noted. These dowries enabled them to marry into gentry families which could make comparable settlements, but they should not be seen as heiresses who married outside their own class. Grace Macartney's husband, Robert Blackwood of Ballyleidy, was her second cousin, and Dorothea Brice who married Henry Maxwell of Finebroague, was a granddaughter of Arthur Upton of Castle Upton, so neither bride married into a different social or economic class. The richest merchant heiress appears to have been George Anderson's daughter Margaret who inherited the fortunes of both her father and uncle and married Cromwell Price of Hollymount; nevertheless, since she was a niece of Hugh Maxwell of Rubane, she was herself part of the gentry of County Down. Thus, most gentry/merchant marriages did not involve significant inequality either of rank or fortune.

The most outstanding alliances were achieved by the family of George Macartney of Auchinleck. Macartney himself married, as his second wife, the sister of Nicholas Butler, a London merchant, who was subsequently knighted and who became a commissioner of the customs and a privy councillor under James II. Macartney's eldest son married a niece of the earl of Longford, and his youngest, one of the daughters and co-heiresses of Sir Charles Porter, lord chancellor of Ireland and lord chief justice. Both sons, however, were councillors (or barristers) and might therefore expect to achieve wealth through their profession, in addition to the wealth and property they inherited from their father. So these marriages, although advantageous, were not entirely unequal.[76]

While the gentry put their younger sons into trade, the Belfast merchants educated sons for professions which recruited almost exclusively from the gentry, namely the law, the church, medicine, the army and estate management. In fact it is rare to find any well-to-do Belfast merchant family apprenticing any of their sons to a craft, although many had cousins who were craftsmen. All gentry professions required a considerable financial outlay, and the ongoing endeavours of parents, relations and friends to promote subsequent careers. The most expensive profession was that of the law. The training of a barrister or councillor involved years of residence in London at one of the inns of court, and could cost £1,000–£1,500.[77] George Macartney of Auchinleck was able to afford this for two of his sons, although there was a twenty year age difference between them which would have helped to stagger the expense. Similarly William Sloane had a brother who was a councillor in London. A cheaper profession was that of solicitor or attorney, which it was possible to practice with no formal legal training. Samuel Martin, a son of George Martin of Belfast, set up as a merchant in

76 Appendix A.18.
77 Earle, *English middle class*, pp 60-1; T.C. Barnard, 'Lawyers and the law in later seventeenth-century Ireland' in *I.H.S.*, xxviii, no.111 (1993), p.259.

3 General George Macartney

Dublin but, with the patronage of Sir Audley Mervyn to whom he was connected by marriage, he became a successful attorney. The family continued in trade, but one of Martin's sons entered the army and he educated another as a physician. The youngest of the Sloane brothers, the future Sir Hans Sloane, also entered the latter profession, as did a son of Brown George McCartney, and George Cromie, a grandson of Black George. It is not possible to estimate the necessary financial outlay for a medical education from the sources available for the Belfast families but Cromie's expenses while at Leyden were a constant source of amazement to his uncles, Isaac Macartney and William Cromie of Dublin.[78] Only a few of the Belfast families had sons in the army but these included General George Macartney, elder son of Black George, whose army career was as successful as it was notorious.[79] Similarly, a scattering of families produced clergymen (Leathes, Rainey, Theaker, Thetford and Waring). The most successful of these, in career terms, was Roger Waring, archdeacon of Dromore, and the most attractive, the unworldly John Leathes, who regularly gave one quarter of his income to the poor. Finally, three members of the Leathes family were agents or employees of three great landlords of Counties Antrim and Down.[80]

Office holders at local and national levels were recruited from the gentry. In this respect too, the Belfast merchants functioned as part of that class. The election of Belfast burgesses as members of parliament has been noted in chapter 1. Between 1660 and 1713 members of eight of the thirty-two families sat in parliament, and members of six were high sheriffs: the two George Macartneys, Thomas Waring, Thomas Knox and Randal Brice for County Antrim, and Hugh Eccles for County Down. Some held other public appointments. Macartney of Auchinleck became surveyor-general of the customs of Ulster in 1683, through the influence of his brother-in-law, Sir Nicholas Butler. Even though dismissed from this position in 1685, he was able subsequently to secure appointment as collector of Belfast. His son James Macartney was a justice of the king's bench in Ireland. William Dobbin, Adam Leathes and David Butle were also employed as collectors, Thomas Pottinger became commissioner of prizes in 1691, William Dobbin and William Leathes were employed by the forfeiture commission in 1703, and Leathes later became a diplomat.[81]

Like the gentry of Counties Down and Antrim, members of the thirty-two families gained military experience during the war years of the 1640s and the Jacobite period. Several held commissions in local troops and are listed among the 'forty-nine officers' – officers who had served in the royalist forces before 1649 and who were one of the groups to be compensated

78 Macartney to William Cromie, 21 Feb. 1704/5, to George Cromie, 3 Mar. 1704/5, 19 Aug. 1706 (Macartney 3, pp 53-4, 64-5, 344).
79 See entry in *D.N.B.*
80 They were Donegall, Conway and Hill; appendix A.15.
81 Appendix A.5, 11, 15, 23.

after the restoration.[82] Similarly, Belfast merchant families played an active part in the resistance to James II. Macartney of Auchinleck was captain of a troop of horse raised at his own expense and both he and Robert Clugston of Belfast are listed in the act of attainder of 1689 as being in arms against the king. Edward Brice and William Dobbin are also known to have been militarily active in this period.[83] In the post-war period, the sovereigns were captains of the Belfast militia and William Craford and Thomas Knox were commissioners of array.[84]

Table 5: The merchants as gentry (based on the 32 families)

land outside Belfast	armigerous	gentry marriages	gentry professions	local or national office	military experience
75%	41%	47%	44%	44%	41%

In the seventeenth century, although many of the thirty-two merchant families held some property outside Belfast they still derived the greater part of their income from trade, urban property and commercial undertakings. Nevertheless, table 5 shows that a high proportion of these families were armigerous, held local or national office, and functioned as part of the gentry. Only 25% of the families studied failed to appear under any of these headings and this proportion may actually have been lower because the surviving source material is uneven. A study of these 'gentry' families reveals that, concurrently with their marriages into landed families and the education of sons in gentry professions, nearly all the families still had one or more member of each generation active in trade. In other words, members of these families were simultaneously merchants and gentry. This is not surprising in the case of Edward Brice and David Butle who were younger sons of local landed families, and who appear never to have been regarded as anything other than members of the gentry who happened to be merchants; nor in the case of the Leathes and Theaker families who, by the end of the seventeenth century, were not actively involved in trade. However, George Macartney of Auchinleck, Black George, Thomas Knox and Hugh Eccles appear to have been regarded as gentry when the greater part of their income was derived from trade and commercial activities. All four were descended from minor landed families in Scotland, but only Macartney of Auchinleck was still in possession of an estate there, so it appears that claims to gentry status, based on ancestry rather than land, could be ratified by financial success.

Many of the families which achieved such success showed no immediate

82 John O'Hart, *Irish landed gentry when Cromwell came to Ireland* (Dublin, 1887), pp 372-411.

83 Appendix A4, 8, 11, 18; members of a number of other merchant families were known as 'captain' but it is possible that some were ships' captains.

84 Letters to Sir Robert Colville about militia in County Antrim, 1691-93 (T.C.D., MS 1178).

desire to quit trade. Successful merchants bred the most suitable of their sons as merchants. Nevertheless, merchant dynasties were not self-perpetuating and three generations in trade appears to have been the maximum for most Belfast families. The English-origin families who were the earliest to trade from Belfast were also the earliest to quit trade, and few of these families were still active in 1700. The Scots who arrived later, also continued later. Both George Macartneys had grandsons in trade, although none of them appear to have achieved anything approaching their grandfathers' success. The main branches of both families acquired estates and subsequently derived their income from land and from their professions. By the mid-eighteenth century, the Brice, Butle, Eccles, Knox, Pottinger and Waring families had become landed gentry, unconnected with trade. Moreover the widening social divide between gentry and merchants is underlined by the fact many descendants of merchant families produced pedigrees with no mention of their ancestors' trading careers. Only a few of the thirty-two families were still active in trade by the mid-eighteenth century, and many of the leading merchant families in Belfast at that date were newcomers who had set up in trade after 1700.[85]

The Belfast merchants belonged to a small close-knit community where families were connected by complex ties resulting from intermarriage, employment and trading partnerships. A clear picture emerges of the hierarchy within this community. The most important family was that of George Macartney of Auchinleck, both in terms of wealth and status, followed by those of Black George and Hugh Eccles. Thomas Knox and the Warings were less important within Belfast, not because they were less wealthy, but because they played a less prominent part in the affairs of the community. Similarly, the presbyterian Chalmers and Smith families, although wealthy, did not serve on the corporation until the end of the period, and no evidence suggests that their social status was as high as that of the preceding families. From the 1690s, David Butle, Edward Brice and William Craford became prominent in the town through wealth, office and social connections. Apart from the Warings, all the above families were of Scottish origin and were presbyterian, or had strong presbyterian connections.

The continuing presence on the corporation of members of four of the oldest Belfast families (Leathes, Theaker, Thetford and Thompson) show that, although less wealthy than the leading Scots, these families retained their high status within the community. The Leathes family in particular produced more burgesses than any other family in the seventeenth century, and one of the most outstanding sovereigns. The career of Robert Leathes spans seventy years. He was a captain in the royalist forces in the 1640s but, like his brother Ensign John Leathes, he felt it necessary to apply for an individual pardon after the Declaration of Breda in 1660. He was a burgess for forty-eight years, resigning in 1717, and served five terms as

85 Gamble, 'The business community and trade of Belfast', pp 25, 184.

4 Captain Robert Leathes

sovereign. Much of his status in the town was derived from his position as comptroller to the first earl of Donegall, as seneschall of the manor of Belfast and constable of Belfast castle, but he also had considerable personal prestige. His career counter-balances the impression, from contemporary sources, that Belfast had become a purely Scots presbyterian town.

In fact, the small group of Church of Ireland merchants was well integrated into the community. Although there were few marriage alliances, they were linked to the presbyterians by trading and ship-owning partnerships, and by the ties of apprenticeship and employment. Where their interests were concerned, the community acted as one. For example, the petition in 1673 for the removal of the customhouse to Belfast was signed by presbyterian and conformist Scots, and by members of English-origin Church of Ireland families.[86] The presbyterian merchants were, on the whole, wealthier but both groups owned land, and members of both groups functioned as members of the gentry. The religious divide in the town eventually led to conflict but attacks on the the presbyterians in the early eighteenth century came from outside the merchant community.

86 Petition of George Macartney, Hugh Eccles, Edward Pottinger, Robert Leathes, George Macartney [of Auchinleck], William Waring, William Anderson and James Chalmers, 19 Feb. 1672/3 (P.R.O., SP.63/333, no.82).

3

Religion in Belfast

THE GROWTH OF PRESBYTERIANISM IN BELFAST

Patrick Adair, minister at Belfast from 1674–94, wrote of Belfast in his narrative of the rise of the presbyterian church:

> It is observable of that place, that, though there was long much opposition to the work of Christ in it, yet by degrees the Lord did wear out the opposers, and make them and their posterity altogether insignificant in the place, and brought in a new people from divers places, who do entertain the gospel and own Christ's interest with equal affection as others.[1]

Although the progress of presbyterianism within Belfast seemed slow to Adair, to other observers it seemed alarmingly rapid. The earliest known presbyterian families to settle in Belfast came from south-west Scotland in the 1630s. Immediately after the occupation of the town by Monro in May 1644 the army established a presbytery there. The majority of the Belfast freemen took the covenant and, perhaps inspired by the democratic organisation of the presbyterian church, petitioned to be allowed to elect the burgesses, and that only those who had taken the covenant should be eligible for election.[2] Nevertheless, since many who were not presbyterians thought it politic to take the covenant, the numbers of active presbyterians in the town may still have been small. As the presbyterian Scots were monarchist and opposed the Commonwealth policy of religious toleration, it was proposed in 1653 to transplant the leading presbyterian Scots in Ulster to another part of Ireland, but the list of proposed transportees only includes eight men from Belfast, in contrast to the large numbers from rural districts of Counties Antrim and Down.[3] However, the presbytery of

---

1 Adair, *Narrative*, p.104.
2 Examination of Thomas Theaker, 16 July 1644 (T.C.D., MS 838, ff 7–8).
3 Young, *Historical notices*, pp 78–83; they included the burgesses Hugh Doake and George Martin; as sovereign, Martin refused to arrange accommodation for Venables's soldiers in 1649, and his property was plundered (Benn, p.129).

Belfast had made a strong protest at the toleration extended to all sects in England in 1649, and this, coupled with their monarchism, led to the town's being regarded as a hotbed of presbyerianism throughout the Commonwealth period.[4] In 1657 the governor of Ulster advised Henry Cromwell that no Scottish minister be admitted to the larger towns and:

> if it could be well done it were advisable that no Scotchman might live in those towns, at least for some years, for your lordship knows there is more danger to be expected from that interest than the Irish in Ulster.[5]

By 1657 this advice was already too late. Scots presbyterians had been arriving at the Ulster ports throughout the 1650s and by the end of the Commonwealth period the change in their religious composition was irreversible. After the restoration, their ministers were ejected and the covenant was burned by the common hangman. Nevertheless religious conformity was not enforced, presbyterian ministers received some financial support from the *regium donum*, and they were able to organise their own ecclesiastical system.[6] The continuing growth of presbyterianism in post-restoration Ulster, in the face of considerable opposition, is well documented, but only a few bare facts are known about the Belfast congregation before the 1690s. The first meeting house was built in the late 1660s and the first minister was William Keyes, an English presbyterian. Keyes was called to be minister at Bull Alley in Dublin in 1673, in spite of opposition from the Belfast congregation, and he was replaced in the following year by Patrick Adair, who had kinship links through marriage with the merchant community.[7]

The religious divide within the town, and within the merchant community, was between protestants. There is no evidence that there were any Roman catholic merchants in Belfast in the seventeenth century. Indeed, very few sources relating to Belfast mention Roman catholics at all. In his extracts from the poll tax returns, Petty stated that there were 223 Irish within Belfast (and 366 English) and listed the most common Irish surnames in the parish. However, at least half of the 'Irish' names in the barony of Belfast appear to be of Scottish derivation, and the same is true

4 [Henry Joy], *Historical collections relative to the town of Belfast* (Belfast, 1817), pp 28–50.

5 J.S. Reid, *History of the presbyterian church in Ireland* (2nd edn, London, 1853), ii, p.215.

6 James McGuire, 'Government attitudes to religious non-conformity in Ireland, 1660–1719' in C.E.J. Caldicott, Hugh Gough, J.-P. Pittion (ed.), *The Huguenots and Ireland, anatomy of an emigration* (Dublin, 1987), pp 256–9; Phil Kilroy, *Protestant dissent and controversy in Ireland, 1660–1714* (Cork, 1994), pp 18–19.

7 *Historic memorials of the first presbyterian church of Belfast* (Belfast, 1887), pp 107–108; see entry for Adair in *D.N.B.*; his third wife Elizabeth was the daughter of George Martin and the widow of William Anderson.

for other baronies in County Antrim. The figure for Irish, and presumably catholics, in Belfast in about 1660 is therefore too large but no other sources enable a more accurate estimate to be reached. It is possible that building along the roads outside the town by 1685[8] may have been the result of the proclamation of 1678 that catholics were not allowed to live within the walls of corporate towns, but Belfast had no 'Irish Quarter' unlike many other Ulster towns. The town book does not mention any Roman catholic townsmen and there are few Irish-sounding names in the freemen's roll. It might be argued that the catholics followed occupations that confined them to the lowest economic class in the town and consequently that they would not have aspired to become freemen. In fact, some 3.6% of the freemen were carmen, porters and labourers, but all have English or Scottish names.[9]

In 1707 the sovereign, George Macartney (youngest son of Macartney of Auchinleck), was instructed to arrest any Roman catholic priests within his jurisdiction. The only such priest, Phelomy O'Hamill, lived some way out of town but came in to surrender himself to Macartney, whereupon a number of protestants, whose goods O'Hamill had been instrumental in saving during the Jacobite period, offered to stand bail for him. Macartney reported 'Thank God we are not under any great fears here' because he had had a return made of all the inhabitants of the town and 'we have not amongst us within the town above seven Papists'.[10]

Two factors may account for the absence of a Roman catholic merchant community in Belfast. First, the town did not exist before the seventeenth century. There was some kind of settlement because the site of the town was at the lowest fordable point of the river Lagan but the indigenous population, living around the mediaeval castle, would have been very small. Second, ease of communication with Scotland, and the existence of networks of kinship, makes it likely that servants and many kinds of labourers were recruited there. Absence of documentation does not prove that there were no Roman catholics in Belfast, but the composition of the James II corporation, described in the next chapter, indicates that no Roman catholic merchant community existed because it was found necessary to appoint all the catholic burgesses from the ranks of the landed gentry.

The Belfast merchants were episcopalians or presbyterians, with the latter forming the great majority. Three factors contributed to the steady

---

8 See page 19.
9 Pender, *Census Ire.*, p.8; Smyth, 'Society and settlement', p.73; George Camblin, *The town in Ulster* (Belfast, 1951), pp 52–3.
10 Craford to Colville, 1 Jan. 1692/3, mentioning O'Hamill's 'civil carriage to the protestants' (T.C.D., MS 1178, no.72); Benn, p.416, the return has not survived; a similar claim was made for Carrickfergus in the 1680s (Hill, *Macdonnells of Antrim*, p.388), but many catholics lived in the Irish Quarter outside the walls.

and undramatic growth of presbyterianism in Belfast. The first and most important was the attitude of the Chichester family. Although the family belonged nominally to the established church, there was considerable sympathy on the part of many family members for presbyterianism. The building of the first meeting house can only have been accomplished with the sanction of the first earl of Donegall. Donegall's third wife was an English presbyterian who used her influence to protect presbyterians in Ulster. However, she strongly opposed the removal to Dublin of Keyes, who was attached to her household, and she bore considerable resentment against the Belfast congregation for failing to prevent it. Before a successor could be appointed, it was felt necessary for the congregation to make a humble address to the earl and countess asking that they should have, in that respect, 'their liberty as other congregations have, without irritation, as far as possible'. Samuel Bryan, Thomas Emlyn and Joseph Boyse, subsequent household chaplains of the Donegall family, were also English presbyterians.[11]

The Donegalls' choice of a vicar for the parish of Belfast was in keeping with their puritanism. Claudius Gilbert who was vicar from c.1671 to 1696 had started his career as an independent, but conformed after the restoration. He remained friendly towards presbyterians; Emlyn often officiated at the parish church, and Elias Travers, preacher at Cooke Street in Dublin, stayed in Gilbert's house when he visited Belfast. The services and sermons which were acceptable to Gilbert's patrons were probably equally acceptable to many of the Scots in Belfast. For example, the two George Macartneys and Thomas Knox were conformists. It is likely that most presbyterians attended the parish church from time to time until the 1690s. The Belfast burgesses were obliged, by a bye-law of 1617, to attend the sovereign to church, on pain of a fine of two shillings, and there were two special pews reserved for them. Although there were several presbyterian burgesses in Belfast, even before the Williamite wars, non-attendance at church by the burgesses never became an issue in Belfast as it did in Coleraine. One presbyterian burgess, Sir Hercules Langford, even had a gallery built in Belfast parish church, although it was actually paid for by Black George Macartney.[12]

The second factor which contributed to the ease with which presbyterianism became established in Belfast was the appointment of Thomas

11 *Historic memorials*, pp 11, 28–9, 54, 108; *Town book*, p.130; C.H. Irwin, *A history of presbyterianism in Dublin and the south and west of Ireland* (London, 1890), p.314; Kilroy, *Protestant dissent*, pp 26–7, 46, 55n.

12 *Town book*, pp 6, 52–3; dissenting burgesses avoided attending the parish church of Coleraine, under pretence of not having gowns (Coleraine minutes, 1682); Macartney to Langford, 5 May 1679 (Macartney 2, p.58); Macartney paid for the building of the gallery and seems to have taken it over from Langford in settlement of a debt, although Isaac Macartney later implied that his father had built it for himself (Macartney to bishop of Down, 2 Oct. 1705 [Macartney 3, p.196]).

Hackett as bishop of Down and Connor in 1672. Hackett was a moderate in his treatment of dissenters and he was also a notorious absentee who spent so much time in London that he was known as the 'bishop of Hammersmith'. Morale and discipline were low among the clergy in his diocese. Consequently, although the growth of presbyterianism was deplored by the government, and the increasing organisation of its sessions and meetings was seen as a threat to the Church of Ireland, the persecution of presbyterians depended largely on the initiative of individual local magistrates and in Belfast there seems to have been little or no persecution of the presbyterian community at an official level.[13]

Thirdly, the Belfast presbyterians were moderate in their beliefs and practices. Merchants are seldom fanatics and members of the Belfast congregation appear to have been more interested in making money than making trouble. Since most of the Scots who settled in Belfast came from the south-west, the most presbyterian area of Scotland from the beginning of the century, it might have been expected that presbyterianism in Belfast would have been rather more fervent and radical. Certainly, those Scots presbyterians who arrived in Belfast in the 1630s may have experienced some persecution, or at least restriction, at home and have emigrated both for religious and economic reasons. However, the majority of the Scots who settled in Belfast left Scotland in the period 1638–60 when the covenanters were in the ascendant, so it could be argued that the economic reasons which caused them to emigrate to Belfast may have been reinforced by a wish to escape from excessive calvinism at home. Patrick Adair, the minister at Belfast from 1674–94, was a known moderate, and the lack of information about his congregation surely indicates that the majority were also moderates, and that the growth of presbyterianism in Belfast was steady but unspectacular.[14]

Most churchmen and the Dublin government however did not distinguish between different kinds of presbyterianism and, from the 1660s to the 1680s, the Ulster presbyterians were constantly expected to support the Scottish covenanters. Some of the Belfast merchants who emigrated from south-west Scotland had connections among the covenanters. Black George Macartney, for example, was the cousin of George Macartney of Blacket, a leading covenanter who was repeatedly fined and imprisoned for his activities in the 1660s–90s.[15] As a largely Scots presbyterian town, Belfast was by

13 J.C. Beckett, 'Irish Scottish relations in the seventeenth century' in J.C. Beckett, *Confrontations, studies in Irish history* (London, 1972), p.37; J.C. Beckett, *Protestant dissent in Ireland, 1687–1784* (London, 1948), p.37; by contrast, conventicles were suppressed in Londonderry in 1683–84 (*Ormonde MSS,* [NS] vii, pp 96, 200).

14 David Stevenson, *Scottish covenanters and Irish confederates: Scottish-Irish relations in the mid-seventeenth century* (Belfast, 1981), p.12; Smout, *Scottish people,* p.98.

15 See for example, correspondence of Col Humphrey Sydenham at Carrickfergus in 1668 (Bodl., Carte MSS 36, ff 203, 206, 209, 486, 488); *Ormonde MSS,* (NS), v, pp 125–6; *Cal. S.P. dom., May 1684–Feb. 1685,* p.261; McGuire, 'Government

definition a potential troublespot. In 1683, the town was described by Lord Arran as 'as fanatic a one as any in Ireland' although he conceded that the sovereign, John Hamilton, a Scot from a County Down family, was 'a very honest man',[16] and Thomas Phillips, in his report on the town's fortifications in 1685, described the town as 'very rich and numerous, and not well affected, having nothing that can any way give a check to anything that might happen, either by foreign or domestic attempts.'[17] As a major port, it was inevitable that suspect cargoes would occasionally be apprehended there, and that unwelcome visitors from Scotland might disembark there, but there appear to have been no particular grounds for anticipating trouble at Belfast, and there is no suggestion that the merchants were suspected of specific seditious activities, as they were in Londonderry.[18]

The town's lack of sympathy for the covenanting cause was demonstrated when a Belfast bookbinder attempted to circulate the 'apologetical declaration' issued by covenanting extremists in Scotland in October 1684. This urged presbyterians not to heed 'indulged' ministers who prayed for the king. Patrick Adair, one of those ministers considered to be indulged by the government, informed the sovereign, John Hamilton, who reported the matter to the authorities. The subsequent examinations of those who were involved show that they were all minor figures and that none of the merchants involved in foreign trade were implicated. The 'plot' was in fact an attack by religious radicals on moderate presbyterianism and found no support among presbyterians of any consequence in Belfast.[19]

RELIGION AND THE COMMUNITY

Although it is possible to determine the religious affiliation of all the leading merchant families, there is no source which throws much light on the part played by religion in their everyday lives. The journals of John Black, the elder, of Bordeaux have a strongly religious tone but date from the mid-eighteenth century.[20] Virtually all the merchant letters which have survived are business letters. Black George Macartney mentioned having attended Bishop Jeremy Taylor's funeral in 1667, and he approved of mea-

attitudes to religious non-conformity in Ireland', p.264; P.H. McKerlie, *The history of the lands and owners in Galloway* (5 vols, Edinburgh, 1870–79), v, p.301.

16 *Ormonde MSS*, (NS), vii, p.132.
17 *Ormonde MSS*, ii, p.319.
18 Thomas Waring to Sir Richard Kennedy, 20 Sept. 1665, concerning seizure of presbyterian pamphlets (Bodl., Carte MSS 34, f.397); *Hastings MSS*, ii, p.386; *Cal. S.P. dom., 1677–78*, p.550; *Ormonde MSS*, (NS), v, p.151, vi, pp 500–1.
19 Kilroy, *Protestant dissent*, p.114; *Ormonde MSS*, (NS), vi, pp 293–4; *Cal. S.P. dom., May 1684–Feb. 1685*, p.259; examinations, Nov. 1684 (Bodl., Carte MSS 40, ff 190, 310–11).
20 Journals of John Black of Bordeaux, 1751–64 (P.R.O.N.I., T1073/7–8, 12, 16).

sures taken against papists in Scotland in 1679[21] but, apart from this, his remarks about religion were confined to pious hopes that ships would arrive safely and that cargoes would find a good market. Similarly, the letter book of David Butle throws no light on his spiritual life, and neither does that of Isaac Macartney. There is no indication that being a successful merchant was thought to be in any way incompatible with being a pious puritan, as was the case in New England at the same date,[22] perhaps because there was seldom such a shortage of imported goods that it was possible to make excessive profits. Two sets of journal extracts throw some light on the organisation of religion at Belfast. The first, written by Robert Leathes between the 1680s and 1713, refers occasionally to the Belfast parish clergy and to special services in the parish church. The second, by William Rainey, a young presbyterian merchant, shows his involvement in the organisation of the congregation in the early 1700s, and notes the occasions on which he received the sacrament and renewed the covenant. By the latter he meant a renewal of faith rather than subscription to the earlier solemn league and covenant, but 'covenant' was still an emotive word which would not have reassured that section of the community which looked upon the presbyterians as a threat. Rainey's journal also notes his purchase from David Chalmers of half a seat in the meeting house, ownership of pews being standard practice in Ulster at that date.[23]

Merchants of both denominations made charitable bequests. Charity was seen as both a religious and a social duty and was of vital importance in Belfast where there was no guild-related provision for widows and the sick, such as existed in many Scottish towns. Most Belfast merchants left money to the poor of the parish. These bequests were surprisingly modest. Only three merchants left as much as £40 to the Belfast poor in the seventeenth century (Edward Holmes, 1631, Thomas Waring, 1665, and Hugh Eccles, 1680), bequests being more often in the region of £5–£10. Many merchants also made small bequests, particularly of rings, to their ministers. The only really large charitable bequest by an Ulster merchant in this period was made by Hugh Rainey, uncle of William Rainey, in 1708 when he endowed a school for poor children at Magherafelt in County Londonderry (which was later attended by his own descendants). Although the Belfast corporation continued to administer funds for the relief of the poor, by the end of the seventeenth century both the parish church and the presbyterian congregation raised separate funds for the poor, and this state of affairs led to charges by the vicar, William Tisdall,

---

21 Macartney to Thomas Hackett, 4 Sept. 1667, to Robert Aickin, 19 Feb. 1678/9 (Macartney 1, pp 598–9, 2, p.24).

22 Bailyn, *New England merchants*, pp 41–4.

23 Extracts from Leathes's journal (L.H.L., Joy MSS, 7); extracts from Rainey's journal (L.H.L., Joy MSS, 10); Gillespie, 'Presbyterian revolution', p.163; and see appendix A.12 for Hugh Eccles's ownership of a pew.

that presbyterians confined their charity to those of their own denomination.[24]

Apart from bequests, many merchants also made charitable donations during their lives. Collections were constantly taken for the relief of the 'algerine slaves', who were seamen or passengers on ships captured by privateers from North Africa. Letters of Black George Macartney suggest that he was co-ordinating collections in the Belfast area in 1680–81, and co-operating with presbyterian ministers in Dublin. From the 1690s, some donations were made specifically for the relief of John Whitehead of Belfast who was captured some time before 1692. The general synod of Ulster raised money for him, and there was at least one individual bequest. Other charitable briefs also met with a good response. The Belfast presbyterian congregation followed Scottish practice in their ownership of a collection of cloaks and palls or 'mort cloths' which they hired out for funerals. This was not the only such collection in the district, but it is the only one which is documented and although the register of hirings does not indicate what was done with this income, it may be presumed that it was spent on charitable purposes. In 1716, the elders reduced the hiring charges by about one third, probably because the initial outlay had long since been recouped and perhaps because they were influenced by the puritan ethic regarding profits.[25]

By the end of the seventeenth century, the leading merchants were presbyterians, and both wealth and power within the corporation were concentrated in their hands, but whatever resentment there may have been at the transformation of what had been an English town into a Scottish one, there can be no doubt that the immigrant Scottish merchants revitalised the town and increased the volume of trade, thus benefitting the entire community. There is no hint that, in Belfast, the episcopalian and presbyterian merchants saw themselves as rivals to any greater extent than was normal in trade and there appears to be no truth in the allegation that the former were driven out of trade by the latter. This, and other similar allegations were made against the presbyterian merchants by the anglican ministers Echlin and Tisdall. Although it can be assumed that many Belfast inhabitants deplored the growth of presbyterianism, and a number, including Robert Leathes, as sovereign, signed a petition supporting the test act, it is interesting to find that there is no record of support for these accusations of discrimination and restrictive practices. On the contrary, in 1713, many of the principal Church of Ireland traders of Belfast, again including

24 There was a board recording charitable donations in the old parish church (R.W.M. Strain, *Belfast and its Charitable Society* [Oxford, 1961], illustration facing p.16) but information from Belfast wills shows that this list was not comprehensive; appendix A.24; Kirkpatrick, pp 440–3.

25 Macartney to Allen, 18 May, 18 Dec. 1680, 23 Apr. 1681 (Macartney 2, pp 256, 403, 453); *Gen. synod Ulster rec.*, i, pp 11, 60; appendix A.21; Kirkpatrick, pp 440–1; Smout, *Scottish people*, p.93; Jean Agnew (ed.), *Funeral register of the first presbyterian church of Belfast*, p.4.

5 Rev. John McBride

Leathes, then in his nineties and the doyen of the Church of Ireland townsmen, signed a statement refuting these charges.[26]

CONFRONTATION AND CONFLICT

In spite of the friendly relations between merchants across the religious divide, Belfast was at the centre of the conflict between the Church of Ireland and presbyterianism in the early eighteenth century. After the accession of William and Mary, presbyterianism went from strength to strength in Ireland in spite of its failure to secure legal toleration. The 1690s saw the rapid growth, both in organisation and numbers, of the presbyterian church in Ireland. The general synod was constituted in 1690 and held meetings at Belfast. Presbyterianism became highly organized, structured and, for a time at least, uniform.[27] The *regium donum* for the support of presbyterian clergymen was re-granted in the same year. The money came from the Belfast customs and was administered from Belfast.[28] In the second half of the decade a combination of famine in Scotland and availability of leases in Ulster attracted massive immigration from Scotland. New congregations were formed and new meeting houses erected. In Belfast, Patrick Adair was succeeded by John McBride, and a new meeting house was built in Rosemary Lane. Within ten years this was too small for the congregation.

The steady growth of the Belfast congregation in the 1690s owed much to the protection and even friendship of the third earl of Donegall. Because there are no surviving Chichester papers, Donegall's relationship with the Belfast presbyterians must be deduced from scraps of evidence, some anecdotal. For example, Tisdall related that Donegall lent him Milton's works and asked his opinion on them, and on his condemning Milton's anti-monarchic opinions and suggesting that such books were distributed in order to debauch the young nobility and gentry, Donegall revealed, with a smile, that McBride had sent him the book. However McBride averred that it was Donegall who lent him the book and that he returned it to one of the earl's brothers. Either way, the impression gained is that McBride and the Chichesters were on friendly book-lending terms. It was at McBride's request that Donegall granted a site in Rosemary Lane for a new presbyterian meeting house and when, in 1704, McBride refused the oath of abjuration, Donegall offered to stand surety for him 'to the value of his estate'.

26 Loyal address to Queen Anne, 17 July 1714 (*B.N.L.*, 30 Nov.–4 Dec. 1792); Kirkpatrick, pp 434–5.
27 Gillespie, 'Presbyterian revolution', p.169.
28 Thomas Craford, a Belfast merchant (appendix A.9), was treasurer of the *regium donum* from at least 1701 and he was succeeded by Brice Blair, a Belfast haberdasher (P.R.O., SP.63/367, nos 145–6).

Donegall also seems to have been on friendly terms with Patrick Adair, and with Dr Victor Ferguson, a leading Belfast presbyterian, both of whom lent him money. These loans indicate commercial interaction between Donegall and the Belfast presbyterians and, as mentioned in chapter two, the earl had a share in trading ventures with a group of presbyterian merchants.[29]

Donegall's friendship was particularly valuable to the Belfast presbyterians because the 1690s saw the revitalisation of the Church of Ireland. The 'bishop of Hammersmith' and many of his clergy were deprived of their livings. A great purge of the venal and the inept in 1694 ushered in a period of reform and renewal.[30] Claudius Gilbert was replaced as vicar of Belfast by James Echlin. Echlin had already assisted Gilbert for a number of years and had been recommended by Lord Longford to the primate in 1691, not only as a person of 'good life and behaviour' but as one who had 'brought over to the communion of the Church of England several persons from the presbyterian meeting'.[31] After this initial success he appears to have made very little impact on the presbyterians of Belfast. In 1698 Bishop King of Derry wrote to the new bishop of Down and Connor:

> I understand the people of Belfast are very refractory, and do many irregu-
> lar things; that they will not consent to enlarge their church lest there
> should be room for all the people; that they bury in spite of the law in the
> Church without prayers, and come in with their hats on; that they break all
> the seats, and refuse to deliver their collection for briefs, according to the
> order of the council, to the church-wardens.[32]

Wearing of hats in church and burying without prayers were, of course, presbyterian practices and if these refractory people were Echlin's regular congregation it underlines the fact that services in Gilbert's time had been exceedingly 'low church'. If Echlin attempted to introduce services more in line with practice elsewhere he doubtless lost more parishioners than he gained.[33]

Since most of the wealthier Belfast inhabitants attended the meeting house, the Church of Ireland congregation and the clergy were poor. When Echlin's curate fell ill it was the presbyterians who helped him financially and Echlin feared that his own indebtedness to the presbyterians would be

---

29 Kirkpatrick, pp 474, 526; Benn, p.405n; bond, Donegall to Ferguson, 1696 (P.R.O., C106/95/15).

30 Reid, *History of the presbyterian church*, ii, p.416 et seq.; J.C. Beckett, 'The govern-ment and the church of Ireland under William III and Anne' in *I.H.S.*, ii, no. 7 (1941), p.289.

31 Extracts from Leathes's journal, 4 Apr., 17 Sept. 1696 (L.H.L., Joy MSS, 7); list of clergy to be commended or blamed, 1693 (P.R.O.N.I., Reeves abstracts, MIC35/5); Benn, p.380.

32 Reid, *History of the presbyterian church*, ii, p.447.

33 Black George Macartney became a presbyterian in the 1690s (Kirkpatrick, p.436).

used as an excuse to arrest him. It was his efforts to improve his financial situation that brought him into into open conflict with the inhabitants of Belfast. Soon after his appointment, he claimed house money – dues paid by dwellers in corporate towns to supplement the income of the vicar. In spite of claims that house money had never been paid in Belfast, it appears that Claudius Gilbert had received it, although not apparently by right but after some sort of negotiation with the townspeople. Echlin's attempts to revive house money were resisted by the entire town, both conformist and presbyterian. In 1698 the corporation employed the rising lawyer, William Conolly, to conduct the town's defence against Echlin.[34]

In 1703, it was alleged that members of the Church of Ireland were being compelled to contribute to a fighting fund to oppose house money. This was denied by the sovereign, the presbyterian David Butle, who wrote 'neither hath any money been raised to oppose our minister but what hath been voluntarily paid as well by conformists as nonconformists'. Butle also defended the largely-presbyterian corporation against charges of allowing dissenters to make unjust rate assessments, of making illegal charges (described emotively as 'ship-money') for use of the town dock, and of failure to make public their accounts. 'Ship-money', which was imposed on all ships discharging directly at the town quay, had actually been introduced in 1696 when Robert Leathes was sovereign and was intended to raise funds for the repair of the quay. Butle defended the charge of 2d per ton, stating that everyone paid voluntarily, that 'the money received hath been applied to every man's satisfaction', and that no coercion was necessary as it was clearly to everyone's benefit not to have to pay gabarts to unload at 12d per ton. He also rebutted a charge of partiality on the part of dissenters making presentments to magistrates.[35]

By 1704, Echlin had 'worn himself out in service of the church' although apparently earning the admiration of the dissenters who were 'the occasion of all his misfortunes'.[36] He exchanged his living for that of William Tisdall and died a few months later. Tisdall, however, was a man who thrived on controversy. The 1690s had seen the emergence of a militant party in the Church of Ireland which saw the structure and organisation of the presbyterian church as as a direct threat to the established church and even to the state. Churchmen deplored the concentration of wealth in the hands of presbyterian merchants, and their appointment to

---

34 Kirkpatrick, pp 442, 484; Benn, pp 376, n.1, 380–1; Butle to Conolly, 5 Mar. 1697/8 (Butle, p.54); for Conolly see entry in *D.N.B.*

35 Case of the corporation of Belfast with respect to byelaws, c.1703 (P.R.O.N.I., Leslie transcripts, T1075/6, p.73); Benn, p.475; *Town book*, pp 189–90, 197; Butle to [unnamed], 6 Nov. 1703 (Butle, pp 67–8); Kirkpatrick also refuted this charge (Kirkpatrick, pp 423, 485).

36 Sophia Hamilton to Bishop King, 8 Apr. 1704 (T.C.D., King correspondence, MS 1995–2008, 1075).

6 Rev. James Kirkpatrick

local office after the abrogation of the oath of supremacy in 1691. Belfast epitomized this state of affairs. By the early eighteenth century the leading presbyterian merchants were both elders and burgesses. Moreover the Belfast burgesses were the only such group in Ireland to resist the test act of 1704, being eventually forced to resign by a ruling of the Irish house of commons in 1707. Tisdall was a leading protagonist in the struggle to combat the presbyterian threat and his anti-presbyterian fervour was fuelled by personal animosity towards the Belfast burgesses and elders who opposed him when he renewed the struggle for house money.[37]

The presbyterian church was defended by the minister John McBride, and his assistant James Kirkpatrick, whose works were printed by the newly established press at Belfast. Belfast had previously imported books and tracts from Scotland, but from 1694 a printing press was set up in the town, with the encouragement of the sovereign William Craford, which appears to have been dedicated to the production of presbyterian devotional works and tracts. In spite of the hostility of local tory magistrates, these were widely disseminated with the active help of the congregation. For example, Tisdall was told by such a magistrate that he had seen the wife of 'the most considerable ruling elder' with a whole apron-full of reprints of a pamphlet by Daniel Defoe.[38]

Only one inhabitant of Belfast can be identified who shared the extremist views of Echlin and Tisdall. Westenra Waring was a grandson of the merchant and tanner, Thomas Waring, and a nephew of William Waring, both of whom had been burgesses and sovereigns of Belfast. Westenra's father had been archdeacon of Dromore. Although he inherited his uncle's substantial commercial and residential property in Belfast, Westenra does not appear ever to have been involved in trade.[39] With the support of Brent Spencer of Lisburn, another zealous high-church tory magistrate, Waring harassed the presbyterians. He and Spencer can be seen heading almost every attack on the Co. Antrim presbyterians in this period. They relentlessly pursued the two non-juring presbyterian ministers, McBride of Belfast and McCracken of Lisburn, both of whom had refused to take the oath of abjuration, and had consequently laid themselves open to the charge of Jacobitism. McBride was warned of his imminent arrest and fled to

37 David Hayton, 'Ireland and the English ministers, 1707–16' (PhD thesis, University of Oxford, 1975), pp 125–6; memorial on the Scots in Ireland, c.1697 (B.L., Sloane MS 2902, no.60, f.218); Tisdall, pp 54–7; McGuire, 'Government attitudes to religious non-conformity in Ireland', pp 268–9; Kilroy, *Protestant dissent*, pp 192–3, 198–202; Tisdall to King, 13 Jan. 1706/7 (T.C.D., King correspondence, MS 1995–2008, 1075); King to Tisdall, 1 Feb. 1706/7 (T.C.D., MS 750/3/2/86).

38 Waring to Kennedy, 20 Sept. 1665 (Bodl., Carte MSS 34, f.397); Benn, pp 316, 425–36; Macartney to Alderman Meade, 29 Dec. 1705 (Macartney 3, p.248); E.R. McClintock Dix, 'List of books and tracts printed in Belfast in the seventeenth century' in *R.I.A. Proc.*, xxxiii, sect.C (Mar. 1916), pp 74–7; Tisdall, p.111.

39 Appendix A.30.

Scotland, and Waring was so enraged at having missed him that he ran McBride's portrait through with his sword. They charged Clotworthy Upton, a member of the County Antrim gentry and brother-in-law of Edward Brice of Belfast, with having commonwealth principles. They missed no opportunity to harass the presbyterians. In 1705, for example, Waring suggested to the bishop of Down and Connor that Isaac Macartney should be deprived of his 'gallery' or family seat in the parish church. Under the last ministry of Queen Anne's reign, harassment of presbyterians, both by magistrates and by the ecclesiastical courts, reached a peak in Ireland.[40] On hearing of her death by express early one morning, Isaac Macartney is said to have capered in the street in his nightgown crying 'Queen Anne is dead'.[41]

In the second half of the seventeenth century, Belfast had become a presbyterian town. With the protection of the earls of Donegall, the presbyterian merchant community had flourished and had established control over the town and the corporation. From the 1690s, the numbers and organisation of Irish presbyterians were seen as a real threat to the established church and to the government. The concentration of power in the hands of presbyterians in Belfast, where the wealthiest merchants were both elders and burgesses, was deplored by the local clergymen and magistrates but there was nothing they could do to combat this situation as long as the Donegall family supported the election of presbyterians as burgesses. In 1707 the widow of the third earl was instrumental in forcing the presbyterian burgesses out of the corporation. Her reasons for this, however, will be shown to have been essentially political.

---

40 *Historic memorials*, p.55; *Commons jn. Ire.*, iii, p.114; Tisdall, pp 120–1; Kirkpatrick, pp 472–4, 527; Macartney to bishop of Down, 2 Oct. 1705 (Macartney 3, p.196); see also note 12 above about this gallery; Hayton, 'Ireland and the English ministers', pp 278–91, 301.
41 This is an anecdote in the Macartney family history (P.R.O.N.I., T2970/12), for which there is corroborative evidence (*Historic memorials*, p.55).

4

Politics and the Corporation

THE CORPORATION OF BELFAST UP TO 1688

Belfast's charter of incorporation gave the earls of Donegall total control over the corporation. Although the burgesses elected a sovereign annually from among their own number, their choice was limited to a list of three candidates (called the leet) supplied by the Chichester family. Since the head of the family (as 'lord of the castle') and the constable of Belfast castle were burgesses *ex officio*, they presumably gave a lead in the voting, and if they did not attend corporation meetings they marked the name of their own nominee in the leet. In theory, the burgesses alone elected a replacement after the death of any of their number, but in practice the earls also controlled these elections although, under the charter, they had no formal right of nomination. There was an element of choice at burgess elections but the family's approval was always sought. Control of burgess elections was essential to the Chichesters because it ensured control over elections of the town's members of parliament.

Since the Chichesters controlled elections and attended and voted at corporation meetings, and their approval was required for new bye-laws, it is not surprising that the town book does not record any major disputes with the family in the seventeenth century. In fact, although the interests of the earls of Donegall were paramount, in most respects they coincided with the interests of the merchant community during this period. The growth of trade and the expansion of the town added to the earls' income and to their prestige. Their control of the corporation was largely benign and, in a later dispute in 1709–10, the corporation wrote that 'The Lord of the Castle have ben heretofore allwayes inclynable to incourage the trade thereof and never interposed in any affaire relating to their Trade'.[1] It is indicative of good relations between the corporation and the Chichester family that the latter's agents and employees among the burgesses served few terms as sovereign, the family being content to leave the running of the town to the merchants.

1 *Town book*, p.208.

It should not be assumed that civic office was universally coveted. It was found necessary to impose a fine on those refusing election, rising from £5 to £10 in 1667. William Leathes refused office as a burgess in 1641 and was fined, and John Chalmers declined to serve a second term as sovereign in 1702. The office of sovereign carried no salary, unlike the office of mayor in Carrickfergus, Coleraine and Londonderry, although the sovereign was not entirely without income. Since he was also clerk of the market he must have received fees and there were various perquisites such as tongues from the butchers, which could be exported profitably. However, even with a salary of £100 p.a., the mayoralty of Londonderry was described as a burden, so it is unlikely that the income of the sovereigns of Belfast exceeded expenses incurred while in office.[2]

The sovereign was unsalaried because Belfast corporation had no endowments, and the main concern of the burgesses during the seventeenth century was to raise enough income, in any way they could, to cover day-to-day expenses. For any extraordinary expenditure it was necessary to impose a rate, which fell most heavily upon the sovereign and burgesses themselves. Their one opportunity to remedy this situation came in 1690 when William III stayed in the town. The sovereign, Robert Leathes, intended to ask the king to endow the town out of forfeited estates but was over-ruled by a majority of the burgesses who thought 'it would be a great shame to begg of his Majtie at his comeinge to Towne'. Later they heard that the King had said 'that if the Magistrates and people of Bellfast had asked anything of him he would have given it them' and Leathes wrote sadly 'the losse is irreparable ... ye old Proverb holds a dum man getts noe land time was and now is Past'.[3] Nevertheless, there was a positive aspect to the corporation's lack of lands. Candidates for burgess-ships were not motivated by greed, and there was no clash of interests within the corporation over the letting of land. Indeed the inability of the Belfast corporation to enrich its members and their associates may explain why the town book does not even hint at conflict between, first, English and Scots burgesses, and later between episcopalians and presbyterians.

Conflict within the corporation is only recorded after May 1644, when Monro and his army occupied the town. In the following month, the covenanting freemen made their petition to be allowed to elect the burgesses, and also that burgesses should be resident. This was an obvious reaction to the election in the previous March of George Rawdon and Roger Lyndon, gentlemen who were officers in local troops, and whose election was revoked two years later. In October 1644, the first two presbyterian burgesses, Hugh Doake and George Martin, were elected. Even with

---

2 *Town book*, pp 1–3, 8, 15, 104, 177, 179; Kirkpatrick, p.422; M'Skimin, *Carrickfergus*, p.186; Londonderry minutes, 3 Feb. 1674/5, 20 Feb. 1701/2.
3 *Town book*, p.243.

these presbyterian reinforcements it is clear that the corporation was barely able to control the town as an enactment was made in the following March against refractory and disobedient persons who might abuse the corporation by their deeds or by malignant and contemptuous words. The town book reveals a bitter quarrel between William Leathes and John Ash, one of the two surviving burgesses named in the original charter, who objected both to Leathes's election as sovereign, and to his being sworn in before one of Monro's officers. In the following year there was a public brawl, which may have been political in origin, between Thomas Hannington, a burgess from a Co. Down gentry family, and John Stewart, a leading merchant. The two presbyterians, Doake and Martin, were elected sovereign in 1647 and 1649 respectively, but under the Commonwealth the sovereigns were chosen from the English-origin, Church of Ireland burgesses, and sworn in before the constable of the castle, by order of Colonel Robert Venables, commander in chief in Ulster.[4]

However, from 1655, the the town book documents the Chichester family's control over all subsequent elections. For example, in 1680, the Donegall agent Gilbert Wye offered to resign his burgess-ship to Colonel John Hill, who as constable of the castle was already a burgess *ex officio*, but Hill wrote to the sovereign 'my Lady is willing to have it for Mr Knox & soe am I'. Some of the burgesses thought Wye's resignation was contrary to the charter, and said so, but there seems to have been no protest at the lack of a proper election. Wye's resignation, and that of Sir Hercules Langford in favour of Edward Harrison at the same date, established the burgess-ship as a transferable office, and thus set a precedent for later resignations.[5]

By the 1660s, so many Scots had settled in Belfast that it was rapidly becoming a Scots presbyterian town but, although some of the immigrant Scots became burgesses within a few years of their arrival at Belfast, the corporation was not swamped by them. Table 6 (overleaf) shows that seven of the eighteen burgesses elected between 1660 and 1688 were Scots. Since burgesses were appointed for life, the change in the composition of the corporation was gradual, but by 1688 there were six Scots burgesses, and seven of English origin, including the sovereign. The only Scottish family to produce more than one burgess before 1688 was that of George Macartney of Auchinleck, and it is an indication of his prestige and the favour with which he was regarded by the Chichester family that his eldest son, a lawyer in his twenties, was elected as burgess in 1676. Macartney was a conformist but some other Scots elected to the corporation in this period were presbyterians.

4 *Town book*, pp 28, 38, 43–4, 46, 240.
5 *Town book*, pp 144–5, 196; Kirkpatrick, p.422.

7 The first earl of Donegall

Table 6: Representation of Scots and presbyterians on Belfast corporation, 1660–88

	English	Scottish	presbyterians
total burgesses (29)	19	10	6
new burgesses (18)	11	7	4
sovereign terms (29)	13	16	1

Since, in Belfast, unlike Coleraine and Londonderry, burgesses were not required to take the oath of supremacy, the office of burgess was, in theory, open to presbyterians, and in practice open to such presbyterians as were favoured by the Chichester family. Between 1660 and 1688, four of the new burgesses were presbyterians. The office of sovereign, however, with the associated magistracy, was a position of national importance which could only be entrusted to someone who was politically sound, and sovereigns were required to take the oath. The sovereign was expected to administer the town in accordance with government policy and to report anything which might threaten national security.[6] Macartney of Auchinleck, although a conformist, was initially regarded as suspect and as sovereign was on the list of justices to be removed in 1663.[7] Table 6 shows that there was a total of six presbyterian burgesses in the corporation between 1660 and 1688. Martin and Doake had been elected while Monro's army was occupying Belfast and they might not have been chosen had Lord Chichester been controlling elections. Both were sovereigns in the 1640s, but being royalists did not serve under the Commonwealth.[8] Two more presbyterians, Sir Hercules Langford and Hugh Eccles, became burgesses in the late 1660s. Langford was a member of the County Antrim gentry and Eccles was a successful merchant of sufficient status to be appointed high sheriff of County Down in 1678. Finally, two presbyterians were elected in the 1680s, after the accession of James II. They were Quarter-Master William Craford, later M.P. for Belfast, and William Lockhart, the son-in-law of George Macartney of Auchinleck.

The only presbyterian to become sovereign between 1660 and 1688 was Hugh Eccles who married into a Church of Ireland family and who may have taken the oath a second time when he became high sheriff.[9] During the period up to 1688, therefore, there were restrictions on presbyterians

6 Thomas Waring to Ormond, 14 Aug. 1663 (N.A., Ormond MS 2331, no.1740); Waring to Kennedy, 20 Sept. 1665 (Bodl., Carte MSS 34, f.397); *U.J.A.*, (2nd series), ii (1896), p.277.
7 Bodl., Carte MSS 32, ff 448–9.
8 Martin has been counted as a Scot in table 6; Lord Chichester was father of the first earl of Donegall, and died in 1648; Roebuck, *Donegall family*, p.128; T.C. Barnard, *Cromwellian Ireland, English government and reform in Ireland, 1649–1660* (Oxford, 1975), p.64.
9 The lists of post-restoration high sheriffs include many other presbyterians and it is questionable whether they were all required to take the oath, bearing in mind that

becoming sovereign but they could be elected as burgesses, and although they were few in number this does not seem to have been a sign of active discrimination but simply that the Donegalls preferred other candidates. Most of the Scots conformists who became burgesses had strong presbyterian connections. Macartney of Auchinleck's first wife, one of his sons, and his son-in-law were presbyterians. Black George Macartney's younger son was a presbyterian, and he himself became a presbyterian in later life. Thomas Knox's wife was the grand-daughter of an ejected presbyterian minister and his brother-in-law Edward Brice was an eminent presbyterian. Moreover, table 6 shows that the Scots served a higher proportion of total sovereign years than the numerically superior English burgesses.

Since the Donegall family were protectors of the presbyterians, there was never any harassment by the corporation such as was practiced by the corporation of Coleraine, which several times appointed presbyterians as burgesses or aldermen, and then tried to fine them heavily for their refusal to take the oath of supremacy.[10] Far from harassing presbyterians, the corporation attempted to alter its own constitution, which must have led to an increase in the number of presbyterian burgesses. In 1671, the corporation drew up proposals for a new charter, apparently with the support of Lord Donegall. In addition to clauses augmenting the corporation's authority and privileges and authorising means of increasing its income, it was proposed that the existing burgesses be styled aldermen, and that a common council of twenty-four new burgesses be elected.[11] This wider form of town government was usual in the older corporate towns in Ireland and also in Londonderry and Coleraine. However, by 1671 it would have been difficult to find an additional twenty-four men in Belfast of sufficient standing to become burgesses without either including the leading presbyterian merchants, or significantly altering the composition of the corporation by appointing second-rank Church of Ireland merchants or non-resident gentry. Although there were only three presbyterians in the corporation at this time (Martin, Eccles, Langford), this proposal clearly had the support of the majority of the burgesses as it included a veiled threat to eject any of their number who refused to contribute to the cost of obtaining the new charter.

In the 1670s, government policy favoured the granting of new charters to tighten control over Irish towns by eliminating any popular element from their constitutions, and 'new rules' were passed for Irish corporations in 1672.[12] Since, under the latter, Donegall's control would have been

the pool of families from which high sheriffs could be chosen was already very small; see also Reid, *History of the presbyterian church*, ii, p.397.
10 Coleraine minutes, 5 Apr., 3 Aug. 1680, and 28 Mar. 1683.
11 *Town book*, pp 118–19.
12 *Essex papers*, i, p.19; Sean Murphy, 'The corporation of Dublin' in *Dublin Historical Review*, xxxviii, 1 (1984), pp 23–4.

diminished and considerable powers would have passed to the corporation, it can be assumed that he subsequently opposed any change. However, if it is accepted that the proposals were intended to lead to wider representation of the community on the corporation, their supporters may have been discouraged when it became clear that adoption of the new rules would also mean the introduction of the oath of supremacy for burgesses. No more is heard of any petition. In 1675, the government was prepared to grant a new charter to Belfast because the town's 'trade and condition' was 'very much altered' from what it had been when the first charter was granted.[13] The fact that this proposal was not taken further suggests that both the Donegall family and the corporation opposed it, albeit for different reasons. Since the corporation showed a readiness to involve presbyterians who were not burgesses where the interests of the whole community were involved, it is unlikely that the Scots presbyterian community of Belfast as a whole felt themselves to be greatly discriminated against or excluded from town affairs, in spite of their low representation on the corporation before 1688. Nevertheless certain individuals may have felt resentment at not being elected burgess, and such resentment probably explains why Thomas Pottinger was prepared to co-operate with the Jacobite government in 1688.

INTERLUDE: THE JAMES II CORPORATION

To gain control of the Irish towns, James II issued new charters naming Roman catholic mayors and burgesses. In Ulster, where there were few urban catholics with wealth or status, the new charters named many presbyterian aldermen and burgesses in a bid for the support of the urban presbyterians who had been under-represented on corporations before 1688, and it was by no means a foregone conclusion that this would be unsuccessful. Although a proclamation announcing James II's accession in 1685 was torn down in Belfast, the corporation had been prompt in producing the customary loyal address. In 1687, however, they made strenuous but unsuccessful efforts to defend their charter against his writ of *quo warranto*.[14] In September of the following year, Robert Leathes, as sovereign, wrote a firm refusal to the request of the bishop of Clogher that the school house or town house of Belfast be used as a chapel by the Roman catholic troops which by then garrisoned the town. Belfast's new charter, dated 16 October 1688, ousted Leathes and most of the other burgesses and named a new corporation of thirty-five burgesses, including Thomas

---

13 *Letters written by his excellency Arthur Capel, earl of Essex, lord lieutenant of Ireland in the year 1675* (Dublin, 1770), p.25; *Cal. S.P. dom., 1675–76*, p.56.

14 Raymond Gillespie, 'The Irish protestants and James II, 1688–90' in *I.H.S.*, xxviii, no.110 (1992), pp 126–7; Benn, p.153; *Town book*, pp 157–8, and see Thomas Knox to Sir Robert Colville, 20 Apr. 1687, about other towns (T.C.D., MS 1178, no.21).

Pottinger as sovereign.[15] The new charter freed the corporation from any formal control of elections by the Donegall family, and did not renew the right of the lord and constable of the castle to be burgesses *ex officio*. This would have been seen as a considerable advantage by the corporation for, no matter how benign the control of the Donegalls may have been in this period, the burgesses would doubtless have preferred to be free of it. However, since the new charter named eighteen members of the Roman catholic landed gentry as non-resident burgesses, and also included a clause by which the sovereign and burgesses could be removed at will by the Dublin government, it was quite unacceptable to the town. Nevertheless, the new burgesses were nominally in office from October 1688 until Schomberg's landing in August 1689, when the old corporation was restored.

It is difficult to ascertain what actually happened in the town during this period because few contemporary sources have survived which refer to events in Belfast, and because most later accounts were either attempts to discredit the presbyterians or to justify their actions. The main sources of information are a summary of events from 1688 to 1690 written by Robert Leathes in the town book, and charges brought by William Tisdall, as part of his offensive against the Belfast presbyterians, which were rebutted by James Kirkpatrick in his book *Presbyterian loyalty*. All these sources are retrospective, and therefore unreliable. They contain two main claims. First, that Thomas Pottinger was responsible for obtaining the new charter for the town; second, that all the presbyterian burgesses were named without their knowledge or consent, and did not act.

Thomas Pottinger's complicity is stated in unequivocal terms by Robert Leathes in the town book:

> That Thomas Pottinger a marcht & ffreeman of Bellfast without ye consent of the Lord of the Castle Soveraigne Burgesses and Commonallity of the Borough of Bellfast procured a new Charter from King James ... and ye said Thomas Pottinger was made ye first Soveraigne and thirty five Burgesses ... in which Charter there is a proviso that ye Lord Deputy generall or other Cheife Governors of Ireland with ye Privy Councell have power to amove or remove the Soveraigne or Burgesses or any of them or any other officer in ye said Borrough at their will and good pleasure from their respective offices and places of trust ... O brave Thomas Pottinger who did not consider the sollem oath of a freeman he had taken to maintain all the rights and priv-elidges of the Corporacon granted by the old Charter ...

Tisdall states that Pottinger 'made Interest to have the Old Charter ... broken'[16] but the town book virtually accuses him of procuring the new

15 *Town book*, pp 158–67; Benn, p.730.
16 The statement is unsigned but is in Leathes's hand (*Town book*, p.242); Tisdall, p.56.

charter on his own initiative. In fact, James II granted new charters to all Irish towns of any importance as a means of controlling them and as a preliminary to the election of a Roman catholic parliament. While it is unlikely that any of his contemporaries seriously believed that Pottinger had any hand in Jacobite policy-making, it must have been immediately obvious that he would not have been named as sovereign unless he had first been sounded out, and had expressed his willingness to serve.

Furthermore, an examination of the composition of the new corporation makes it clear that those burgesses who were protestants had been chosen with considerable care. Including Pottinger himself, they totalled sixteen or seventeen, and thus could have been outvoted if necessary by the Roman catholics, who were mostly drawn from the County Antrim gentry because there were no catholic townsmen of sufficient status.[17] The protestant burgesses were as follows:

Henry Chads	William Dobbin	(?Peter Knowles)	Black George Macartney
John Chalmers	Hugh Eccles	Thomas Knox	Edward Pottinger
William Craford	John Eccles	William Lockhart	Thomas Pottinger
Humphrey Dobbin	John Fletcher	George Macartney	James Shaw
		of Auchinleck	David Smith

They included five out of the six Scottish burgesses of the old corporation, namely the two George Macartneys, Knox, Craford and Lockhart. The inclusion of these five, three of whom were the richest and most eminent merchants in the town, gave the new corporation some continuity with the old, and all five were either presbyterians, or had presbyterian connections. Although Tisdall states that there were eleven or twelve dissenters in the new corporation, only seven are claimed as such in *Presbyterian loyalty*, namely Chads, Chalmers, Craford, John Eccles, Lockhart, Shaw and Smith.[18] Others may have conformed after the test act and it would have been impolitic to have named them. For example, the Dobbin brothers were from a presbyterian branch of an Old English family. Captain Hugh Eccles was the son of Hugh Eccles, the presbyterian burgess, but appears to have been a conformist. Edward Pottinger may have been a presbyterian but one of his daughters married a son of the archbishop of Tuam. Nothing is known of Knowles's religion. He was appointed collector for Belfast by James II in place of George Macartney of Auchinleck, and had been a merchant there since at least 1677 when he became a freeman. John Fletcher probably belonged to the established church, because his wife,

17 Sir Neill O'Neill, Mark Talbot, Daniel O'Neill, Charles O'Neill, Felix O'Neill, three John O'Neills, John O'Neill of Ballyboran, Daniel and John McNaghton, James Wogan, James Savage, Martin Gernon, Eneas and Patrick Moylin, Charles Mulalan, Abraham Lee; lists of Irish Jacobites (*Anal. Hib.*, xxii [1960], pp 1–230).
18 Tisdall, p.50; Kirkpatrick, p.423.

Elizabeth Dawson of Armagh, had a large circle of clerical connections.[19] Fletcher appears to have been related to a Dublin family of aldermanic rank and his inclusion in the group may reflect his disappointment at his failure to achieve similar rank in the Belfast corporation. Similarly, the Dobbin brothers came of a family which held office in Carrickfergus corporation throughout the century.

Family connections linked many of the James II burgesses. There were two pairs of brothers (Pottingers and Dobbins), while Hugh and John Eccles were cousins. William Dobbin was married to Hugh Eccles's sister, and Thomas Pottinger's wife, Esther Eccles, was probably the aunt of both Hugh and John Eccles. Edward Pottinger's wife was a distant cousin of the Dobbin brothers. James Shaw had married the widow of a Chalmers. Lockhart was Macartney's son-in-law. William Craford and David Smith had married the sisters Janet and Grissell Clugston, whose mother was a Shaw.[20] The protestant part of the new corporation was therefore made up of men who either from religious affiliation, personal ambition or family loyalty, or a combination of all three, might be expected to accept office and to serve under Thomas Pottinger's leadership. There is no doubt that this group was carefully chosen by someone with local knowledge and in all probability this was Pottinger himself. In addition, contemporaries believed that he had not only co-operated with the Jacobites, but that he had in some way put himself forward and initiated negotiations. This is unlikely in view of his later career in government service under William and Mary.[21]

There is no direct evidence as to Pottinger's own motive for co-operating with the Jacobites. Although it has been suggested that he acted through public spirit,[22] it is more reasonable to suppose that he simply wanted to be sovereign. Under normal circumstances he would have needed, first, to become a burgess. No details survive of burgess elections so it is not known whether, or how often, he had been put forward for that office. Since other presbyterians had become burgesses, Pottinger's failure to reach that position may have been because his economic and social status was insufficiently high, or it may reflect his relationship with the Chichester family and the other burgesses. Whereas most of the Scottish settlers in Belfast came from the south-west, all the evidence suggests that Pottinger was from the Orkneys, and he appears to have stood a little way apart from the rest of the presbyterian community. For example, in spite of his marriage into two Belfast families, he is not named as an executor or administrator in any surviving Belfast wills and he was never an elder or commissioner of the Belfast presbyterian church.

19 Abstracts of wills of Elizabeth Fletcher, 1722, and her sister Mary Forster, 1735 (P.R.O.N.I., Leslie abstracts, T1075/12, pp 258, 270).
20 Appendix A.7, 8, 9, 11, 12, 23, 26.
21 Appendix A.23.
22 Nelson, 'Belfast presbyterians', p.20.

Whatever motives led him to seek office, his behaviour as sovereign was exemplary – and the restored Belfast corporation actually wrote a statement to that effect which has not survived. He played an active and successful role in protecting the property of Belfast inhabitants from the Jacobite troops and, after the act of attainder was passed in 1689, he negotiated for an extension of the period of grace for those townsmen who had fled.[23] His co-operation with the Jacobite authorities led to his being called a Jacobite by his enemies, but he was active in obtaining supplies and transport for Schomberg's army in the winter of 1689–90, partly at his own expense. He was rewarded for this by a grant, from the Williamite government, of the office of commissioner for prizes at Belfast. When this office proved to be less lucrative than he had hoped, John Ellis, the under-secretary of state, helped him to petition for relief, and in 1703 he was in the Netherlands, apparently waiting on the Duke of Marlborough. After spending some years in London, he returned to Belfast, probably early in 1710, and lived in reduced circumstances until his death in 1715.

In spite of his exemplary conduct as sovereign, Pottinger was regarded with almost universal opprobium by the Belfast townspeople because he had disregarded his freeman's oath. In accepting the office of sovereign without first serving as a burgess, he was disobeying the laws and statutes of the town, and by collaborating in the drawing up of a charter which included a clause giving the Dublin government the power to dismiss the sovereign or burgesses at will, he was breaking his oath not to 'doe or suffer to bee done anie thinge that may bee to the hurte and hindrance of this Corporacon'.[24] His co-operation with the Jacobites was seen as a betrayal which no subsequent good conduct could excuse. The Belfast presbyterian merchants, who vigorously denied all Tisdall's charges against themselves, made no attempt to exculpate Pottinger, but merely stated:

> ... because Mr Pottinger having been a Considerable Dealer in Town, and now in Declining Age (near 80) as well as Circumstances, and being marry'd in a Family of good Respect, Interest, and Loyalty, Protestants of all Persuasions wav'd taking any Notice of the Matter, further than Declaring in all Companies, and upon all Occasions, and frequently to his face, that they did not Approve, but Condemn the said Practice.[25]

This passage confirms that the charges against Pottinger were broadly true. However his subsequent career in government service shows that the Williamite administration took a less severe view of his co-operation with the Jacobites than did the Belfast community.

23 [Charles Leslie,] *An answer to a book entituled the state of the protestants in Ireland under King James's government* (London, 1692), pp 148–52, app. pp 74, 75, hereafter cited as Leslie, *Answer to King.*
24 *Town book*, p.78.
25 Kirkpatrick, p.425.

Although the presbyterian community was unable either to deny Pottinger's involvement or to defend his conduct, the presbyterian burgesses appointed by the James II charter claimed to have been named without their prior knowledge and never to have acted. *Presbyterian loyalty* contains a declaration, dated 2 September 1713, by five presbyterian ex-burgesses of Belfast, including William Craford and John Chalmers, both of whom were burgesses under the James II charter. They stated:

> ... that our Names were made use of without our Knowledge, Consent or Privity, and that we never accepted of, or serv'd in the Office of Burgesses in Belfast, by Virtue of the said Charter: And 'tis hereby Certify'd and Declar'd by all of us, that we have heard (and do verily believe) all the Rest of our Persuasion who were Nominated Burgesses in the said Charter solemnly protest and Declare, that their Names were likewise inserted and made use of without their Knowlege, Consent and Privity; and we know and Certify that none of them did ever Accept or Serve in the Office of Burgesses in this Corporation, by Virtue of the said Charter, the said Thomas Pottinger only excepted.[26]

Craford and Chalmers were speaking only for the presbyterians among the burgesses and it is not known how far their statement could have been applied to the other protestant burgesses. There is no suggestion, let alone evidence, that any of the James II burgesses had sought office, but it would have been odd if some of them had not been sounded out first by Pottinger. Since this cannot be documented, the truth of their claim to have been named without their knowledge or consent cannot be proved or disproved. However, their claim never to have acted can be investigated through an examination of their activities and whereabouts in 1688 to 1689.

However unpopular the new charter was, at the date of its issue on 16 October 1688 James II was the lawful king and the invasion of William of Orange was still three weeks away. The glorious revolution and the accession of William and Mary may, with hindsight, have seemed inevitable but in October 1688 the new protestant burgesses must have been in a quandary, for although there had been rumours about a possible invasion, its actual date was a closely-kept secret. The new charter was legal. *Quo warranto* proceedings had been used by Charles II for the same purpose, and the presence of a Jacobite garrison would have ensured that opposition to the charter was not expressed publicly. The town book contains no record of the proceedings of the new corporation. The only official document signed by any of the burgesses in this period dates from five months after the new charter. It is the town's letter of submission to the Jacobite commander, General Richard Hamilton, written immediately after the rout of the protestant forces of the northern association at the 'break of

26 Kirkpatrick, p.424.

Dromore' on 14 March 1689.[27] There are twenty-two signatures which include those of two burgesses of the old corporation (Robert Leathes and Lewis Thompson), one of both old and new (Black George Macartney), and two future burgesses (James Buller and Neil McNeil). The leading signatory was Colonel John Hill, who as constable of the castle was an *ex officio* burgess under the old charter.[28] The fact that Thomas Pottinger did not sign this document is probably not significant. The Belfast inhabitants were reacting to an emergency. News of the break of Dromore was brought to the town by express causing many of the townspeople to flee.[29] The town had given considerable support to the association, and with Hamilton and his army only hours away, no time could be wasted in waiting for more signatures to their submission. It is unlikely that the signatories chose not to include Pottinger as this would have been an exceptionally bad moment to have slighted him.[30]

Since only one of the burgesses named in the new charter signed the submission, where were the others and what had they been doing in the meantime? A state of near panic had prevailed long before the break of Dromore. The inevitability of conflict between James II and the northern protestants had led to the formation of 'associations', ostensibly for defence, led by the protestant gentry. The fact that these units were ill prepared and badly led, due in part to internal factiousness, meant that little reliance was placed upon them locally. By January 1689 there was a widescale exodus from the countryside, with those who remained anticipating that 'vile merciless, bloody enemies' would fall on them 'like a thunderclap'.[31] A plot to disarm the Jacobite garrison at Carrickfergus had been discouraged by the 'gentlemen of Belfast' because they feared reprisals if it was unsuccessful, but townsmen of Belfast openly mustered and drilled.[32] Most of the Belfast merchants were active in their support of William and Mary although the town did not declare for them until 9 March, upon an assurance that an army was coming to their assistance from England. Many were involved in the northern association or contributed money or supplies. The act of attainder passed by James II's 'patriot parliament' in 1689 divided the attainted into categories according

27 Letter of submission (N.A., M 2541, f.21).
28 Hill, who was about 65 in 1689, was Lord Donegall's steward, and was subsequently governor of Fort William; Leslie, *Answer to King*, p.148; abstract of chancery bill, Cary v. Donegall, 1679 (P.R.O.N.I., Tenison Groves abstracts, T808/7122); account of William III's landing, 1690 (P.R.O.N.I., copies of documents from Society of Friends, Dublin, T1062/49/12).
29 Journal of John Black, 18 Aug. 1752 (P.R.O.N.I., T1073/7).
30 Pottinger may have made a separate representation to Hamilton (Leslie, *Answer to King*, p.149).
31 Johnston to Crumpe, 15 Jan.–17 Feb. 1688/9 (Bodl., Carte MSS 40, f.522).
32 *Mackenzie's memorials of the siege of Derry including his narrative and its vindication*, ed. W.D. Killen (Belfast, 1861), p.18, hereafter cited as Mackenzie, *Memorials*.

to their involvement in resistance to the king. The first, consisting of those who had notoriously joined in the rebellion against James II, included Macartney of Auchinleck, a burgess under both the old and new charters, Captain James Shaw, one of the new burgesses, and Edward Harrison, one of the old. A second category, consisting of those whose absence from Ireland could be construed as treason, included Henry Chads, William Craford and David Smith, all of whom can be supposed to have contributed to the Williamite cause. Notable contributions of money, supplies and ammunition were also made by the two George Macartneys, James Macartney and Thomas Knox.[33]

The act of attainder states that all persons named were out of the country in the summer of 1689. Most of the Belfast burgesses who were Scots went back to Scotland. George Macartney of Auchinleck, who had raised a troop of horse at his own expense, was 'with many others forced to leave the kingdom in a great hurry' on 12 March 1689[34] and was in Scotland in April. He had held the office of collector of Belfast, but had been replaced in December 1688 by Peter Knowles. Like many other collectors he had handed over the revenue to the protestant forces, and appears to have taken some to Scotland with him. In his absence, Knowles seized much of Macartney's personal property, claiming that he had embezzled the revenue.[35] Macartney had previously been dismissed from the office of surveyor-general of the customs of Ulster for helping merchants to evade the navigation acts.[36] He was married to Elizabeth Butler, who came of a recusant family in Lancashire, and who was the sister of Sir Nicholas Butler, a privy councillor of James II.[37] These circumstances combined to place Macartney in a vulnerable position, laying him open to charges of both embezzlement and Jacobitism. The charge of Jacobitism was speedily dismissed, but it was not until several years after his death that his wife and son were able to clear his name of all charges.

Of the other Belfast burgesses named in the act of attainder, Henry Chads was in Glasgow in June 1689, seeking permission to sell a cargo of arms and ammunition which he had bought for the use of a company in

33 William King, *The state of the protestants under the late King James's government* (Dublin, 1730), pp 199–244; Mackenzie, *Memorials*, p.62; claim by James Hamilton of Tollymore, commander of one of the northern association regiments, from the treasury for sums advanced to him in 1688 (*Cal. treas. bks*, ix, p.801).

34 Petition of George Macartney, 27 Sept. 1689 (P.R.O., T1/5, p.105).

35 Leslie, *Answer to King*, p.91; William Stannus to James Hamilton, 8 Apr. 1689, which also mentions Edward Brice, future burgess, raising a company in Scotland (P.R.O.N.I., Roden MSS, MIC 147/8, vol.16, no.55); Knowles also pressed some gabarts belonging to Macartney, Lewis Thompson and Robert Martin into Jacobite service (*Reg. privy council of Scotland*, xvi, pp 309–10, 697).

36 See chapter 5.

37 There is no evidence which suggests that either Elizabeth or her brother were Roman catholics.

Belfast in which he was concerned. He had diverted these goods to Ayr after the rout of the protestant forces. William Craford and David Smith also fled to Glasgow with their wives, who were sisters, and were still there in December 1689.[38] Other burgesses are also easy to trace. Black George Macartney was in Belfast on 14 March, when he signed the letter of submission, but he may not at that point have realised that the defeated army had abandoned letters and accounts as they fled, which would enable the Jacobites to identify supporters of the association. He left soon after with his family and he was in Lancashire in June. By that time, he and Edmund Harrison, his chief correspondent in London, were probably involved in supplying Schomberg's artillery train.[39] Thomas Knox was certainly still in Ulster on 4 December 1688 when he was one of the gentlemen who sent copies to Dublin of a mysterious letter, dropped in Comber, warning Lord Mountalexander of an imminent protestant massacre. He was in Glasgow by the following May, and he and his family appear to have spent several years there.[40] Captain Edward Pottinger was at Coleraine in March 1689, where by his skill with artillery he beat off a Jacobite attack. He subsequently went to London with his wife and daughters and was made captain of a yacht which was at Carrickfergus during the siege by Schomberg.[41] Both William and Humphrey Dobbin were at the siege of Londonderry. William Lockhart was in Glasgow. John Eccles appears on the list of protestant refugees who made claims for their losses; since his name is bracketed with that of the Belfast merchant John Black, who was married to his cousin, he may have fled to Ayr with the Blacks. The whereabouts of Hugh Eccles is not known, but his mother was in England with one of her sons in 1689. Similarly, there is no direct information about John Chalmers, but other members of the family were at Ayr.[42]

From March 1689 therefore, almost all of the new protestant burgesses were absent from Belfast, the majority being in Scotland. Even though the anticipated sack of the town by the Jacobite forces never took place, and Thomas Pottinger sent them reassuring messages, they could not be prevailed upon to return until after Schomberg had landed in August. Their absence was doubtless the reason why Belfast's representatives to the 'patriot parliament' were not returned until 20 May 1689 when most other members of parliament had been returned almost a fortnight earlier. There is no source which mentions the election of the members for Belfast but there were so few burgesses remaining there that the election would have

38 *Reg. privy council of Scotland*, xiii, pp 450, 537; appendix A.9, 26.
39 *A faithful history of the northern affairs of Ireland* (London, 1690), p.38; appendix A.19.
40 Mackenzie, *Memorials*, pp 8–9; appendix A.14.
41 *Reg. privy council of Scotland*, xvi, p.4, and see appendix A.23.
42 Appendix A.3, 7, 11, 12, 17.

had to have been deferred until the arrival of the Roman catholic burgesses, who were almost all in the Jacobite army.[43]

However, the fact that the protestant burgesses, except presumably Thomas Pottinger, were not present at the parliamentary election in May 1689 does not prove that they were all unwilling to act in less important matters. Although many of the wealthiest townsmen had fled, Belfast was not abandoned, and the organization of the town, its markets and its courts, can hardly have been at a standstill for almost a year. Pottinger himself must have been assisted by Peter Knowles the collector, by John Hill,[44] who was a burgess *ex officio* under the old charter, and possibly also by John Fletcher whose whereabouts remain untraced. There is however a hint of wider co-operation in the burgesses' statement from *Presbyterian loyalty*, quoted above. Craford and Chalmers stated that 'we know and Certify that none of them did ever Accept or Serve in the Office of Burgesses in this Corporation, by Virtue of the said Charter [i.e. the James II charter]'. However, Craford, the Macartneys, Knox and Lockhart had been elected burgesses for life under the old James I charter. If they had continued to share in the running of the town, at least until the break of Dromore, they could later have claimed to have done so by virtue of the old charter, rather than the new. Direct proof is lacking but the careful wording of the statement in *Presbyterian loyalty* suggests that this may have been a partial solution to the problems that faced the community after the new charter was issued.

THE CORPORATION OF BELFAST FROM 1689 TO 1707

Because the former sovereign and corporation were restored after Schomberg's landing in August 1689, the period of Jacobite control can be treated as an interlude which had no lasting effect on the town. It was, in fact, the Williamite victory that had wider implications for change, as it ushered in a period of toleration towards presbyterians which, although short-lived, had far-reaching effects. The abrogation of the oath of supremacy in Ireland in 1691 opened all offices to presbyterians and changed the composition of the corporations in the Ulster towns. Table 7 (overleaf) shows that in the period 1689–1704 increasing numbers of Scots presbyterians were elected as burgesses at Belfast.

William Tisdall asserted that the rapid growth of presbyterian representation on the corporations of the northern towns could not have been

43 Leslie, *Answer to King*, pp 148–9; there was a similar situation in Carrickfergus where the aldermen had fled on account of 'the ruggedness of the times', (P.R.O.N.I., statement by Richard Dobbs, D162/1); Walter Harris, *History of the life and reign of William Henry ... king of England, Scotland, France and Ireland* (Dublin, 1749), app.xi.

44 Hill to Pottinger, May 1689 (Leslie, *Answer to King*, p.75).

Table 7: Representation of Scots and presbyterians on the Belfast corporation,[45]
1689–1704

	English	Scottish	presbyterians
total burgesses (22)	8 or 9	12 or 13	11
new burgesses (12)	3 or 4	8 or 9	8
sovereign terms (14)	6	8	7

achieved without trickery,[46] and he accused the presbyterian burgesses of the Ulster towns of refusing to admit any churchmen once their numbers were sufficient to control the elections. However, the rapid change in the composition of the Belfast corporation was the result of the deaths, between 1690 and 1693, of five elderly burgesses, all of whom were members of the established church. The town book shows that their presbyterian successors were elected unanimously. Kirkpatrick, in his reply to Tisdall's accusations, not only gave details of every burgess election in Belfast between 1686 and 1703, but stated that the presbyterians were 'Elected not only with the Consent, but by the Interest and Recommendation of the Right Honorable Family of Donegal'.[47] The friendliness of the third earl towards presbyterians has been noted previously and, with his sanction, not only did the Belfast corporation become largely presbyterian, but both members of parliament for the town, elected in 1703, were also presbyterians.[48] Moreover, this change in the composition of the corporation reflects the change within the merchant community. The leading merchants, from whom the burgesses were normally elected, were by 1700 almost all presbyterians. In addition to their election as burgesses, a number of presbyterians held office as sovereign from 1691 to 1704. In eight out of these fourteen years the sovereign was a presbyterian, again with Lord Donegall's approval. It was normal for election of the mayors or sovereigns of corporate towns to be approved by the Dublin government. The town book contains no mention of any formal approval being sought before 1726,[49] let alone refused, so it appears that the government was willing to accept Donegall's nominees, even when they were presbyterians.

This is in contrast to the situation in Londonderry during the same period. There too, a number of burgesses and aldermen had been elected to replace those who had died in the siege or left the country, and the pre-

45 It is not known whether the presbyterian James Buller was Scots or English; for a complete list of burgesses and sovereigns within this period, see appendix D.
46 Tisdall, pp 58–9.
47 Kirkpatrick, p.422.
48 William Craford and William Cairnes; when in June 1704, it was thought likely that parliament would be dissolved, Ormond was recommended to ask Donegall to change them (*Ormonde MSS*, [NS], viii, p.85).
49 Licence for John Clugston to serve was sought in 1726 (Young, *Historical notices*, p.167).

ponderance of presbyterians in this number was explained by the financial decline of many of the conformist citizens. As in Belfast, a number of the leading presbyterians were elected mayor but there was a perpetual struggle to get these appointments approved. Alexander Lecky and James Lennox, two leading presbyterian merchants, each served one term, but their re-elections were not confirmed by the government. Throughout the 1690s the Londonderry corporation spent considerable sums to defend their choice, generally without success. Simultaneously, the corporation was at odds with Bishop King of Derry, and the rejection of the presbyterian mayors was attributed to his influence. The Londonderry corporation minutes reveal considerable friction between presbyterians and conformists when one of the latter accused the corporation of excluding him from the office of mayor. It was also rumoured that the sword and mace had been carried before some of the presbyterian mayors to the meeting house, although this was denied by the corporation. There was conflict between presbyterians and episcopalians, both inside and outside the corporation and, in 1699, Charles Norman, a conformist, wrote to Bishop King to inform him that he and some others of the established church proposed to set up in trade there as the virtual trading monopoly of the dissenters had given them the 'means and power to oppose and injure us'.[50]

By 1695, the presbyterians were in the majority in the Belfast corpora-tion, although the sovereign for that year was Edward Harrison, a member of the Church of Ireland. The other Church of Ireland burgesses were Robert Leathes, Lewis Thompson, Thomas Knox, James Macartney, and Lord Donegall. Donegall had secured his own election as burgess in 1692 because, although the long drawn-out lawsuit with his cousin, the countess of Longford (daughter of the first earl of Donegall), was settled in that year, Lady Longford retained the title 'lord of the castle' for life. It was therefore she, not Donegall, who was an *ex officio* burgess of Belfast and both she and her husband attended meetings of the corporation.[51] For Donegall to have an equal voice in the town's affairs it was necessary for him to be an elected burgess, to offset the influence of the Longfords, and his brothers were also elected in 1697 and 1698. Donegall's relations with the corporation seem to have been consistently good, and all the evidence suggests that he was quite satisfied with the conduct of the presbyterian burgesses. When, for example, he was absent in London during his year of office as sovereign, David Smith acted in his stead, and he asked John Chalmers to serve a second

50 Burgesses of Londonderry were chosen from those who had previously served as sheriff, and this was apparently a very costly office (Kirkpatrick, pp 426–7); Conolly to Lennox, 11 Nov. 1693 (P.R.O.N.I., Lenox-Conyngham papers, T3161/1/3); Londonderry minutes, 12 Jan. 1697/8, 2 Jan. 1701/2; petition on behalf of Thomas Moncrieff, 1698 (P.R.O.N.I., Lenox-Conyngham papers, D1449/12/19); Robert Rochfort to James Lennox, 6 Dec. 1701 (ibid., D1449/1/6); Norman to King, 1 Jan. 1698/9 (T.C.D., MS 1995–2008/590).
51 *Town book*, p.190.

term as sovereign.[52] Not only was there no friction between Donegall and the presbyterians, there is no record of any animosity towards the presbyterians from the Church of Ireland burgesses, a situation quite unlike that within the corporations of Londonderry and Coleraine.

Apart from the increasing number of presbyterian burgesses, another change had taken place in the composition of the corporation. The majority of those elected still came from local merchant families, many now producing a second or third generation of burgesses. It was the families themselves that had changed. In the 1650s, the burgesses were a group of able and successful businessmen, but few were of much importance outside their own locality. From the 1670s to 1690s the status of the sovereign had increased, and the office had been held by a number of outstanding men. The leading merchants functioned as members of the gentry, becoming high sheriffs and members of parliament, educating sons for the gentry professions and making marriage alliances with local gentry families. In the 1690s, the sons of George Macartney of Auchinleck were members of parliament and married into influential families; James Macartney became a justice of the king's bench in 1701. The presbyterians William Craford and Edward Brice were also members of parliament. Both Brice and David Butle were related to many of the gentry families of County Antrim. From the early eighteenth century it was inevitable that, when the interests of the Chichester family diverged from those of the corporation, there would be a struggle for control between the family and the burgesses. This situation was masked by the friendly relations between Lord Donegall and the corporation, but his early death and the test act crisis precipitated the struggle.

The test act, passed in 1704, required all holders of office to take the sacrament in the established church. Promptly after the passing of the act, the presbyterian David Butle resigned as sovereign of Belfast,[53] and the sovereign-elect, George Macartney, youngest son of George Macartney of Auchinleck, was asked to serve for the remainder of Butle's term. Although he had only been elected burgess in 1702 on the death of Black George Macartney, Macartney quickly emerged as the leader of the corporation, and acceptable to both conformists and presbyterians. He was at this date in his early thirties, a barrister and member of parliament for Newtownlimavady. He was the Donegalls' principal tenant-in-chief in Belfast, he had recently married an heiress, and was clearly destined for a successful career, helped by the advice and support of his elder half-brother, Justice James Macartney.

However, Butle did not resign as burgess and neither did the other seven presbyterian burgesses. The sacramental test was an innovation. It was by no means clear who would have to take it and, since the burgesses

---

52 Kirkpatrick, p.422.
53 Butle to the corporation, 29 July 1704 (*Town book*, pp 194–5, where his name is printed as Buller).

of Belfast had never been obliged to take the oath of supremacy, there were some grounds for assuming that they would not be obliged to take the test either.[54] Moreover, since the act had been originally intended to debar Roman catholics from office and the clause which extended the test to protestant dissenters had not originated in the Irish house of commons, there was some possibility that this part of the act might be repealed. There is no source detailing events at Belfast in 1704, but it is most likely that the burgesses consulted Lord Donegall and, with his assent, decided to wait and see what would happen.

In Carrickfergus, a junta of four presbyterians or quasi-presbyterians was said by Tisdall to hold the office of mayor in rotation.[55] In the absence of any surviving corporation minutes it is impossible to determine their reaction to the test act. Like that of Belfast, the Carrickfergus corporation was largely controlled by the earl of Donegall. Presumably he would have been content for the presbyterian members of the corporation there to continue in office initially, but as there do not seem to have been any subsequent resignations[56] any presbyterian members must eventually have conformed. In other corporations presbyterian burgesses and aldermen were given no chance to hold on to office. In Coleraine, at least seven presbyterians refused to qualify themselves and were promptly replaced.[57] In Londonderry, as in Belfast, there appears to have been some uncertainty as to which office-holders had to resign. Presbyterian justices, the mayor of the staple and one of the constables resigned immediately, but the aldermen and burgesses were uncertain whether their offices came within the act and applied to the recorder, Robert Rochfort, for his advice. Rochfort gave his opinion that all who would not qualify themselves by taking the sacramental test should resign, and although the presbyterians in the corporation were hopeful that the act would be repealed, they resigned soon after.[58]

In Drogheda, there was only one dissenting alderman who had just been elected. Upon his refusing to qualify himself, the unsympathetic corporation attempted to fine him £66 13s 4d.[59] In Dublin, only one alderman, Thomas Bell, failed to qualify himself and his place was declared vacant. Bell, a presbyterian who had assisted the Londonderry corporation to present their case about mayoral elections, may have come from Belfast as

54 Richard Cox to Southwell, 24 Oct. 1706 (B.L., Add MS 38,154, ff 86–7); I am indebted to Ian Mongomery for this reference.
55 Tisdall, pp 57–8.
56 I am indebted to Sheela Speers for this information.
57 There may have been as many as twelve dissenters who were replaced (Mullin, *Coleraine*, pp 160, 163).
58 Londonderry minutes, 20 July 1704; *Ormonde MSS*, (NS), viii, p.104; 9 aldermen and 17 burgesses were presbyterians (Hayton, 'Ireland and the English ministers', p.40); King to Lindsay, 30 Oct. 1706 (T.C.D., MS 750/3/2/62–3).
59 He appealed and the fine was halved (Thomas Gogarty (ed.), *Council book of the corporation of Drogheda, i, 1649–1734* [Drogheda, 1915, repr. 1988], pp 286, 288, 290).

he was related in some way to the Belfast Hamiltons.[60] William Cairnes, one of the presbyterian M.P.s for Belfast, whose election as sheriff of Dublin in the previous year had failed to win the approbation of the lords justices, requested to be excused from all offices in the city and further attendance on the city's affairs, as did Thomas Kirkpatrick, another presbyterian, and almost certainly another Ulsterman.[61] Therefore, although there may have been initial uncertainty about the implications of the test act, these doubts appear to have been swiftly resolved in towns with less supportive patrons.

Lord Donegall left with his regiment for Spain in November 1704. He appears to have remained content with the situation in Belfast and sent money for the corporation to drink his health in 1706.[62] The test act was petitioned against, and its repeal was supported by a pro-presbyterian faction in the Irish house of commons.[63] The presbyterian burgesses of Belfast continued to sit tight but were aware of their anomalous position. When David Smith, one of their number, died in 1705, none of them voted at the election of his successor, Michael Harrison. Harrison was a member of the local Church of Ireland gentry but, since he was the son of a burgess and had a house in Belfast, there is no reason to assume that the presbyterians would have opposed his election.

On 10 April 1706 Lord Donegall was killed in action in Spain at the age of forty. The news was greeted in Belfast with genuine regret. Isaac Macartney wrote to William Cairnes 'this place and particularly myself hath lost a good friend'.[64] The earl appears to have been well liked and was something of a benefactor to the town, and the burgesses copied King Charles of Spain's letter commending his conduct and valour into the town book.[65] George Macartney, who had served as sovereign since July 1704 when he took over from Butle, was re-elected as sovereign in June 1706 and his election may have been approved in advance by Lord Donegall. Thereafter, the corporation had to deal with Lady Donegall and even before Donegall's death it may have been realised that there would be changes if she survived him.[66] It was probably clear from the start that the

---

60　Londonderry minutes, 31 Mar. 1693; for Bell see appendix A.13, 16.

61　Minutes, 13 July 1703, Sept.–Oct. 1704 (Dublin Corporation Archives, Monday book, i, 1658–1712, pp 155B–159A); Kirkpatrick/Kilpatrick was a trustee for the Capel Street congregation in 1718 (Registry of Deeds, Dublin, 22 444 12536).

62　Macartney to William Sloane, 11 Nov. 1704, to Donegall, 29 Mar. 1706, (Macartney 3, pp 9–10, 291–2).

63　*Commons' jn. Ire.*, iii, p.279, David Butle was one of the signatories; Hayton, 'Ireland and the English ministers', p.39.

64　Macartney to Cairnes, 8 June 1706 (Macartney 3, p.320).

65　Benn, pp 144–9, 292–3, 533; Roebuck, 'Landlord indebtedness', pp 152–3; *Town book*, p.195.

66　For example, Isaac Macartney advised William Sloane to have nothing to do with a mortgage of Sir Robert Colville on land leased from Lord Donegall as 'it is a lease

anomalous state of affairs regarding the presbyterian burgesses would not be allowed to continue and they immediately sought counsel's advice.[67]

Although her actions led to the ousting of the presbyterians from the corporation, Lady Donegall was not hostile to presbyterianism. In many respects her religious background was similar to that of the Chichester family. Her father, the first earl of Granard, was instrumental in obtaining the original *regium donum* in 1672. Her mother was a presbyterian who regularly attended the Capel Street meeting house in Dublin.[68] An examination of events between 1704 and 1707 suggests that her objective in 1707 was not primarily to force the presbyterian burgesses to resign, as they should have done in 1704 after the passing of the test act, but was to oust George Macartney and regain control of the corporation.

Lady Donegall's first action was to get her younger son, a child of six, elected burgess in December 1706, on the death of Arthur Macartney, a presbyterian and half-brother to the sovereign.[69] The following June, she presented the corporation with a leet consisting of Michael Harrison, Edward Brice and John Chalmers, from whom they were to elect the next sovereign. Since Brice and Chalmers were both presbyterians this was tantamount to an order to elect Harrison, a member of the established church (and a grandson of Bishop Jeremy Taylor). The corporation elected Brice who, predictably, refused to qualify himself and they then asked Macartney to continue to serve.[70] At this point it must have been clear to the countess that it would to be impossible to dislodge Macartney as sovereign unless she could replace the non-voting presbyterian burgesses with her own nominees.

In the following month, William Cairnes, member of parliament for Belfast, died. The countess proposed, as his successor, his brother Alexander Cairnes, merchant and banker of London, whom she may have expected to be acceptable to the corporation. However, the Macartney brothers supported the candidature of Samuel Ogle, an English presbyterian with property in Ireland. Cairnes, although a presbyterian, was no crusader and was unlikely to challenge the establishment. Ogle, on the other hand, was an active campaigner on the presbyterians' behalf striving

Lady Donegall designs to do her utmost to break if she survives him', 17 Jan. 1704/5 (Macartney 3, pp 41–2).

67 Macartney to Messrs Cairnes, London, 10 Aug. 1706 (Macartney 3, pp 338–9); Macartney copied the charter into the back of his letter book.

68 McGuire, 'Government attitudes to religious non-conformity in Ireland', p.263; Beckett, 'Irish Scottish relations', pp 36, 43; Irwin, *Presbyterianism in Dublin*, pp 11–12, 266.

69 He was disqualified as a minor and replaced at the same time as the presbyterian burgesses.

70 *Town book*, pp 196, 244; Lady Donegall took counsel's advice as to whether her son, the fourth earl, who was a burgess *ex officio* as lord of the castle, had a vote during his minority (Donegall minority accounts, pt 2, p.13).

8 The Irish House of Commons, c.1708

for the repeal of the test act. In the ensuing election only six burgesses voted and Ogle was returned because George Macartney claimed (on the advice of his brother Justice James Macartney) that he was entitled to vote twice, once as sovereign and once as burgess. By allowing the presbyterian burgesses to continue as non-voting members of the corporation Macartney had taken control of the Donegalls' pocket borough. The countess now attempted to oust Macartney as sovereign and to ensure he was not re-elected. Cairnes petitioned parliament against Ogle's election, the countess (in the name of her son, the fourth earl) brought a petition accusing Macartney of improper actions as sovereign, and Dr William Tisdall seized the opportunity to re-open the house money question.[71]

The Irish house of commons considered the disputed election first. Robert Leathes, Lewis Thompson and Patrick Duffe, as constable of the castle, had voted for Cairnes; the Macartney brothers and John Haltridge had voted for Ogle. The presbyterians did not vote, and neither did Michael Harrison nor the third earl's brother, John Itchingham Chichester,[72] who were presumably not in Belfast. Haltridge, who was M.P. for Killyleagh, had become a burgess in April 1707 when his brother-in-law Isaac Macartney resigned his burgess-ship in his favour. He was a conformist but came of a Scots presbyterian family, two of his uncles being ministers. Macartney's resignation is unlikely to have been because he was more realistic than his colleagues about the presbyterians' chances of continuing as burgesses. He can hardly have been better informed than Macartney, Brice and Craford who were all M.P.s, and in the event, when the matter was put to the vote, the presbyterian support-ers were narrowly defeated. It is however possible, because he was on friendly terms with the Cairnes family, that he already knew in April 1707 that William Cairnes was terminally ill and resigned in order to transfer his burgess-ship to Haltridge so that the latter could vote with the Macartneys for Ogle. In addition to claiming that Ogle had had four votes in his favour, the Macartney faction also challenged Patrick Duffe's right to vote as he had never been sworn as a burgess, had not qualified himself as constable of the castle under the test act, and his appointment as con-stable had not been renewed by deed since Lord Donegall's death.[73] The house accepted the objections against Duffe and found in favour of Ogle. However, as George Dodington, chief secretary to Lord Pembroke, wrote: 'In the examination of the merit of that election it appeared several burgesses being dissenters had not taken the sacrament nor acted for some

71 Although Swift later called Cairnes 'a Scot and a fanatic', he was, in fact, a moder-ate who was rewarded with a baronetcy in 1708 (Tenison, 'Old Dublin bankers' p.121); Robert Johnson to Ormond, 18 Oct. 1707 (*Ormonde MSS*, [NS], viii, p.312); the session ended before Tisdall's petition could be heard.

72 He was elected burgess in 1698, was M.P. for Gorey, had estates in County Wicklow, and died in 1721.

73 Duffe was Donegall agent for the Belfast estate; he was a conformist and died in or before 1709.

years past', and it was established that the sacramental test extended to burgesses of corporations.[74]

The Donegall petition was heard a few days later. The charges brought against Macartney are not detailed, but apart from his failure to secure the resignation of the presbyterian burgesses and to fill up their places, his 'unwarrantable and illegal practices' appear to have been much the same as those with which the Belfast corporation was charged several years previously, namely the levying of 'ship money' at the town dock, compelling the Belfast parishioners to contribute to the fund for opposing the claim for house money, unjust and unequal levying of rates and failure to present proper accounts. All these charges pre-dated Macartney's election as sovereign and have been discussed above. Although Lady Donegall produced many witnesses, it is clear that Macartney was able to put up a good defence. The hearing on 24 October was full of drama. Lady Donegall and her entourage had hoped to hear the proceedings but their presence was objected to and they were virtually driven from the gallery. Justice James Macartney elected to stay, and exchanged heated words with Captain Philips, a connection of the Chichester family, who had to be prevented from assaulting him. Finally it was resolved, *nemine contradicente*, that Macartney had 'fully acquitted himself of the several matters alledged against him ... to the satisfaction of the House'. Three days later, however, the house resolved that the burgesses of Belfast were obliged to take the sacramental test, and that those who had not done so were deemed no longer burgesses; and furthermore, it was ruled that the taking of 2d per ton at Belfast quay was arbitrary and illegal. The house, in fact, accepted that the Belfast corporation was acting against the law, but did not hold Macartney responsible.[75]

The countess's proceedings against the corporation were later regarded as anti-presbyterian but they can be better interpreted as being anti-Macartney, and this was in fact the interpretation of contemporaries.[76] Robert Johnson, baron of the exchequer, who wrote an account of the hearing of the Donegall petition against George Macartney, described Justice James Macartney as:

> one of the three electors of Ogle, the chief manager for him, who together with his brother, the sovereign, do set up to have the great power over the corporation, to the prejudice of the Countess Dowager and the young Earl.

74 *Commons' jn. Ire.*, iii, pp 520–22; Dodington to [?Sunderland], 2 Nov. 1707 (P.R.O., SP.63/366, no.252); [Anderson Saunders] to Edward Southwell, 18 Oct. 1707 (B.L., Add. MS 9715, f.205).

75 For the countess's expenses, see Donegall minority accounts, pt 2, pp 8–9, 15; *Ormonde MSS*, (NS), viii, pp 312–13; *Commons' jn. Ire.*, iii, pp 537–39.

76 See Young, *Historical notices*, p.175, for a rather confused anecdote; [Saunders] to Southwell, 29 Oct. 1707 (B.L., Add. MS 9715, f.219).

It is true they were raised by a dependence and by the favour of that
family, but it will not be strange to your grace if one should say that sometimes signifies nothing.[77]

The Donegall petition, therefore, was seen as the culmination of a struggle
between the Macartneys and Lady Donegall for control over the corporation. The countess inherited a situation in which power in the corporation
was passing into the hands of the most important burgesses, a situation
which had been masked in her husband's lifetime because no clash of interests had arisen. In acting against George Macartney, the countess was protecting the interests of her young son. Had she not done so, there was a real
possibility that the Donegall family would have lost control of parliamentary
elections in the borough. There is no indication of actual personal dislike of
the Macartneys although, as a protegé and kinsman of the earl of Longford,
James Macartney may have been unpopular with the third earl. Nor, as has
been noted above, does anything in the countess's background suggest that
that she was anti-presbyterian. Although she was prepared to use the testimony of a tory high-flyer like Westenra Waring at the hearing before the
Irish commons, she did not reward him with a burgess-ship subsequently,
even though he came of a burgess family.[78] Although the Macartney brothers
were members of the established church, they had aligned themselves with
the presbyterian majority on the corporation and, by choosing Ogle as
member of parliament in Cairnes's place, showed their intention to work for
the repeal of the test act. Unable to control the corporation through George
Macartney, Lady Donegall next set about replacing him. Of the conformist
burgess, Leathes and Thompson, although loyal, were old and not of sufficient weight to oppose the Macartneys. Michael Harrison was the only
burgess of sufficient standing to balance the Macartney interest in the corporation. He was member of parliament for Lisburn, commissary-general of
the musters in Ireland, and his wife was the daughter of a former secretary
of state. When Lady Donegall's attempt to replace George Macartney as
sovereign with Michael Harrison failed, and when Macartney's refusal to
replace the presbyterian burgesses allowed him to control a bye-election, she
attacked him directly in the house of commons. Her attack was unsuccessful, but it was established that members of corporations had to take the
sacramental test, and the countess was thus able to regain control of the
corporation by replacing the presbyterians.

The presbyterian burgesses were faced with a choice. They could either
take the sacramental test or lose all direct influence over the town's affairs.
Two of the Eccles family had faced this decision in 1704 and had conformed. John Eccles and his brother James, nephews of Hugh Eccles of

77 *Ormonde MSS*, (NS), viii, pp 312–13.
78 She paid his travelling expenses to Dublin (Donegall minority accounts, pt 2, p.15),
    and see appendix A.30.

Belfast, were members of the corporations of Dublin and Waterford.
Rather than resign after the test act, both took the sacramental test and
both subsequently became mayors.[79] By 1707, it was clear that, although the
English administration favoured repeal of the test act, and the Irish whigs
supported the ideal of religious toleration, there would never be a majority
in the existing Irish commons in favour of repeal, and that presbyterians
who refused to conform would be barred from office for the forseeable
future.[80] George Dodington, the chief secretary and a whig, met the presbyterian burgesses of Belfast who were in Dublin for the hearing and had
hopes that they would conform: 'I have sent for and discoursed the leading
dissenters of Belfast and pressed them to qualify themselves and they give
me great hopes they will comply and promise to exhort all their brethren in
the North to do the same'.[81] Whether Dodington's optimism was the result
of wishful thinking on his part or politeness on the part of the burgesses, it
was soon found to be misplaced. Occasional conformity was unacceptable to
the majority of Scots presbyterians and John McBride, the minister at
Belfast, was strongly opposed to it. The presbyterian burgesses could not
have taken the sacrament without betraying McBride and the congregation
of which they were the elders. However much they may have regretted
losing the control and direction of the town's affairs, no other option was
open to them.[82]

Dodington also stated that the house's decision would be a rule for
purging all the corporations of Ireland. Since the Belfast presbyterians
appear to have been the last to go, he must have been referring to the fact
that in many corporations no successors had been elected after the presbyterian aldermen and burgesses resigned. In Belfast, elections to the vacant
burgess-ships were held immediately, but the loss of the presbyterians left a
gap which was hard to fill. There were simply not enough suitable candidates from the old Church of Ireland families within the town. There was
no rising generation of Leatheses, Theakers and Thompsons to re-establish
the position of these families as leaders of the community. Nicholas
Thetford, whose father and uncle had both served as burgesses, refused 'a
Burgessship coming in such a manner'[83] which underlines the good relationship which existed between presbyterians and Church of Ireland merchants.

79 Appendix A12.
80 Hayton, 'Ireland and the English ministers', pp 127, 130, 273; McGuire,
    'Government attitudes to religious non-conformity in Ireland', pp 274–5; there were
    subsequent appeals against the test act, for example, William Craford and Isaac
    Macartney were signatories to one in 1711 (P.R.O., SP.63/367, no.157).
81 Dodington to [?Sunderland], 2 Nov. 1707 (P.R.O., SP.63/366, no.252).
82 Kilroy, *Protestant dissent*, pp 189–92; it was said that Isaac Macartney was ready to
    qualify himself if he were elected a burgess in 1726 (Young, *Historical notices*,
    p.166).
83 *Town book*, p.236; he was elected again in the following year on the death of Lewis
    Thompson, and this time accepted.

9 George Macartney, M.P. for Belfast

Many of the new burgesses elected in 1707 and in the next decade came
from families with no previous experience of local government (Richard
Wilson, George Portis, James Gurner), and most of those who had such
experience (Nathaniel Byrt, Henry Ellis and Edward Clements) had
acquired it in Carrickfergus rather than Belfast. Continuity was not entirely
lost. Two of the grandsons of Macartney of Auchinleck became burgesses,
as did two grandsons and a great-grandson of Black George Macartney.

The countess's main objective had been achieved. She had broken the
control of the Macartney family over the corporation by replacing the presbyterian burgesses. Her relationship with the new corporation was far from
smooth but she had won back the family's control over elections.[84] The
Macartney brothers remained burgesses, but when George Macartney finished his fourth term of office as sovereign in 1708 the new corporation did
not re-elect him. Although he lived until 1757, and was by far the most
distinguished member of the corporation, he was never again elected sovereign. His exclusion from this office can only have been the result of the
Donegall family's refusal to nominate him, although they were content that
he should represent the town in parliament.[85] Similarly, James Macartney
did not serve again. It would be unkind to suggest that the sovereigns
thereafter were complete nonentities but the exclusion of the presbyterians
from representation on the corporation and from the direction of the
town's affairs resulted in the election of mediocre burgesses and the decline
in authority of the corporation.[86]

The effects on the town were far reaching. Membership of the corporation became an honour with few duties apart from the election of the
town's members of parliament. By the 1760s, the corporation's influence
was confined principally to matters of market regulation, and the sovereign
was unable to deal with problems inherent in the town's rapid growth.[87] To
some extent, this was inevitable. Such a primitive and narrow form of town
government was inadequate by the early eighteenth century and would
never have been able to meet the needs of the growing town, but had it
still been composed of the leading presbyterian merchants it is unlikely that
the town's affairs would have been conducted with the lethargy and lack of
initiative which characterised the corporation in the eighteenth century.

---

84 *Town book*, p.208; there was another disputed election in 1711, but the claim of the
    countess's candidate was upheld (Donegall minority accounts, pt 2, p.45).
85 The town book gives the leet from 1707–27, and Macartney's name was not includ-
    ed (*Town book*, pp 244–5).
86 Robert Green to earl of Barrymore, 7 May 1726, about the sovereign John Clugston:
    'All he wants is a book to teach him the law, resolving to read much, as he hears our
    late Sovereign did, but he understood not what he read, and I believe mr Clugston's
    understanding will be abundantly less' (Young, *Historical notices*, p.166).
87 Gamble, 'Business community and trade of Belfast', pp 156, 175–6.

5

Trade

EXPORTS, IMPORTS AND MARKETS

Throughout the seventeenth century, the Belfast merchants were primarily provisions merchants, concerned principally in the export of butter, beef, grain and fish. The most important of these commodities was butter. The butter handled by the Belfast merchants was the best 'English' butter and was highly praised, particularly by those trying to sell it. In 1666 Black George wrote to a merchant at Ostend, 'this is a great country for butter ... I furnish most of all the merchants with butter that goes to all places in France and Flanders'.[1] By 1683, Belfast had become a leading Irish port for butter, and exports continued to rise.

After the civil war period, cattle stocks recovered in the late 1650s and beef looked likely to become as important a commodity as butter. As early as 1661 Macartney contracted to slaughter 1,000 cattle and in 1665 he wrote that he had sent large quantities to Cadiz, Tangiers, La Rochelle and Barbados.[2] By the 1660s, the West Indies had become dependent on imported provisions and provided a steady market for beef. In addition to their exports, Belfast merchants frequently supplied the royal navy, and the general increase in transatlantic trade brought an increased demand for salt beef for consumption at sea. Although, overall, beef was to prove 'neither a remunerative nor a profitable export', in Belfast, at least, the evidence points to its having been a fairly reliable commodity with an acceptable rate of profit, and the demand was such that local supplies could not always meet it.[3] The failure of beef to achieve the same kind of export figures as butter lies in its failure to find a steady European market as agricultural conditions in Europe improved and prohibitive tariffs prevented its import into France for domestic consumption.

1 Macartney to Jacobus van Houtte, 28 Apr. 1666 (Macartney 1, p.348).
2 Macartney to Thomas Moore, 14 Aug. 1661, to Claude Gobaignon, 21 Jan. 1664/5 (Macartney 1, pp 16–17, 150).
3 Cullen, 'Economic trends', pp 393, 397; in 1679 Macartney was obtaining large quantities of beef from Ballyshannon, County Donegal, (Macartney to Harrison, 13 Sept. 1679 [Macartney 2, p.144]).

Moreover, beef cannot be considered in isolation, as it was so closely linked with the trade in tallow, hides and tanned leather. The merchant frequently bought his beef on the hoof, disposed of the tallow to a chandler, sometimes contracting to take the finished product, and salted the hides himself for export or sold them to a tanner. This was explained by George Macartney in October 1680 when, faced with two large orders for salt hides from Dutch merchants in London and Amsterdam, he wrote 'most of our butchers, what hides they kill, is engaged beforehand to merchants that ventures them and the merchants hath them from them [sic] green [i.e. unsalted] and salts them themselves. There is not any buys and salts here to sell here again...'[4]

The third foodstuff that could be salted for export was fish. The bulk of the trade was in herrings and, again, the demand exceeded local supply. In the 1660s Black George was regularly sending a boat up the Scottish coast to collect locally caught and salted herrings. He supplied several Dublin merchants and also exported directly to Barbados, Bristol and France. The trade in herrings fluctuated. Black George was not dealing in them in the early 1680s because they were cheaper at Dublin. Later in the same decade, Belfast merchants were importing considerable quantities from Scotland, and in the early 1700s they were buying herrings from Scotland, Carlingford and Ballyshannon, principally for export to the West Indies.

Salmon, which was in shorter supply, was a luxury. The great fishings of the Bann and the Foyle were owned and leased out by the City of London and, in addition, there were a number of 'small fishings'. It was also possible for Belfast merchants to obtain salmon from County Donegal, although the supply was limited. Italy was reckoned to be the best market for salmon but it was difficult to get freight there for small quantities. Total quantities available however were very small. In the 1680s the whole Bann fishing was normally expected to produce only 200 tons and the catch was often less than this. In 1680, Macartney was negotiating for 80–100 tons. He was unsuccessful as the catch was poor and it transpired that the lessee of the fishings had already promised over 100 tons annually to a London merchant. A year later the lease of the Bann fishing came into the hands of Lord Massereene who promised the whole catch to Londoners.[5] From the small quantities available it is clear that most of the Belfast merchants were not involved in the salmon trade and that it was of minor importance to the port.

Of far more importance to the whole merchant community was the trade in grain and oatmeal. This is poorly documented in the Macartney

4 Macartney to Gerrard Wymans, 26 Oct. 1680, and to Dehulter & Vanhomrigh, same day (Macartney 2, p.368).
5 Macartney to Daniel Arthur, 6 July 1680, and to Joshua Allen, 14 May 1681 (Macartney 2, pp 280, 465).

letter books but other sources indicate a sizeable trade. Scandinavia provided a regular market for oatmeal. In March 1677, Thomas Bell of Belfast petitioned the lord lieutenant for passes to Denmark to be issued speedily to a number of ships waiting at Belfast. Ten ships are listed, including the two largest in the town's fleet.[6] Both Macartney and Lewis Thompson refer to the quantities of oatmeal sent to Norway in the 1670s[7] and this continued throughout the period. Although the principal export was oatmeal, wheat and barley were also exported. In the 1690s, when there was famine in Scotland and surpluses in Ireland, David Butle's letter book reveals that he and the Macartneys were involved in the shipping of barley to Scotland from Drogheda.

Similarly, although there is little in the earlier Macartney letter books about the export of timber, quantities exported rose throughout the century, much of it being in the form of barrel staves. These exports, coupled with the demand at home for timber to make barrels for the provisions trade, for fuel for smelting iron, and for bark for the tanning industry, were causing official concern as early as the 1650s. Even though this concern reached a crescendo in the 1690s, giving the impression that Ireland was virtually denuded of trees, a considerable export continued into the eighteenth century. In the early 1700s Isaac Macartney was regularly sending consignments of 8,000–10,000 barrel staves to Bristol, and in 1705 he wrote to his correspondent there that he would be able to send 100,000 the next year and asked him to find out whether coopers would contract for that quantity. It is likely that Macartney himself had contracted to buy from a landlord who was selling his timber to settle his debts. For example, in 1704, Macartney recommended William Sloane to buy an estate near Portadown with 'above £8,000 worth of woods thereon which would yield ready money, that commodity being very scarce in Ireland, especially the bark of it'.[8]

The second half of the seventeenth century saw improvements in the manufacture of linen, particularly in Ulster. Even though the quantities produced were small, it was nevertheless an important export because the cost was high, relative to the bulk. It was reckoned to be the best commodity to send to Virginia and New England, where there was a diminishing demand for agricultural surpluses. Otherwise, the best market was England,

6 Petition of Thomas Bell, 17 Mar. 1677 (P.R.O., SP.63/338, no.33); although oatmeal is not specified, it was the normal outwards cargo to Scandinavia.
7 Thompson to Jacob David, 6 Nov. 1675 (P.R.O., Marescoe David papers, C114/76[2]:6); Macartney to Messrs Dulinch, 24 May 1679 (Macartney 2, p.74).
8 Robert Dunlop (ed.), *Ireland under the commonwealth: being a selection of documents relating to the government of Ireland, 1651–59* (2 vols, Manchester, 1913), ii, pp 564–5; Eileen McCracken, *The Irish woods since Tudor times, distribution and exploitation* (Newton Abbot, 1971), pp 98, 137; Macartney to Sloane, 27 Nov. 1704, to William Galbraith, 9 July, 27 Aug. 1705, to James Hillhouse, 9 Mar. 1705/6 (Macartney 3, pp 20–1, 140–1, 176–7, 285).

but quantities exported there remained small until the English government removed the duty on Irish linens imported for domestic use in 1696. The first detailed figures for exports, covering the years 1683–86, show that Belfast and Dublin, between them, accounted for approximately 73% of all linen exports, each port exporting more-or-less equal quantities over these four years, and that the total quantity exported rose six fold during the period. Dublin was to handle 70% of the linen trade by the 1690s but much of the linen from south-east Ulster reached Dublin via Belfast, giving the town a larger share in the trade than is apparent from the customs figures. Considerable quantities of linen yarn were exported to England and this continued to be profitable after the development of a home industry manufacturing a quality product. For example, David Butle was exporting yarn to Liverpool in the 1690s, and Isaac Macartney to Bristol in the early 1700s. Nevertheless, Belfast was not a major exporter of yarn, the leading ports for this trade being Drogheda and Dublin.[9]

Throughout the seventeenth century, merchants were equally concerned in the import and export trades and most freight was arranged on that basis, although imports were never on the same scale as exports. Imports fell into three main categories. First, there were essential materials such as deals, that is sawn softwood planks,[10] and tar, which were brought from Scandinavia, salt which came from France, Portugal and England, and coal from Scotland and England. The second category was luxury goods, the most important of which were wine and brandy from France and Spain, sugar from the West Indies and tobacco from America, although the latter rapidly became seen as a necessity rather than a luxury. Third, a large variety of manufactured goods, not obtainable locally, were imported from Europe, Scotland and Dublin, for example, pots and pans, wire, glasses, paper, haberdashery, and a wide range of textiles from silk to canvas, including vast quantities of linen from Scotland for the Irish market.

By trading both ways, merchants were able to make double profits. In many cases they also doubled their problems. Although much of the surviving source material for Belfast trade relates to the Macartneys it is possible to identify both the problems which were experienced by the whole

---

9   Table of exports and imports into Ireland, Dec. 1682–Dec. 1686 (B.L., Add. MS 4759, ff 1, 2, 3, 6, 17, 19, 31, 44, and Sloane MS 2902); David Dickson, 'The place of Dublin in the eighteenth century Irish economy' in Devine and Dickson, *Scotland and Ireland 1600–1850*, p.183; Macartney to Daniel Walker, 31 Jan. 1678/9, to William Sargeant, 8 Feb. 1678/9 (Macartney 2, pp 16, 19); Liverpool port books, 1690s (P.R.O., E190/1353/1 ff 33, 35, 37, 39, 41 et seq., 1355/5 ff 15–17, 20, 24, 26, 27 et seq., 1359/11 ff 5, 9, 12, 13, 16 et seq., 1360/17 ff 3, 6, 8, 9, 11 et seq.); Butle to Levinus Houston of Liverpool, 22 Aug. 1696, 23 Sept. 1697 (Butle, pp 37, 51); Macartney to Galbraith, 9 July 1705 (Macartney 3, pp 140–1); tables of exports from Ireland from 1698 (P.R.O., CUST 15).

10 It was cheaper to import sawn deals than to cut them in Ireland (McCracken, *Irish woods*, pp 119, 125).

merchant community and the methods they used to improve and extend trade. The principal aims of the Belfast merchants were to send goods to the most profitable markets abroad, to ensure that these goods were in a saleable condition on arrival, to import only what they could sell, and to find a way around any impediment to trade.

In the first half of the seventeenth century, Ireland was largely dependent on English markets, but the progressive closing of these markets to Irish goods[11] forced Ireland to identify and develop markets in Europe and the New World. Similarly, although Ulster also had a thriving trade with Scotland, this too was subject to embargoes and as Scotland was also a producer of provisions for export, the two countries were in effect competing for markets. There can seldom have been a period when trading conditions in Europe changed more rapidly. The most striking feature of the tables of Irish exports and imports for 1683–86 is the fluctuation from year to year both of amounts exported and of the markets. This can in part be attributed to restrictions on trade when the navigation acts were re-imposed in 1685, but it also reflects major variations in supply and demand. Figures for Irish exports and imports from 1698 show similar fluctuations.[12] Lack of a steady home market meant that trade in agricultural surpluses from Ireland was not only affected by fluctuations in supply but was also particularly vulnerable to changes in market conditions, whether caused by European wars, embargoes against Irish imports or the state of the harvests abroad. Good harvests in Europe had disastrous effects on demand, or, in the words of Black George Macartney, 'our butter dear at home and cheap abroad will make us sad merchants'.[13]

A combination of the effects of war, cattle plague and poor harvests established France as the major customer for Irish provisions between the 1660s and the 1680s and, in addition to purchases for domestic consumption, Irish provisions were also bought for shipment to the French colonies. However, from the late 1680s, this export trade with France was reduced by the high duties imposed on imported beef and butter for home consumption in France and French Flanders. Spain was seen as one of the best markets for butter. There was keen competition to arrive there with the first cargo of new butter each summer, and Belfast was the major exporter in the period 1683–85.[14] In addition, Spain was a leading market for tanned leather although there was also considerable demand at home and in Dublin. Scandinavia was a reliable market for oatmeal and the ships brought back deals and tar. As wars and embargoes affected European

11 There were restrictions or bans on the import of Irish cattle in 1663 and 1667, and butter in 1681, and there were tariffs against wool and linen.
12 Tables of Irish exports and imports from 1698 (P.R.O., CUST 15).
13 Macartney to Delap, 25 Sept. 1680 (Macartney 2, p.345).
14 Table of exports and imports into Ireland, Dec. 1682–Dec. 1686 (B.L., Add. MS 4759, ff 6, 21, 35).

markets, transatlantic trade offered an alternative market for Irish provisions. From the 1650s, trade with the West Indies and America was the fastest growing sector of Irish overseas trade. In the West Indies, the adoption of a sugar monoculture based on slave labour made the islands dependent on imported provisions.[15] However, by the end of the century, the Irish provisions merchants faced increasing competition in the West Indies from the American mainland. Apart from such long-term changes, all markets varied from year to year and even from month to month. Merchants were therefore pragmatists, accustomed to route and re-route cargoes on the advice of their factors overseas to ensure that their goods eventually reached a good market.[16]

In addition to the main commodities described above, the merchants traded in anything that would yield a profit. For example, cheese, pork, bread and beer were all exported from Belfast according to availability. Other exports included iron, soap, rabbit skins, shoes, stockings and hats. It was also profitable to convey people, both willing and unwilling, to the West Indies. In 1679 for example, Macartney and his partner Humphrey Jervis of Dublin were making up a shipload of 100–150 disbanded soldiers, and in 1706, Brown George McCartney contracted to transport several prisoners from Carrickfergus.[17] Every opportunity was grasped to enquire about alternative outlets for Belfast's goods. Every new business contact abroad was asked about the prospects for trade. The following is typical of such letters:

> Pray let me know what goods of our country would sell with you and what your goods are, if any good be got I would gladly drive some trade with you if it would turn to account.[18]

Letters frequently close with lists of commodity prices and many give details of the goods available and those to new clients stress the seasonal character of the provisions trade.

Even when provisions were sent to a good market there would be little or no profit if they arrived in poor condition. Butter, Belfast's principal export, would last at least a year if properly packed, but a series of regulations at national and local level about the making of casks shows that in

15 Vincent T. Harlow, *A history of Barbados, 1625–1685* (Oxford, 1926), pp 164, 169; because of the market for provisions in the West Indies, the Belfast merchants were not involved in the slave trade at this date.

16 For example, in 1705 butter was being sent to Norway and thence to France to save the duty payable there on Irish butter (Macartney to Daniel Hays, 22 Aug. 1705 [Macartney 3, p.175]).

17 Macartney to Jervis, 1 Mar. 1678/9 (Macartney 2, p.31); Macartney to Richard Cadell, 28 Jan. 1705/6, to John O Neile, 18 Apr. 1706 (Macartney 3, pp 260, 298–9; the latter contains interesting details of Brown George's expenses).

18 Macartney to Andrew Marjoribank, Danzig, 15 May 1679 (Macartney 2, p.69).

practice a lot of butter reached its destination in poor condition. The common fault seems to have been the use of green or unseasoned casks which made the butter taste unpleasant. Butter was normally packed at source which gave the merchants little opportunity to ensure that casks and barrels were of the right standard although they generally sampled each consignment. Some, at least, of the producers were eager to improve their product. Sir George Rawdon asked Macartney's advice on the best way to preserve butter and wrote to his brother-in-law, Lord Conway:

> I have set out advice to all in our parts to put up their butter in seasoned casks. This is a copy of it wherein I had G McCartney's advice and approbation, and many thanks to him and our small merchants at Lisburn.[19]

Similarly fish was also packed at source and once again the merchant could only advise and entreat the supplier to see that the catch was salted without delay. Although it might be possible to dispose of a cargo of dubious herrings if they could be got to France before the end of Lent,[20] salmon was a different matter as it was a luxury and only fetched a good price if it was in good condition. However, since the supply of salmon was always far less than the demand, it was difficult for the purchaser to bring pressure to bear on the supplier. Macartney, who purchased salmon for Daniel Arthur of London, was blamed when a consignment of salmon was found to be 'bad, old and rotten', and he in turn blamed the factor at Rouen for not draining the fish and washing it in strong salt pickle to restore the colour and take away the oily taste, adding rather lamely 'Rouen is a very curious market for salmon for they scruple upon salmon really good and right and will call them nought'.[21] As far as he was able, Macartney tried to ensure that fish were packed fresh and that each cask was marked so that individual suppliers could be identified, but it is not until 1706 that a letter can be found stating that a purchase of fish would be conditional upon the suppliers being willing to guarantee them to market.[22]

The preservation of beef posed fewer problems because merchants bought it on the hoof, or through local butchers, and were able to supervise the packing. Under good conditions salt beef would last two years. The best quality white salt from France or Portugal was preferred as it preserved the colour and made the meat look appetising. Beef was a surprisingly fragile commodity that needed careful handling. For example, in 1665, George Macartney refused to send beef for re-loading at Dublin:

19 *Cal. S.P. Ire., 1666–69*, p.594.
20 Macartney to William Barron, 14 Mar. 1665/6 (Macartney 1, p.322).
21 Macartney to Wyse, Lombard & Ley, 15 Dec. 1679, and to Arthur, 27 Dec. 1679 (Macartney 2, pp 205, 211).
22 Macartney to Delap, 21 Mar. 1680/1 (Macartney 2, p.441); Macartney to Caldwell, 11 Feb. 1705/6 (Macartney 3, p.268).

being pickled beef is a great weight and putting it aboard here and discharging it in gabarts and may be ill look[ed] to there, if it were never so good it
will look ugly when the cask[s] are broke and then the pickle runs out.[23]

As with butter, regulations were needed to ensure that the barrels were
made of well-seasoned wood.[24] Even with the larger merchants employing
their own salters and packers a certain proportion of beef reached its destination in poor condition, needing re-packing in fresh brine, and some was
past even this remedy.

In the period covered by the first two Macartney letter books (1661–81),
the provisions trade was strictly seasonal. The season lasted from the early
summer, when negotiations began for the first butter, until the end of
December. By January virtually all goods had been exported and trade was
dead. The impression given in the third Macartney letter book (1704–06) is
that beef and butter were available for a longer period. It seems reasonable
to assume that the growth in the volume of exports had been accompanied
by some improvement in standards of packing and preserving, and that
provisions could be kept reliably for longer periods.

If some of the problems of the Belfast merchants as exporters eased by
the end of the century, their problems as importers remained the same. In
order to buy only those goods that would sell, it was necessary not only to
know the needs and tastes of the home market, but also to time the arrival
of cargoes so that the market, which was small, would not be glutted.
Factors abroad were often asked to undertake not to load a similar cargo
for any other merchant at the same port. Even so, because imports such as
wine, tobacco and sugar were seasonal, or because some voyages could only
be made at certain times of the year, it frequently happened that several
cargoes of the same commodity arrived within a short time of each other,
making it a 'drug on the market'. Even the market for basic supplies such
as deals and tar was limited. For example in 1670 there was a surplus of
deal boards in Belfast which were sold off cheaply, and in 1706 there were
enough deals in the town to last a year. Also in 1706, so much tar had been
sent to both Belfast and Dublin that the merchants were trying to re-export
it to Bristol, Liverpool and Whitehaven, and the small market for copper
was also glutted.[25] In spite of the large amounts used in the provisions
industry, salt too could glut the market. Its usefulness as ballast may have
led to its being imported in excess of demand.

The market was even smaller for imported luxury goods. Wine was the
most important of these throughout the seventeenth century. It was essential for the merchant to know his market and to import only the type and

23 Macartney to Langford, 28 Feb. 1664/5 (Macartney 1, p.162).
24 *Town book*, pp 155, 186.
25 *Cal. S.P. Ire., 1669–70*, p.247; Macartney to Latin, Hammond and Innis, 1706
    (Macartney 3, pp 266, 310, 332, 336).

Mr James Thruston   Belfast ye 17th of June 1665

My last to yow was the ... Currant wherein I gaue
yow an acctt of the aryuall of the mari of Goshcko
since I haue vnladen hor and tasted the wyne the
whyte wyne is indifferent onlie the vnrackt wyne is
nowe flat and foylie which I doubt shall not be worth
right : but for the Clarrett it is the worst that euer I
tasted ft martins Clarrett is better now it I doubt I shall
nouer gett a logshead of it soe as for whyte though
small they loue it best here but Clarrett they will
drinke none except it be exeellant good and ... fine
if I thought that yow wold haue laid on for ...
Clarrett I wold haue ton of the best Cost what it wold
this is both rugh and of a dull cullor I know not as yett wo
I shall doe with it the worst I tell most of hor to
fraught home to bvrdraue to ... Cauws man who is
here and reeceiued the goods from ... owne vpon
acctt of some debt vnto the last yeare the fraught
... is to pay for his goods is
and I haue payed the master hir ... shillings and he
payed the ... for the worst of the remaind of ye
must be payed out of the goods which I haue sent
being 2 small Caskes of tallow ... 5 barrells of tallow
65 tanned hyds whereof 23 ar small hyps and 38
and ... hyd they wright in all here 7 ... lbs wright the
tallow weight, nett 42 ... I wold haue sent more
but ... owne was vnwilling to gett in this goods for
... Cauws and ther was some dutch Liuers in the
Channell which made me afrayd the goods is all
Consignd in on bill of loadin with ... here is to ...

10 Letter from George Macartney to James Thruston of Bordeaux
about import of wine, 17 June 1665

quality that would sell. In 1667, Black George advised Joshua Allen of Dublin that 'salt will do no good here neither will bad Spanish wine [there are] few drinkers of wine and what they drink they would have it good'.[26] French wines sold best and there was a reasonable market for brandy but there was very little sale for poor wine even at low prices. Time and time again the Macartneys stressed the discerning palate of their clientele and the importance of sending only the best wine; in 1665, for example, Black George wrote 'but claret they will drink none except it be excellent good and pleasant'.[27] Unfortunately most wine travelled badly and did not necessarily improve with keeping and many cargoes were described on arrival as 'the worst I ever did taste'. Because the import duty on wine was so high, a poor quality cargo automatically meant a loss for the importer, and complaints to suppliers of wine frequently end with the wish that they had sent the ship home empty to save the duty. Brandy travelled better but the duty was so high that unless it could be sold well and quickly it could also make a loss. For example, Black George diverted one cargo to Danzig in 1679 rather than pay the duty at Belfast. There was no improvement in the situation by the early 1700s. In 1705, Isaac Macartney described wine which George Boyd of Bordeaux had sent him as 'sour crabbed small trash' and the market in 1706 was glutted with wine and brandy, much of it being re-exported from Scotland where it could be imported freely, in spite of the war, under the wine act of 1703.[28]

Tobacco and sugar posed less of a problem because they travelled better and could be stored longer. Even so, the year to year fluctuations of both crops could lead to an imbalance between demand and supply. Sugar was seen as a luxury, although demand was such that a sugar refinery was set up in Belfast in the 1660s, but tobacco rapidly became one of the necessities of life. Imports into Ireland doubled between 1665 and 1685 and continued to rise. From the 1670s most tobacco was imported from America as the West Indian planters had gone over entirely to sugar production. As with wine, local preferences made merchants selective: 'When any sweet scented tobacco comes hither we are forced to send it to Dublin ... the tobacco fit for this place is a thick stout tobacco ... Raphanick [Rappahannock, Virginia] tobacco is generally best liked here'.[29] But even though large quantities of tobacco were bought by all classes of society the market could still be glutted.

---

26 Macartney to Allen, 6 July 1667, and to Huishe, 4 July 1666 (Macartney 1, pp 570, 380).
27 See p.113; Macartney to James Thruston, 17 June 1665 (Macartney 1, pp 189–90).
28 Smout, *Scottish trade*, p.65; Macartney to George Boyd, 28 Nov. 1705, to René St Fleurant, 21 July 1705, and to Robert Gordon, 23 Feb. 1705/6 (Macartney 3, pp 147, 233, 273).
29 Macartney to John Earle, 28 Nov. 1705 (Macartney 3, p.232).

Luxury foods including oranges and lemons, prunes, chocolate, raisins and almonds were imported in small quantities and presumably sold well enough to encourage their import. Similarly there was a limited market for manufactures such as paper, silk, tapestries, and glassware. A typical cargo ordered from the Low Countries in the 1660s included soap, madder, sugar, alum, indigo, galls from Smyrna, currants, thread, tiles, starch, whalebone, ginger, pepper, and aniseed.[30] Surpluses of luxury goods might be sent to another port. In 1666, for example, Black George found he had imported enough liquorice to supply Belfast for seven years ('the worst bargain that ever I dealt in') and sent some to Dublin and to Scotland.[31] Although, in the late seventeenth century, there was a significant increase in the demand for luxury manufactured goods,[32] the Belfast merchants were generally cautious of importing such goods unless they were ordered in advance by the nobility and gentry, and they were careful to stress that anything sent should be 'of the newest fashion such as they use now at London' and that textiles should be in the most up-to-date colours. Sales were small as many of the gentry families were regular visitors to Dublin where a wider range of goods was available. Some Dublin merchants sent such goods to be sold in Belfast but they faced competition from direct imports. For example, Macartney accepted a consignment of Dublin-made flint glass to sell in 1679 and 'built a little house a purpose for glasses and put shelves round about it thinking to drive a sale' but his hopes were dashed by the arrival of cheaper and clearer glasses direct from Holland and France which sold better.[33] A different venture in the same year was more successful. Both George Macartneys were involved in the import of arms for the militia, in response to the Popish Plot, and even here, Black George insisted that only the best would do ('coarse arms will not off here').[34] Similarly, in 1689, the needs of Schomberg's army prompted a dash from Belfast by every available small ship to load hose, gloves, horse-shoes and nails, aquavitae, beer, biscuits, brandy, pipes and tobacco.[35] The successful merchant needed not only to know his market but to make the

30 Macartney to David Agnew, 17 Dec. 1663 (Macartney 1, p.86).
31 Macartney to Allen, 17 Nov. 1666 (Macartney 1, p.473).
32 T.C. Barnard, 'The political, material and mental culture of the Cork settlers, c.1650–1700' in Patrick O'Flanagan and Cornelius G. Buttimer (ed.), *Cork, history and society, interdisciplinary essays on the history of an Irish county* (Dublin, 1993), pp 327–31.
33 Macartney to Captain Nicols, 2 July 1679 (Macartney 2, p.91); I am indebted to Peter Francis for his interpretation of the technical content of this letter which contains the earliest known reference to the manufacture of flint glass in the British Isles.
34 *Ormonde MSS*, ii, p.257; Macartney to Dehulter & Vanhomrigh, 29 Mar., 19 Apr., 7 and 17 May, 1679, and to Robert Bridges, 7 May, 28 June 1679 (Macartney 2, pp 41, 51, 60, 71, 89).
35 Ayr port book (exports), June – Nov. 1689 (S.R.O., E72/3/19).

most of any opportunity for trade that presented itself.

By the early eighteenth century the increase in the population of Ulster and better living standards should have ensured an improved home market for imports but the effects of war on exports, rising rents, and the revaluation of the coinage, had brought about a period of recession and stagnation.[36] Sales of luxury goods became even more difficult. As Isaac Macartney explained in 1705 to Edmund Harrison of London, whose raisins and chocolate he had failed to sell:

> I cannot help it for I did my utmost and if these goods had all been my own I'm sure could not manage them to better advantage considering the deplorable condition of poor Ireland, that many good families cannot get as much as will buy them necessary bread and clothes out of their rents.[37]

The home market did not recover and expand until a series of good harvests in the years 1711–14, and the end of the European war in 1713. Until then, the market for imports was small, so it was essential for the merchants to know exactly what would sell, to import goods that would be attractive or inexpensive or, if possible, both, and to bring them in at a time when the market was not already swamped with similar goods.

FOREIGN EMBARGOES AND ENGLISH LEGISLATION

In addition to all the other problems which faced seventeenth-century merchants, their trade was continually impeded by wars and embargoes. Many embargoes were for political reasons and were not seriously enforced. For example, in 1666 when trade from France into England was prohibited, Black George wrote: 'I believe they will hardly do so in Ireland being the French will do what they can to have it come in and the nobles to get wine for themselves', and to alleviate distress caused by the cattle acts Irish ships were allowed to trade with the French.[38] Political restrictions on trade did not impose any kind of moral obligation on the merchants and trading with the enemy was not seen as unpatriotic. In the war years of the 1690s, Belfast's trade links with France were connived at officially as merchant ships could supply intelligence about the enemy. Even without official sanction, trade restrictions were circumvented wherever possible. Ships routinely carried false papers to show if they were stopped by naval frigates or privateers, and the masters and crew were coached in the parts they were to play. This was not always successful as privateers sometimes resorted to torture. In addition to the risk from enemy privateers in

36 Cullen, *Econ. hist. Ire.*, pp 33–4, 36, 42–3.
37 Macartney to Harrison, 14 Apr. 1705 (Macartney 3, pp 85–6).
38 Macartney to William Watt, 24 Oct. 1666 (Macartney 1, p.452).

wartime, the Algerian privateers or 'Biscayers' were a constant threat throughout the period and their operations at times extended as far north as the southern coast of Ireland. Normally only the French were immune from the Biscayers so ships trading to Spain often sailed as French ships. For example, in 1681 Macartney's partner Humphrey Jervis 'made a French ship' of their ship, the *Dublin Merchant*, and picked up a French-speaking crew in Jersey to sail her to the Straits.[39] The normal practice was to put the ship and cargo into the name of some co-operative Frenchman and the reverse also applied, some ships sailing as 'French' in French, Spanish and Mediterranean waters, and 'English' on their return to England or Ireland. There was a brisk traffic in all kinds of false papers, passes and certificates. It was inevitable, therefore, that when restrictions on trade were imposed by the English government the same methods would be used to circumvent them.

From the 1650s, the English parliament passed a series of acts, which were designed to protect English trading and commercial interests. The consequent effects on Irish trade, though caused by indifference rather than design, were far reaching.[40] The overall result of these restrictions was to discourage trade generally, but the effects of each individual act varied from port to port. The first of these pieces of legislation, the cattle acts of 1663 and 1667, which culminated in a total ban on the export of live cattle into England from Ireland, damaged, in the short term, the economy of the south of Ireland, but had little effect on the Belfast merchants whose involvement in the trade appears to have been minimal. The Liverpool port books, for example, do not enter any Belfast merchants as cattle importers in the 1660s. In 1665, George Macartney attempted to remit money to London via some cattle drovers who were to draw bills payable in London when they had sold their cattle. There is no indication in his letters that Macartney himself had any interest in the cattle; on the contrary, the unsatisfactory outcome of the arrangement and the lack of communication between Macartney and the drovers suggest rather that he had no regular involvement with the livestock trade.[41] Similarly, in the period of Macartney's second letter book (1679–81) when the prohibition lapsed temporarily, a lack of suitable cattle in the north and uncertainty about the duration of the liberty to export made him hold back from investing in this

39 Macartney to Harrison, 11 Oct. 1679, and 2 Mar. 1680/1 (Macartney 2, pp 162, 436).
40 Cullen, 'Economic trends', pp 386–7.
41 Donald Woodward, 'Anglo-Irish livestock trade of the seventeenth century' in *I.H.S.*, xviii, no. 72 (1972–3), p.502; Macartney to Arthur, 19 July 1665, to Thomas Hackett, 5 and 29 Aug., 16 Sept., 4 Oct. 1665, 2 June, 11 Aug. 1666 (Macartney 1, pp 205, 212, 225, 237, 243, 367, 405); James Biggar of Belfast had a similar experience with some drovers a year later (Macartney to Michael Lincoln, 19 Dec. 1666, and 12 Jan. 1666/7 [Macartney 1, pp 486, 497]).

new branch of trade and his chief interest in the trade seems to have been its effect on the rate of exchange between Dublin and London.[42]

The principal port for the export of cattle from the Lagan valley was Donaghadee, which offered easier loading for livestock than at Belfast, and a shorter crossing to the English ports of the north-west; Strangford had similar advantages. Much of the cattle exported from County Antrim went out through the ports of the Antrim coast or through Coleraine. These ports were all affected by the cattle acts. The effect on Coleraine appears to have been far reaching and the port of Donaghadee never recovered.[43] Belfast's lack of involvement in the trade may be partly attributed to the unsuitability of the harbour, but may also be because many of the greater landlords in the Lagan valley did not use the merchants as middlemen but organised the export of cattle from their own estates, sending their own men as drovers. In fact, the ban on the export of live cattle was seen by one such landlord as a blessing in disguise, for it would encourage investment in better breeds of cattle and enable the landlords to participate in the more profitable export of beef.[44] The export of live cattle raised the price of beef for salting and, by improving the quantity and quality of beef, the cattle acts may actually have benefitted the Belfast merchants.

The effects of the navigation acts of 1663 and 1671 were more serious and far reaching. In order to protect English industry and English shipping against competition, principally from the Dutch, all colonial imports and exports had to be carried in English ships, manned by English crews, via English ports. Irish-built ships counted as English, as did Irish crews, but Irish ports counted as foreign. Until the act of union in 1707, Scotland was treated as a foreign nation under the acts, primarily because of the substantial investment by the Dutch in Scottish ships and trade. However, because of the dependence of the West Indies and, initially, the American colonies on imported foodstuffs, the direct export of provisions to the colonies from both Ireland and Scotland was still permitted. A proportion of Belfast's exports were carried to the colonies for London merchants in English ships (particularly at the beginning of the period), but even the goods sent by Belfast merchants, on their own account and in their own ships, were unaffected because the greater part of the town's fleet counted as English under the acts. Therefore the major export trade of the town was little affected.

The navigation acts, however, also banned the direct export to the colonies, other than from English ports, of all manufactured goods. In 1667, Macartney wrote to Joshua Allen of Dublin that they had previously

42 Macartney to Robert Contales, 7 June 1679, to Harrison, 14 June 1679, to Jervis, 14 June 1679, (Macartney 2, pp 79, 80, 83).

43 Mullin, *Coleraine*, pp 109–10; Cullen, 'Economic trends', p.392; Donaghadee remained an important port for the export of horses (tables of exports [B.L., Add. MS 4759, ff 2, 18, 32, 45]).

44 *Hastings MSS*, ii, pp 373–5.

sent linen, frieze and drugget (both coarse woollen cloths), to the Leeward Isles.[45] Friezes were not being made at Belfast in the 1660s, but by the 1680s there was a woollen industry in the town. In 1685, a renewal of George Macartney of Auchinleck's lease of the town's mills stated that he had laid out £300 in repairing and altering the old mills, and in building a new corn mill and a new tuck mill,[46] and about 5% of Belfast freemen were dyers, felt makers and other textile workers. Macartney may have profited by the brief suspension of the navigation acts during the early 1680s when the trade figures show an increase in exports of friezes from Belfast to the colonies.[47] The trade figures for 1698 show that Belfast was exporting modest amounts of friezes to Scotland, the Plantations, Norway, Portugal and Spain, but the woollen act of 1699 banned the export of woollen cloth to markets other than in England where the duties had become prohibitive. Belfast friezes were not diverted to England where there would have been no market for them but it is possible, since the amount exported was small,[48] that the town's output could be absorbed by the growing home market.

In addition to the friezes and drugget mentioned above, Macartney included shoes and stockings in his list of goods sent to the Leeward Islands before 1663. In 1681–84, while the navigation acts were suspended, exports of manufactured goods to the plantations were resumed. In 1684, such exports from Belfast had risen considerably since the previous year, and accounted for 23% of all shoes and stockings sent from Ireland to the plantations in that year. Since these export figures are characterised by wild fluctuations it would be rash to assume that this was a rising industry later crushed by the navigation acts. Although the large numbers of Belfast freemen involved in the manufacture of clothing and footwear throughout the period 1636–82 point to a sizeable local industry, it is probable that items of clothing and footwear manufactured at Belfast were largely for the home market. Apart from textiles and clothes, very little else was manufactured at Belfast during this period. Items such as pots and pans, soap, starch, needles, pins, and nails, which were in constant demand in the colonies, were actually imported into Belfast from Scotland, Dublin and England.

At Belfast, the export trade most affected by the navigation acts was that of linen. The growth of the trade, and Belfast's part in it, have been discussed above. As increasing quantities of a quality product became available for export, the profitability of the trade to the Belfast merchants was considerably reduced by its enforced channelling through English ports.

45 Macartney to Allen, 20 June 1666 (Macartney 1, p.374).
46 Memorial of lease, 9 July 1685 (N.A., Lodge's records of the rolls, viii, p.219).
47 213 yards in 1682/3, 1, 180 in 1683/4, the latter figure being just under 10% of the total exported from Ireland in that year (B.L., Add. MS 4759, ff 3, 19).
48 2367 yards in 1698.

Their attempts to have this part of the acts repealed will be discussed later in this chapter.

The effect of the prohibition of direct imports from the colonies was initially far more serious and its wider implications caused bitterness, not just among the merchants. Sir George Rawdon wrote 'It is very severe that all foreign goods must first be landed in England and here we the retailers only, and they in England, the merchants. We shall be niderlins till Doomsday ...'[49] However the full effects were not felt until the last loophole had been closed by the act of 1671, when Rawdon wrote:

> We are more undone in this poor kingdom by a late Act, that all goods from America, Africa, and Asia are to be landed after last Michaelmas at some port of England or Wales and pay custom there or forfeit ship and goods, than we were by restraint of our cattle trade.[50]

Thereafter all enumerated goods, which included sugar and tobacco, had to be landed at English ports where the duty was paid. Imports from the colonies which were intended for the Irish market were unloaded at ports such as Bristol, Chester, Liverpool and Whitehaven, and then shipped to Ireland. Belfast's proximity to the English ports meant that the town suffered less than Galway and Limerick on the west coast, but even so the delays which resulted from landing goods in England were expensive.[51] Merchants at all Irish ports resented the prohibition on direct imports. In an attempt to win support from the Irish urban communities, the 'patriot parliament' of James II drew up an act for the advance and improvement of trade which would have permitted direct trade between Ireland and the colonies but the defeat of the Jacobites meant the loss of this, and other legislation which would have benefitted Irish merchants.[52] When William III spent five days at Belfast in June 1690, a deputation of Belfast merchants, consisting of George Macartney, Edward Pottinger, William Dobbin and James Shaw, drew the king's attention to the difficulties caused by the provisions of acts of parliament, particularly that of 1671. The king is said to have discussed the matter with them freely and to have promised that due consideration would be given to their views.[53]

With the onset of a series of wars against the French in 1689, Liverpool developed into the safest and most convenient port for landing goods before re-shipment to Belfast. Ships sailing 'northabout' round the north

---

49 *Cal. S.P. Ire., 1666–69*, p.574.
50 *Cal. S.P. Ire., 1671*, p.585.
51 For example, the additional cost of unloading tobacco was reckoned to add at least a halfpenny per pound to the price in Ireland (*Cal. S.P. col. [America and West Indies], 1685–88*, nos 613, 670).
52 Simms, *War and politics in Ireland*, pp 78–9.
53 Notes on Dobbin family (P.R.O.N.I., T367); it is not clear which of the George Macartneys is meant.

coast of Ireland, and putting at in at Liverpool, were at less risk from French privateers and, under optimum conditions, the crossing from Liverpool to Belfast could take only two or three days.[54] However there were often considerable delays in discharging goods there. For example, in November 1705, Isaac Macartney asked his Liverpool agent to hasten the unloading of the *Laurel* which had returned from an eventful and unlucky voyage with a cargo of tobacco, and deplored the time it took for the customs formalities to be completed and the fact that no priority was given to ships belonging to other ports:

> if she had been sent to Blewmoris [Beaumaris] she would have been discharged in the time she was with you ... which would save a great deal of wages and less charge than is otherways at your port. We hope your interest may prevail for her immediate dispatch that she may be here by Xmas, their own ships they pay no wages to and save likewise their meat and drink and surely the Collector will consider it the benefit to his port to encourage strangers.[55]

The Huguenot linen manufacturers at Lisburn also complained of excessive charges at Liverpool and found it easier to send their goods to London via Dublin and Chester. The Belfast merchants continued to land some cargoes at Bristol, Milford Haven and Falmouth, particularly when there was no market at Belfast for the goods. Isaac Macartney's letter book shows that he regularly landed sugar and tobacco at these ports and shipped up to Belfast in small craft only such quantities as he could sell on the home market. For the outward journeys he sent small cargoes of tallow, salt hides, staves and linen.

The restrictions on trade imposed by the navigation acts were a perpetual source of grievance for the Irish merchants, and time did nothing to reconcile them to the situation. It was only to be expected that the methods they used to circumvent the embargoes and restrictions arising from European wars would also be used against the limitations resulting from the acts. Avoidance of the acts was on a large scale. Between 1678 and 1681, for example, at least one hundred vessels in Irish-colonial commerce were seized for violations of the acts of trade and navigation.[56] Not all seizures were justified. Since the acts were intended to exclude the Scots from colonial trade, a perpetual problem for Ulster merchants, who were nearly all either first or second generation Scottish immigrants, was to convince the authorities that their ships and crews were free under the acts. In 1671, for example, the *James* of Belfast was seized as unfree by Sir Charles Wheler in Nevis, and the four Belfast merchants who owned her petitioned

---

54 Ralph Davis, *The rise of the English shipping industry in the seventeenth and eighteenth centuries* (London, 1962), p.270; P.G.E. Clemens, 'The rise of Liverpool 1665–1750' in *Econ. Hist. Rev.*, 2nd series, xxix (1976), pp 214–16.
55 Macartney to John Cunningham, 20 Nov. 1704 (Macartney 3, pp 14–15).
56 Thomas M. Truxes, *Irish-American trade, 1660–1783* (Cambridge, 1988), p.10.

in the following year for damages amounting to £5,000. Similarly, in 1686, Robert Johnson, a Scotsman who had settled in Antigua, claimed that he was a freeman of Belfast and that his ship, the *Mayflower*, was built at Coleraine and should be counted as an English ship.[57]

Although, in a few such instances, Belfast merchants were unjustly accused, there can be no doubt that the whole community avoided the provisions of the navigation acts where it seemed safe to do so. Apart from falsifying the status of 'unfree' ships (which was not normally necessary because most of the town's ships and those of their clients were free), there were other ways of getting around the acts. The most common involved the use of false papers, usually certificates relating to return cargoes. For example, in 1682 the *Adventure* of Whitehaven was freighted by John Fletcher of Belfast for a voyage to Virginia and Maryland, and was seized on her return with a cargo of tobacco because Fletcher had given the master a forged certificate.[58] Forged certificates could only be obtained by bribing or suborning customs officials but this seems to have been easily accomplished. Standards of honesty and efficiency were low among revenue collectors, and peculation and embezzlement were commonplace. Petty fraud was endemic at most customhouses. At Belfast however, it was revealed in 1684 that fraudulent certificates were being issued on a large scale with not only the connivance but the active participation of the most senior customs official in the north.

George Macartney of Auchinleck had become surveyor-general of customs of Ulster early in 1683. He owed his appointment to the influence of his brother-in-law, Sir Nicholas Butler, one of the commissioners of the customs in London, and to that of the earl of Longford. According to Sir George Rawdon, Macartney's appointment was not popular with the Belfast merchants[59] although they may have been won over by his willingness to help them to avoid the restrictions imposed on their trade by the navigation acts. In fairness to Macartney it must be said that he may have been conniving at an established practice as Fletcher's false certificate, mentioned above, pre-dates his appointment and may have come from the Belfast customhouse. The main culprit appears to have been William Dobbin, the deputy collector. Dobbin confessed to counterfeiting seals and forging officers' hands in issuing false certificates, and in the subsequent inquiry he implicated Macartney, but not the collector, Henry Davis, who appears to have been absent for much of the time. Dobbin's subsequent dismissal is not surprising, but that Macartney could be dismissed in spite of his connections indicates a degree of involvement which the treasury was unable to condone.

57 *Cal. S.P. col. (America and West Indies)*, *1669–74*, nos 631, 660, 813; *Cal. treas. bks*,
        iii, p.1138, viii, p.521; *Anal. Hib.*, iv (1932), p.270.
58 *Cal. treas. bks*, vii, p.1525.
59 *Cal. S.P. dom., 1683 Jan. to July*, p.56.

Their complicity in fraud did not prevent either man from holding office subsequently. Macartney had influential patrons. Two years later he petitioned the treasury lords who were 'so sensible of the hardship of his case' that they desired the revenue commissioners in Ireland to give him some employment equal to that from which he had been dismissed. This proved impossible but the revenue commissioners did appoint him collector at Belfast, even though this meant re-deploying their own appointee. Similarly William Dobbin became collector at Strangford and Donaghadee in 1689, and was a receiver for the forfeiture commissioners from 1700–03.[60]

Another method used by Belfast merchants to avoid the restrictions of the navigation acts involved special pleading, where the master of a returning ship claimed that circumstances had forced him to put into Belfast and to unload there. For example in 1675, William Amys, commander of the *Unicorn* of Belfast, put into Belfast on his return from the Leeward Islands and Virginia, and subsequently claimed that storm damage to his ship made it too dangerous to proceed to England to unload. Amys' claim was not allowed 'being a matter of dangerous consequence and an ill precedent'[61] but other later claims appear to have been more successful. The *William and John* of Belfast, owned by a group of Belfast merchants, was the subject of two similar claims arising from events in 1689 and 1694. In both years, circumstances had obliged the master to unload his cargo in Belfast. In each case the master's story was accepted, or he was at least given the benefit of the doubt, and the merchants who owned the cargo were allowed to pay duty in Ireland, after it had been stressed that the rule should be applied strictly in future.[62]

Strict enforcement of the navigation acts was in reality impossible, in spite of the penalties of seizure and confiscation, as the officials were reluctant to penalize honest merchants who were the victims of circumstance. Seventeenth-century merchants were accustomed to acting first and pleading afterwards and every possible excuse was seized upon which might be used to justify unloading at Belfast instead of at an English port. Moreover, since in the 1690s the merchants and traders of Bristol and Liverpool complained that ships were regularly going from the plantations to unload in Scotland and Ireland, it looks as though very few cases of ships unloading cargoes in Ireland were actually being referred to the English authorities. Certainly the central government appears to have had very little information about the enforcement, or lack of enforcement, of the acts in Ireland as in 1696, when the collector at Belfast reported that a rich ship from

60 *Cal. treas. bks*, vii, pp 1430, 1440–1, 1514, viii, p.1419.

61 Declaration by Hugh Eccles, sovereign of Belfast, 5 Aug. 1675 (B.L., Stowe MS 208, f.227); *Acts privy council, colonial series, 1613–80*, no.1047.

62 *Cal. treas. bks*, ix, pp 985, 990, x, pp 879, 899; *Cal. treas. papers, 1556–7–1696*, pp 156, 423; petition of Belfast merchants, 14 Jan. 1694/5, and related papers (P.R.O., T1/31, p.53 et seq.).

Virginia was expected there, the lords justices were ordered to make enquiry whether it was the practice in Ireland for ships to come thither directly from the plantations. Evasion probably reached a peak in the early 1690s when the naval war with France provided opportunistic ship's masters with excuses to by-pass English ports. However, the navigation act of 1696 forbade all direct imports from the colonies which brought legal two-way trade to an end, and evasion based on false customs certificates or special pleading became rare.[63]

There can be no doubt that Belfast's trade suffered as a result of the restrictions on direct importation imposed by the navigation acts. The town was prominent as an importer of tobacco in the early 1680s, when the act of 1671 had lapsed, but quantities imported declined soon after the reimposition of the colonial ban. The acts deprived Belfast of a share in the valuable re-export trade in colonial goods. Profits from the re-export of sugar would have been limited because Europe was supplied by the produce of the French and Dutch colonies which was generally cheaper, but sugar was being re-exported from Belfast to the Glasgow refinery until prohibited by the act of 1671.[64] Although the trade in sugar from the West Indies became increasingly dominated by the London sugar merchants, Belfast was ideally situated to become the leading tobacco re-exporter in the north. The merchants struggled to import tobacco against the provisions of the acts in the 1690s until finally defeated by the total ban on direct colonial imports, and by the act of union between England and Scotland in 1707 which legalized direct importation into Scottish ports and made Glasgow the leading entrepôt port of the north.[65]

By the 1690s, it was not only Belfast's imports which were seriously affected by the navigation acts. By that date, the settlement of the Huguenots at Lisburn and the Flemish at Waringstown, and subsequent improvements in the manufacture of linen, had increased both the quality and quantity of linen available. In 1696, England, starved by the war with France of linens from Holland and Saxony, abolished the duty on plain linens from Ireland which gave a boost to both manufacture and trade, and thereafter it was English policy to encourage the Irish linen trade.[66] In

---

63 Harper, *English navigation laws*, pp 60, 74, 103; *Cal. S.P. dom., 1695 (Addenda)*, p.355; Truxes, *Irish-American trade*, p.12.
64 Cargo of *William* of Greenock, 23 Feb. 1670 (S.R.O., Glasgow port book, E72/10/2).
65 L.M. Cullen, 'Merchant communities, the navigation acts and Irish and Scottish responses' in L.M. Cullen and T.C. Smout (ed.), *Comparative aspects of Scottish and Irish economic and social history, 1600–1900* (Edinburgh, 1977), p.171; L.E. Cochran, *Scottish trade with Ireland in the eighteenth century* (Edinburgh, 1985), pp 9–10.
66 W.H. Crawford, 'The rise of the linen industry' in L.M. Cullen (ed.), *The formation of the Irish economy* (Cork, 1969), pp 25–6; H.F. Kearney, 'The political background to English mercantilism' in *Econ. Hist. Rev.*, 2nd series, xi (1959), pp 491–2, 495).

1698, for example, Belfast was exporting ten times as much linen as in 1682/3.[67] In October 1703, a committee which included Edward Brice, Thomas Knox and William Craford, was appointed by the Irish house of commons to prepare the heads of a bill for the encouragement of linen manufacture, and the queen was petitioned to free the export of linen from the restrictions of the navigation acts. The direct exportation of linen from Ireland to the colonies was finally permitted from 24 June 1705. In anticipation, Isaac Macartney had written to a correspondent in Bideford in the previous March:

> now when the Parliament of England is pleased to let poor Ireland export directly linen to the English plantation, for which trade this is the only fit port in the Kingdom of Ireland, the north of Ireland being the chief part for the linen manufactory there being very little made elsewhere in the Kingdom, if you incline to be concerned in that trade either for the West Indies or Virginia, the months of June, July, August and September is the only season for buying the same.[68]

In other letters he stressed that linen was always 5% cheaper at Belfast than in Dublin. In 1705 therefore, Macartney was clearly aware of the potential of the trade. Exports from Belfast continued to rise, particularly after the Treaty of Utrecht in 1713, with a high proportion being sent to the plantations. Within twenty years linen had become 'the best branch of trade this kingdom has'.[69]

Although the volume of Belfast's trade increased enormously in the course of the seventeenth century, the goods exported remained much the same. The Belfast merchants were provisions merchants, dealing in agricultural surpluses, and struggling to sell highly perishable cargoes at volatile markets. Their trade was seasonal, but by the end of the century there are indications that salted provisions were available for most of the year, which suggests that attempts to improve packing and preservation had been successful. For much of the period, trade was considerably impeded by foreign wars and embargoes, and by English legislation. The navigation acts, which forbade direct trade with the colonies, had serious consequences at Belfast. Even though the major export, provisions, was not affected, the acts restricted the emerging linen trade and the importation of tobacco and sugar. Consequently evasion of the acts was widespread. In 1707, the act of union freed Scotland from the restrictions of the navigation acts and opened the way for Glasgow to become the major re-exporter of colonial goods in the north. Nevertheless, the lifting of

---

67 Tables of Irish exports, 1698 (P.R.O., CUST 15/1)
68 Macartney to Buck, 12 Mar. 1704/5 (Macartney 3, p.68).
69 James Hamilton Maxwell to Agmondesham Vesey, 21 July 1722 (N.A., Sarsfield Vesey letters, 175).

restrictions on the direct export of linen to the colonies contributed to the development of Belfast as a major international port, and for the Belfast merchants it meant that, in 1707, they were on the threshold of a new era in which they had a high quality non-perishable product for which there was a steady demand.

6

Business Practice

PARTNERSHIPS, SHIPS AND SHIPPING

The trade of the Belfast merchant community in the seventeenth century followed the normal pattern of the time, being financed by partnerships, with merchants taking shares in cargoes of individual ships. No agreements have survived from Belfast for such partnerships in the seventeenth century but the Macartney letter books show that there were normally between two and eight partners, that partnerships were temporary (lasting only until the return of the ship in which the goods were freighted), that it was customary to share any accidental loss or damage to goods, and that, even at the end of the period, the partners were not obliged to adopt a common policy towards insurance. The leading merchants were usually involved in several ventures with different partners at any one time. The advantages of partnerships were shared outlay and shared risk. Shared outlay meant that no merchant was obliged to find the necessary funds to load an entire vessel but could spread outlay and returns over a longer period by investing in a number of different cargoes to different markets. Shared risks applied not only to such obvious disasters as shipwreck or capture by privateers, but to all the factors which could result in a loss rather than a profit, such as delay, poor condition of goods on arrival, variable markets abroad, poor choice of goods for the return cargo, and glutted markets at home. Even when human inefficiency was not to blame, simple bad luck could turn profits into losses. By sharing freight on a number of voyages the disasters could be offset by the successes. Freight-sharing partnerships worked best when all the partners were at the same port. In 1705, Isaac Macartney wrote to a correspondent at Bruges '... I do consider partners being in different places it's troublesome when their trade to employ their ship lies different ways'.[1]

Ships were owned by similar, but more permanent partnerships. There are striking differences when ship-ownership in Belfast is compared with

---

1 Macartney to Mathew Prosser, 1 Oct. 1705 (Macartney 3, pp 193-4).

common practice in England. The first is that ships were divided into a small number of shares. The larger trading ships in England were frequently divided into sixteen or even thirty-two shares and, although some merchants had shares in these ships, most of the partners were passive investors. Most Belfast ships in the 1650s–70s were divided into two, three or four shares and even the largest ships had only seven partners. The reasons for the limited numbers of shares are straightforward. First there were limited numbers of people with money to spare for investment purposes. Belfast was still a very small town and there are no signs that the Ulster gentry was interested in investing in ships at this date. Second, and more important, is the fact that there seems to have been no such thing as a 'sleeping partner' in Belfast shipping in the seventeenth century. The merchants who owned the ships intended to use them, wherever possible, to ship their own goods, and partnerships involving large numbers were often strained by the conflicting interests of the partners. Although it was common for one of the leading partners to undertake most of the actual loading and paperwork, the others were seldom content to be sleeping partners and let him proceed as a 'ship's husband' would at a later date.

This kind of ship-owning partnership was still customary in Belfast in the early eighteenth century. Such a partnership owned the *Laurel* in 1704 and Isaac Macartney, who had an eighth share, frequently bewailed the lack of a common policy and shared responsibility for the ship, even though most of the partners were close business associates. There is some evidence that this was a period of transition between merchant partnerships and investment partnerships at Belfast. The *Donegall* of Belfast, for example, was divided into twenty parts, and the owners in 1711 included local gentry.[2] However the papers of the Belfast merchant Daniel Mussenden show that smaller merchant ship-owning partnerships were still the norm in the 1720s.[3]

Another difference in ship-ownership at Belfast, compared to practice in England, is that few ships' masters owned a share in their ships. In a list of c.1661 showing twenty-nine Belfast ships, only eleven masters were part-owners, and eight of these ships were of below 50 tons.[4] Lack of investment by the masters presumably indicates a shortage of capital. It was quite common, however, for ships' masters to have a share of the cargo, in addition to the customary privilege of loading some goods on their own

2 Sale of 1/20 part of the *Donegall* of Belfast, by Richard Dobbs of Castle Dobbs to Alexander Moore of Belfast, 1711 (P.R.O.N.I., Brett papers, D271/4)
3 Charter parties, 19 Aug. 1718, 14 Sept. 1720, 5 Feb. 1722/3 (P.R.O.N.I., Mussenden papers, D354/369, 373, 381).
4 List of Belfast shipping (P.R.O.N.I., Young [Pinkerton] MSS, D2930 addnl. MS 9/16P), printed in Benn, p.310, without names of masters); although dated c.1663 by Benn, this list probably dates from the first half of 1661 before the purchases of the *Angel Gabriel*, the *Unicorn* and the *North Star* by Belfast merchants (see table 8); no other list shows both owners and masters.

account. Several ships' masters were also merchants. The most notable was Edward Pottinger, captain of the *Insiquin*, at 150 tons one of Belfast's largest ships in the 1660s–70s, and captain of the *Donegall* in the 1680s. Other Belfast families also produced both merchants and mariners, notably the Chalmers, Holmes, Leathes, Smith and Whiteside families.

Table 8 (overleaf) is a list of Belfast ships between c.1661 and c.1675, with tonnages and owners, derived mainly from lists compiled by customs officials which included shipping from both Belfast and Carrickfergus.[5] Ships which can be identified as belonging to Carrickfergus have been omitted from this table. While these lists may have been accurate statements of the town's shipping on the dates when they were compiled, they do not contain a complete record of Belfast ships between these dates. References to further Belfast ships are to be found in a number of sources, and five are described in sufficient detail to be included in table 8.[6] Excluding the garbarts, the total number of individual ship-owners appearing in the table is fifty, counting both George Macartneys.[7] Very few ships had a single owner, and those few were of low tonnage.

Table 9 is a breakdown of ownership showing both the percentages of owners who were mariners, merchants or members of the thirty-two families, and also the percentage of ship shares that each group held. In addition to those ships' masters who were also owners named in the list of c.1661, a further four are identifiable from other sources bringing the total to 20% of the fifty owners. However, mariners only held 12.5% of ship shares, and two, Edward Pottinger and Anthony Wild, who were both merchants and mariners, owned more than half of the mariners' shares between them. Twenty-one of the thirty-two families studied in depth owned shares in ships, and these twenty-one families owned, between them, more than 65% of the town's shipping. Nineteen of the owners had shares in two or more ships, and eleven owners had shares in three or more ships. Ownership of ship shares was concentrated in the hands of the merchants, in particular James Chalmers, Hugh Eccles, the two George Macartneys, Thomas Pottinger and William Smith. Gabarts, which were used for unloading ships, have not been included in table 9, but, in addition to the shares in ships shown there, Chalmers, Eccles, Smith, Knox, Lewis Thompson and George Macartney all either owned or had a half share in a gabart.

The picture that emerges from the merchant letter books and the various shipping lists is of a group of merchants who took shares in numer-

5 See note 4 above for list of c.1661; list of Carrickfergus shipping, [c.1675] (N.L.I., MS 8110, printed in Benn, p.311).

6 *North Star* and *Unicorn* (*Town book*, pp 94–6); *Angel Gabriel* (Macartney to Arthur, 14 July 1665 [Macartney 1, pp 201–2]); *James* (1666) (Macartney to McKinney, 9 Jan. 1665/6 [Macartney 1, p.306]); *James* (1672) (*Anal. Hib.*, iv [1932], pp 270–3).

7 It is not possible to distinguish between the two George Macartneys in the shipping lists.

Table 8: Belfast shipping, c.1661–c.1675

ship	tons	owners
Antelope	200	c.1661: G. **Macartney**, H. **Eccles**, T. **Knox**, T. **Pottinger**, Jas **Chalmers**, Jn **White**, T. Martin c.1675: minus **White** and Martin
Insiquin	150	c.1661: H. **Eccles**, *E. Pottinger*, T. **Pottinger**, T. **Young** c.1675: minus **Young**, plus **Macartney**
Belfast Merchant	150	c.1675: T. **Knox**, Jas **Chalmers**, Jn **Hamilton**, A. Maxwell, J. Burnie, W. **Lockhart**, T. Aitkin
Adventure	120	c.1661: W. **Smith**, Jn **White**, W. Arthur, *Jn Gregge* c.1675: minus *Gregge*, plus Jas **Young**
Rose	80	c.1675: T. **Pottinger**, H. **Eccles**, E. **Pottinger**
North Star	80	1662: W. **Smith**, W. Thomb, W. **Moore**
Unicorn		1662: W. **Smith**, W. Thomb, H. **Eccles**, M. **Biggar**
Angel Gabriel	70	1665: Black George **Macartney**
Anne	70	c.1675: W. **Smith**, G. **Macartney**
William	50	c.1661–75: T. **Knox**, W. **Lockhart**
Margaret	50	c.1661–75: T. Owen, L. **Thompson**
Fullwood	50	c.1661: T. **Pottinger**, E. **Pottinger**, Jn **Black**, Jn **Martin**, *N. Trimble*
John	50	c.1675: J. McBryde, W. Thomson
James		1672: J. **Clugston**, W. **Anderson**, J. **Chalmers**, T. **Pottinger**
James	45	1666: G. **Macartney**, H. **Eccles**, G. **Macartney**
Charlemont	40	c.1661–75: *R. Whiteside*, T. **Chads**
Olive Branch	40	c.1661: G. **Macartney**, A. Wild, E. Wilson
Providence	40	c.1661: T. **Aitkin**, W. **Lockhart**, *Jn Adam*, A. Sinkler, A. Wild, W. **Rainey**
Andrew	40	c.1675: J. **Hamilton**, A. Gregg, W. **Craford**
Isabell	40	c.1675: W. **Smith**, Jas **Chalmers**, T. **Pottinger**, Jn White
Katherine	40	c.1675: W. **Smith**, G. Holmes, R. Holmes
Diamond	40	c.1675: G. **Macartney**, A. Wild, E. Wilson
Phoenix	40	c.1675: J. **Chalmers**, J. Burnie, A. Maxwell, H. Speir, T. Hoome
Plain Dealing	40	c.1675: Jn Browne
Salmon	35	c.1675: Jas Bodkin
Grizell	30	c.1661: Jas **Young**; c.1675 W. **Smith**
Dolphin	25	c.1661–75: Lewis **Thompson**
James	25	c.1661–75: *Jas Glasgow*
Mayflower	24	c.1661: E. McBryde, M. Johnson
Ossory	20	c.1661–75: C. Jones, J. Fletcher
Salmon (gabart)	16	c.1661: Widow **Leathes**
Resolution (gabart)	16	c.1661: G. **Macartney**, Lewis **Thompson**
Mary (gabart)	12	c.1661: Jn **Hamilton**, Jas **Chalmers**
Isabell (gabart)	12	c.1661: H. **Eccles**, Jn McFerran
Mouse (gabart)	10	c.1661: Widow **Leathes**
Betty (gabart)	8	c.1661: T. **Knox**
Anne (gabart)	6	c.1661: Widow **Leathes**
Elizabeth (gabart)	6	c.1661: Jas McAdam
Jane (gabart)	6	c.1661: G. **Macartney**
Martha (gabart)	6	c.1661: G. **Macartney**

Names of members of the thirty-two families are shown in **bold**.
Ships' masters' names are shown in *italics*.

ous trading ventures and who, between them, owned virtually the whole of the Belfast shipping. Their involvement in the latter appears to have been, at times, reluctant (Black George sometimes stated that he would have preferred to freight) but it was necessary because the supply of vessels available for freighting was limited and availability was frequently out of step with demand. Owning shares in ships did at least ensure that it would be possible to ship cargoes when and where the merchants wanted. It is also clear that without merchant investment the town's fleet would have been almost non-existent in the seventeenth century.

Table 9: Shipowners and ship shares, c.1661–c.1675

	mariners	merchants	the 32 families
owners	20%	80%	46%
ship shares	12.5%	87.5%	65.6%

The growth in trade from Belfast is reflected in the growth of the town's shipping. In 1661 there were twenty-nine ships, totalling 1,102 tons burden, and in 1675 there were twenty-seven, totalling 1,527 tons. However, the first list of ships includes gabarts. If these are subtracted, the town had eighteen ships in 1661, totalling 998 tons. By the mid-1670s therefore, both ships and tonnage had increased by about 50%, most of this increase being in ships of between 40 and 80 tons burden. A third list of ships dated 1682–86 lists sixty-seven ships with a total tonnage of 3,307.[8] The increase in the twenty years between 1661 and the early 1680s was therefore in the region of 350%. The town's shipping appears to have exceeded that of Cork at the same date, and probably compared very favourably with that of any Irish port other than Dublin.[9] However, even by the 1680s there were only nine ships of 100 tons and upwards. The average was about 50 tons, and there were ships of less than 20 tons used for trade within the Irish Sea.

Moreover, the three lists of Belfast (and Carrickfergus) ships give a false impression of the volume of shipping from the town because many cargoes were carried in ships from neighbouring coastal towns, including Larne, Holywood and Strangford, but principally from Donaghadee. Indeed, the first Macartney letter book refers more frequently to ships from Donaghadee than from Belfast. In 1675, Donaghadee had a fleet of about eighteen ships ranging from 20 to 60 tons, and in 1697 the total of seafaring people (i.e. seamen and fishermen) living there out-numbered those at

8 List of Belfast shipping, 1682–86, including names of masters but not owners (*B.N.L.*, 24–28 May 1793); like the previous lists this includes a few vessels from Carrickfergus.

9 Dickson, 'Economic history of the Cork region', p.492; William Petty, *The political anatomy of Ireland* (1691, repr. Shannon, 1969), p.110.

Belfast and Carrickfergus combined.[10] Since the trade of Donaghadee was small in scale after the ban on live cattle exports in 1667, the town's ships and seamen can be regarded virtually as an extension to Belfast's home fleet.

Only the first Belfast shipping list gives precise details of where each ship was built. Of the twenty-nine ships listed, fifteen were built at Belfast. This however includes all the gabarts and none of the ships of 100 tons or over. In the list of the 1670s about half the ships listed were built in Ireland, and most of the rest were from England. All but five of the town's fleet were free under the navigation acts although in the case of two of the largest which were foreign-built, this may have been the result of false statements about their date of purchase. The list including this information was signed by the obliging William Dobbin as deputy collector at Belfast.[11] Of the four largest ships (120–200 tons) only one was Irish-built. Belfast-built ships may have been small because the ship builders lacked access to the great oaks of County Londonderry. Belfast had a ship-building industry throughout the seventeenth century, but imported all the necessary masts and rigging. The scale of operations appears to have been small, as in the rest of Ireland. However, the industry recovered after the Williamite wars, larger ships were built, and Belfast was supplying ships to Scotland for trade with the colonies at the time of the act of union.[12] The size of the town's fleet in the early eighteenth century is not known. However, totals for ships and tonnage employed at the major Irish ports from 1698 show that although more ships were employed in Belfast's trade than at Cork or Waterford, the total tonnage of these ships was only a third to a half of that at Cork, and that the tonnage of ships employed at Waterford frequently excelled those at Belfast.[13] These comparisons make it clear that

10 There were 268 at Belfast and Carrickfergus of whom 194 were seamen, and 313 (no breakdown) at Donaghadee (antiquarian notes [L.H.L., Joy MSS, 7, and P.R.O.N.I., Young (Pinkerton), D2930 addnl. MS 9/12]); Joy says that skippers of many Belfast ships lived at Donaghadee; report on state of port of Donaghadee, 1675 (Stevenson, *Two centuries of life in Down*, p.253, from Rawlinson MS B510, f.7b [Bodl.]).

11 The signatures of Dobbin and other customs officials are at the foot of the account of ships belonging to the port of Carrickfergus, n.d. (N.L.I., MS 8110), but not in the partial transcript printed in Benn, p.311.

12 McCracken, *Irish woods*, pp 65–7; the cargo of the *James* of Irvine included cables, ropes and anchors, etc. for a new vessel building at Belfast, 20 Apr. 1681 (S.R.O., Ayr port book, E72/3/6); the ropemaker at Belfast was supplied with hemp from Dublin (Macartney to John Vernon, 15 Feb. 1678/9 [Macartney 2, p.22]); only nine men in the freemen's register are described as shipwrights or ship carpenters between 1639 and 1681; George O'Brien, *The economic history of Ireland in the seventeenth century* (Dublin, 1919), pp 169–173; extract from Leathes's journal, 15 Nov. 1700 (L.H.L., Joy MSS, 7); Macartney to Messrs Cairnes, 16 Mar. 1705/6 (Macartney 3, pp 286–7); *Ormonde MSS*, (NS), viii, p.274.

13 Estimates of the tonnage of shipping employed in the trade of Ireland, 1698–1714 (P.R.O., CUST 15/1–17)

11 Merchant shipping at Liverpool, 1680

most ships involved in Belfast's trade were smaller than those at Cork and Waterford.

Although the tendency in England in the seventeenth century was for increasing specialisation, with ships and masters repeating the same journey with the same cargo in successive years, there is no sign that this was true in Belfast at the same date for specialisation was not encouraged by the constant changes imposed on trade by embargoes and other restrictions. Nevertheless there were three main trade routes for ships from Belfast and the other Ulster ports. In the spring, as soon as it was practicable, Belfast ships sailed to Norway with oatmeal; in the early autumn they went to France and Spain for wine, and in the winter they sailed to America for tobacco and to the West Indies for sugar, generally returning before July when the hurricane season started. Most Belfast ships were used on all of these routes, as the markets dictated, and even ships as small as 40 tons were used for transatlantic trade. Very complicated voyages were quite common, with ships loading and discharging at several consecutive ports.

Trading and ship-owning partnerships were necessary to spread the risks of shipping which were high throughout the period. Even crossing the Irish Sea was a considerable undertaking in bad weather and the Macartney letter books abound in stories of ships which were blown off course and lost sight of for weeks. The percentage of ships lost was high and a number of providential escapes are recorded in the lives of the merchant families. Hugh Rainey of Magherafelt, brother of William Rainey of Belfast, left money to found a school in recognition of his providential escape from shipwreck, and John Black of Bordeaux spent each anniversary of a similar escape in grateful prayer. Another Belfast merchant, James Stewart, made his will in 1693 because he was setting out on a journey to England; since it was proved about six months later his pessimism was well-founded although it is not recorded whether he was actually lost at sea. Added to the hazard of shipwreck was the danger in wartime from privateers and the press. For example, the *James* of Belfast, owned by the two George Macartneys and Hugh Eccles, sailed for Antigua in 1666 but was pressed into carrying troops for the re-taking of St. Kitts. She was subsequently captured by the French and taken to Martinique and her owners were still claiming compensation in 1668.[14] Even when there was peace, the Biscayers posed a perpetual threat.

From the 1690s, war with France brought French privateers into the Irish Sea, and the problem was especially acute in the first years of the eighteenth century, when privateers actually came into Belfast Lough. In response to the complaints of the merchants, there was a sporadic naval presence over the next few years which proved to be a mixed blessing, for

---

14 Appendix A.3, 24; abstract of will of James Stewart, 1693 (P.R.O.N.I., Stewart abstracts, D1759/3B/1, p.71); Macartney to John Read, 27 Apr. 1667 (Macartney 1, pp 537–8); *Acts privy council (colonial series), 1613–80*, no. 755.

the frigate captains, although protecting Belfast shipping from privateers, generally had to be paid to convoy ships, and they pressed seamen at every opportunity. The danger of pressing grew so acute that in 1705 Isaac Macartney was sending letters to Ballyshannon to await the arrival of ships from the West Indies and America, instructing the masters to put in at Larne and to send an express to him at Belfast so that he could warn them if there were any men-of-war in Belfast Lough.

Although merchant letters abound with fervent prayers for the safe arrival of ships, many merchants took more practical steps to safeguard their interests. As Bartholomew Vanhomrigh of Dublin wrote, in 1685, to a correspondent in London, 'I am sorry for this disaster but God's will must be done to whose providence we must submit. I hope you have insured your interest ...'.[15] From the 1660s Black George and other Belfast merchants were regularly insuring ships and cargoes in time of war. It was not possible to arrange insurance in Dublin at this date, let alone at Belfast, and Black George normally asked Daniel Arthur in London, or his correspondents in Antwerp, Rotterdam, Rouen or St Malo to set it up. Insurance was not a complete answer to hazards at sea as the underwriters seldom paid more than 75–85% of the sum insured and recovering even this proportion could be a lengthy process. The uncertainty and unreliability of the insurance market led many merchants to prefer to take risks rather than waste money on premiums, and for those who did insure it was a way of mitigating rather than covering risks. Because underwriters never paid more than a proportion of the sum insured, it was normal for merchants to insure only about two-thirds of the total value of their interest, and insurance of cargoes was, initially, more common than insurance of ships. Marine insurance became more widely adopted in the 1690s when there was an increased risk of capture from French privateers and there were gradual improvements in the organisation and reliability of the London insurance market. Nevertheless, insurance did not become reliable or routine until the eighteenth century and merchants were frequently dissatisfied with the outcome. As late as 1706, when Isaac Macartney asked Messrs Cairnes of London to arrange certificates and protection against pressing for the ship *Hopewell* for Barbados, he added 'We are discouraged from making any insurance in London for any of our interest by reason of the uncertainty of your insurers by which we are generally disappointed in case of loss', and he suggested getting insurance in Holland instead.[16]

Problems in shipping partnerships frequently arose from the fact that it was impossible to impose a common policy on insurance since the uncertainty of recovering adequate insurance money made many merchants disinclined to pay premiums, even in time of war. This depended to a great

15 Vanhomrigh to Peter de Best, 18 Apr. 1685 (T.C.D., Vanhomrigh letter book, MS 3961, f.241v).
16 Macartney to Messrs Cairnes, 16 Mar. 1705/6 (Macartney 3, pp 286–7).

extent on the personality of the individual merchant. For example, when David Butle asked Alexander Cairnes in London to insure goods between Milford Haven and Glasgow in 1698 he wrote 'one other reason why I delayed writing was waiting for my partners to join but they have more courage than I have and will not be at further charge'.[17] A good illustration of the complex problems arising from differing attitudes to insurance appears in Isaac Macartney's letter book. Macartney was one of the partners involved in the *Elizabeth* of Dublin which was freighted in 1706 to bring a cargo of wine, brandy, prunes, rosin, vinegar and cork from Bordeaux. She was taken by privateers from Flushing in June but brought into Falmouth. There appear to have been at least seven partners in Belfast, Bordeaux, Dublin and Scotland and, in addition, wine had been loaded for John Black and John Hamilton of Belfast, who were not among the original partners, to make up the freight although the factors at Bordeaux had been instructed not to include goods for anyone else at Belfast. Because of the war the ship was trading illegally so there was little prospect of recovering anything by law, and the partners could not agree to negotiate with the privateers because Black and Hamilton had taken out insurance and preferred to claim rather than to try to buy back the cargo.[18]

The Macartney letter books contain two good 'case histories' of ships, forty years apart, which illustrate the pattern of trade from Belfast and many of the hazards encountered. The first ship is the *Angel Gabriel*. She was purchased by Black George Macartney in 1661, having been sent on approval by Edward Moore, a Bristol merchant living at La Rochelle. She was of 65–70 tons burden, with a crew of eleven plus master and mate, and the ratio of men to tonnage suggests that she was expensive to run.[19] Certainly Macartney was already wishing to be rid of her in the following year ('the worst bargain that ever I bought'). She was sent to France for wine, then to the West Indies for sugar, and from 1663 was making regular runs down to Cadiz and the Straits. Macartney was her sole owner and frequently loaded at least half of the cargo on his own account. In the summer of 1665 a friend of Daniel Arthur wanted to freight her for the West Indies but Macartney had already made plans to send her to Cadiz again and asked Arthur to arrange insurance for £400 for the goods and £200 for the ship, which was half the value of the ship and considerably less than the value of the cargo, adding 'I pray let it be with honest and able men that if ought but well should happen that there be no wrangling to get the money'. Insurance proved hard to find because of the plague in London and a rate of 16% was quoted. Macartney eventually managed to get £150 insured for £9 3s [i.e. at approximately 6%]. The *Angel Gabriel* was taken by privateers outside Cadiz in the autumn of 1665. The recovery

17 Butle to Alex. Cairnes, 9 Nov. 1698 (Butle, pp 58–9).
18 Macartney to John Cossart, 20 June [?*recte* July] 1706, to Robert Gordon, 5 Aug. 1706, to Messrs Cairnes, 26 Aug. 1706 (Macartney 3, pp 334–8).
19 Davis, *English shipping industry*, p.378.

of the insurance money was a protracted affair as the master had been imprisoned when the ship was taken and several months elapsed before he was freed and able to give evidence to the underwriters. Macartney eventually received £120 13s 3d for the £150 insured but this was not until the end of 1667, after he had threatened to sue. He was a heavy loser as he had loaded three quarters of the cargo on his own account. Thereafter he was careful to spread the risks in partnerships.[20]

The second ship that is well documented in the Macartney letter books is the *Laurel*. She was a ship of 130–140 tons and ten guns, built in 1700 and, unlike the *Angel Gabriel*, was intended for a specialised trade having been 'sheathed on the stocks for the guinea trade'.[21] She cost £1,700 including her original outfitting and was owned by eight partners in March 1703, when she sailed for America. On the way there she was taken by privateers but escaped through the enterprise of her master. She then put into Newfoundland where various bonds were given to stop her being taken back to England as salvage. Most of her crew was pressed and new seamen had to be hired at top wages so that the season for tobacco was over by the time she reached Virginia. She remained there for seven months, waiting for the next crop, and picked up a 'touch of the worms'. Because of the loss of part of her outwards cargo of provisions, the master and supercargo could not afford to buy a full return cargo and they could not find any freight to carry. When she arrived back at Plymouth, a year later than expected, she was delayed waiting for a convoy to Liverpool. On reaching Liverpool, she lay for weeks before being cleared by the customs while Isaac Macartney, who was acting for the owners, organised a claim against the insurers and at the same time tried to ensure that bills for her 'outrigg' and expenses while in Virginia were met by the various partners. The cargo, like the ship, was divided into eighths (although not all the partners in the cargo were owners) and at least one of these shares was further divided as the supercargo had a 1/16 share. In October 1704 Macartney wrote 'I am plagued with a parcel of partners that does not pay their parts' and he finally resorted to instructing his correspondent in Liverpool to impound their shares of the cargo until the bills had been paid. At this stage the partners were ready to sell, even though ship prices generally had dropped since the *Laurel* was built. In January 1705, Macartney wrote to William Cairnes in Dublin, '... if all the partners will take my advice they will sell her for £600 for I am truly tired of shipping'. The insurance when finally paid proved, as usual, to be less than anticipat-

20 Macartney to Edward Moore, 20 Apr. 1661, to Thomas Lewis, 20 Feb. 1661/2, to Barron, 24 Sept. 1662, to Arthur, 14 and 29 July 1665, to Sexton 25 Aug., 25 Oct. 1665, to Arthur, 28 Sept. 1667 (Macartney 1, pp 3–4, 45–6, 55, 201–2, 210, 222, 253, 604).

21 i.e. she was intended for tropical waters; the Guinea Coast was the west coast of Africa so the *Laurel* may have been built as a slaver although she was not being used as one.

ed. The *Laurel* was eventually sold for £532 to James Arbuckle, another Belfast merchant, in January 1706.[22] The misfortunes of the *Laurel* can be ascribed largely to bad luck rather than bad management, but the problems arising on her return were due to the large number of partners with a share in either the ship or the cargo.

FRIENDS AND FACTORS

In the 1660s, most Irish merchants were trading on commission; that is, they were loading cargoes for merchants abroad. As late as 1686 Lord Clarendon wrote:

> whoever considers the trade of this kingdom, will tell you that five parts of six of it are carried on by commission; many men have made good estates by that way of dealing; but few merchants who trade upon their own accounts, think it worth their while to be here.[23]

Although the Scots who settled at Belfast may be seen as a part of the widespread migration of Scottish merchants in the seventeenth century, seeking better trading prospects abroad, they did not, unlike many other expatriate Scottish communities, specialise in loading cargoes for Scottish markets or in handling Scottish goods. The Belfast merchants were chiefly employed in the export of agricultural surpluses, the best market for which was not normally Scotland. Although there was a steady and profitable trade between Ulster and south-west Scotland, the leading merchants in both countries were those who traded with Europe and the New World. The Scots who emigrated to Belfast did not settle there in order to act as factors for, or even to trade in partnership with merchants at their ports of origin. In spite of the constant trade between Belfast and Glasgow, there is no indication from the Glasgow port books that Thomas Knox, the Smiths or William Anderson acted on behalf of, or in partnership with their kinfolk in Glasgow. Those few merchants in Belfast who can be identified as having set themselves up as the 'Belfast end' of existing partnerships were not Scots. John Fletcher who traded in partnership with Charles Jones of Bristol for a number of years, appears to have come from Dublin,[24] and Cornelis van Weede, a Dutch merchant who lived at Belfast for several years, can be assumed to have been acting as factor for other Dutchmen.[25]

22 Macartney to Cromie & Stevenson, 21 Oct. 1704, to Cunningham, 8 Nov. 1704, 19 Jan. 1705/6, to William Cairnes, 20 Jan. 1704/5, to Messrs Cairnes, 8 Jan., 26 Mar. 1705, 3 June 1706 (Macartney 3, pp 2, 6–7, 34–5, 44, 76–7, 255–6, 318).
23 *The correspondence of Henry Hyde, earl of Clarendon, and his brother, Laurence Hyde, earl of Rochester, with the diary of Lord Clarendon from 1687–90*, ed. S.W. Singer (2 vols, London, 1828), i, p.571, hereafter cited as *Clarendon corr.*
24 Fletcher and Jones were co-owners of the *Ossory*.
25 *Town book*, p.270; *Cal. S.P. Ire., 1669–70*, p.321; Van Weede returned to the

The Scottish merchants who settled at Belfast acted as factors for merchants in London and Europe, but in the 1660s 40% of Ireland's foreign trade revenue derived from Dublin, with Dublin merchants acting as middlemen and obtaining commodities from a wide hinterland and from merchants at the provincial Irish ports. Black George Macartney's two letter books show how he built up connections in the 1660s, with his recorded out-letters rising from 32 in 1661 to 312 in 1666. He obtained and loaded cargoes of provisions, receiving a commission of 2½%. Some of these goods were shipped in locally freighted ships but it was common for vessels to be sent from abroad. Economists of the day deplored the dependence of Irish merchants on foreign ships, particularly Dutch, the freighting of which was said to discourage Irish shipbuilding, and at least £60,000 p.a. was paid to foreign shipowners in freight charges.[26] Ships freighted abroad arrived with a cargo to be sold, also on commission, and it was part of the duty of a factor to give advice about the most suitable goods to send. Sometimes it was better to send no cargo at all; in 1675, Lewis Thompson advised Jacob David of London 'We have our returns to this place often in wines both French and Spanish and in brandy, but money is the best commodity that we have.'[27]

Working on commission was extremely beneficial to the Belfast merchants as it helped them to build up capital, without risk, to finance trade on their own accounts, and offered them opportunities to extend this trade because they were offered shares in the cargoes which they loaded for merchants in Dublin and abroad. The arrangement was advantageous to all parties because it ensured that goods loaded would be of the best quality available and it spread the risk of the venture. In the 1660s, Belfast merchants also initiated partnerships with merchants abroad. Apart from shares in such cargoes, the Macartney letter books also document an increasing trade by partnerships within the community. Where possible, this trade was carried in Belfast's own fleet, and merchants either shipped goods in their own ships or took shares in cargoes. A comparison between the letter books of George Macartney and those of Isaac Macartney and David Butle shows a considerable change in trading patterns. In 1667, for example, Black George was involved in at least twenty-seven trading ventures and had shares in about one third of these. By contrast, in 1705 Isaac Macartney was involved in at least twenty-five ventures and had shares in about four-fifths. Although it is not possible to document this change over the entire

Netherlands and was at Rotterdam in 1675 when he had dealings with both George Macartney and Lewis Thompson of Belfast; he was broke in 1678; Thompson to Charles Marescoe, 26 June, 4 Sept. 1675, Van Weede to Jacob David, 20 Sept. 1675 (P.R.O., C114/77(1):9, C114/76(1):5, C114/72(2):5); see also Henry Roseveare (ed.), *Markets and merchants of the late seventeenth century, the Marescoe-David letters, 1668–1680* (Oxford, 1987), pp 180, 504.

26 Petty, *Political anatomy*, p.110; Lawrence, *Interest of Ireland*, pt 1, p.83; Simms, *War and politics in Ireland*, p.55.

27 Thompson to David, 6 Nov 1675 (P.R.O., C114/76(2):6).

period, Isaac Macartney's and Butle's letter books suggest that by the early eighteenth century most of their trade was in partnership with other Belfast merchants.

The Belfast merchant letter books also show increasing contact with Irish ports other than Dublin. In the 1660s, Black George Macartney had dealings with merchants in Londonderry and Coleraine, especially the latter, when he needed extra butter to make up cargoes or had goods for which there was no sale at Belfast. From the late 1670s, however, he extended his operations to Ballyshannon in County Donegal where James Delap, a local man, acted as his factor, buying butter, beef, tallow and salmon to be shipped from Ballyshannon and Killybegs. It is clear from his letters to Delap that this was a recent development. For example he warned him to supply only English butter, such as was produced at Enniskillen, and to make sure his tallow was hard, white and sweet 'being the beginning of that trade with you and if bad at first will for ever discourage'.[28] The advantage of buying from Ballyshannon was that prices were generally lower than at Belfast and the difference was enough to outweigh the higher rates for freight from the north-west coast. The disadvantage was that there were fewer ships there to freight and masters of ships were unwilling to sail 'northabout' after the end of October which made the trading season shorter. Many of the cargoes loaded by Delap at the time of the second letter book were divided three ways between Daniel Arthur of London, Joshua Allen of Dublin and Black George. The letter books of Isaac Macartney and David Butle show that, from the late 1690s, Belfast merchants were in regular contact, not only with Ballyshannon, but also with correspondents at Cork and Waterford.

When the Belfast merchants were trading in partnership with a merchant abroad the outwards cargo would be consigned to him to sell, but in ventures where none of the partners lived at the port of destination it was necessary to employ someone to sell the goods and buy the return cargo. Many merchant partnerships entrusted the sale of goods to the ship's master, or they, or the ship-owners, employed a merchant to sail with goods as supercargo. Established merchants did not normally accompany their own goods unless they combined the professions of merchant and mariner, so the supercargo was frequently a young merchant who was setting up in business on his own and who had a small share in the cargo. The voyage gave him useful experience and he received a salary and expenses. Thomas Pottinger was later to claim to have been the first Belfast merchant to go to foreign parts to trade. This claim may not have been strictly accurate, but he was the first of these young supercargoes mentioned in the Macartney letter books, when he sailed on the *Angel Gabriel* to Nevis in 1662.[29] Other young merchants mentioned in Macartney's

28 Macartney to Delap, 25 Oct. 1679 (Macartney 2, p.177).

letters are John Hamilton, who had been his apprentice, and who accompanied Macartney's goods on the *Swan* of Donaghadee to Cadiz in 1667, and James Burnie who sailed to Holland at the end of the same year as Macartney's factor because he had 'a fancy' to see the country.[30] Because no seventeenth-century merchant apprenticeship indentures have survived for Belfast it is not known whether apprentices were sent on voyages as part of their training, as was common in Scotland, but it seems very likely.[31]

The young merchants travelled for experience and possibly for adventure. Two who met with more adventure than they had anticipated were David Agnew and Hugh Lundie, both of whom had served their apprenticeship at Belfast, and who sailed to Antigua in 1666 on the *James* of Belfast with a cargo belonging to the two George Macartneys and Hugh Eccles. Before the *James* could return she was pressed by Major-General Henry Willoughby into carrying troops for the re-taking of St Kitts and was subsequently captured by the French and taken to Martinique. Although Agnew was wounded he managed to get home on another ship but Lundie was still missing a year later. The anxiety of his employers was the more acute because he had in his possession the certificate issued by Willoughby which would enable them to claim compensation from the government.[32] Although voyages gradually became both faster and safer there was a continued risk from privateers and pirates. In 1700, for example, Joseph Bigger of Belfast, then aged 24, who was travelling on the *Friendship* of Belfast, was taken prisoner by pirates who attacked and looted the ship off the coast of Virginia.[33]

On many voyages the ship's master was trusted to sell and buy for his employers[34] but if a supercargo sailed with the goods he was normally in charge of their sale and the purchase of the return cargo. Since this generally involved transactions on credit, instructions to the master or supercargo always stressed the importance of only trusting honest men and of not leaving any debts uncollected. Ideally, the whole operation should be rolled up behind them like a carpet because it was generally extremely difficult to collect debts in a foreign country. However, even an experienced

29 Benn, p.166; Macartney to Pottinger, 17 Dec. 1661, and to Lewis, 20 Feb. 1661/2 (Macartney 1, pp 35–8, 45–6).

30 Macartney to Creagh, 17 Dec. 1667 (Macartney 1, p.640).

31 Smout, *Scottish trade*, p.77; John Hamilton had been apprenticed to Macartney, and Hugh Lundie (see below) to Hugh Eccles, but it is not clear whether they were still apprentices when they sailed as supercargoes.

32 Harlow, *History of Barbados*, p.182 et seq.; Macartney to John Read, 27 Apr. 1667 (Macartney 1, pp 537–8); *Cal. S.P. Ire., 1666–69*, p.389; *Acts privy council (colonial series) 1613–80*, no.755; Lundie returned to Belfast and became a merchant of the staple in 1668 (*Town book*, p.267, printed as Lendey).

33 Deposition of Joseph Bigger (P.R.O., HCA1/26, p.14).

34 This was particularly true of voyages to Scandinavia where ships' masters chose the timber for the return cargo; Smout, *Scottish trade*, p.99; Vanhomrigh to John

captain and a competent supercargo would be instructed to take the advice
of a local merchant at their port of destination because only he could
supply them with up-to-date information about the state of the market, and
about the credit-worthiness of possible purchasers.

Many merchants preferred to consign their goods directly to a correspondent or factor at the point of sale. Although young merchants frequently sailed on ships in which Macartney had a share of the cargo, he
himself more often relied on his correspondents at the ports of destination.
A typical letter to a correspondent instructed him as follows:

> I pray you receive and dispose of all to good and honest men that will pay
> ready money or, if to time [i.e. sold on credit], to such as will pay punctual-
> ly, let them lie unsold before you deal with shuffling men.[35]

In spite of their local knowledge, Macartney's correspondents did not
always live up to his expectations. In 1679 he wrote to Robert Contales at
Ostend about a bad debt:

> I am so ashamed that such miscarriages should fall out upon me, and others
> that send little boys abroad have their concerns all secure, and that you
> living in the place should meet with such misfortune it troubles me.[36]

A code of practice for factors is revealed in the business letters of the
Belfast merchants, which applied equally to their own conduct as commission agents and to that of their factors abroad. The ideal factor should
advise his client what goods to send, sell the cargo at the best possible
price to individuals whose credit he could vouch for, and load a return
cargo of the best quality goods he could obtain. He should not load a
another cargo of similar goods for the same port if there was a chance that
they would arrive first and glut the market. He was expected to keep in
touch with the merchants who employed him, to advise them of the appro-
priate times to order goods if they were seasonal, to inform them about the
state of the markets and local conditions, and to give them as much
warning as possible about goods that would not sell. In brief, he should
handle his employer's affairs as though they were his own and act as a
friend – which was the term contemporaries normally used to describe a
correspondent abroad – preferring to lose his commission rather than have
his employer make a loss. When circumstances beyond his control led to
reduced profits, or even losses, it was important that his employer should
be satisfied that he had done his best. Macartney frequently ended his
letters to correspondents abroad 'but question not that you have done your
endeavour'. The relationship between employers and factors was usually a

Whitelock, 22 Apr. 1684 (T.C.D., Vanhomrigh letter book, MS 3961, ff 45v–46);
Macartney to Robert Holmes, 27 Apr. 1705 (Macartney 3, pp 94–5).
35　Macartney to Nicholas Lee, 10 Sept. 1680 (Macartney 2, p.333).
36　Macartney to Contales, 19 Apr. 1679 (Macartney 2, p.53).

reciprocal arrangement which lasted for years. Macartney's letter books show that he was regularly in partnership with many of his 'friends' abroad, and expected them to take as good care of his concerns as he did of theirs, although this did not always seem to him to be the case. In 1680, for example, he wrote to Contales 'If you were as forward for my good as I am for yours it would be better for me'.[37] Nevertheless he continued to deal with Contales because their trade was reciprocal and because he could count on his honesty, if not always his judgment.

Enormous care was taken in the choosing of factors abroad because the success or failure of a venture might depend on their abilities. Getting rid of an untrustworthy or inefficient factor could pose problems because it was usually difficult to get clear of him financially. For example, Isaac Macartney's correspondent in Bergen in 1704 was so unsatisfactory that Macartney declined to recommend him to anyone else but he was himself obliged to continue to employ him because there were still debts outstanding from previous ventures to Bergen. He explained this to Alexander Carstaires of Rotterdam: 'we are of your opinion that we are ill dealt by Mr Christy and if could get clear would not employ him again and do intreat the favour of you to advise on who is the fittest man to employ there'.[38] Employing an incompetent or dishonest factor could have far-reaching implications as a merchant could be asked to take responsibility for the performance of his correspondents. For example in 1684 Vanhomrigh of Dublin asked Black George Macartney to arrange a cargo of butter from Coleraine, which they would share, but wrote cautiously 'since I am a stranger to your correspondent at Coleraine I depend to be kept harmless if he should do amiss [sic] in his direction or capacity'.[39] The successful merchant needed to maintain a network of competent and trustworthy correspondents abroad. This meant not only selecting them with care but also, if the correspondence had lapsed, getting an up-to-date assessment of their credit-worthiness and abilities. In 1667, for example, Macartney wrote to Richard Huishe of Dublin asking if he had any recent correspondence with Edward Moore of La Rochelle for he intended to consign a cargo to him 'if he be as he used to be'.[40]

COMMERCIAL MORALITY

If a merchant could not believe his factor's excuses for failure, he had no alternative but to find another factor. It was therefore essential when choosing a factor, or indeed a business partner, to make careful enquiry

37 Macartney to Contales, 16 Jan. 1679/80 (Macartney 2, p.218).
38 Macartney to Carstaires, 28 Nov. 1705 (Macartney 3, pp 233–34A).
39 Vanhomrigh to Macartney, 15 July 1684 (T.C.D., Vanhomrigh letter book, MS 3961, f.85r–v).
40 Macartney to Huishe, 24 Dec. 1667 (Macartney 1, p.643).

about his reputation. Since all transactions between merchants were based upon trust, a reputation for honesty was essential for success in trade. No merchant would entrust his goods or his business to another who was unknown to him, without first making enquiries about his reputation. Merchants therefore took every opportunity to demonstrate their trust-worthiness. For example, their letter-books show the Macartneys to have been scrupulous in their dealings with other merchants, as they frequently pointed out errors in accounts in their correspondents' favour, and remind-ed their factors when they had forgotten to charge their commission. Black George's own standard was stated in a letter of 1666: 'I do not care what people say I shall do the thing what's just and shall expect the like'.[41] However, merchant letters do not make it clear whether scrupulous honesty was seen as a moral imperative or a necessary code of conduct; and although the Belfast merchants professed high standards of business mora-lity they did not always live up to them.

The careers of two merchants illustrate real rather than ideal standards. John Davies was a burgess of Belfast between 1642 and his death in 1667, although he came of a Carrickfergus merchant family and was alderman and mayor for that town. As a businessman, Davies appears to have been a pike among minnows at Carrickfergus. For example, he was said to have brought about the ruin of the merchant Joseph Harris, who 'dealt much in French wines until alderman John Davies by buying the Country Butter giving them a greater price, selling the wine he imported cheaper, and Mr Harris loosing the Ships with the Cargo ... and other losses Spoiled his trade, and reduced him and his family to low circumstances'. When Carrickfergus cor-poration received £3,000 from the crown in 1637, in payment for the sur-render of its third part of the customs, Davies was entrusted with £1,300 of this money to invest on the town's behalf, but a list of grievances dated 1659 complained 'that neither stock nor interest has been paid by any' while 'eminent men had gayned & purchased to themselves vast Estates, and the poore Sort Scarce able to feede or maintaine their families with food'. By the time of the restoration Davies had become too important for the cor-poration to bring to book. He had been a noted royalist during the Commonwealth period, and his social and economic status was confirmed by his election as knight of the shire for County Antrim in 1660. He died an extremely wealthy man, having made a fortune provisioning the army in Ulster in the 1640s, and his sons married into titled families.[42]

The second example is that of William Sloane of Belfast and London who began his career as a merchant in Black George Macartney's counting house. By 1704 Sloane had moved his trading operations to Portsmouth having left considerable debts in Ulster. Black George's son, Isaac Macartney, Sloane's friend and relation by marriage, was acting as his agent

41 Macartney to Watt, 20 Sept. 1666 (Macartney 1, pp 429–30).
42 M'Skimin, *Carrickfergus*, pp 122, 323, 341, 393–5; Lodge, *Peerage*, i, pp 150–1.

in Belfast. Macartney urged Sloane to settle his debts, stressing that this was not from self interest, because his father's name was on the list of creditors. The total owed by Sloane is uncertain; in one letter Macartney said that £1,000 would clear it, and in another he stated that Sloane was trying to raise £1,500 to £2,000. Sloane's creditors were not all merchants. For example, Mr Montgomery of Gransha had been 'an extraordinary friend' to Sloane and 'a great sufferer by it'.[43] Sloane's debts were finally paid in 1708 but it is clear from Macartney's letters that he thought Sloane was morally wrong not to settle his debts earlier, when his financial position would have allowed him to make some repayments, for although he had money tied up in a loan to Lord Donegall, he still had access to funds for investment purposes. At the same time that Macartney was urging him to settle his debts, he was also sending him details of estates in Ulster which were currently on the market. Davies and Sloane were exceptional in that they offended against contemporary standards of morality without suffering ill consequences, but neither man appears to have been overtly dishonest before becoming well established and successful. It appears therefore that while strict adherence to a code of conduct was essential for the majority of merchants, and in particular for young merchants starting in trade, the morality of the rich and successful was a reflection of their own personal standards.

In addition to a reputation for honesty and trustworthiness, it was also important for a young merchant to be 'active' or hard-working and this was usually stressed in letters of recommendation and, indeed, in letters of self-recommendation. For example, in his letters to clients, Black George frequently stressed his own diligence in handling their business. Indolence led directly to failure.[44] Honesty and hard work, however, were not enough, and certainly no guarantee of success. Macartney sometimes employed the Belfast merchant Will Biggar but felt it necessary to excuse his poor performance saying 'I will engage for his honesty but his slowness makes me ashamed';[45] and Biggar never achieved more than moderate success in trade. Honesty and hard work had to be accompanied by 'punctualness', that is speed, both in performance and in settling debts. A typical letter of recommendation, between merchants, stated in 1679 that Humphrey Jervis was 'an able, honest and punctual man in whom you may confide for a good correspondent in Dublin and able to do any business'.[46] Similarly, when John Cunningham of Liverpool asked Isaac Macartney to recommend him to the firm of Burton & Harrison of Dublin, Macartney wrote 'I have had considerable business with him in his both buying and selling goods for

---

43 Lord Mountalexander to Hans Sloane, 4 Dec. 1706 (B.L., Sloane MS 4040, f.266).
44 John Black of Bordeaux attributed his nephew's failure to his lying in bed until ten or eleven o'clock (Black to Priscilla Arbuckle, 31 May 1737 [P.R.O.N.I., Black papers, D1950/12]).
45 Macartney to Watt, 3 July 1667 (Macartney 1, p.569).
46 Macartney to Harrison, 9 May 1679 (Macartney 2, p.64).

me, and found him always just and punctual'.[47] Since Cunningham was the brother-in-law of Macartney's close friend and business associate Robert Lennox, and acted for a number of Belfast merchants, Macartney could hardly have refused to recommend him. However he was aware that punctuality was not Cunningham's strongest suit and he felt sufficiently worried to write to him by the same post entreating him to be punctual if Burton & Harrison gave him any business.

Moreover, a merchant's reputation was only as good as his last few transactions and his performance was the subject of constant scrutiny. For example, confidence in the abilities of Anthony Hall of Carrickfergus, who was eventually ruined, was declining by 1667 when Sir George Rawdon wrote 'I hear [?some] are suspicious he is not so able as he was esteemed formerly' and he advised Lord Conway to make enquiries about Hall in London.[48] Merchants were constantly asked to report on both the ability and credit of other merchants. When, in 1675, Lewis Thompson was asked about the credit and circumstances of John Clugston of Belfast, who had lost heavily when the *James* of Belfast, of which he was part-owner, was seized under the navigation acts in 1671, he warned his London correspondent 'if you be clear of him keep so and if he owes you money I cannot see any probability how it will be had'.[49] It was seen as a merchant's duty to warn correspondents when any other merchant with whom they had dealings was in trouble. Clugston's circumstances would have been well known to the whole community, but in less extreme cases the problem was to strike a balance between duty and friendship. In 1667 Macartney hinted to Thomas Hackett of Dublin that he should be careful in his dealings with John McKinney of Londonderry but, fearful that what was intended as a hint might turn into a rumour that would damage McKinney, the brother of his close friend Alexander McKinney of Nevis, he wrote in his next letter to Hackett:

> As to what I said concerning Mr McKinney [it] was only I heard trading did not do so well as formerly and he was slow in paying and so I gave you a hint to be wary but I make no doubt but he will be punctual with you for I found him very honest in what I had to do with him.[50]

The second half of the seventeenth century saw the evolution of the bill of exchange as a means of transferring credits between trading centres. The smooth running of this system depended on the honesty and 'punctualness' of all concerned. Such credit transactions between merchants were generally straightforward. Bills of exchange promised payment within a stated period. When a bill was about to fall due it was presented for payment and

47 Macartney to Burton & Harrison, 19 Jan. 1705/6 (Macartney 3, p.255).
48 Rawdon to Conway, 4 Jan. 1666/7 (P.R.O., SP.63/322, no.4).
49 Thompson to David, 6 Nov. 1675 (P.R.O., C114/76(2):6).
50 Macartney to Hackett, 12 and 22 June 1667 (Macartney 1, pp 558, 560-1).

in most cases was accepted and paid, or the term might be re-negotiated and interest charged. If it was not accepted it was protested by a formal statement before a notary public, and non-payment after acceptance could similarly be protested. A protest served as a public warning to the rest of the community that an individual was unable to pay a debt. Having a bill protested struck at the personal credit of any merchant and was to be avoided whenever possible. Merchants were careful of each other's credit and would give each other as much warning as possible of impending bills and would avoid drawing on someone who was not 'in cash', but even leading merchants occasionally had their bills protested, usually when these were part of complex transactions. Since the most important asset any merchant had was his reputation, a protest was considered extremely damaging, even when it was the result of a misunderstanding or failure to synchronise payments, and it frequently led to indignant letters and angry recriminations. If it was known that a merchant had a number of bills protested, other merchants would be reluctant to extend credit to him and his business would suffer. However, protests and debt did not inevitably lead to ruin. Robert Whiteside of Belfast, for example, had serious debts in 1681, when Macartney wrote to his creditors, 'I'll assure [you] he hath nothing and is in above £160 in debt, he was at home all this last winter and durst not come out of doors, now he's gone abroad in a ship',[51] but Whiteside recovered and continued to trade.

Since many bills were presented when merchants had no funds to meet them, all kinds of techniques were used to delay acceptance and payment without protest, to the embarrassment of the presenter of the bills. Macartney's letters reveal that evasion and prevarication were by no means unusual, and it is probable that he used the same techniques himself. Most bills between merchants, however, were paid without undue delay and protests were not common. In theory, a protest might be followed by arrest for debt, but in practice this course was seldom taken as it was recognized that imprisonment made it less likely that the defaulter would ever be in a position to pay. Rather than going to law, terms were generally negotiated privately (it being very common to 'abate' the interest if the principal could be paid, if necessary in instalments), and creditors were usually sufficiently realistic to settle for the best offer the defaulter and his friends could make.

The readiness of the merchants to negotiate sprang from a profound mistrust of the law. Although they were capable of pursuing debtors with tenacity and taking swift action to protect their interests, most merchants would have agreed with Black George Macartney that the law was a lottery.[52] Lawsuits were expensive and lawyers were seen as battening on society.[53] Disagreements between merchants were normally settled before

51 Macartney to Chandler, 14 May 1681 (Macartney 2, p.464).
52 Macartney to Allen, 15 Jan. 1680/1 (Macartney 2, p.412).
53 Barnard, 'Cork settlers', p.342.

arbitrators, and going to law to recover a debt was seen as a last resort which by no means guaranteed success, because many merchants had powerful friends to protect them. While it cannot be claimed that the Belfast merchants were less litigious than any similar group in Ireland it is certain that they entered into law suits with extreme reluctance, and Isaac Macartney might have been speaking for the whole community when he replied to a letter from Charles Campbell, a Dublin lawyer, 'I doubt not your readiness to serve me, but hopes never to be plagued with law suits which [I] shall always endeavour to avoid'.[54]

Although it is clear that high standards of commercial morality were adhered to by the Belfast merchant community through conscience, expediency, or a combination of both, these standards were not always applied in their transactions with others outside the community. In their dealings with their suppliers, the merchants' aim was to buy at the lowest possible price. Prices for provisions varied according to the demand abroad and the supply at home, the butter market being the most volatile with variations in the price throughout the season. Merchants abroad occasionally stipulated the maximum rate they would pay for butter, but generally instructed their factors to purchase at the 'ruling price current'. That price was normally reached after weeks of patient negotiation with a number of middlemen, in market towns such as Lisburn, who dealt with the suppliers. Black George Macartney impressed Sir George Rawdon with his fairness in these negotiations:

> George McCartney is so honest that he told me he could not in conscience drive [?hard] bargains beforehand, but would have them keep it, and he would give the market rates for it when it was ready ... He only factors for others, and would not have the country undone.[55]

This cannot however be the whole truth. Certainly such passive dealing would not have attracted a large clientele in Dublin, and Macartney's letters to these clients are full of tales of heroic negotiations. Richard Mildmay, one of Lord Conway's agents, gave a hostile account of these negotiations, accusing the Belfast merchants of sharp practice:

> I am often at Belfast and am now pretty well acquainted with their juntoes and counsels about beating down the price of butter, in the beginning of the season of the year, for the last two years past, I was straitened for money and was forced to put hard on your tenants for supplies, so that some were forced to sell their butter for 16s ... I have not been pressed for money this year and therefore have given the tenants notice from time to time of all the false reports dispersed from the merchants of Belfast as of war with France,

54 Macartney to Campbell, 14 Jan. 1705/6 (Macartney 3, p.254).
55 Rawdon to Conway, 28 Mar. 1674 (P.R.O., SP.63/335, no.54).

embargoes of their ships, that they would buy no butter this year, etc., and now they are forced to buy and to give 23 or 24s per hundred to begin with, which is of great advantage to this country, for it is the only commodity that brings money, and the quantity that is vented at Belfast is almost incredible.[56]

While there is no direct evidence, apart from this letter, that the merchants deliberately misled the suppliers, it is certainly true that they did their best to stop merchants from London and Dublin from dealing directly with the suppliers as the high prices offered by outsiders generally had the effect of raising the market rate. On one occasion Macartney and three other merchants got together 30 tons of butter for a visiting Londoner to stop him dealing directly with the butter merchants and raising the price for everyone else.

It was in their dealings with the collectors of revenue that the departure of the merchants from their code of commercial morality was most marked. It was felt to be the responsibility of the customs officials to collect the revenue rather than that of the merchants to proffer it. Since the complexity of the laws governing imports and exports made possible genuine mistakes on the part of the merchants, the penalties for evasion were not necessarily severe and did not serve as much of a deterrent. There is sufficient evidence in the Macartney letter books to show that a degree of evasion of duty on exports was routine. Ships normally carried more goods than the quantities entered at the customhouse and as it was difficult to check the full lading of a large ship the customs officials either failed to notice, or were prepared to connive at any disparity. Occasionally the merchants were too greedy. In 1661, for example, William Smith made the entry at the customhouse for a whole cargo, as he had the greatest share, but entered so short that the discrepancy was obvious and 550 firkins of butter were seized. As a result, Macartney was obliged to explain to clients in Dublin that for the time being he and his partners were having to enter everything, making it clear that this was not their usual practice.[57] Similarly, goods of all kinds entering the port were concealed from the customs men. In 1666, for example, soap was being brought in from Scotland under coals thus escaping the duty and underselling supplies in Belfast. Many cargoes by-passed the customhouse altogether and were landed along the Antrim coast. Macartney himself was involved in some illegal shipments but it is difficult to estimate how far the merchant community was involved in outright smuggling as naturally enough little evidence has survived. Certainly smuggling was widespread and increased in the eighteenth century so it is likely that Belfast merchants regularly by-

---

56 Mildmay to Conway, 4 July 1677 (P.R.O., SP.63/336, no.67).
57 Macartney to Alderman Ridge, 12 Nov. 1661, and to Thomas Lewis, 25 Nov. 1661 (Macartney 1, pp 24–5, 26–7).

passed the customs although commodities such as wine would have been difficult to sell on a large scale without proof that duty had been paid.[58]

The use of false papers and passes by the Belfast merchants and their widescale evasion of the effects of the navigation acts has been discussed in chapter 5. Their expertise was also shared with trading partners in Europe. For example, in 1706, Isaac Macartney wrote to Matthew Prosser, who operated in Bruges and Rotterdam, that he would take a quarter share in a cargo of wine, brandy, rosin and vinegar from France, and recommended that Prosser should 'get a dutch pass ... to save her from the biscayers but when she comes to this side to discharge she must be called a ship belonging either to England or Ireland to save the paying foreign duty'.[59] Macartney was an elder of the presbyterian church, with a reputation for honesty and trustworthiness in all his business dealings. His advice to Prosser did not represent a breach of his code of conduct because it is clear that he saw no moral difference between deceiving pirates and deceiving customs officials.

PROFIT AND LOSS, SUCCESS AND FAILURE

The Belfast merchants' income from trade was derived from profits on shares in trading ventures and from ship-owning, and from commission paid on goods which they loaded or sold for merchants in other ports. It is extremely difficult to calculate profits from the surviving letter books. Profits on outgoing cargoes were not generally remitted home but used to purchase the return cargoes and there is little information in the merchant letter books about the sale of return cargoes even when the merchant was working on commission. Even where detailed account books have survived, seventeenth-century rates of profit are difficult to determine because it is normally impossible to calculate overheads. Nevertheless, it is possible to make some generalisations on rates of profit based on contemporary sources other than accounts. For example it can be assumed that investment in trade was expected to bring in more than the normal lending rate in Ireland. This was nominally 10% in the second half of the seventeenth century although from the 1680s it was possible to borrow money at 8% on reasonable security. Contemporary economists agreed that the high rate of interest compared with that in England (6%) and in Holland (3%) had a detrimental effect on Irish trade, and that the rate in Ireland encouraged those with capital to be usurers rather than merchants.[60] This suggests that the annual return on investment in trade sometimes failed to reach 10% or

58 L.M. Cullen, 'The smuggling trade in Ireland in the eighteenth century' in *R.I.A. Proc.*, lxvii, sect. C, pp 149–50.

59 Macartney to Prosser, 2 Mar. 1705/6 (Macartney 3, pp 280–1).

60 Lawrence, *Interest of Ireland*, pt 1, p.7, pt 2, p.13; Petty, *Political anatomy*, p.127.

was so little above it as not to justify the risk and effort involved. In England, profits of between 6% and 25% on individual trading ventures were normal, with a probable average of 6%–12%.[61] Although nothing is known about the profit levels achieved by the wealthiest Belfast merchants in this period, clues about expection of profit on individual voyages are provided by correspondence about insurance rates. In times of war insurance rates soared, and the level at which they became unacceptable to the merchants is some indication of the profit levels anticipated. George Macartney was prepared to pay a premium of 10–16% on a cargo to Barbados and Antigua in 1666 but thought that 40%, which Daniel Arthur was quoting, was far too high. However he nowhere stated that it would wipe out his entire profit on the voyage. Since Macartney can be assumed to have been making at least 8–10% on top of insurance, these figures suggests a profit level on transatlantic voyages of at least 40% to 50% and possibly more. The round trip to the West Indies generally took about nine months, so the level of profit expected on those voyages would have been higher than on voyages to Europe which afforded a quicker return on capital laid out and the opportunity to reinvest in the same season.

There are a few accounts in the second Macartney letter book for European ventures in the 1670s, including sales of wine, which show modest profits of between about £3 and £114 per voyage, but also losses on the same scale. However European trade could be very profitable when conditions were favourable. For example, in 1679 Black George wrote to Jervis that it was unfortunate that delays had prevented their ship the *Dublin Merchant* from going to Cadiz as 'Thomas Pottinger will make £1,000 profit this voyage and had but a small stock out'.[62] Even allowing for some exaggeration of the profitability of a lost opportunity, Macartney seems to be suggesting a profit level well in excess of 50%, although his figure may only have meant the profit on the goods sold without taking freight charges and other overheads into account. There is even less information available as to profits of trade with England and Scotland. However, since the surviving port books for the west coast ports of England and Scotland contain few references either to the largest ships belonging to Belfast or to the wealthiest merchants it seems likely that profit levels were modest and that such merchants made their money by trading voyages to Europe and the New World.

A substantial part of the income from trade of all the Belfast merchants came from commissions, paid at the rate of 2½%. Since merchant letters contain details of the value of goods loaded, it is possible to calculate what individual merchants earned as factors for individual ventures. For example, Thomas Owen of Belfast twice loaded £900 worth of goods for a

61 Grassby, 'Rate of profit', pp 728–33.
62 Macartney to Jervis, 1 Mar. 1678/9 (Macartney 2, p.31).

single client in 1668–69 which would have earned him £44 10s, and a cargo
of beef and butter loaded by Macartney for Dehulter & Vanhomrigh of
Amsterdam cost £2,124 19s 4d, so would have brought him slightly over
£53 in commission.[63] Since Macartney was acting as factor for at least six
of the leading Dublin merchants from the 1660s, this must have generated
a considerable income but although his commission can be calculated for
many ventures, it is not possible to say how much of this was actual profit
since it is impossible to estimate his overheads.

Profits from ship-owning are also hard to calculate. Although Belfast
merchants may have purchased shares in ships in order to carry their own
goods, they also expected to make a regular profit from freighting to others.
Rates for freight were fairly stable in the seventeenth century, except in
times of war, although they were to decline sharply from the beginning of
the eighteenth century. Ships could be acquired cheaply. A new flyboat of
300 tons burden cost £800–£1,000 in 1684[64] but most trading vessels were
considerably smaller and could be acquired second hand; for example, Black
George Macartney reckoned that the *Angel Gabriel* (65–70 tons) was worth
£400 in 1665.[65] With luck, ships could last for at least 20 years; several of
the ships which appear in the list of Belfast shipping of c.1661 are also in
the list for the 1680s. This may not always have been an advantage as the
Belfast ships of 1661 would have been expensive to run in view of the ratio
of men to tonnage. The ships in the earlier list, excluding the gabarts,
carried one man to every 5.1 tons. There was a decreasing ratio of men to
tonnage on trading ships in the second half of the seventeenth century
which is attributed partly to the use of Dutch prizes – the flyboats which
needed smaller crews in relation to their cargo – and partly to subsequent
improvement in the design of English ships. Ralph Davis gives figures for
men per ton for London ships in 1686 showing that even the most heavily
manned ships trading to Spain and Portugal had a ratio of one man to 7.9
tons of cargo, and ratios of one man to 9.3 to 9.8 tons were achieved on
ships trading to the New World.[66] It would be difficult for the owner of a
heavily manned ship to offer competitive rates for freight as seamen's wages
were the largest element within the freight charge.

Against the income from freight had to be set not only the wages of the
crew, but the expenses of regular re-fitting and repairs. A good example of
such expenditure appears in the second Macartney letter book. Macartney
had a share in the *Dublin Merchant*, a ship of 200 tons, with 16 guns and
22 men, in partnership with Captain Edward Tarleton, a ship's master

63 Owen to Marescoe, 19 Apr., 1 June 1669 (P.R.O., Marescoe David, C114, tempo-
    rary box D, bundle 3, C114/74(1):1); Macartney to Dehulter & Vanhomrigh,
    23 Aug. 1680 (Macartney 2, p.313).
64 Vanhomrigh to Lionel Herne, 14 Feb. 1683/4 (T.C.D., Vanhomrigh letter book,
    MS 3961, f.16).
65 Macartney to Arthur, 14 July 1665 (Macartney 1, pp 201–2).
66 Davis, *English shipping industry*, p.59.

from Liverpool, and Alderman Humphrey Jervis, and others, of Dublin. His share in this ship appears to have been an investment rather than a means of extending his own trade. The *Dublin Merchant* was principally employed in trade to France and Spain, although like most Irish ships at that time she carried goods to a variety of destinations as the partners thought fit. At the end of 1679 she brought a cargo to London from the West Indies, and delayed there trying to pick up freight. Even though she was efficiently manned, at a ratio of one man to just under 9.1 tons, the wages of the crew and other expenses mounted up alarmingly and Macartney wrote to Jervis 'her long stay at London eats up all so that we cannot expect much to remain to be divided'. His share of the profits (which is not specified) was further reduced by the cost of re-fitting. This, by current standards, does not seem to have been excessive but Macartney wrote 'its admiration to me that so much money can be spent as £1,015', although having worked through the account in detail he was unable to object to a single item.[67] Ralph Davis estimates that the earnings of a normal English ship in peacetime, in the 1680s, was £5 per ton per annum.[68] It is not possible to make even a rough estimate of Macartney's income from shipping as the Belfast shipping lists do not distinguish between the two George Macartneys. However, James Chalmers of Belfast owned approximately 90 tons in shares in four Belfast ships in the mid-1670s so he could have had an income from ship-owning of £450 p.a. He may also, like Macartney, have had shares in ships outside Belfast. Merchant investment in shipping therefore was both convenient and profitable even though the rate of profit frequently fell below expectation. It also carried a high level of risk for those at the start of their careers who were unable to balance losses against profits. For example, John Clugston the younger of Belfast was a part owner, in 1671, of the *James* of Belfast, but did not, as far as is known, have shares in any other vessel. His fortunes never recovered from the seizure of the *James* in the West Indies,[69] for in 1675 his estate and reputation were 'both very low in esteem with the most that know him for he hath been out of credit, stock and trade these four years' and was in hiding from his creditors.[70]

The successful merchant was one who spread risks by taking shares in cargoes and ships and who could thus absorb the impact of losses and other disasters. Only merchants operating on a large scale could afford small profits. It was usually easier to stay rich than to become rich, but even the wealthiest merchants could occasionally fail. For example, Anthony Hall, mayor of Carrickfergus in 1665, was 'a merchant of good Account, and lived many Years in this Towne, till brocken by bad servents and misfortunes at Sea, to the loss of Great numbers of people that he had money

---

67 Macartney to Jervis, 30 Apr., 29 June 1680 (Macartney 2, pp 244, 277).
68 Davis, *English shipping industry*, p.389.
69 See chapter 5.
70 Thompson to David, 6 Nov. 1675 (P.R.O., C114/76(2):6).

from on Interest'.[71] Reliance on bad servants implies inattention to business and this charge is levied at Isaac Macartney who went under in the 1730s. Macartney's débâcle owed much to his involvement in the affairs of his brother-in-law John Haltridge, but probably also to his generosity and opulent lifestyle. Macartney's contemporary, Robert Gardner of Carrick-fergus, was of a very similar character, 'a man of great hospitality, doing many offices of sincere friendship to all those that made application to him', but after many successful years as an agent in London, he became involved in the South Sea Bubble 'losing then the most of all he had, so that he died in low circumstances, and his affairs very much encumbered'.[72] Although honesty, hard work and 'punctualness' could lead to success, success itself could become a distraction and lead to ruin.

The majority of unsuccessful merchants however had never succeeded in becoming rich. Although bad luck was seen as contributing to failure it was never thought to be the sole cause. There is very little information about unsuccessful merchants, most of whom sank without trace, but what there is follows a common pattern. For example, Archibald Little became a freeman of Belfast in 1678 but was in financial difficulties two years later: 'some ventures he sent out is not returned and he hath a deal of goods in the shop which he cannot make money of'.[73] In the same year, James Biggar was forced to make over a lease of property in Belfast to his creditors, who were mainly his kinsmen, being unable to pay his debts 'by reason of many debts are owing unto me'.[74] In 1706, Isaac Macartney wrote: '[Thomas] Erwin is an honest man but constantly pinched by over trading himself in this country where no money is stirring for any manner of goods'.[75] A combination of unsold merchandise and unpaid debts could tie up a merchant's capital so that he was unable to pay his own creditors and could lead to financial ruin.

Although originally operating as commission agents, the Belfast merchants increasingly traded on their own accounts in the second half of the seventeenth century. All trade was handled by partnerships, generally lasting for a single voyage, and the town's shipping was also owned by merchant partnerships. Trading in several partnerships simultaneously spread risks. The necessary ingredients for success were seen as honesty, hard work and 'punctualness'. Reasons for failure were more complex. Spectacular financial débâcles were generally attributed to inattention to business. Failures of minor merchants were caused by debts to suppliers, because money owing could not be collected, and capital was tied up in unsold goods. Cash flow, credit and debt, and their effects on the Belfast merchants, will be discussed in the next chapter.

71 M'Skimin, *Carrickfergus*, p.323
72 M'Skimin, *Carrickfergus*, p.146n.
73 Macartney to Allen Wilkinson, 29 Dec. 1680 (Macartney 2, p.407).
74 *Town book*, p.140.
75 Macartney to Galbraith, 8 June 1706 (Macartney 3, p.319).

Cash and Credit

Although by the middle of the seventeenth century it was still quite normal for a merchant to entrust a ship's master with a large sum in cash to lay out in the purchase of goods on his arrival at his port of destination, the possibility of capture or looting by privateers, and the prospect of recovering only a fraction of such loss through insurance, combined to make transactions on credit attractive to merchants. Whererever possible, Irish merchants traded both ways, the return cargo being purchased with the proceeds of the sale of the outward cargo. Purchasers, however, generally demanded credit, and, increasingly, the return cargo was not purchased at the point of sale. Two-way trading would therefore have been impossible without a system of buying and selling on credit. Bills of exchange promising payment within a stated period became the standard method of payment in most transactions, so much so that by the end of the century the purchaser with cash thought himself entitled to a considerable discount. Even purchasers on credit could expect the price to vary according to the length of time allowed for payment, the seller usually being willing to reduce the price if his need was pressing.

Promissory notes and bonds of all sorts had long been common between merchants but the bill of exchange, as it evolved in the seventeenth century, was negotiable; that is, it could be endorsed by the payee and used by him to settle another debt. Where the debt was owed to a creditor at another trading centre, the bill could be exchanged for one which was payable there. Bills of exchange therefore allowed the exchange of debits and credits between centres of commerce by a system which was both complex and flexible. Provincial centres benefitted by these credit dealings. The earliest reference to a Belfast merchant using bills of exchange dates from 1629 and concerns Lewis Thompson (as Louijs Tomas) drawing bills on Amsterdam merchants.[1] Thompson/Tomas, however, was a Dutchman and is not therefore representative of the Belfast community at that date.

---

1 Statement of Cornelius Pietersz Werden, 23 Oct. 1631 (Municipal Archives,

There is little information surviving about Belfast trade for the next thirty years but by the 1660s bills of exchange were in frequent use and are mentioned throughout the first Macartney letter book. The provisions trade from Belfast was largely financed from London and Dublin, often with Belfast merchants taking a share in the cargoes. The latter took advantage of the sophisticated arrangements for payments by credit to which their partners were accustomed and, when trading on their own accounts, used the same network of correspondents to arrange the exchange of bills in London and Dublin.

Black George Macartney was a frequent correspondent and partner of Daniel Arthur of London. Arthur, an Irishman in his forties in the 1660s, was by then a leading banker with dealings with most of the Irish aristocracy. He also acted as banker for many of the leading Dublin merchants. The first two Macartney letter books document a business relationship lasting at least twenty years which survived Arthur's presumed involvement in the Popish Plot and his subsequent retreat to Paris.[2] Arthur eventually became permanently resident in Paris where he acted as banker for the Irish Jacobites, but even in the early 1700s Isaac Macartney still had occasional correspondence with him. In Dublin, Black George had dealings with the bankers Elnathan Lumm and Abel Ram and with merchants who specialised in the handling of bills of exchange. The Macartney letter books also throw a certain amount of light on the contacts and activities of other Belfast merchants, making it clear that they too had correspondents in London and Dublin. The provisions trade therefore provided the merchant community of Belfast with the infrastructure necessary to facilitate the change to trading on credit.

The change to a credit system was gradual. In the 1660s, the use of bills of exchange varied according to the hazards to be encountered at sea. For example, in time of war in 1665, Macartney was angry with the master of the *Angel Gabriel* for bringing cash home with him from Cadiz because he could not get any bills, but two years later, in peacetime, he instructed the supercargo on the *Swan* of Donaghadee that if he sold his cargo for more than he needed to buy sherry, malaga wine, raisins, olives, oranges and lemons at Cadiz, he was to bring the surplus home in 'good plate cobs'.[3] 'Trucking', or trading goods for goods, was often preferred for simple transactions and remained customary in the West Indies.

Amsterdam, Not. Arch. 842, notaris J.C. Hoogeboom); I am indebted to Rolf Loeber for this reference.

2 Macartney to John Hodson, 12 Feb. 1679/80, to William Squyre, 6 July 1680 (Macartney 2, pp 21, 281); *Ormonde MSS*, (NS), iv, p.475; *Ormonde MSS*, ii, p.255; petition of Sir Daniel Arthur (P.R.O.N.I., Annesley MSS, petitions to parliament, 1701–04, D1854/2/20, f.124); A.E. Murphy, 'Richard Cantillon, an Irish banker in Paris' in Murphy, *Economists and the Irish economy*, pp 46–8.

3 Macartney to Arthur, 3 May 1665, to Hamilton, 16 Oct. 1667 (Macartney 1, pp 174, 609); a plate cob was a Spanish-American eight reale piece.

Manufactured goods too could be trucked. Macartney stated in a letter to Joshua Allen that before the navigation acts they had been able to exchange drugget at 16–18lb of sugar or tobacco per yard in the Leeward Isles.[4]

However the first two Macartney letter books make it clear that the merchant community at Belfast was regularly using bills of exchange from the 1660s, although the volume of bills through Belfast was frequently inadequate and some merchants resorted to entrusting money to cattle drovers to remit to London. By the 1680s almost all Macartney's remittances were made by bills of exchange and he took full advantage of the flexibility of the system. Prices of goods were negotiable in direct relation to the length of credit allowed, and as circumstances changed bills were discounted, using the term in its loosest sense to describe the sale of bills at less than their face value in return for speedy payment. They were not only used for merchant transactions abroad. The insufficient supply of specie at home, which circulated in fits and starts, and the hazards of transporting large sums in cash, combined to make bills of exchange the most attractive method of inland remittance.

In spite of the participation of all the leading Belfast merchants the system did not work smoothly. Trade at Belfast was seasonal and so was the supply of bills. The limitations of the system, and also the extent of George Macartney's credit dealings, are revealed in a letter of 1680 to Elnathan Lumm, in which he wrote 'I can get no bills for Holland, Flanders nor France, neither for London, our country goods have not sold well abroad so little money returned yet but goods'.[5] There was generally a dead period, lasting several months, from the beginning of the year when the last of the provisions had been exported. In January 1680, Macartney explained to a correspondent in Dublin: 'trade is now over upon a sudden and none can draw [i.e. on Dublin] and their effects being unsold they cannot draw for London'.[6] In addition to seasonal variations, the market in bills between Ireland and London depended to some extent on the rate of exchange between England and Ireland which was affected by external events such as war, plague, and the imposition and lapsing of the cattle acts, and these fluctuations of the exchange rate were monitored anxiously. Although most credit transactions with London went via Dublin, it was possible to remit money directly between Belfast and London, and Belfast was probably the only provincial town, apart from Cork, to develop an independent bill trade with London in this period.[7] The rate of exchange was slightly higher between London and Belfast than London and Dublin.[8]

4 Macartney to Allen, 22 June 1667 (Macartney 1, pp 561–2).
5 Macartney to Lumm, 16 Nov. 1680 (Macartney 2, p.389).
6 Macartney to Owen Price, 3 Jan. 1679/80 (Macartney 2, p.215).
7 Macartney to Price, 11 Oct. 1679 (Macartney 2, p.162); Dickson, 'The place of Dublin in the eighteenth century Irish economy', p.184.
8 For example, it was 11% as opposed to 9½% in 1683 (*Cal. S.P. dom., 1683 Jan.–June*, p.224).

This was reflected by an inland exchange rate between Belfast and Dublin which was also subject to seasonal fluctuations.

Although bills of exchange were in widespread use in Belfast by the 1680s, some cash payments, and even trading goods for goods, continued into the eighteenth century. As late as 1705, it was possible for a Glasgow merchant of substance to write 'I abhorred to send a Ship in her Ballast to purchase Goods on Credit, which hath destroyed many unthinking men, when Bills of Exchange has come upon them like a Thunder-Clap, although I confess at times it cannot be evited'.[9] However, bills of exchange and promissory notes were made both safer and easier to use by some major legal changes in the late seventeenth and early eighteenth centuries which encouraged their adoption by the more conservative merchants, and in the same period facilities were expanded for the clearing of international payments.[10] Surviving sources suggest that by the early 1700s, virtually all Belfast trade was financed by bills of exchange with remittances going through London. David Butle, who was trading on a smaller scale than the Macartneys, was using bills of exchange in the 1690s, and for trade with the West Indies he used letters of credit from the Cairnes brothers in London.

However, Butle seems normally to have paid cash for goods from Scotland and only suggested using bills of exchange in 1696 when guineas temporarily commanded a higher price in Ireland and would thus have lost value if exported. Since the method of payment he set up involved an agent in Scotland drawing on his and his partners' bankers in London it appears that, in spite of the close links between Belfast and Scotland, it was not easy to remit money there by bill of exchange. In the 1660s, George Macartney had had problems remitting money to Scotland, and in 1667, he advised a correspondent in Dublin 'I can give no bills for Edinburgh neither is there any man here that can do it. If you order your money to London you may draw to Edinburgh and get good exchange'.[11] So little Scottish trade is recorded in the first two Macartney letter books that it is not possible to document merchant remittances from Belfast to Scotland until the period covered by Butle's letter book in the 1690s. In the next decade Isaac Macartney was able to remit money to Scotland and to draw on a correspondent in Edinburgh, but even so, bills were not always available and it could be more advantageous for Macartney's correspondent to

---

9 John Spreul, *An accompt current betwixt Scotland and England* (Glasgow, 1882), p.49, quoted in Smout, *Scottish trade*, p.117.

10 J. Milnes Holden, *The history of negotiable instruments in English law* (London, 1955), pp 30, 33, 47–8, 54; same, 'Bills of exchange during the seventeenth century' in *Law Quarterly Review*, lxvii (1951), pp 232–6, 247–8; J. Sperling, 'The international payments mechanism in the seventeenth and eigththeenth centuries' in *Econ. Hist. Rev.*, 2nd series, xiv (1961–2), p.468.

11 Macartney to Rowan, 21 Jan. 1665/6, to Huishe, 20 July 1667 (Macartney 1, pp 317, 576).

draw on his bankers in London. Macartney's bills of exchange appear to have been remittances for the gentry rather than merchant transactions and his business dealings in Scotland were normally on a cash basis. As he explained to the Dublin bankers Burton & Harrison in 1704, 'no trade here from England, what little trade we have is from Scotland and the money is brought over in specia'.[12] So, although the use of bills of exchange for external trade was common in Scotland, it seems that there was no regular flow of bills directly between Scotland and Ulster and that merchants in both countries dealt through correspondents in London.

Apart from their dealings with Scotland, Macartney and his various partners were accustomed to organising credit payments for complex transactions but there could still be problems in obtaining bills when required at Belfast, particularly at the end of the winter. As trade had become less sharply seasonal delays in obtaining bills were usually short, but the underlying problem in the early 1700s was the reduction of trade, largely as a result of the war of the Spanish succession. As Isaac Macartney wrote to William Cairnes, the Dublin banker, in 1706, 'Its purely the decay of trade that makes so little drawing or remitting from hence, if doth not mend I believe half our town will be forced to leave this place if knew where to go'.[13] By the end of the seventeenth century, bills of exchange had become the standard method of financing most business transactions, but in spite of the readiness of the Belfast merchants to trade on credit wherever possible, it is apparent that even when trading conditions were favourable the volume of trade at Belfast was insufficient to support the system throughout the year.

SPECIE AND CASH FLOW IN IRELAND

Throughout the seventeenth century there was normally a shortage of specie in Ireland. Contemporaries usually attributed this to the outward flow to England of the rents of Irish estates, but although the drain on the Irish economy was severe, with an estimated £100,000 p.a. being spent in England, it is probable that only a small proportion of this sum was exported as bullion, as the gentry normally remitted their money by bills of exchange.[14] Export of rents in cash may have contributed to the shortage of specie in Ireland, but shortages also occurred in England and Scotland and the principal cause was that insufficient coins were minted. From the 1650s

---

12 Macartney to William Blackburn, 15 Jan. 1704/5, to Burton & Harrison, 22 Nov. 1704 (Macartney 3, pp 16, 38–9).
13 Macartney to Cairnes, 9 Feb. 1705/6 (Macartney 3, p.265).
14 Petty, *Political anatomy*, p.127; *Discourse concerning Ireland*, p.9; Michael MacCarthy-Morrogh, 'Credit and remittance: monetary problems in early seventeenth century Munster' in *I.E.S.H.*, xiv (1987), p.12.

12 Trade tokens of William Smith, 1657, John Steward or Stewart, 1656, and Robert Whiteside, 1667, about twice actual size. The ship and the bell are parts of the arms of Belfast.

to 1680 there was an acute shortage of small denomination coins in Ireland, which need was met by the issue of tokens of brass or copper, generally for the value of one penny, by individual merchants and tradesmen. The issue of tokens not only solved the problem of the shortage of small change but their production, at a fraction of their face value, may have been a form of speculation by the issuers and may, to some extent, have created their own demand. In Belfast, virtually all such tokens were issued by the leading merchants of the town rather than by tradesmen or retailers.[15] In 1680, a mint was established at Dublin which produced copper halfpence, ending the need for tokens, but was not allowed to strike coins in precious metals. Political upheavals from 1685 led to an outflow of cash. This was reversed for a short period from 1696 when coin commanded a higher price in Ireland than in England and guineas poured into Ireland, but silver and gold coins remained in short supply, even though augmented by foreign coins which circulated freely.

In the early 1700s, the recession led to the hoarding of gold and silver coins but there was an abundance of small denomination coins in circulation which led to problems when payments were made in cash. Isaac Macartney regularly presented bills of exchange to the collectors of the revenue on behalf of the Dublin bankers Burton & Harrison. Since the collectors received most of their revenue in brass halfpence they insisted on giving these to Macartney rather than silver. Macartney's reluctance to accept brass arose not so much from any expressed dislike of brass money *per se*, but rather from the expense of transporting to Dublin large sums in halfpence, and when entreaties to the collectors to pay in silver failed, he resorted to subterfuge and even bribery. But although constantly bemoaning the shortage of specie of all kinds (except halfpence) Macartney was himself contributing to that shortage. Throughout the period covered by the third letter book (1704–06) he was steadily buying up dollars, ducats and ducatoons, which circulated freely in Ireland, and sending them at the rate of several hundred pounds worth a year to Daniel Hays of London[16] who was probably supplying bullion for the East Indies trade. Macartney summed up the situation as regards the flow of specie in Ulster in 1705 when he wrote to Hays:

> all sorts of species are very scarce here that its a rare matter to see a dollar, ducatoon or plait cobe, not one to be had but what is in rich grubbs' hands

15 George C. Williamson, *Trade tokens issued in the seventeenth century in England, Wales and Ireland by corporations, merchants, tradesmen, etc.* (2 vols, London, 1889–91), ii, pp 1360–2; at least twelve of the thirty-two Belfast merchants in appendix A issued trade tokens; Robert Heslip, 'Lisburn seventeenth century tokens' in *Lisburn Historical Society Journal*, vi (1986), pp 7–10; I am indebted to Robert Heslip for advice on this section.

16 Daniel Hays was a Frenchman and a former alderman of Dublin who had moved to London in 1694 (Dublin Corporation Archives, Monday book, i, 1658–1712, ff 126A, 133A).

> who will not part with them without the highest allowance that has been given ... and some will choose to keep them another year expecting their rise.[17]

The perpetual shortage of specie was solved to some extent by the use of bills of exchange, but all provisions exported had ultimately to be paid for in cash. The existence of a class of middlemen in the butter trade made it possible for merchants to make stage payments for butter using bills, and some payments were made in advance, amounting to short term loans. The middlemen however had to find specie to pay the 'country people' (i.e. the actual producers) and so they usually demanded part payment in cash. Since Belfast merchants were frequently buying on commission for merchants in Dublin, it was often necessary for the latter to send bullion to Belfast, although this could be a risky undertaking. For example, in September 1679, Black George explained his delay in sending butter to Peter Cossart of Rouen, thus:

> I cannot get the money from Dublin by exchange and I dare not hazard to bring it by land for fear of tories which puts me to a strait as none will part with butter and tallow without ready money.[18]

At other times there was money in Belfast which had to be transported to Dublin. The cost of transporting cash by land varied according to its destination. For example, in 1666 Black George offered to fetch some cash from Londonderry to Belfast for the Dublin merchant Thomas Hackett, writing 'if you are pleased I will send a man and a horse for it, it will not cost above 16s to bring it hither and there is no danger by land at all for this is a very peaceable country'.[19] However it was far more expensive to send money between Belfast and Dublin where the country was less peaceable and, for most of the seventeenth century, an armed escort was considered necessary. To reduce costs, Macartney sometimes only hired an escort for the most dangerous section of the journey which lay between Newry and Dundalk, or he delayed until he could send it in convoy with some member of the gentry who was travelling to Dublin. Even in the early 1700s when the danger of highway robbery was much reduced, Isaac Macartney only used a carrier to collect cash in Coleraine and Londonderry when he was unable to remit the money in bills because it was so expensive.

    The problem of highway robbery, although serious, could be dealt with by sending bullion with an armed escort. A less serious problem, but one which it seemed impossible to solve, was that however carefully the money was counted, packed and sealed, it was frequently found to be short when the bags were opened at their destination. The sums involved were general-

17 Macartney to Hays, 22 Oct. 1705 (Macartney 3, p.214).
18 Macartney to Cossart, 30 Sept. 1679 (Macartney 2, p.160).
19 Macartney to Hackett, 2 June 1662 (Macartney 1, p.367).

ly small. For example, in 1679, the sum of £800 which Black George sent to Robert Bridges of Dublin was found to be 3s 3d short on arrival 'which I much admire being [sic] I first counted it over myself and two after me and found it right' and, in 1681, £3 was found to be missing from a sum sent to Abel Ram of Dublin, although Macartney wrote 'I'll assure you I never was so careful in counting money as in this'.[20] Twenty-five years later Isaac Macartney was still having much the same problem and writing in identical terms. All kinds of devices were used to disguise the containers which held cash and to conceal from the escort what they were carrying but nothing seems to have prevented the pilfering of small sums, and in these circumstances, the merchant who sent the money had no alternative but to make good the shortfall. Since the sums stolen were usually trifling they probably amounted to less than the commission which would have been charged to remit the money by bills of exchange but, added to the costs of actually sending the money by land, they constituted an unwelcome charge which merchants were determined to avoid wherever possible.

However erratic the flow of specie around Ireland might be throughout the seventeenth century, it followed a predictable course. As Bishop King wrote, 'most of the current Coyn in the Kingdom came into the Treasury once in a year'.[21] Merchants therefore could tap this flow of cash as it came into the hands of the local collectors of revenue. The Macartney letter books record a stream of bills of exchange from Dublin merchants to be presented to the local collectors but, since these collectors too had some problems with cash flow, it was not always easy to get these bills accepted. Macartney's letters in the 1660s document his dealings with a particularly elusive customs official at Carrickfergus which led him to advise a Dublin correspondent to 'meddle with no Excise man for they are nought', although he had dealings with customs officials in the 1670s.[22] In the early 1700s, Isaac Macartney also had problems in his dealings with the collectors, as described above, but these problems did not usually include getting the bills accepted in the first place.

MERCHANTS AND GENTRY

The other predictable element in the flow of cash around the country was the payment of rents every May Day and All Saints with the subsequent demand by the gentry to remit this money to Dublin or London by bills of exchange. As far as remittances were concerned, merchants and gentry had

20 Macartney to Bridges, 5 Mar. 1678/9, to Ram, 12 Feb. 1680/1 (Macartney 2, pp 32, 426).
21 King, *State of the protestants*, p.97.
22 Macartney to Allen, 3 July 1667, to Hackett, 17 Dec. 1667 (Macartney 1, pp 567, 639).

a symbiotic relationship. The gentry had cash in Ulster and needed it in Dublin or London. The merchants had credit in Dublin and London from the sale of their goods but needed cash at home. Without the regular flow of gentry remittances to England and to Dublin it would have been difficult for the Belfast merchants to finance most of their ventures through bills of exchange. However since the gentry were also both creditors and customers of the merchants, most financial transactions between gentry and merchants were extremely complex and it is not always possible to distinguish the different elements.

The simplest form of transaction between merchants and gentry was the remittance of money, the merchant at Belfast giving a bill drawn on a correspondent in Dublin or London in return for cash. When remitting money to London the gentry took as keen an interest in fluctuations in the exchange rate as any merchant. Sir George Rawdon's letters to Lord Conway constantly note its rise and fall. This general awareness of the exchange on the part of the gentry could affect the flow of money to England. In 1679, for example, the lapsing of the ban on live cattle exports was expected to lead to a fall in the exchange rate and the gentry were unwilling to remit until this happened. Macartney explained to Edmund Harrison that he had

> sent to all the gentry abroad to see if they would remit any money to London but since the proroguing of the parliament and the rumour of cattle going over they expect exchange to fall to nothing so all wait for the opportunity of the time and will give no exchange.[23]

As expected the exchange rate fell steadily until the autumn of the following year. Fluctuations in the rate of exchange, and the difference in the rates of interest in England and Ireland,[24] meant that it was possible to make money grow simply by moving it about. Such money dealing was explained to Sir George Rawdon by the merchant Humphrey Jervis with whom he frequently stayed when he was in Dublin:

> Mr Jervis and I have been speaking of exchanging money between England and Ireland, and I think it demonstrable that any that has money at interest may make above 20% per annum by that traffic without any danger of loss, if there be a stock of [£]9,000 or 10,000.[25]

When remitting money, Rawdon dealt principally with Black George Macartney who seems to have offered very competitive rates, but he also had dealings with the Dutch merchant Cornelis van Weede, who was living

23 Macartney to Harrison, 14 June 1679 Macartney 2, p.83).
24 6% in England and 10% in Ireland until 1704.
25 Rawdon to Conway, 6 Dec. 1673 (*Cal. S.P. dom., 1673–75*, p.48).

at Belfast in the early 1670s.[26] All substantial merchants were involved in gentry remittances. For example, Macartney arranged bills for the earl of Donegall and Sir George Rawdon in the 1660s, Lewis Thompson was remitting money to London for Sir Randal Beresford in 1675–76, and in 1687 Thomas Knox remitted money to Dublin for Sir Robert Colville.[27] Because of the fluctuation in the supply of bills members of the gentry could not deal exclusively with any one merchant, and there was in any case competition between merchants to attract this business. In view of the shortage of cash at Belfast throughout this period, no merchant was willing to let such an opportunity slip, apart from the benefits arising from obliging someone influential. For example, in 1665 Macartney drew £20 on William Watt of Dublin at eight days sight to give to John Topham,

> being he is a gentleman who I would willingly please in such a small business, Chancellor of the bishop's courts, if my men be working on a holiday he will excuse me. I would not have drawn on you without advice if that he had not been going upon a sudden to Dublin and durst not take his money with him

and two years later he apologised to Thomas Hackett of Dublin for drawing on him for £50 at five days sight for Michael Harrison of Magheralave, saying 'it is seldom I can have money here'.[28] The seasonality of trade at Belfast meant that at times it was impossible for any merchant to make remittances for the gentry. In April 1666, for example, Adam Leathes, Lord Conway's agent at Lisburn, had to travel to Dublin to remit money to England as he was unable to get any bills from Belfast owing to lack of trade. Similarly, in September 1677, another Conway agent was unable to remit £500–600 from Belfast because none of the merchants could draw bills on London, and he attributed this to the wet weather which had affected the supply of provisions.[29] However, by the early eighteenth century, the volume of bills of exchange handled at Belfast had increased and delays were normally only for a few days.

Although rents were payable on May Day and All Saints, it could take weeks, if not months, for all the money to come in. It was common for gentry to obtain bills from the merchants before all their rents had been paid, and although most of these bills would not have been payable imme-

26 *Cal. S.P. Ire., 1669–70*, pp 228, 321; *Cal. S.P. dom., 1680–81*, p.76; for van Weede see also chapter 6.

27 Macartney to Barron, 21 Sept. 1664 (Macartney 1, p.119); Thompson to David, 4 Sept., 7 Oct., 22 Dec. 1675, 29 Jan. 1675/6 (P.R.O., C114/76(1):5, C114/76(2):6); Knox to Colville, 20 Apr. 1687 (T.C.D., MS 1178, no.21).

28 Macartney to Watt, 29 Nov. 1665, to Hackett, 15 Nov. 1667 (Macartney 1, pp 281, 620).

29 Leathes to Conway, 18 Apr. 1666 (*Cal. S.P. Ire., 1666–69*, p.94); Mildmay to Conway, 26 Sept. 1677 (*Cal. S.P. dom., 1677–78*, p.378).

diately, many of these transactions were, in effect, short-term loans against the gentry's own bills, bonds or promissory notes for payment within a fixed term. Most gentry anticipated their income to solve the problem of cash flow but income from land was adversely affected by civil war, by uneconomic letting policies which reduced rents in the long term, and by the fall in agricultural prices in the early eighteenth century. In order to live in the style which their rank demanded many noble and gentry families slid ever deeper into debt.

In theory the same rules of acceptance and protest applied to all bills of exchange. In practice there was little a merchant could do, without great expense, to recover money from a debtor who was his social and economic superior. As Black George wrote in 1666, 'there is very ill getting money out of great men's hands'.[30] Moreover, protested bills had less serious effects on the credit of the gentry than on that of the merchant class. Because it was so difficult to recover money from defaulting members of the gentry their personal credit and financial reputation were of paramount importance to prospective lenders of money. The merchants who remitted their rents could supply information both about their income from their estates and their 'punctualness' in accepting bills. George Macartney was continually asked by his Dublin correspondents about the 'credit rating' of the Ulster gentry and his replies were extremely frank. For example, even after the marquess of Antrim had regained control of his estates in 1665 his credit rating remained very low and a Dublin merchant was warned that if he advanced him any money he should be sure to get his wife's signature on the bond too, as she was 'a very careful woman of her credit'.[31] In 1679, Macartney warned a correspondent that Lord Ardglass's bills were seldom paid and described him in the following year as 'a man scarce of money very often'.[32] In the early 1700s Isaac Macartney was replying to similar enquiries in similar terms. For example he wrote to Messrs Cairnes of London 'Charles O'Neile['s] bill, drawn by his lady, is paid, have a care of advancing more money without good endorsers, this I pray to yourself'.[33]

Merchants' advice about the credit of the gentry was given in the knowledge that they themselves might eventually be asked to present the bills for acceptance and payment. The presentment of bills was a routine task for all merchants throughout this period but it never became any easier or less unpopular. Even in dealings within the Belfast merchant community getting bills accepted often proved to be time-consuming and embarrassing. Nevertheless since protested bills swiftly undermined business credit, payment was generally forthcoming, and interest was paid

30 Macartney to Price, 30 Oct. 1666 (Macartney 1, p.459).
31 Macartney to Hackett, 6 Apr. 1666 (Macartney 1, p.336); Antrim's debts in the 1660s totalled roughly £40, 000 (Ohlmeyer, *Civil war and restoration*, p.268).
32 Macartney to Cole, 30 May 1679, to Lumm, 28 July 1680 (Macartney 2, pp 77, 297).
33 Macartney to Cairnes, 23 May 1705 (Macartney 3, p.114).

where this was late. There was very little leverage however that could be used against the gentry, short of going to law, and merchants were reluctant even to protest bills of the gentry if it could be avoided. A letter of Isaac Macartney to Captain Arthur Magenis in 1706 explained the dilemma of the merchants. He wrote:

> Its a surprizal to me you take no care in discharging Mr O'Hara's bills on you ... the profit got by exchange is small, but the punctual payment makes quick returns, but where the payment is dilatory it were better for the person that lends his money to put it out at interest which will yield double advantage than any gotten by these bills. Indeed if [I] did as usual amongst merchants protest the bills and recover damages [it] would give good profit but out of respect to you I would not protest said bills therefore desire your answer. If you will not pay them then I must protest them.[34]

Magenis, who had the name of a good payer, settled the bills. Many bills were only accepted and paid because of the patience and tact of the presenter, and legal proceedings, although hinted at, were seen as a last resort. An ability to deal with the gentry was therefore recognized as an essential attribute for any merchant who wanted business from the Dublin and London bankers. For example, in 1705 Isaac Macartney recommended Alderman James Lennox of Londonderry to the Dublin bankers, Burton & Harrison, as

> the man I do make use of there who is a substantial honest man and has good interest with both nobility and gentry in that country and if he will take your business, as I doubt not but he will, none can do it better in that country.[35]

The high social standing of Ulster merchants such as Lennox must have helped them to be firm in their dealings with the gentry. Macartney himself was tenacious in pursuing debts owed by such gentry as the Chichesters and Uptons, assuring his Dublin correspondents that they would not escape 'true dunning', but had difficulty in dealing with his own brother-in-law, John Haltridge, and avoided presenting bills to him whenever possible, explaining that a stranger was more likely to get money from him than a relation. However, Macartney's inability to take a firm line with Haltridge stemmed not from any difference in social status but from their relationship, and this eventually led to his becoming responsible for Haltridge's debts which contributed largely to his own eventual downfall in the 1730s. Haltridge had inherited a considerable fortune and property from his father, the merchant William Haltridge of Dromore, but had unfortunately failed to inherit any of the latter's financial acumen. Although

34 Macartney to Magenis, 20 Feb. 1705/6 (Macartney 3, pp 271–2).
35 Macartney to Burton & Harrison, 11 June 1705 (Macartney 3, p.125).

his difficulties were in part caused by a ruinous lawsuit to recover his wife's dowry, Haltridge's main problem was one which he shared with most of those described as bad payers by the merchants, namely an inability to live within his income, leading inevitably to a slide into debt.

Apart from the regular presentment of bills of exchange to the gentry, Isaac Macartney was deeply involved in the affairs of two notable debtors, Sir Basil Dixwell and Lord Conway. In neither case was Macartney himself a creditor. He was involved as the agent of two firms of Dublin bankers, William Cairnes and Burton & Harrison. Dixwell's problems were on a far smaller scale than Conway's but they arose from the same cause – both men drew bills faster than their rents could come in. Macartney, whose job it was to collect the rents from their agents, found himself in sympathy with the agents rather than the bankers. In 1705 he wrote to Cairnes that John Jelly, who was Dixwell's agent, said that if 'Dixwell does not leave off drawing he will quit his employ ... he wishes you would stop advancing any more money till the bills already drawn are near cleared'.[36] Similarly, he defended the efforts of Lord Conway's agents to clear his increasing debt to Burton & Harrison which rose from £7,668 in February 1705 to £9,542 in October 1706, these sums being the principal only. However, in that period of recession, he could see no prospect of Conway being able to pay off his debts unless he raised money by selling the wood on his estate.[37]

The distinction between debts and loans to the gentry was blurred. The high lending rate in Ireland encouraged those who had surplus cash to invest it in loans. As Bishop King of Derry commented, 'Tis not thought prudent in Ireland where money is at 10 per cent for anyone to keep cash by him, & perhaps he that hath £1000 per annum hath often not £100 in cash'.[38] The lending rate remained at a nominal 10% until the early eighteenth century, dropping to 8% in 1704. Wealthy merchants with capital to spare invested it in loans to the gentry. Loans were negotiated on a personal basis, with friends and business contacts putting those who had cash to lend in touch with those who needed to borrow it. Money was normally lent on the security of a rent charge, a mortgage or a bond with a penalty clause. Plenty of evidence exists to show that Belfast merchants made loans to the gentry, both in Ulster and Scotland. For example, in the 1670s–80s George Macartney, John Hamilton, Gabriel Holmes, James Chalmers and William Craford, all lent sums ranging from £200–£600, secured by rent charges, to gentry in Counties Antrim and Down,[39] and John Clugston the

36 Macartney to Cairnes, 10 Oct. 1705 (Macartney 3, p.206).
37 Macartney to Burton & Harrison, 28 Feb., 23 June 1705, 6 May, 5 Oct. 1706 (Macartney 3, pp 62–3, 129, 309, 363).
38 King, *State of the protestants*, p.233.
39 Indentures, Lord Mountalexander to Macartney, 24 June 1674, Sir Hans Hamilton and James Hamilton to Gabriel Holmes, 12 Dec. 1678, James Hamilton to John

elder and Thomas Knox both lent money to gentry in Scotland.[40] A schedule of the debts of James Montgomery of Rosemount, in County Down, made in the 1690s shows that, in addition to many smaller sums owing to Belfast merchants, he owed nearly £500 to the executors of the Belfast merchant Thomas Aitkin, and the size of this sum suggests a loan rather than a debt for goods supplied. Montgomery's affairs went from bad to worse and Isaac Macartney eventually bought up the mortgages on the Rosemount estates for the sum of £1,077, and conveyed them to James Bailie of Inishargie in 1719 for £2,600, the total owed him by Montgomery.[41] Isaac Macartney's father-in-law, William Haltridge of Dromore, appears to have been lending money on a large scale in the 1680s. In 1706 Isaac Macartney wrote:

> I have a mortgage settled on Dundalk lands by Lord Dungannon and [James Hamilton of] Tollymore ... grounded on two judgments entered 26 years ago of £1,000 each by father Haltridge which was assigned over to me now I do get the interest of one ½ year past when [the] other becomes due [it is] punctually paid without charge.[42]

Another of William Haltridge's loans is revealed by the claim of his widow and son to the forfeiture commissioners in 1702, against the estate of Patrick and Rowland Savage in County Down. In 1688, Haltridge had lent £525 to the Savages, and others, on a bond with a 100% penalty clause, but only £105 had been repaid. Nor was it only the wealthiest merchants who made loans to the gentry. In 1709, John Black the elder of Belfast lent £500 to one of the Shaws of Ballytweedy by bond, which debt was eventually repaid over forty years later.[43]

The last example shows that gentry loans were always something of a calculated risk. Merchants dealing with the powerful and influential were always reluctant to go to law. The problems they might face were underlined by George Macartney to Joshua Allen of Dublin who was in dispute with Sir Robert Colville in 1680–81:

Hamilton, 12 Dec. 1678 (N.A., Lodge's records of the rolls, vii p.452, viii p.55), Mountalexander to James Chalmers, 1 Nov. 1677 (N.A., D 15274); exchequer bill, 21 June 1722 (N.A., Crosslé abstracts, Smith vii, pp 1340–7); see also rent accounts for properties in Cultra and the Falls, 1672–78, and Macartney to Harrison, 31 Jan. 1679/80 (Macartney 2, pp 5–8, 500 et seq.).

40 Deeds relating to loan by Clugston to John Carsan of Sanick, 1660s (*Kirkcudbright sheriff court deeds 1623–75*, ed. M.B. Johnston and Catherine Armet [Edinburgh, 1939], nos 270, 325); registered deeds concerning loans by Knox to the Cockburns, lairds of Langtown, etc., 1691 (S.R.O., Register of Deeds, DAL 72, 833, 835–6).

41 Schedule of debts of James Montgomery of Rosemount, c.1691 (P.R.O.N.I., Montgomery papers, T1030/9A); Hill, *Montgomery manuscripts*, p.419.

42 Macartney to William Sloane, 19 Aug. 1706 (Macartney 3, pp 346–8).

43 Report on claim of Elizabeth and John Haltridge, and judgment (P.R.O.N.I., Annesley MSS, D1854/2/18, ff 125–6, D1854/2/35, p.15); journal of John Black of Bordeaux, 18 Aug., 4 Nov. 1752 (P.R.O.N.I., T1073/7).

You have one to deal with that delights in law and if you could dispose of your money otherwise its good to be free of trouble and of such a man as Sir Maurice is and take Sir Robert's money without spending more at law which is but a lottery.[44]

Since the Belfast merchants had money to invest it might have been expected that they would have lent some to the earls of Donegall who were almost perpetually in debt throughout this period. There are no details extant of loans raised locally by the first two earls to meet their liabilities, but papers survive relating the affairs of the third earl from the 1690s to his death in 1705.[45] The third earl had been involved since his accession to the title in 1678 in a law suit started by his father to recover the Donegall estates from the female descendants of the first earl. In 1692 a settlement was finally reached with the first earl's daughter, Lady Longford, although the estate continued to pay substantial allowances to the Longfords. By this date, Donegall was already heavily in debt, and he raised money by selling the Dungannon estate to the Belfast merchant, Thomas Knox. In the mid-1690s, as his need for money to advance his political and military career grew greater, he entered into a number of short-term bonds with 100% penalty clauses. The fact that he was unable to get money on easier terms underlines the wariness of his creditors at this date. With the death of Lady Longford in 1697 and that of her husband in 1700, the earl's long-term financial prospects (and those of his creditors) improved but his death in action in 1705, and the extravagant terms of his will which settled generous allowances on all members of his family, changed his creditors' prospects and resulted in some of them still being unpaid thirty years later.[46]

As late as August 1705, Isaac Macartney assured a London correspondent that a bill of the earl for £1,000 would be accepted by his agent Patrick Duffe: 'my lord has a good estate here so do believe if [he] has drawn no more bills of late his bill will meet with due honour.' Duffe, who was better informed, took evasive action and left for Dublin.[47] Nevertheless, although Macartney was not aware of the full extent of Donegall's debts before his death, it is clear that Donegall's affairs did not inspire confi-

44 Sir Maurice Eustace was the son of the lord chancellor of Ireland and Colville's son-in-law; Macartney to Allen, 15 Jan. 1680/1, and see letters to same of 27 Sept. 1680 and 9 Feb. 1680/1 (Macartney 2, pp 412, 350, 426); Colville letters, 1680–84 (N.A., M 485).

45 Papers relating to debts of third earl of Donegall (P.R.O., C106/95/15).

46 John McBride to Hans Sloane, 30 Dec. 1700, 'My Lord Longford died last week, whereby the earl of Donegall is richer than he was more than £1, 000 per annum' (B.L., Sloane MS 4038, f.117); Roebuck, 'Landlord indebtedness', pp 140–2.

47 Macartney to Messrs Carbonells [*recte* Cardonells], 4 and 6 Aug. 1705 (Macartney 3, pp 161–2, 165); Macartney might have replied differently had he been consulted before the money was advanced.

dence in the local business community as only two merchants from local families appear to have been his creditors, and neither of these men actually lived in Belfast.[48] It is interesting to note that the only two Belfast men who are known to have lent him money were not merchants.[49]

To raise money, the third earl had sold life annuities from his estate at 'ruinously cheap prices'.[50] William Sloane had purchased one of £50 for his young son, and he had also advanced money to Donegall, secured by a deed of mortgage. In 1705, Sloane was in England and Isaac Macartney, his friend and cousin by marriage, was acting as his agent. On the news of Donegall's death, Macartney wrote to Charles Campbell of Dublin, who was handling Donegall's affairs, to ask whether Lady Donegall had been a party to the deed of mortgage, and whether it was safe from any claims for her jointure:

> nothing being more sure than that there is not estate enough to answer jointures, life rents and interest of money, Belfast estate not being liable for one penny but the young ladies' portions, so that most sure some of the creditors will suffer for the present.[51]

Campbell's reply enabled Macartney to send Sloane a detailed breakdown of the charges on the Donegall estate which show that, apart from the extravagant annuities, interest was already being paid at 8% on debts totalling £20,000.[52] Although Sloane's debt, being one of the oldest, was considered one of the safest, Macartney advised him to persuade Donegall's brothers, who could draw on any part of the estate for their annuities, to relinquish their title to his mortgage. Sloane, of course, was not seeking repayment of principal, just the regular payment of interest. The Donegall rental of 1719 shows that the rents paid were servicing a number of loans, including Sloane's which is shown as £4,000 at 7%; however as he was only being paid £70 8s 4d per annum from rents, it seems that the interest was not being fully paid, and the principal was still owing in the 1730s.[53] Although other horror stories could be told of the debts of the nobility and the gentry, it must be supposed that loans from merchants to gentry were normally repaid with some kind of return on the investment as it is difficult to see how any other considerations, such as the wish to oblige a social superior, could have been sufficient to induce merchants to lend large sums on unfavourable terms.

48 They were William Sloane, and Hugh Whyte of London who was related to the Belfast Whites.
49 They were the presbyterian minister, Patrick Adair, and Dr Victor Ferguson.
50 Roebuck, 'Donegall family', p.130.
51 Macartney to Campbell, 14 Aug. 1706 (Macartney 3, pp 340–1).
52 Macartney to Sloane, 19 Aug. 1706 (Macartney 3, pp 346–8).
53 Donegall estate rental, 1719 (P.R.O.N.I., D2249/61, nos 249–54); Donegall minority accounts (P.R.O., C106/95/15).

Any consideration of gentry indebtedness to merchants, however, must take into account one important and complicating factor, which is that the gentry were themselves the main market for most imported goods. Apart from timber, tar and tobacco, practically all imports were luxury goods which would only sell to the gentry and merchant classes. Since the home market was small and easily glutted, buyers could always demand credit. Those who continually exceeded their incomes were generally considerable consumers of luxuries and any attempt to withhold credit from the gentry would have led to a reduction in trade. In many cases the importers of these goods dealt directly with the gentry. Importers of wine generally disposed of part of each cargo direct to the gentry and nobility and the rest to the vintners who would bottle it. Even the vintners expected six months credit. The gentry were frequently as bad at paying for their wine as they were at accepting bills of exchange, but here too it was hard to apply any leverage as the merchant who dunned his customers too vigorously would find that they dealt with more obliging suppliers in future. Once again a combination of tact, patience and outright supplication was needed to encourage the gentry to pay their debts. For example, in 1676, Black George Macartney wrote to George Maxwell of Orchardton who had settled part of his account, 'I do intreat you do me the kindness to send me the rest for I am exceedingly straitened at this time'.[54] Where patience and tact failed other expedients were tried. In the same year, Macartney, who had been owed money for wine, sugar and spices for five years by Lord Ardglass, instructed James Sloane, elder brother of William and Hans and a barrister in London, to take Ardglass to a London tavern and spend eight or ten shillings or more on his entertainment in order to induce him to sign a bond to settle his debt within the next twelve months, and although he hoped that fair words would persuade Ardglass to do what was 'right and just' he told Sloane 'I think it better to have him to the tavern ere you deliver my letter to him'. In case this tactic failed, Macartney was simultaneously discussing the possibility of getting a writ against Ardglass's real or personal estate, although he doubted if this would be possible as the sub-sheriff was one of Ardglass's tenants.[55] The Ardglass affair is an excellent illustration of the impotence of even a substantial merchant in dealing with a determined non-payer from the nobility.

Although the extended credit demanded by the gentry probably led to prices being adjusted accordingly, gentry debts ate into the profit margins on luxury goods. Prosperous merchants with large turnovers could afford to carry what amounted to loans to the gentry but small merchants usually

54 Macartney to Maxwell, 4 Jan. 1675/6 (S.R.O., Maxwell of Orchardton, RH15/91/60).
55 Macartney to Sloane, 30 Apr. 1679, to Bridges, 14 May 1679 (Macartney 2, pp 56, 65).

failed when unpaid debts made it impossible for them to pay their own creditors. Lawrence gives the bad payment of the gentry as one of the principal reasons for the 'ill-performance' of Irish merchants with their creditors abroad, and their generally low credit'.[56] However, the short-comings of the gentry as customers were offset by the advantages of gentry remittance business and the interest paid on loans, and merchants and gentry were frequently involved in several kinds of transactions simultaneously. For example, a detailed account of Sir Robert Maxwell with the Belfast merchant Allan Corbett shows that in addition to a formidable list of luxury goods, Corbett was also billing him for cash lent for a bill of exchange to England, for 'exchange for your money' and for interest on a loan of £46 10s.[57] Moreover, not all loans were made to the gentry. The gentry themselves, when in funds, were also prepared to lend money at interest. The letters of Sir George Rawdon reveal that he lent £100, in 1665, to a merchant who was in need of cash to buy beef for the navy, and in a letter of 1679 Macartney informed Edmund Harrison of London that the countess of Donegall had 'let to interest £1,000 of her money', although he does not say to whom.[58] The financial involvement of merchants and gentry therefore consisted of numbers of inter-locking transactions and the financial affairs of some of the Ulster gentry were known to be so complex that the state of their health was enquired after with bated breath. As Isaac Macartney commented to William Sloane, in November 1704, if James Hamilton of Bangor were to die 'there would be as great an outcry of losses as there was on Sir Robert's death'.[59]

MERCHANTS AND BANKERS

The complexity of merchant/gentry transactions led, to some extent, to mutual dependence. In 1676, Lord Arran wrote to his father, not entirely in jest, 'We are afraid that next post we shall hear that Abel Ram's English correspondent is broke; if so I shall break ...'[60] Abel Ram was a leading

56 Lawrence, *Interest of Ireland*, pt 1, p.10.
57 Account of Maxwell with Corbett, 28 Apr. 1683, for buttons, stockings, a french hat, soap, nutmegs, sugar, bridle bosses, tortoiseshell, calico, corks, serge, oil, cloves, mace, ginger, cinnamon, silk buttons, a pan and colander, stockings, tape, pins, raisins, currants, paper, pepper, rice, brandy, a cask of sturgeon, a sword with a silver hilt and handle, broadcloth, looking glass, gold and silver thread, etc. (S.R.O., Maxwell of Orchardton, RH15/91/60).
58 *Cal. S.P. Ire., 1662–65*, p.638; Macartney to Harrison, 8 Nov. 1679 (Macartney 2, p.183).
59 Macartney to Sloane, 27 Nov. 1704 (Macartney 3, pp 20–1); Sir Robert Hamilton had died in 1703.
60 *Ormonde MSS*, (NS), iv, p.9.

Dublin merchant, goldsmith and banker, with a large gentry clientele. Another such was Elnathan Lumm, also originally a goldsmith, who was described as 'one of the chief bankers in Dublin' in 1699.[61] This term was not in common use in the seventeenth century and many who were operating as bankers continued to call themselves merchants, seeing banking as one activity among many. Goldsmiths were involved in banking because the gentry lodged sums of money or plate with them, and drew on them as they needed funds. In Dublin, however, the chief purpose of banking was to transmit rents to London and although goldsmiths continued to be involved, a new type of Dublin banker had emerged by the beginning of the eighteenth century, originating in the landed classes. Foremost among these were three Ulstermen: Francis Harrison, the partner of Benjamin Burton from c.1700, was the son of Edward Harrison of Magheralave, one of the few non-merchant burgesses of Belfast; Hugh Henry was the son of the presbyterian minister of Carrickfergus, and William Cairnes came of a landed presbyterian family and was the brother of Alexander and Henry Cairnes, the London bankers. All three had considerable personal fortunes, and were members of parliament.[62]

The volume of bills of exchange handled at Belfast in the seventeenth century was insufficient for any Belfast merchant to have acted as a banker in this period, and most remittances to London went via Dublin. Nevertheless, although bills of exchange were in common use by all merchants, there was a markedly different degree of involvement in the activities they generated, between individual merchants. A comparison of the letter books of the Macartneys (father and son) and that of David Butle underlines this difference. Although, in the 1690s, Butle was in regular correspondence with Alexander Cairnes of London and paid for his goods with bills there is no indication that he dealt in bills beyond what was necessary to finance his trading operations. The Macartneys, on the other hand, were from the 1660s continuously engaged in the supply, exchange and presentment of bills, principally on behalf of a number of leading Dublin merchants and bankers; indeed Isaac Macartney's letter book contains more letters about bills than about trade. Since a commission of 1½% was paid on the bills they handled, this represented a regular and not inconsiderable addition to their income.

There are some indications in the letter books that Black George found himself to be ahead of his time in his use of bills of exchange. For example, in 1666, he tried to remit money directly to Scotland and was rebuked by a Glasgow merchant for his rashness in trusting him with

61 Tenison, 'Old Dublin bankers', pp 120–1.
62 Cullen, 'Landlords, bankers and merchants', pp 26, 31 et seq.; appendix B.4;
    Tenison, op. cit., pp 36–8, 120–1, 194–5.
63 Macartney to Rowan, 21 Jan. 1665/6 (Macartney 1, p.317).

another man's money.[63] In the following year, when the Dublin merchant Edward Yard offered to pay the Belfast tallow merchants half in Belfast and half in London, he suggested asking Sir George Rawdon to take Yard's bills to London and to order money to Belfast so that the whole sum could be paid there, only to be told by Yard that 'he does not use to go a begging [his] bills'.[64] That Macartney saw himself as being particularly active in this field is clear from a letter he wrote to Robert Bridges of Dublin in 1679, in which he discussed the non-payment of a bill to Sir John Frederick & Co. of London, adding 'for charge of protests and interest I will refer myself to their wills and suppose considering my forwardness to send bills that they will demand nothing'.[65] Macartney's dealings with Frederick consisted of the supplying of bills rather than actual trade, and he was beginning to make a similar distinction between his correspondents in Dublin. In the same year he wrote to Edmund Harrison of London recommending several Dublin merchants thus:

> I deal with several good men in Dublin as Sir Joshua Allen, Robert Bridges, William Sergeant and 7 or 8 others, if it be but for remitting of money I find Mr Sergeant very active, you have had a trial of him, but if for buying goods I may appoint another if you be not settled.[66]

Nevertheless Macartney's business with Sergeant was not confined to remittances as he frequently made purchases of butter and beef on his behalf. Twenty-five years later this kind of division between correspondents was more marked. Isaac Macartney's chief agent in Dublin for matters of trade was the merchant partnership of Cromie & Stevenson but his remittances were mainly handled by Burton & Harrison, and by William Cairnes. Moreover, every few months he made up a statement for each of the two latter firms listing bills of exchange paid and unpaid, and deducting his commission of 1½%. He had become the agent in Belfast for each of these firms, handling a steady flow of incoming bills, and sending down to Dublin what bills he could obtain to balance the accounts.

Isaac Macartney did not call himself a banker although the title was later claimed for him by his son. Although he was active in the discounting and transmitting of bills of exchange, he never issued bank notes. Nevertheless, considering his activities as agent of the Cairnes brothers, he has some claim to be considered as another 'branch' of their bank, which operated in London, Dublin and Limerick. Not only did he deal extensively in bills of exchange, he was also active in the creation of credit. The recession of the early 1700s meant that the supply of bills in and around

64 Macartney to Yard, 15 Nov. 1667 (Macartney 1, p.622).
65 Macartney to Bridges, 31 Jan. 1678/9 (Macartney 2, p.18).
66 Macartney to Harrison, 19 Apr. 1679 (Macartney 2, p.53).

13 Letter from Isaac Macartney to Burton & Harrison,
showing dealing in bills, 5 September, 1705

Belfast was still sometimes inadequate and he did what he could to increase the volume. For example he wrote to his correspondent in Cork,

> I have desired several linen drapers to lodge what money they have to remit to these parts in your hands and take your bills on me from time to time for the same, which I beg the favour of you to give as short sight as you please and your bills shall meet due honour, and what money you receive for the same please to send me good bills on London at as easy Exchange as you can and if find said bills do turn to account it may prove an advantage to us both.[67]

Many merchants in provincial towns dealt in bills as a profitable sideline, but there are indications that Macartney was seen as the leader in this field in Belfast. In 1721, Agmondisham Vesey, who was projecting the formation of a bank, wrote to his brother-in-law John Hamilton Maxwell of the Drum, County Down, for advice as to a suitable agent in Belfast. Hamilton Maxwell replied 'Mr Isaac Macartney is certainly the fittest person in Belfast to be your correspondent and can best promote it and he is a very honest worthy gentleman'. However, this project came to nothing and the first private bank in Belfast was not established until 1752.[68]

In banking and economic organisation, Ireland lagged far behind Scotland where the Bank of Scotland had been founded in 1695, and where merchant and commercial undertakings were financed by joint-stock companies. Ireland had more in common with New England where there was also a chronic shortage of money and an outflow of specie to England. In Ireland, various proposals to establish a land bank, or bank of credit, in the 1680s had come to nothing. In New England, a bank of credit had been set up in 1681 but had collapsed after a few years. The weakness of the financial infrastructure in both Ireland and New England in contrast to Scotland is a reflection of the unfavourable colonial status of the two former.[69]

Nevertheless, by 1707, trade in Belfast was largely financed by bills of exchange and, because of the shortage of specie and the problems of transporting it, bills were also used for inland transactions. The Belfast merchants were also involved in the remitting of rents to England and in the handling of gentry bills of exchange. Their dealings with the gentry were complex. Many of these bills of exchange amounted to short-term loans without which the gentry would have been unable to purchase imported luxury goods, and the merchants also made them long-term loans as a form

67 Macartney to Hugh Mitchell, 4 Aug. 1705 (Macartney 3, p.163).
68 Maxwell to Vesey, 21 Mar. 1721/2 (N.A., Sarsfield Vesey letters, 170); Benn, p.465.
69 Cochran, *Scottish trade with Ireland*, p.8; Smout, 'Development and enterprise of Glasgow', p.202; Lawrence, *Interest of Ireland*, pt 2, p.3; Petty, *Political anatomy*, p.75; *Ormonde MSS*, (NS), vii, p.27; Bailyn, *New England merchants*, pp 100, 184–5, 188.

of investment. There were always problems inherent in dealings with the gentry, who were notoriously bad payers, but these dealings were an essential part of the system of remitting money by bills, and it was the regular flow of gentry remittances that made possible the sophisticated credit transactions which were routinely used by the Belfast merchants by the end of the seventeenth century.

8

The Merchant Community Abroad

Apart from the emergence of the linen trade, Belfast's trade was much the same in the early eighteenth century as it had been fifty years earlier. It had increased in volume rather than in essentials. However, there had been one notable change in this period. By the early eighteenth century most of Belfast's trade at foreign ports was handled by a network of merchants from Belfast or Ulster who had settled abroad. This fundamental change can be illustrated by contrasting the correspondents of Black George Macartney with those of his son, Isaac. The Macartneys' choice of factors was broadly typical of that of the whole community. Black George frequently indicated in his letters that his factors were acting for other Belfast merchants, and David Butle's letter book of 1696–1703 reveals an almost identical choice of correspondents to that of Isaac Macartney. Indeed, at this date, the merchant/factor relationship was seldom exclusive. Factors resident abroad handled the business of large numbers of merchants, including many from the same ports, and aimed at complete impartiality in their dealings.

Black George's two letter books reveal that he had, at any one time, about twenty regular factors abroad, and at least six major clients in Dublin. The majority of his letters relate to trading voyages to Europe. This is because these voyages were frequently complex and involved dealings at more than one European port, and because voyages to non-European ports appear to have generated little correspondence with resident factors. On voyages to Norway, the ship's master was frequently commissioned both to buy and sell, while in the New World, the slowness of communications coupled with the seasonality of trade made it impossible to get up-to-date intelligence about the markets or about the competence and credit of local merchants.[1] Supercargoes normally accompanied goods because there was no point in consigning them to a factor who might not even be alive, let alone solvent.

1 Ian K. Steele, *The English Atlantic 1675–1740, an exploration of communication and community* (New York and Oxford, 1986), pp 215–7.

All seventeenth-century trade was carried on within a framework of extended kinship groups. The widespread migration of merchants from Scotland seeking better trading prospects abroad had resulted in the establishment of Scottish communities across Scandinavia and Europe. Some of these merchants set themselves up as factors specialising in handling Scottish goods, and by the mid-seventeenth century there was a network of expatriate Scots acting as correspondents for merchants at home. Similarly there was an outflow of Roman catholic merchants from Ireland, principally from Galway, Limerick and Waterford, who also settled abroad. They were the dominant group in France, where the Scots were few in number before the eighteenth century, and also in the West Indies until after the act of union of 1707. Like the Scots, they too were strongly represented in London. Since most of the Belfast merchants were Scots it would be reasonable to expect that most of their factors abroad would also be Scots. However, George Macartney's letter books show that both he and others in the community traded mainly with Irishmen abroad and with foreign nationals.

In the early 1660s Macartney was closely associated with merchants in Bristol, and he consigned goods to Thomas Lewis at La Rochelle and to Edward Moore, a merchant from Bristol who operated both at La Rochelle and Bordeaux. However, he gradually built up a considerable clientele in Dublin and consolidated these links by regular visits to Dublin in the early spring when trade at Belfast was dead. He normally spent several weeks there, generally staying at the house of Humphrey Jervis who was a distant kinsman. As his trade on behalf of the Dublin merchants increased, so his dealings with the English factors in France declined and, from the mid-1660s, the majority of Macartney's factors in France can be linked directly with his Dublin clients. For example, his agent at Rouen was a brother of Thomas Hackett of Dublin, and after this man's death he dealt with Peter Cossart of Rouen and Le Havre who had business and family links with Dublin and other parts of Ireland. From the 1660s Macartney was also doing business with a group of inter-related Roman catholic merchant families who had originated in Waterford and who had family members settled in France and Dublin. His contacts with this group in Dublin were Nicholas Lincoln and Michael Garreldin, and it was through them he first made contact with Nicholas Lee and Andrew Garreldin at Nantes, Nicholas Garreldin Redmond at St Malo and Messrs Wyse, Lombard and Ley at Rouen.

It was preferable to employ countrymen who had settled abroad rather than foreign factors who might act in the interests of their own community, if not their own country. The kind of measures taken by the Belfast community to protect their own interests looked less admirable when encountered abroad. For example in 1679, when Macartney and Jervis sent their ship the *Dublin Merchant* to the West Indies, Macartney wrote 'I hope you have got a smart man to go with her [as] supercargo that will not be fooled with these cunning men in Barbados'.[2] Even Londonderry, with which the Belfast merchants had frequent contact, was reckoned to be a difficult port for outsiders to trade at:

> It is the worst place that ever men sent goods to for I never heard any man speak well of that place for when any men's goods comes there except their own they will strive to break the price as low as they can.[3]

However, this kind of xenophobia was presumably tempered by contact with the cosmopolitan Dublin community, which included groups of Dutch and French merchants, and Macartney numbered several foreigners among his factors. One foreign national who handled goods for the Belfast merchants throughout this period was Henry Lavie of Bordeaux, a French protestant.[4] In the early 1660s, Macartney and a number of other Belfast merchants were dealing with James Thruston of Bordeaux who may have been a member of the Thruston family of Bristol. Macartney was dissatisfied with the quality of the wines that Thruston loaded for him and by 1665 was consigning goods in secret to Lavie who was already factor for other Belfast merchants. Macartney did not sever his connection with Thruston, and was still recommending him in 1667, but by the 1680s Lavie appears to have been acting for most of the Belfast merchants and also for merchants in Scotland.[5]

Although few Scots settled in France before the 1690s, they abounded in the Low Countries. Nevertheless, in the 1660s–80s, Macartney dealt with Patrick Creagh at Flushing, an Irishman who was originally recommended to him by Thomas Hackett of Dublin, with John Brouwe at Ostend who acted as factor for Joshua Allen, and with Dehulter and Vanhomrigh at Amsterdam who handled the business of a number of Dublin merchants. Vanhomrigh visited Dublin in 1679, and settled there in 1681, with Macartney continuing as both factor and partner. An analysis of Macartney's correspondence shows that although he had dealings with a few expatriate Scots, for example James Cunningham at Cadiz, Andrew Marjoribank at Danzig, and William Fife at Stockholm, the majority of his factors abroad were business connections or kinsmen of his Dublin clients. Many of these Dublin merchants were inter-related. They recommended Macartney to each other but he himself appears to have had kinship ties with only one of this group, namely Humphrey Jervis. The same appears to have been true of his contemporaries at Belfast who also employed their

---

2 Macartney to Jervis, 9 Mar. 1678/9 (Macartney 2, p.33).

3 Macartney to Allen, 7 Sept. 1666 (Macartney 1, p.421).

4 Shaw, *Letters of denization*, p.216.

5 *Town book*, pp 115–15; *Cal. S.P. Ire., 1666–69*, pp 382, 587; Samuel Moore, Ayr, to Andrew Russell, asking him to remit to Lavie in Bordeaux, for account of Robert Doock of Ayr, 14 Apr. 1680 (S.R.O., Russell papers, RH15/106/371/14).

Dublin clients' factors. Marriages between merchant families in Belfast and Dublin were extremely rare before the 1690s. Most Belfast merchants therefore were employed by members of a kinship network originating at Dublin to which they did not themselves belong, and their relationships with the factors who were part of this network, even in ports where Scottish merchants were settled, underlines the dependence of their trading activities on their Dublin employers.

Between 1681, when Black George's second letter book ends, and 1704, when that of Isaac Macartney begins, a significant change had taken place. Virtually all the correspondents of the latter were Scots presbyterians, and a high proportion were from Ulster. There appears to be very little overlap with the correspondents in the two earlier Macartney letter books. There are two letters to Daniel Arthur, who was by then in his eighties, two to Henry Lavie of Bordeaux, although this may not have been the same man who was active in the 1660s–80s, and two to Edmund Harrison of London, with whom Black George had been in partnership on numerous occasions, including the supplying of Schomberg's artillery train.[6] The largest group of letters to one of Black George's former correspondents is to Elnathan Lumm of Dublin and comprises eighteen letters relating to Lumm's banking activities. Some change was inevitable since many of Black George's correspondents would have been dead or in retirement by 1704 but their replacements indicate that this change was fundamental. Isaac's major correspondents were Alexander and Henry Cairnes at London, William Cromie, James Stevenson, and William Cairnes at Dublin, James Eccles at Waterford, Hugh Mitchell at Cork, William Galbraith and James Hillhouse at Bristol, John Cunningham at Liverpool, Alexander Carstaires at Rotterdam, George Boyd and Robert Gordon at Bordeaux, and the Moore brothers in Barbados. Apart from Carstaires and Gordon, who were Scots from Scotland, all the rest were Scots from Ulster.

David Butle's letter book covers a longer period (1696–1703) but contains far fewer letters, addressed to a total of only twenty-seven correspondents.[7] Twelve of these also appear in Isaac Macartney's letter book and letters to several of the remainder do not relate to trade. Like Macartney he was dealing with Alexander Cairnes at London, Cromie at Dublin, Eccles at Waterford, Carstaires at Rotterdam, Boyd at Bordeaux, Moore at Barbados, and with William Blackburn and Andrew Lees in Glasgow.[8] Moreover, not only were Macartney's and Butle's trading networks almost identical, but Macartney's letters contain frequent references to other Belfast merchants consigning goods to these same factors.

6 Harrison became one of the directors of the East India Company and was knighted in 1698; *Cal. S.P. dom., 1690–91*, p.530.
7 There are letters to c.250 correspondents in Macartney 1 and 2, and c.150 in Macartney 3.
8 Edward Brice's account book, c.1686–96 (P.R.O.N.I., D1556/16/7) contains even

14 Sir John Eccles

A significant change had taken place since the period covered by the first two Macartney letter books. The merchant community at Belfast, which was largely Scottish in origin, was dealing, by the mid-1690s, with a network of factors who were mostly Ulster Scots and, although Dublin remained central to their trade and financial dealings, they were no longer trading primarily as factors for Dublin merchants. Their trading network now consisted of their own connections and countrymen rather than those of their employers in Dublin, and the Dublin merchants with whom they did the most business were themselves expatriate Ulster men, and so part of this same network.

Colonies of provincial merchants in Dublin developed in the seventeenth and early eighteenth centuries. Leonard Thompson was the first Belfast merchant to live there in the 1630s.[9] However, the Thompsons had emigrated to Belfast from the Low Countries a few years previously and so are not typical of the Belfast merchant community. The first identifiable member of a Belfast merchant family living in Dublin after the restoration was Samuel Martin, son of the burgess George Martin. However, although Martin appears to have started his career as a merchant, he soon established himself as an attorney, aided by his marriage to a relation of Sir Audley Mervyn, sergeant-at-law and speaker of the Irish house of commons.[10] He built up a thriving legal practice handling the business of Belfast merchants and of many of the Ulster gentry and was greatly in demand as an executor or administrator of wills. Sir John Eccles, nephew of the burgess Hugh Eccles, is the first Dublin merchant who can be identified as belonging to a Belfast family. He settled in Dublin before 1682, and subsequently became alderman, mayor and collector for the port. Thomas Bell was another Dublin alderman who came from an Ulster presbyterian background.[11] Since he was a freeman by 1683 he must have settled in Dublin at least as early as Eccles. In the mid-1680s, Black George Macartney attempted to set up his eldest son in Dublin, but this son rejected a career as a merchant in favour of the army.[12] However, at much the same date, Macartney's son-in-law Francis Cromie settled in Dublin. Although Francis died in 1692, his brother William Cromie

---

less information but it does reveal that he had dealings with Eccles at Waterford, and also with Alexander Mitchell at Dublin and William Brown at London, both of whom are included among Butle's correspondents, although not among Macartney's in the period 1704–06.

9 D.R. Hainsworth (ed.), *Commercial papers of Sir Christopher Lowther* (Surtees Society, clxxxix, Gateshead, 1977), pp 2–3; and see appendix A.29.

10 See *D.N.B.* for details of Mervyn's career.

11 Since he was related to John Hamilton of Belfast he may perhaps be identified with Thomas Bell of Belfast who petitioned, in 1677, for passes to Denmark for a number of Belfast ships (*Cal. S.P. dom., 1677–78*, p.33).

12 He became a freeman of Dublin in 1686, see appendix A.19 and entry in *D.N.B.* for his subsequent career.

became a freeman of Dublin in that same year and married into a Dublin merchant family. By the mid-1690s he was handling the business of a number of Belfast merchants and in the early 1700s was in partnership with James Stevenson from County Down.

From 1672, 'protestant strangers' were allowed to become freemen of Dublin 'by special grace' and this encouraged an influx of settlers from the north although it is not possible to identify an Ulster community in Dublin before the 1690s. In that decade, many Belfast and Ulster merchants appear in the rolls of freemen.[13] None are noted as having served an apprenticeship in Dublin, although this was so in other trades, so these merchants already had some experience, capital and contacts when they settled in Dublin. By the end of the seventeenth century there was a considerable, and expanding, group of Ulster merchants settled in Dublin. At this date they were virtually all still presbyterians and attended the Capel Street meeting house which belonged to the synod of Ulster.[14] Capel Street, on the north side of the River Liffey, was in the most rapidly developing area of Dublin, near the law courts. Many of the presbyterians from Belfast lived in this district, which lay in the parish of St. Michan's, and it is clear that this was the nucleus of the community. Among this presbyterian group were Samuel Martin and his sons, William Biggar, Hugh and Archibald White, Thomas Bell, William Montgomery and James Anderson. Many of the trustees of the Capel Street congregation listed in 1718 came from Belfast families.[15] Other notable members of the Ulster community were William Cairnes, brother of Alexander and Henry Cairnes, the London bankers, and M.P. for Belfast, Hugh Henry of Carrickfergus, who was to become one of Dublin's leading bankers, Charles Campbell, whose family came from County Down, and who handled the legal affairs of the Donegall and Hamilton families, and the lawyer and politician William Conolly.

By the 1690s there were also Belfast men in other ports in Ireland. James Eccles of Waterford, who became a freeman there in 1693, was a brother of Sir John Eccles of Dublin, and he acted as factor for the Belfast merchants until his death in 1707. John Black's brother David settled in Cork but died in 1696, and Hugh Mitchell of Cork, with whom the Belfast merchants dealt from the mid-1690s, was a member of the Mitchell family of Glenarm, in County Antrim, which also expanded into Dublin.

Most of the leading Belfast merchants visited London and established personal contacts there. Only one, George Macartney of Auchinleck, is known to have married into a London merchant family.[16] Others dealt with merchants from Belfast or Ulster who had settled there. The earliest

13 Roll of freemen, typescript by G. Thrift, 1919 (Dublin Corporation Archives).
14 Francis Iredell, the minister from 1699, was from County Antrim and married a grand-daughter of George Macartney of Auchinleck in 1716 (appendix A.18).
15 Registry of Deeds, Dublin, 22 444 12536.
16 Elizabeth Butler had three brothers in London in 1664 (Sir William Dugdale, *The*

known of these is Hugh Whyte, who was established in London by 1677 when he was referred to as 'Mr Hugh Whyte in London in whose hands is most of the money the Belfast merchants have in London'. No dealings with Whyte are recorded in Black George's letter books, but he recommended him to Sir George Rawdon.[17] Whyte was a member of the Belfast Whyte/White family, and was the brother-in-law of William Smith of Belfast. Whyte's transactions as banker for the Belfast merchants are not well documented but his probate inventory, and the subsequent case papers, show dealings with Lord Donegall, Arthur Upton, Sir Arthur Rawdon and other members of the Ulster gentry.[18]

After Whyte's death, most Belfast merchants dealt with either William Brown or the Cairnes brothers. Brown, who was the brother-in-law of Edward Brice and Thomas Knox, was the London agent and banker of a number of Belfast and Ulster merchants, and his success enabled him to set up a son in trade in Venice. In his will of 1712 he named Robert Gardner of Westminster as trustee for his daughter.[19] Gardner can be identified as Robert Gardner of Carrickfergus whose unlucky investment in the South Sea Company is mentioned in chapter six. Isaac Macartney corresponded with Gardner, but as a personal friend rather than a London agent. Both Brown's and Gardner's business dealings were small, however, compared with those of the Cairnes brothers, the eldest of whom had established himself in London by the early 1690s. By the early 1700s their business was run by Alexander and Henry in London and William in Dublin. They were bankers for a wide circle of merchants and Ulster gentry and were also personal friends of several of the Belfast merchants. Alexander is known to have visited Londonderry and Belfast in 1705 and, as M.P. for Belfast, William had frequent contact with the leading merchants, and acted as banker in Dublin for many of them. The Cairnes brothers were presbyterians but, apart from William, were not militant in support of their faith. Nevertheless they were helpful to their co-religionists. For example, when Francis Iredell, minister of the Capel Street congregation in Dublin, was sent to London in 1711 to present an address to the queen, he was instructed to wait on Sir Alexander Cairnes (created a baronet in 1708) who would advise him in the management of the business.[20]

visitation of the county palatine of Lancaster made in the year 1664–5, ed. F.R. Raines [Chetham Society, 84, 85, 88, Manchester, 1872–3] p.64); appendix A.18.

17 *Cal. S.P. dom., 1676–77*, p.577, *1677–78*, p.4.

18 Copies of inventory of goods of Hugh Whyte and case papers (P.R.O., PROB.4/4465; N.A., Crosslé abstracts, Smith viii, pp 895–7).

19 Copy will of John Gamble of Strabane, 9 Apr. 1706 (N.A., prerogative will book, 1706–08); Butle to Brown, 9 May 1696 (Butle, p.33); there is evidence in the letter books of Isaac Macartney and David Butle that Brown had dealings with Brice, Chads, James Arbuckle and William and John Rainey; copy will of William Brown, 1712 (P.R.O., PROB.11/530).

20 Tenison, 'Old Dublin bankers', pp 120–1; Lawlor, *History of the family of Cairnes*,

15 Sir Hans Sloane

Another Ulster family to settle in London in the seventeenth century were the Sloanes. James Sloane, a barrister, was there in the 1680s, and his brothers Hans from the 1690s, and William from the early 1700s. Although neither James nor Hans was concerned in trade both were seen as part of the Belfast merchant community's network of friends and relatives abroad. For example James helped Black George to recover a debt from Lord Ardglass in 1679, and Hans was in correspondence with Dr Victor Ferguson and John McBride of Belfast in the 1690s–1700s, both of whom wrote letters of introduction for a stream of young men from Belfast and County Down who were either studying medicine or travelling to London for pleasure.[21] Although other Ulster and Belfast merchants settled in London, their numbers were comparatively small and they did not stand out as a distinct community there as they did in Dublin. Since there was, in London, a substantial community of expatriate Scots, large numbers of whom were involved in trade and banking, it is likely that the Ulster merchants were seen as a subdivision within this group, and that they worshipped at the Scots presbyterian church at Founder's Hall. By the early eighteenth century, the Belfast merchants' factors in the English outports were also Scots or Ulster presbyterians. For example, William Ferys of Whitehaven, who acted for a number of Belfast merchants, was a presbyterian whose family owned land in Dunmurry, just outside Belfast, while John Cunningham of Liverpool was a brother-in-law of Robert Lennox of Belfast, and James Hillhouse of Bristol was Lennox's nephew.[22]

By the end of the seventeenth century the Belfast network had spread to France. In 1679, John Black of Belfast travelled out to Bordeaux and chose some wines which proved to be excellent on arrival at Belfast. Subsequent visits also proved profitable. Black established a distant cousin, George Boyd, in Henry Lavie's counting house and by the early 1700s Boyd was operating in partnership with Robert Gordon. Gordon, who was

pp 81–2; Cullen, 'Merchant communities, the navigation acts and Irish and Scottish responses', p.165; abstract of prerogative court case papers, Hamilton v. Hamilton, 1704 (P.R.O.N.I., Tenison Groves abstracts, T808/6117, 6453); Robert Holt to James Hamilton, 20 Feb. 1695/6 (P.R.O.N.I., MIC147/8, vol. 16, no. 132); Thomas Pottinger to John Ellis, 31 July 1697 (B.L., Add. MS 28,881, f.375); John to William Leathes, 28 Sept. 1713 (Suffolk R.O., Ipswich branch, de Mussenden-Leathes papers, T1039/6/11); Macartney to Messrs Cairnes, 26 July 1705 (Macartney 3, p.151); *Gen. synod Ulster rec.*, i, pp 281–2, 313, 341.

21 Macartney to James Sloane, 30 Apr. 1679 (Macartney 2, p.56); Ferguson to Sloane, 14 July 1691, 27 Mar. 1704/5, McBride to Sloane, 1700–13 (B.L., Sloane MS 4036, f.106, MS 4038, ff 117, 189, 288, MS 4039, f.229, MS 4040, f.122, MS 4043, ff 68, 202).

22 Abstracts of Ferys wills etc., 1712, 1714 (P.R.O.N.I., Hill abstracts, T719/1, T731/21, T732); D.R. Hainsworth (ed.), *The correspondence of Sir John Lowther of Whitehaven, 1693–98: a provincial community in wartime* (Oxford, 1983), no.123; Macartney to Cunningham, 20 Nov. 1704, and to Hillhouse, 17 Aug. 1706 (Macartney 3, pp 14–15, 342).

a Scot, also had a network of kinsmen in trade. His wife's brother Robert Byres was a merchant in Dublin, and another of Byres's sisters was married to William Souper of Aberdeen, who was Isaac Macartney's agent there.[23] Boyd and Gordon supplied wine for many of the Belfast merchants from the profits of the sale of their outward cargoes of provisions. The principal import was beef for re-export to the French colonies, although there was a boom in butter following the peace of Ryswick. Boyd and Gordon were joined at Bordeaux by Black's son John who settled there in 1699, and who founded one of the most successful and dynamic of the merchant houses in Bordeaux in the eighteenth century.

Less is known about the earliest Belfast settlers in the West Indies. Macartney's friend Alexander McKinney went out to Barbados in 1661 and Robert Johnson had a plantation on Antigua in 1686,[24] but no further information has been found about them or their descendants so it is possible that they succumbed to the West Indian climate. A grandson of George Martin of Belfast settled in Antigua but no contacts with the Belfast community are recorded. However, by 1698, the brothers William and Robert Moore had settled in Barbados and were handling the business of Belfast merchants. There is no direct evidence that they were related to the Belfast Moores but this seems likely as William Moore of Barbados was the brother-in-law of James Arbuckle of Belfast.[25]

By the beginning of the eighteenth century, therefore, not only did the trading network of the Belfast merchants consist largely of Ulster presbyterians, but many of them were actual kinsmen linked by blood or marriage. This network had expanded rapidly after the Williamite wars and included members of many of the thirty-two Belfast families in appendix A. The growth of this network is demonstrated in the following two tables. Table 10 (overleaf) shows that in the period 1660–89 only seven, or appproximately 22%, of the thirty-two families had a relation by blood, with the same surname, in another trading centre, excluding Scotland. A further eight families had a similar connection by marriage, bringing the total to fifteen, or 46%. However, the actual number of individuals represented by these figures is small as four of the families related by marriage were related to the same person, namely John Eccles of Dublin. By beginning of the eighteenth century, seven of the thirty-two families had died out, or appear to have had no active connection with trade.[26]

23 Journal of John Black of Bordeaux, 14 June 1763 (P.R.O.N.I., T1073/16); details of children of Robert Gordon, 1689–1713 (P.R.O.N.I., Black papers, D1950/2); will pedigree of Robert Byres (P.R.O.N.I., Betham will pedigrees, T559/14, p.156).
24 Macartney to McKinney, 16 Dec. 1661 (Macartney 1, p.34); for Johnson see chapter 5.
25 Butle to William Moore, 10 Jan. 1697/8 (Butle, p.53); Macartney to William Moore, 18 Jan. 1704/5 (Macartney 3, p.43); Arbuckle was also son-in-law to John Black.
26 Doake, Dobbin, Hamilton, Leathes, Lockhart, Theaker, Waring.

Table 10: Belfast merchants with relations at other trading centres, 1660–89
(based on 32 families)

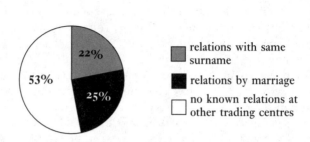

Table 11 (below) shows that by 1700 there had been a considerable increase in the numbers of Belfast merchants at other trading centres. It is based on the twenty-five families still in trade in the early eighteenth century. Eighteen of these, or 72%, had a relation (by blood or marriage) settled elsewhere, most of whom were active in trade and had dealings with the Belfast community. At least thirteen of these families had a kinsman in Dublin, which underlines the central position of the city in Belfast's trade, and at least eleven had kinsmen in more than one trading centre.

Table 11: Belfast families with relations at other trading centres in 1700
(based on 25 families)

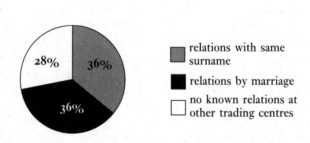

Outstanding among these were prolific families such as the Martins, Whites and Eccleses whose younger sons, cousins and nephews settled in several cities and ports. Moreover, the percentages given in tables 10 and 11 may be understated because the marriage alliances of a number of families are poorly documented and because kinship networks in the seventeenth century would have included kinship through several marriages, which is not shown here.

L.M. Cullen's study of the Dublin merchant community in the eighteenth century demonstrates that '... if the merchant's foreign correspondents by blood and marriage are analysed, his activities fit into a pattern of trade conducted on the account of an entire family group in several centres'.[27] A detailed study of Belfast merchant families has shown that this was equally true of the Belfast merchant community at the end of the seventeenth century. A brief description of two such family networks will illustrate this:

Members of the Eccles family, which originated in Ayrshire, had been in Ulster since the 1630s, although it appears to have been members of the second generation who settled in and around Belfast by the 1650s. By the 1690s the family was represented at Belfast by John Eccles whose marriage to Jane Rainey had brought important trading contacts in Coleraine and Londonderry. His cousin Alderman John Eccles had been in Dublin since the 1680s, and the latter's brother James was established in Waterford. Both were to become mayors of their adoptive cities. Their sister Jane was married to John Black of Belfast, whose brother David was trading from Cork in the 1690s; Black settled first a cousin, then a son at Bordeaux, and two other sons were to settle at Cadiz. By contrast, Robert Lennox did not settle in Belfast until after the Jacobite wars although he had previously been active as a merchant in Londonderry. He was a brother of Alderman James Lennox of Londonderry, who was married to Elizabeth Galt of Coleraine. Robert Lennox's third wife, whom he married in 1702, was a cousin of Alderman Thomas Bell of Dublin. Lennox was also a brother-in-law of John Cunningham of Liverpool and an uncle of James Hillhouse of Bristol, both of whom acted as factors for a number of Belfast merchants.

Every one of the Belfast merchant families with members in other trading centres was of Scottish origin and almost all were presbyterian. They were seen as part of the great Scots presbyterian trading network, and the growth of this network was viewed with alarm by members of the government. A memorandum of c.1697 in the papers of Abraham Hill, commissioner of the board of trade,[28] begins by stating that the Scots had got into their hands two-thirds of the trade of Ireland. This was said to have arisen from their victualling the English armies during the Williamite wars. They were then said to have gone 'boldly into France, and had, for many years, connivance for all they imported, as it brought help and increase to the Publick Revenue'. Belfast received particular mention:

> That although Belfast is now counted the second place of trade in Ireland, yet the Scotch merchants are spread into all other the trading towns of that kingdom, and are made magistrates in their turnes. They are generally frugal, industrious, very national, and very helpful to each other against any

27 Cullen, 'Dublin merchant community', p.195.
28 Memorandum on the Scots in Ireland (B.L., Sloane MS 2902, no.60, f.218).

third. That this temper is the same in their gentry, who have gotten great
authority in the Army, and in the parliament of that kingdom.

The memorandum concludes: 'Whether this growing wealth and power, if
found true, will centre at last in England or in Scotland, is worth consideration'. The Belfast merchants were seen as part of a Scots presbyterian
network which posed both a political threat to the Anglo-Irish establishment in Ireland, and an economic threat to English trade, threats which
were to lead to the passing of the test act in 1704 and the act of union in
1707.

   Within a period of forty years there had been a considerable change in
trading practice. In the 1660s the Belfast merchants acted mainly as factors
or partners of merchants in Dublin, and they consigned goods to the
factors abroad employed by the latter, many of whom were expatriate
Irishmen, connected to the Dublin merchants by blood or marriage, or
were foreign nationals with connections in Dublin. This was particularly
true in France, but even in those parts of Europe where a network of
Scottish merchants existed, the Belfast merchants appear to have made
little use of them in the 1660s–80s. By the end of the century a fundamental change had taken place. By 1700, almost all of the factors who handled
the goods of Belfast merchants in other trading centres were Scots and
presbyterians. Although they were seen as part of the Scottish trading
network, many can be identified as coming from Ulster, and a high proportion of these were from Belfast. The colony of presbyterian merchants
which is identifiable in Dublin in the 1690s included many Belfast men,
some of whom had been there since the 1660s. Dublin continued to play a
dominant role in trade and banking but the Belfast merchants now dealt
with a group of their own kinsmen and connections who had settled there.
Belfast men had also settled in Waterford and Cork and handled the business of the Belfast merchants there. Similarly Belfast or Ulster men acted
as bankers in London for the Belfast community. There were Belfast men
in the West Indies from the 1660s, and by the 1690s settlement had begun
in Bordeaux. The first generation of merchants from Scotland had established Belfast as the major port in Ulster for the export of provisions and
linen. The second generation established a network of Belfast merchants
abroad to extend that trade.

Epilogue

By the end of the seventeenth century, Belfast had developed from a minor port, with a poor harbour, into the fourth largest trading centre in Ireland. The next century was to see a further expansion of trade through the enterprise of the merchant community. The community remained close-knit, with family ties reinforcing business partnerships, but new leaders emerged as the original families retired from trade. By the middle of the century, most of the thirty-two families no longer had any connection with business, apart from the Black family which went from strength to strength. The Andersons, Crafords, Theakers, Thompsons and the Belfast branch of the Warings had died out. The Brices, Butles, Knoxes, Macartneys, Raineys and Pottingers had become landed families.

The merchant community, like the town, remained predominantly presbyterian, but it was no longer united. Controversy over subscription to the Westminster Confession of Faith led to a permanent rift between the New Light and the Old Light parties in the presbyterian church. In the middle of the century, those who attended the parish church were still from the poorer section of the community. Numbers of Roman catholics within the town increased slowly; the first catholic church was built in 1784, with presbyterians contributing to the building fund.

The population increased to over 8,000 by the middle of the eighteenth century. The town spread but the centre was falling into decay because the incapacity of the fourth earl of Donegall had prevented renewal of the leases issued in the 1690s when the Donegall/Longford lawsuit was settled. When the new leases were finally issued they carried considerable rent increases, but the centre of the town was renewed, and by the end of the century Belfast boasted new buildings such as an exchange and assembly rooms, a new parish church, a theatre and a poor house. The Donegall family were now absentee landlords, but the fifth earl contributed generously towards the new public buildings.

The test act remained in force for almost eighty years. The Belfast corporation was ineffectual and incapable of dealing with the problems of the rapidly growing town. It was the presbyterian merchants who founded the

Belfast Charitable Society in 1752, and who built and ran the poor house. The wealthy merchant families were leaders of the social and intellectual life of the town. Their exclusion from office resulted in alienation from the British government and this, coupled with their contact with revolutionary doctrines in both America and France, led members of these families to support first, the Belfast Volunteers, and later the United Irishmen, leading members of the latter being descendants of seventeenth-century Belfast merchants.

The growth of the linen industry changed the pattern of Belfast's export trade. Close links developed with the American colonies, with members of many Belfast merchant families settling in American ports. Belfast ships carried emigrants to America from the surrounding countryside. The quays and docks were improved, largely as result of the enterprise of individual merchants. The first bank was set up in Belfast in 1752, although this was short-lived, and the Chamber of Commerce was founded in 1783. However, by the end of the century merchants no longer dominated the town which was becoming an industrial rather than a commercial centre. Nevertheless it was the achievements of the Belfast merchant community which laid the foundations for the town's development as a major industrial city.

Bibliography

IRELAND

BELFAST
Belfast Central Library
  Bigger papers
Linen Hall Library
  Belfast Newsletter
  Blackwood pedigrees
  'Genealogical history of the family of the Rt. Hon. Sir George Macartney ...
    1773'
  Antiquarian papers of Henry Joy
  Letter books of George Macartney, 1661–68, 1679–81
Public Record Office of Northern Ireland
A. *Major sources*
  Annesley (records of forfeiture commission) (D1854)
  Belfast town book (MIC556)
  Black (T1073, T2420, D719, D1838, D1950)
  Brice, account book of Edward Brice, c.1686–96 (D1556/16/7)
  Butle, out-letter book of David Butle, 1696–1703 (D1449/13/1)
  Coleraine corporation, minutes, 1672–1710 (T3380/1)
  Dobbs (T431, T707, D162)
  Donegall (D509, D2249/61, MIC4B, MIC385)
  Londonderry corporation, minutes from 1673 (MIC440/1)
  Macartney, out-letter book of Isaac Macartney, 1704–06 (D501)
  Macartney (of Auchinleck and Lisanoure) (D572, D1062, D1184, D3000/109/1)
  Macartney (of Blacket) (T2970, D3649, D2092, D3513)
  Registry of Deeds (MIC7 and MIC311)
  State Papers (Ireland) (MIC223, T448, T546)
B. *Minor sources*
  Adair (D929)
  Antrim (D265)
  Ash (T989)
  Biggar (D3905)
  Brett (D271)
  Burges (T1007, T1147)
  Castle Stewart (D1618)
  Clanbrassil (T761)
  Clements (D3860)

Conolly (T2826)
Dobbin (T367)
Downshire (D671)
Gaussen (D2315)
Granard (T3765)
Hamilton (T741, T890, T919, D1460)
Hearth money rolls, 1666 (T3022/4/1), 1669 (T307A)
Innis (T1514, D3562)
Land purchase commission (T810)
Lennox (Drennan) (T468, T710, T765, T1116, D729, D270)
Lenox-Conyngham (T313, T420, T498, T500, T3161, D1449)
Leslie (D3406/D)
Londonderry (D654)
Magenis (T185)
Massereene (D562)
Maxwell (D1556)
Montgomery (T1030)
Mussenden (D354)
Murray of Broughton (D2860)
Perceval-Price (T2473)
Roden (Hamilton of Tollymore) (MIC147/8)
Rossmore (T2929)
Sloane (T1512, T2974/3)
Society of Friends (Dublin) (T1062)
Trevor (D778)
Vesey (T1998, T3738)
Ward (T1128, D2092)
Waring (D695, MIC385)
Weir (D298)
White (D2861)

C. *Antiquarian papers, etc.*
Benn (D3113)
Betham (T559)
Chart (D1246)
Clarke (D1430, MIC92)
Crosslé (T283, T618, T748, T780, T845)
Given (D2096)
Graham (T1289)
Hill (T719, T731, T732)
Irish Genealogical Research Society (T777)
Leslie (T552, T1075)
Mathews (T681)
Millin (T811)
Nicholson (T828)
Reeves (MIC35)
Society of Genealogists (T581)
Steele (T277)
Stewart (T403, D1759)
Stewart Kennedy (T700)
Tenison Groves (T808)
Young (D2930)

DUBLIN
Dublin Public Libraries (Corporation Archives)
  Roll of freemen, City of Dublin, (typescript by G. Thrift, 1919)
  Dublin corporation, Monday books
Genealogical Office
  Will abstracts
  Funeral entries, grants, etc. (GO MSS 67, 69, 76–8, 85–7, 103)
National Archives
  Betham abstracts
  Brice, counsel's opinion (M1325)
  Chancery bill books
  Colville letters, 1680–84 (M 485)
  Crosslé abstracts
  Ferguson transcripts
  Letter of submission by Belfast corporation, 1689 (M 2541, f.21)
  Lodge's records of the rolls
  Miscellaneous (M 15274)
  Prerogative will books
  Record Commissioners' transcripts
  Sarsfield Vesey letters
  Tenison Groves abstracts
  Thrift will abstracts
National Library of Ireland
  Brice (MS 21,961)
  Carte MSS (microfilm)
  List of Carrickfergus shipping (MS 8100)
  Ormond MSS (2331, no.1740, 2439, no.8536)
Registry of Deeds
  Indexes and memorials
Trinity College Dublin
  Antrim militia papers and letters to Sir Robert Colville, 1687–93 (MS 1178)
  Claims of protestant refugees, and brief for protestants of Ireland at Chester,
      1689 (MS 847)
  Examination of Thomas Theaker, 1644 (MS 838, ff 7–8)
  Molyneux's journey to the north, 1708 (MS 883/2)
  Stewart-Kennedy notebooks
  Archbishop King's correspondence (MS 750, 1995–2008)
  Bartholomew Vanhomrigh, out-letter book, 1684–85 (MS 3961)

SCOTLAND

EDINBURGH
General Register Office for Scotland
  Old parish registers of Ayr, Dumfries, Irvine and Glasgow
Scottish Record Office
  Admiralty Court records (AC/7)
  Register of Deeds
  Registers of Sasines
  Commissary Court records
  Port books, Ayr and Glasgow (E72/3, 10)
  Agnew of Lochnaw papers (GD154/935)
  Maxwell of Orchardton papers (RH15/91)
  Russell papers (RH15/106)

KIRKWALL
Orkney Archives Office
    Traill papers (D14/2/6)
    Notes on Pottinger family (D20/3/10)

ENGLAND

IPSWICH
Suffolk Record Office, Ipswich Branch
    De Mussenden-Leathes papers (T1039)

LONDON
British Library
    Bonnivert's journal (Sloane MS 1033)
    Letters from Sir Richard Cox to Sir Robert and Edward Southwell (Add. MSS
        38,153–7)
    Declaration of Hugh Eccles concerning ship *Unicorn* 1675 (Stowe 208, f.227)
    Letters to John Ellis from Thomas Pottinger (Add.MSS 28,881 f.375, 28,890
        f.397, 28,891 f.145), from George Macartney (Add. MS 28,876 ff87, 115, 141),
        from Humphrey Jervis (Add. MSS 28,875 f.191, 28,877 f.397, 28,892 f.113,
        28,893 f.37)
    Papers and letters relating to proceedings of the Irish Parliament (Add. MS 9715)
    Report from Thomas Knox on wool smuggling from south of Ireland to France
        c.1706 (Add. MS 21,133 f.62)
    Martin of Antigua (Add. MSS 41, 474)
    Monck's tour, 1637 (Harleian MS 2138, ff.164–89)
    Petitions of Thomas Pottinger to Earl Godolphin, c.1700 (Add. MSS 28,940, ff 297,
        298)
    Letters to Sir Hans Sloane (Sloane MSS)
    Papers of Abraham Hill (Sloane MS 2902)
    Table of exports and imports into Ireland, Dec. 1682–Dec. 1686 (Add. MS 4759)
Lambeth Palace Library
    Bishop Gibson's letters (MS 1742)
Public Record Office
        Chancery Masters' exhibits: Papers about debts of third earl of Donegall
            (C106/95/15)
        Donegall minority accounts (C107/16)
        Marescoe David letters (C114)
    Colonial office papers (CO1/xxviii, 46)
    High Court of Admiralty papers (HCA1, 13, 15)
    Port books, Bristol, Chester, Liverpool, Whitehaven (E190)
    Prerogative wills and administrations
    State papers (SP 63)
    Tables of Irish exports and imports from 1698 (CUST 15)
    Treasury books and papers (T1, 4, 14, 27)

OXFORD
Bodleian Library
    Carte MSS 31–40

CONTEMPORARY PRINTED SOURCES

A discourse concerning Ireland and the different interests thereof in answer to the Exon and Barnstable petitions (London, 1698).

Arthur Dobbs, *An essay on the trade and improvement of Ireland* (Dublin, 1729).

A faithful history of the northern affairs of Ireland (London, 1690).

William King, *The state of the protestants under the late King James's government* (London, 1691; Dublin, 1730).

James Kirkpatrick, *An historical essay upon the loyalty of presbyterians in Great Britain and Ireland from the reformation to this present year* (Belfast, 1713).

Richard Lawrence, *The interest of Ireland in its trade and wealth stated* (Dublin, 1682).

[Charles Leslie], *An answer to a book intituled the state of the protestants in Ireland under King James's government* (London, 1692).

Sir William Petty, *The political anatomy of Ireland* (1691, repr. Shannon, 1969).

William Sacheverall, *An account of the Isle of Man ... with a voyage to I Columb-Kill* (London, 1702).

George Story, *An impartial history of the wars of Ireland* (London, 1693).

William Tisdall, *Conduct of the dissenters of Ireland with respect to both church and state* (Dublin, 1712).

Sample of true-blue presbyterian loyalty in all changes and turns of government (Dublin, 1709).

PRINTED PRIMARY SOURCES AND COMPILATIONS

Acts of the privy council of England (colonial series) 1613–1720 (2 vols, London, 1908–10).

Patrick Adair, *A true narrative of the rise and progress of the presbyterian church in Ireland*, ed. W.D. Killen (Belfast, 1866).

Jean Agnew (ed.), *Funeral register of the First Presbyterian Church of Belfast, 1712–36* (Belfast, 1995).

Henry F. Berry (ed.), *The registers of the church of St Michan, Dublin*, (2 vols, Dublin, 1907, 1909).

Calendar of the Carew manuscripts preserved in the archiepiscopal library at Lambeth, 1515–1624 (6 vols, London, 1867–73).

Calendars of state papers, colonial series (America and West Indies), 1661–1708 (16 vols, London, 1880–1916).

Calendars of state papers, domestic series, 1660–1704 (London, 1860–1972).

Calendars of state papers relating to Ireland, 1633–70 (7 vols, London, 1901–10).

Calendars of treasury books, 1660–92 (vols i–ix, London, 1904–31).

Calendar of treasury papers 1556–7–1696 (London, 1868).

S.T. Carleton (ed.), *Heads and hearths, the hearth money rolls and poll tax returns for Co. Antrim, 1660–69* (Belfast, 1991).

[Clarendon], *The correspondence of Henry Hyde, earl of Clarendon, and his brother, Laurence Hyde, earl of Rochester, with the diary of Lord Clarendon from 1687–90*, ed. S.W. Singer, (2 vols, London, 1828).

Robert Dunlop (ed.), *Ireland under the commonwealth: being a selection of documents relating to the government of Ireland, 1651–59* (2 vols, Manchester, 1913).

[Essex], *Essex papers 1672–79*, ed. Osmund Airy, (vol. i, London, 1890).

Letters written by Arthur Capel, earl of Essex, lord lieutenant of Ireland, in ... 1675 (London, 1770).

J.T. Gilbert (ed.), *Calendar of ancient records of Dublin, in the possession of the municipal corporation* (vols i–vi, Dublin, 1889–96).

Thomas Gogarty (ed.), *Council book of the corporation of Drogheda* (2 vols, Drogheda, 1915, repr. Cork, 1988)

D.R. Hainsworth (ed.), *Commercial papers of Sir Christopher Lowther* (Surtees Society, clxxxix, Gateshead, 1977).

> *The correspondence of Sir John Lowther of Whitehaven, 1693–98: a provincial community in wartime* (Oxford, 1983).

[Hastings] *Report on the manuscripts of the late Reginald Rawdon Hastings Esq., of the Manor House, Ashby de la Zouche* (4 vols, H.M.C., London, 1930–37).

Anthony Hewitson (ed.), *Social life and national movements in the seventeenth century 1688–89–90, diary of Thomas Bellingham, an officer under William III* (Preston, 1908).

George Hill (ed.), *The Montgomery manuscripts 1608–1706: compiled from the family papers by William Montgomery of Rosemount esquire* (Belfast, 1869).

[Irvine] *Muniments of the royal burgh of Irvine* (2 vols, Edinburgh, 1890–1).

Journals of the house of commons of the kingdom of Ireland (Dublin, 1763).

Journals of the Irish house of lords (vols i–ii, Dublin, 1783).

[Kirkcudbright] *Kirkcudbright sheriff court deeds 1623–1700*, ed. Mary B. Johnston and Catherine Armet (3 vols, Edinburgh, 1939, 1953).

> *Kirkcudbright town council records 1606–58* (2 vols, Edinburgh, 1958).

T.K. Lowry, (ed.), *The Hamilton manuscripts, containing some account of territories of Upper Clandeboye, Great Ardes, Dufferin in the county of Down, by Sir William Hamilton, afterward Viscount Clandeboye* (Belfast, 1867).

[John Mackenzie], *Mackenzie's memorials of the siege of Derry including his narrative and its vindication*, ed. W.D. Killen (Belfast 1861).

T.W. Moody and J.G. Simms (ed.), *The bishopric of Derry and the Irish Society of London, 1603–1705* (2 vols, I.M.C., Dublin, 1968, 1983).

[Ormonde] *Calendar of the manuscripts of the marquess of Ormonde, preserved at Kilkenny Castle* (11 vols, H.M.C., London, 1895–1920).

Seamus Pender (ed.), *A census of Ireland circa 1659, with supplementary material from the poll money ordinances (1660–61)* (I.M.C., Dublin, 1939).

Records of the general synod of Ulster from 1691 to 1820, i, 1691–1720 (Belfast, 1890).

The register of the privy council of Scotland 1660–91 (3rd series, 16 vols, Edinburgh, 1908–70).

Henry Roseveare (ed.), *Markets and merchants of the late seventeenth century, the Marescoe-David letters, 1668–1680* (Oxford, 1987).

[Strafford] *The earl of Strafforde's letters and despatches*, ed. William Knowler (2 vols, Dublin, 1740).

Harold Williams, *The correspondence of Jonathan Swift* (vol. i, Oxford, 1963).

R.M. Young (ed.), *The town book of the corporation of Belfast, 1613–1816* (Belfast, 1892).

> *Historical notices of old Belfast and its vicinity* (Belfast 1896).

SECONDARY SOURCES

E.D Atkinson, *An Ulster parish, being a history of Donaghcloney* (Dublin, 1898).

Bernard Bailyn, *The New England merchants in the seventeenth century* (Cambridge, Mass., 1955).

Violet Barbour, 'Marine risks and insurance in the seventeenth century' in *Journal of Economic and Business History*, i (1929), pp 561–70.

T.C. Barnard, *Cromwellian Ireland, English government and reform in Ireland, 1649–1660* (Oxford, 1975).

> 'Lawyers and the law in later seventeenth-century Ireland' in *I.H.S.*, xxviii, no.111 (1993), pp 256–82.

'The political, material and mental culture of the Cork settlers, c.1650–1700' in Patrick O'Flanagan and Cornelius G. Buttimer (ed.), *Cork history & society, interdisciplinary essays on the history of an Irish county* (Dublin, 1993), pp 309–65.

Thomas C. Barrow, *Trade and empire: the British customs service in colonial America, 1660–1776* (Cambridge, Mass., 1967).

J.C. Beckett, *Protestant dissent in Ireland, 1687–1784* (London, 1948).

'The government and the church of Ireland under William III and Anne' in *I.H.S.*, ii, no.7 (1941), pp 280–302.

'Irish-Scottish relations in the seventeenth century' in J.C. Beckett (ed.), *Confrontations, studies in Irish history* (London, 1972), pp 26–46.

'The seventeenth century' in J.C. Beckett and R.E. Glasscock (ed.), *Belfast: the origin and growth of an industrial city* (London, 1967), pp 26–38.

'William King's administration of the diocese of Derry, 1691–1703' in *I.H.S.*, iv, no.14 (1944–5), pp 164–80.

Earl of Belmore, *The history of the Corry family of Castlecoole* (London and Dublin, 1891).

George Benn, *A history of the town of Belfast* (2 vols, Belfast, 1877).

I. Budge and C. O'Leary, *Belfast: approach to crisis: a study of Belfast politics 1613–1970* (London, 1973).

Bernard Burke, *A genealogical and heraldic history of the landed gentry of Ireland* (London, 1912).

Paul Butel, *Les négociants bordelais, l'Europe et les îles au xviiie siècle* (Paris, 1974).

R.A. Butlin, 'Irish towns in the sixteenth and seventeenth centuries' in R.A. Butlin (ed.), *The development of the Irish town* (London, 1977), pp 61–100.

George Camblin, *The town in Ulster* (Belfast, 1951).

P.G.E. Clemens, 'The rise of Liverpool, 1665–1750' in *Econ. Hist. Rev.*, 2nd series, xxix (1976), pp 211–25.

L.E. Cochran, *Scottish trade with Ireland in the eighteenth century* (Edinburgh, 1985).

W.H. Crawford, 'The rise of the linen industry' in L.M. Cullen (ed.), *The formation of the Irish economy* (Cork, 1969), pp 23–25.

L.M. Cullen, *Anglo-Irish trade, 1660–1800* (Manchester, 1968).

An economic history of Ireland since 1660 (London, 1972).

'The Dublin merchant community in the eighteenth century' in Paul Butel and L.M. Cullen (ed.), *Cities and merchants: French and Irish perspectives on urban development, 1500–1900* (Dublin, 1986), pp 195–209.

'Economic development, 1691–1750' in T.W. Moody and W.E. Vaughan (ed.), *A new history of Ireland, iv, Eighteenth-century Ireland 1691–1800* (Oxford, 1986), pp 123–58.

'Economic trends, 1660–91' in T.W. Moody, F.X. Martin, F.J. Byrne (ed.), *A new history of Ireland, iii, Early modern Ireland 1534–1691* (Oxford, 1978), pp 387–407.

'Galway merchants in the outside world, 1650–1800' in Diarmuid O'Cearbhaill (ed.), *Galway: town and gown, 1484–1984* (Dublin, 1984), pp 63–89.

'The Huguenots from the perspective of the merchant networks of W. Europe (1680–1790): the example of the brandy trade' in C.E.J. Caldicott, Hugh Gough, J.-P. Pittion (ed.), *The Huguenots and Ireland, anatomy of an emigration* (Dublin, 1987), pp 129–49.

'The Irish merchant communities of Bordeaux, La Rochelle and Cognac in the eighteenth century' in Paul Butel and L.M. Cullen (ed.), *Négoce et industrie en France et en Irlande aux xviiie et xixe siècles* (Paris, 1980), pp 51–63.

'Landlords, bankers and merchants: the early Irish banking world, 1700–1820' in A.E. Murphy (ed.), *Economists and the Irish economy from the eighteenth century to the present day* (Dublin, 1984), pp 25–44.

'Merchant communities, the navigation acts and Irish and Scottish responses' in

L.M. Cullen and T.C. Smout (ed.), *Comparative aspects of Scottish and Irish economic and social history, 1600–1900* (Edinburgh, 1977), pp 165–76.

'Population trends in seventeenth century Ireland' in *Economic and Social Review*, vi, no. 2 (Jan., 1975), pp 149–65.

'The smuggling trade in Ireland in the eighteenth century' in *R.I.A. Proc.*, lxvii, sect. C, pp 149–75.

Ralph Davis, *The rise of the English shipping industry in the seventeenth and eighteenth centuries* (Newton Abbot, 1962).

T.M. Devine, 'The Scottish merchant community, 1680–1740' in R.H. Campbell and A. Skinner (ed.), *The origins and nature of the Scottish enlightenment* (Edinburgh, 1982), pp 26–41.

'The social composition of the business class in the larger Scottish towns, 1680–1740' in T.M. Devine and David Dickson (ed.), *Ireland and Scotland 1600–1850: parallels and contrasts in economic and social development* (Edinburgh, 1983), pp 163–76.

David Dickson, 'The place of Dublin in the eighteenth century Irish economy' in T.M. Devine and David Dickson (ed.), *Ireland and Scotland 1600–1850: parallels and contrasts in economic and social development* (Edinburgh, 1983), pp 177–92.

David Dickson, Cormac Ó Grada, Stuart Daultrey, 'Hearth tax, household size and Irish population change 1672–1821' in *R.I.A. Proc.*, lxxxii, sect.C., no.6 (1982), pp 128–81.

Dictionary of National Biography, ed. Leslie Stephen and Sydney Lee (66 vols, London, 1885–1901; reprinted with corrections, 22 vols, London, 1908–09).

E.R. McClintock Dix, 'List of books and tracts printed in Belfast in the seventeenth century' in *R.I.A. Proc.*, xxxiii, sect.C. (1916), pp 73–80.

John Dubourdieu, *Statistical survey of the county of Antrim* (Dublin, 1812).

James Duchal (ed.), *Sermons of the Reverend John Abernethy* (London, 1762).

Sir William Dugdale, *The Visitation of the county palatine of Lancaster made in the year 1664–5*, ed. F.R. Raines (Chetham Society, 84, 85, 88, Manchester, 1872–73).

Peter Earle, *The making of the English middle class, 1660–1730* (London, 1991).

Peter Francis, 'The Belfast potthouse, Carrickfergus clay and the spread of the delftware industry' in *Transactions of the English Ceramic Circle*, xv, pt 2 (1994), pp 267–282.

Raymond Gillespie, *Colonial Ulster: the settlement of east Ulster 1600–41* (Cork, 1985).

The transformation of the Irish economy, 1550–1700 (Dublin, 1991).

'The Irish protestants and James II, 1688–90' in *I.H.S.*, xxviii, no.110 (1992), pp 124–33.

'Landed society and the interregnum in Ireland and Scotland' in Rosalind Mitchison and Peter Roebuck (ed.): *Economy and society in Scotland and Ireland* (Edinburgh, 1988), pp 38–47.

'The origins and development of an Ulster urban network, 1600–1641' in *I.H.S.*, xxiv, no.93 (1984), pp 15–29.

'The presbyterian revolution in Ulster, 1660–1690' in W.J. Sheils and Diana Wood (ed.), *The churches, Ireland and the Irish* (Oxford 1989), pp 159–70.

Richard Grassby, 'English merchant capitalism in the late seventeenth century, the composition of business fortunes' in *Past and Present*, xlvi (1970), pp 87–107.

'The personal wealth of the business community in seventeenth-century England' in *Econ. Hist. Rev.*, 2nd series, xxiii (1970), pp 220–34.

'The rate of profit in the seventeenth century' in *E.H.R.*, lxxxiv (1969) pp 721–51.

'Social mobility and business enterprise in seventeenth century England' in Donald Pennington and Keith Thomas (ed.), *Puritans and revolutionaries* (Oxford 1978), pp 355–81.

Vincent T. Harlow, *A history of Barbados, 1625–1685* (Oxford, 1926).

L.A. Harper, *The English navigation laws* (New York, 1939).

Walter Harris, *History of the life and reign of William Henry ... king of England, Scotland, France and Ireland* (Dublin, 1749).

Robert Heslip, 'Lisburn seventeenth century tokens' in *Lisburn Historical Society Journal*, vi (1986), pp 7–10.

George Hill, *An historical account of the Macdonnells of Antrim* (Belfast, 1873).

Historic memorials of the first presbyterian church of Belfast (Belfast, 1887).

J. Milnes Holden, *The history of negotiable instruments in English law* (London, 1955).
'Bills of exchange during the seventeenth century' in *Law Quarterly Review*, lxvii (1951), pp 230–48.

Edward Hughes, 'The eighteenth-century estate agent' in H.A. Cronne, T.W. Moody, D.B. Quinn (ed.), *Essays in British and Irish history* (London, 1949), pp 185–99.

R.J. Hunter, 'Ulster plantation towns 1609–41' in David Harkness and Mary O'Dowd (ed.), *The town in Ireland* (*Historical Studies*, xiii, 1981), pp 55–80.

John De Courcy Ireland, *Ireland and the Irish in maritime history* (Dublin, 1986).
Ireland's sea fisheries: a history (Dublin, 1981).

C.H. Irwin, *A history of presbyterianism in Dublin and the south and west of Ireland* (London, 1890).

F.G. James, 'The Irish lobby in the early eighteenth century' in *E.H.R.*, lxxxi (1966), pp 543–57.

[Henry Joy], *Historical collections relative to the town of Belfast* (Belfast, 1817).

H.F. Kearney, 'Mercantilism and Ireland, 1620–40' in T. Desmond Williams (ed.), *Historical Studies*, i (1958), pp 59–68.
'The political background to English mercantilism' in *Econ. Hist. Rev.*, 2nd series, xi (1959), pp 484–96.

Colum Kenny, *King's Inns and the kingdom of Ireland, the Irish inn of court, 1541–1800* (Dublin, 1992).

Phil Kilroy, *Protestant dissent and controversy in Ireland 1660–1714* (Cork, 1994).

H.C. Lawlor, *A history of the family of Cairnes* (London, 1906).

John Lodge, *The peerage of Ireland or a genealogical history of the present nobility of that kingdom* (7 vols, London, 1789).

W. Macafee and V. Morgan, 'Population in Ulster, 1660–1760' in Peter Roebuck (ed.), *Plantation to partition, essays in Ulster history in honour of J. L. McCracken* (Belfast, 1981), pp 46–63.

Michael MacCarthy-Morrogh, 'Credit and remittance: monetary problems in early seventeenth century Munster' in *I.E.S.H.*, xiv (1987), pp 5–19.

Eileen McCracken, *The Irish woods since Tudor times, distribution and exploitation* (Newton Abbot, 1971).

Patrick McGrath (ed.), *Merchants and merchandise in seventeenth-century Bristol* (Bristol, 1955).

James McGuire, 'Government attitudes to religious non-conformity in Ireland, 1660–1719' in C.E.J. Caldicott, Hugh Gough, J.-P. Pittion (ed.), *The Huguenots and Ireland, anatomy of an emigration* (Dublin, 1987), pp 255–84.

P.H. McKerlie, *The history of the lands and owners in Galloway* (5 vols, Edinburgh, 1870–79)

Edward MacLysaght, *Irish life in the seventeenth century* (Dublin and London, 1939; 2nd edn, Cork, 1950).

Samuel M'Skimin, *The history and antiquities of the town of Carrickfergus* (3rd edn, Belfast, 1829, with addenda and appendix 1833, 39).

John McUre, *A view of the city of Glasgow* (Glasgow, 1736).

S. Shannon Millin, *Additional sidelights on Belfast history* (Belfast and London, 1938).

Rosalind Mitchison, 'Ireland and Scotland: the seventeenth century legacies compared' in T.M. Devine and David Dickson (ed.), *Ireland and Scotland 1600–1850: parallels and contrasts in economic and social development* (Edinburgh, 1983), pp 1–11.

T.H. Mullin, *Coleraine in by-gone centuries* (Belfast, 1976).

Antoin E. Murphy, 'Richard Cantillon, an Irish banker in Paris' in Antoin E. Murphy (ed.), *Economists and the Irish economy from the eighteenth century to the present day* (Dublin 1984).

Sean Murphy, 'The corporation of Dublin' in *Dublin Historical Review*, xxxviii, no.1 (1984), pp 22–35.

George O'Brien, *The economic history of Ireland in the seventeenth century* (Dublin, 1919). 'The Irish staple organization in the reign of James I' in *Economic History*, i (1926), pp 42–56.

John O'Hart (ed.), *Irish landed gentry when Cromwell came to Ireland* (Dublin, 1887).

Jane H. Ohlmeyer, *Civil war and restoration in the three Stuart kingdoms, The career of Randal MacDonnell, marquis of Antrim, 1609–1683* (Cambridge, 1993).

James Paterson, *History of the county of Ayr with a genealogical account of the families of Ayrshire* (2 vols, Ayr 1847, Paisley 1852).

Michael Perceval-Maxwell, *The Scottish migration to Ulster in the reign of James I* (London, 1973; repr. Belfast, 1990).

J.S. Reid, *History of the presbyterian church in Ireland* (vol. ii, 2nd edition, London, 1853).

Philip S. Robinson, *The plantation of Ulster, British settlement in an Irish landscape* (Dublin, 1984).

Peter Roebuck, 'The Donegall family and the development of Belfast, 1600–1850' in Paul Butel and L.M. Cullen (ed.), *Cities and merchants: French and Irish perspectives on urban development, 1500–1900* (Dublin, 1988), pp 125–36. 'Landlord indebtedness in Ulster in the seventeenth and eighteenth centuries' in J.M. Goldstrom and L.A. Clarkson (ed.), *Irish population, economy and society* (Oxford, 1981), pp 135–154. 'The making of an Ulster great estate: the Chichesters, barons of Belfast and viscounts of Carrickfergus, 1599–1648' in *R.I.A. Proc.*, lxxix, sect. C (1979), pp 1–25.

William A. Shaw, *Letters of denization and acts of naturalization for aliens in England and Ireland 1603–1700* (Lymington, 1911).

Anthony Sheehan, 'Irish towns in a period of change 1558–1625' in Ciaran Brady and Raymond Gillespie (ed.), *Natives and newcomers, essays on the making of Irish colonial society, 1534–1641* (Dublin, 1986), pp 93–119.

J.G. Simms, *Jacobite Ireland 1685–91* (London, 1969). *War and politics in Ireland 1649–1730*, ed. D.W. Hayton and Gerald O'Brien (London, 1986). *The Williamite confiscation in Ireland, 1690–1703* (London, 1956, repr. Connecticut, 1976).

J.G. Simms (ed.), 'Irish Jacobites, lists from T.C.D. MS N.1.3' in *Anal. Hib.*, xxii (1960), pp 1–230.

James Simon, *Essay on Irish coins, and of the currency of foreign monies in Ireland: with Mr Snelling's supplement* (Dublin, 1810).

Charles Smith and Walter Harris, *Ancient and present state of the county of Down* (Dublin, 1744).

T.C. Smout, *A history of the Scottish people, 1560–1830* (Glasgow and London, 1970). *Scottish trade on the eve of union, 1660–1707* (Edinburgh and London, 1963). 'The development and enterprise of Glasgow, 1556–1707' in *Scottish Journal of Political Economy*, vii (1960), pp 192–212. 'The Glasgow merchant community in the seventeenth century' in *Scottish Historical Review*, xlvii (1968), pp 53–71. 'The overseas trade of Ayrshire, 1660–1707' in *Ayrshire Collections*, vi (1958–60).

W.J. Smyth, 'Society and settlement in seventeenth century Ireland: the evidence of the

1659 census' in W.J. Smyth and Kevin Whelan (ed.), *The common ground, essays on the historical geography of Ireland, presented to T. Jones Hughes* (Cork, 1988), pp 55–83.

J. Sperling, 'The international payments mechanism in the seventeenth and eighteenth centuries' in *Econ. Hist. Rev.*, 2nd series, xiv (1961–62), pp 446–68.

Ian K. Steele, *The English Atlantic 1675–1740, an exploration of communication and community* (New York and Oxford 1986)

David Stevenson, *Scottish covenanters and Irish confederates: Scottish-Irish relations in the mid-seventeenth century* (Belfast, 1981).

John Stevenson, *Two centuries of life in Down, 1600–1800* (Belfast, 1920).

David Stewart, *The Scots in Ulster, their denization and naturalization, 1605–34* (2 vols, Belfast, 1952, 1954).

Lawrence Stone, 'Social mobility in England, 1500–1700' in *Past and Present*, xxxiii (1966), pp 16–55.

R.W.M. Strain, *Belfast and its Charitable Society* (Oxford, 1961).

Robin Sweetnam, 'The development of Belfast harbour' in Michael McCaughan and John Appleby (ed.), *The Irish Sea: aspects of maritime history* (Belfast, 1989), pp 101–9.

C.M. Tenison, 'The old Dublin bankers' in *Cork Historical and Archaeological Society Journal*, series 1, iii (1894), pp 36–38, 104–5, 120–3, 194–5.

Joan Thirsk, 'Younger sons in the seventeenth century' in *History*, liv (1968–69), pp 358–77.

Thomas M. Truxes, *Irish-American trade, 1660–1783* (Cambridge, 1988).

J.C. Walton, 'The merchant communities of Waterford in the sixteenth and seventeenth centuries' in Paul Butel and L.M. Cullen (ed.), *Cities and merchants: French and Irish perspectives on urban development, 1500–1900* (Dublin, 1986), pp 183–94.

George C. Williamson, *Trade tokens issued in the seventeenth century in England, Wales and Ireland by corporations, merchants, tradesmen, etc.* (2 vols, London, 1889–91).

Thomas Witherow, *Historical and literary memorials of presbyterianism in Ireland (1623–1731)* (London and Belfast, 1879).

Donald Woodward, 'Anglo-Irish livestock trade of the seventeenth century' in *I.H.S.*, xviii, no. 72 (1972–3), pp 489–523.

'A comparative study of the Irish and Scottish livestock trades in the seventeenth century' in L.M. Cullen and T.C. Smout (ed.), *Comparative aspects of Scottish and Irish economic and social history* (Edinburgh, 1977), pp 147–74.

'Irish-Scottish trade and English commercial policy during the 1660s' in *Scottish Hist. Rev.*, lvi (1977), pp 153–74.

'Irish sea trade and shipping from the later middle ages to c.1660' in Michael McCaughan and John Appleby (ed.), *The Irish sea: aspects of maritime history* (Belfast, 1989), pp 35–44.

THESES

David J. Dickson, 'An economic history of the Cork region in the eighteenth century' (PhD, Trinity College Dublin, 1977).

Norman E. Gamble, 'The business community and trade of Belfast 1767–1800' (PhD, Trinity College Dublin, 1978).

David William Hayton, 'Ireland and the English ministers, 1707–16 (PhD, University of Oxford, 1975).

T.F. McCarthy, 'Ulster Office, 1552–1800' (M.A., Queen's University Belfast, 1983).

John Wallace Nelson, 'The Belfast presbyterians 1670–1830, an analysis of their political and social interests' (PhD, Queen's University Belfast, 1985).

Appendix A

These profiles are headed by the name of the senior member of the family and other members of the family are listed with their relationship to him, unless their names are indented. Indented material relates to the person named immediately above, generally a son or brother of the senior member. The profiles have been simplified by the omission of family members for whom there is little information, and of most offspring who were only active after the 1720s. Most families held property in Belfast and only property outside the town is noted in the profiles. Where surnames of connected families are printed in capitals, these families are the subject of separate profiles. Wherever possible, contemporary sources have been used in the compilation of these profiles, together with transcripts and abstracts of documents which are no longer extant. If several abstracts exist of a document such as a will, the fullest of these has been cited. Where original source material has not survived, even in the form of abstracts, printed works and some collections of genealogical notes have been used. These sources are frequently unreliable and this is indicated in the footnotes. A number of sources have been used throughout the profiles, and to avoid repetitious footnotes, these are listed below:

Belfast burgesses and sovereigns	R.M. Young (ed.), *The town book of the corporation of Belfast, 1613–1816* (Belfast, 1892), pp 232–45.
Belfast freemen	ibid., pp 246–86
Gravestone inscriptions	*Gravestone inscriptions series*, ed. R.S.J. Clarke, County Antrim (2 vols), County Down (20 vols), Belfast (4 vols) (Belfast, from 1978); and *Journal of the Association for the Preservation of the Memorials of the Dead in Ireland* (13 vols, Dublin, 1892–1934).
Hearth money rolls	S.T. Carleton (ed.), *Heads and hearths, the hearth money rolls and poll tax returns for County Antrim, 1660–69* (Belfast, 1991), pp 36–9.
High sheriffs of County Antrim	R.M. Young (ed.), *Historical notices of old Belfast* (Belfast 1896), pp 257–8

High sheriffs of County Down   George Hill (ed.), *The Montgomery manuscripts 1608–1706* (Belfast, 1869), pp 437–8

Members of parliament   *Journals of the house of commons of the kingdom of Ireland* (Dublin, 1763).

Prerogative administration bonds   P.R.O.N.I., index, T490

Prerogative marriage licence bonds   P.R.O.N.I., index, T932

Presbyterian ministers   J. & S.G. McConnell (ed.), *Fasti of the Irish presbyterian church, 1613–1840* (Belfast, 1935).

Shipowners   Chapter 6, table 8

T.C.D. *alumni*   G.D. Burchtaell and T.U. Sadleir (ed.), *Alumni Dublinenses, 1593–1860* (Dublin, 1935).

T559   P.R.O.N.I., Betham's will pedigrees

T808   P.R.O.N.I., Tenison Groves abstracts

I
William ANDERSON, merchant and shipowner of Belfast
career: merchant stapler of Belfast 1659, paid 15s; assessed at £3 in subsidy roll of
1661 and at £2 in 1666; had 2 hearths in 1666, 5 in 1669; signed petition for
customhouse to be moved to Belfast 1673; died 22 Mar. 1676 and left £1 to poor of
Belfast; prerogative will dated 13 Mar. 1676.[1]
religion: presbyterian[2]
place of origin: Stobcross, Glasgow
wife: Elizabeth, daughter of George MARTIN; she = (2 Patrick Adair, presbyterian
minister of Belfast; he died 1694.[3]
sons: incl. George, servant of Black George MACARTNEY 1680, merchant of Belfast,
died 9 June 1705.[4]
    wife: Grissell Maxwell, sister of Hugh Maxwell of Rubane, County Down
    children: William and Jane, died c.1708–09, minors; Margaret, a minor in 1715 and
    heiress of her father and uncle, = (1720) Cromwell Price of Hollymount; buried at
    Downpatrick, 14 July 1740.[5]
    executors: wife and brother James; the latter appointed Isaac MACARTNEY to
    succeed him.
James, merchant or attorney of Belfast and Dublin, will dated 4 Sept. 1706, proved
6 Dec. 1706, left over £900 in cash bequests including £20 towards building a new
meeting house in Belfast 'for the poorer sort'.[6]
    property: purchased 732 acres in County Antrim, 558 acres in County Down, 257
    acres in County Kildare, and 36 acres in County Kilkenny from forfeiture commis-
    sioners in 1703.[7]
    wife: Elizabeth, daughter of William LOCKHART, alive 1698
    daughter: Elizabeth, presumably dead by 1706[8]
    cousins: Dr George MARTIN, Arthur MACARTNEY, Jemy Dingwell, Betty
    Dingwell als THETFORD, John Caldwell (carpenter in Dublin), William BIGGER.
    executors (and trustees for brother's children): uncle Samuel MARTIN and
    Thomas CRAFORD[9]
    overseers: cousin James Anderson of Stobcross, Alexander Adair
    witnesses: William CRAFORD, Neile McNeile, David CHALMERS
daughters: Sarah, and Margaret = (possibly) William CHALMERS, of Belfast.[10]
brother: James Anderson of Stobcross, Glasgow[11]
apprentice: Daniel Harper, merchant stapler 1670
executors: George MACARTNEY and Thomas KNOX

1 Benn, pp 296, 314–5; petition, 1673 (P.R.O., SP.63/333, no.82); Strain, *Belfast and its
  Charitable Society*, opp. p.16; will pedigrees (P.R.O.N.I., T559/5, pp 287, 349).
2 *Historic memorials*, p.108.
3 Ibid., p.54; notes on Martin family (L.H.L., Joy MSS, 10).
4 George Anderson to Joshua Allen, Dec. 1680 (Macartney 2, p.397); *Reg. privy council of
  Scotland*, xiii, 1686–89, pp 467, 583; Macartney to William Cairnes, 9 June 1705 (Macartney 3,
  p.120).
5 Disbursements by Hugh Maxwell for the Anderson children (P.R.O.N.I., Perceval-Price papers,
  T2473/1); Price pedigree (L.H.L., Blackwood, lxxvi, p.8); registers of Down cathedral
  (P.R.O.N.I., MIC1/38).
6 Butle to Anderson, 13 Feb., 20 Feb. 1702/3 (Butle, pp 65–6); copy will of James Anderson
  (N.A., prerogative will book 1706–08, ff 24–25).
7 Forfeiture commission rentals, incl. purchasers, 1702–03, (P.R.O.N.I., Annesley MSS,
  D1854/2/29, nos 344, 542, 543, 568, 604, 643, 776, 817, D1854/2/29a, ff 33, 140, 152);
  Reports of the commissioners into the public records of Ireland (Dublin, 1820–25), 15th R. iii, pp
  352, 360.
8 Prerogative administrations sub Lockhart 1698, 1708, and see 6 above.
9 Registry of Deeds, Dublin, 1 477 371; Donegall minority accounts, pt 1, p.3; and see 6 above.
10 Extracts relating to Anderson family (N.A., Crosslé abstracts, Anderson).
11 Will pedigree (P.R.O.N.I., T559/5, p.287).

2

The **BIGGAR/BIGGER** family, merchants and shipowners of Belfast
religion: presbyterian
place of origin: probably from Irvine, Ayrshire[1]
older generation:
James Biggar, merchant of Belfast, merchant stapler 1661, paid 10s; had 1 hearth in
1666 and 1669; issued tokens 1666; in London 1666; alive in 1681.[2]
William Biggar, brother of James, merchant of Belfast, merchant stapler 1669 *gratis*;
employed by Black George MACARTNEY who wrote: 'I will engage for his honesty
but his slowness makes me ashamed'; dead by 1679.[3]
James and William Biggar were brothers or close relations of Michael and John Biggar
(below)
Michael Biggar, merchant and shipowner of Belfast, merchant stapler 1654, 10s paid
by 'Jo & Michaell Biggart'; issued tokens in 1657; had 1 hearth in 1666, and 2 in 1669;
prerogative will dated 26 June 1674 at Edinburgh, proved 3 Dec. 1674.[4]

> **religion**: presbyterian[5]
> **wife and executor**: Agnes Stewart, who survived him; children not named in his
> will.[6]
> **brother-in-law**: Thomas Stewart, merchant of Belfast, merchant stapler 1661,
> having served apprenticeship; had 2 hearths in 1666 and 6 in 1669.[7]
> **executor** to will of Robert NEVIN, 1661
> **servant**: Alexander Woods

John Biggar, probably brother of Michael, merchant of Belfast, merchant stapler 1654,
issued trade tokens 1657; had 1 hearth in 1666, and 2 in 1669; presbyterian; held
property in Belfast jointly with William Biggar (above), alive in 1677; possibly related to
Thomas Biggar of Irvine.[8]

younger generation:[9]
Alexander Bigger, merchant of Belfast, prerogative will dated 8 June 1696, proved
17 June 1696.[10]

> **wife**: Jane, who survived him
> **son**: James, merchant of Belfast = (before 1727) Margaret, daughter and co-heiress
> of Robert LENNOX of Belfast, merchant.[11]
> **daughters**: incl. Anne = (1730, dowry £200) James Woodside of Belfast, mariner,
> who died before May 1743.[12]
> **mother**: Elizabeth, possibly NEVIN, Connor will dated 5 May 1694, proved
> 28 May 1694; her overseers were William LOCKHART and cousin William
> BIGGER, witnesses John and James Bell; she was a cousin of George

1 *Town book*, p.140.
2 Benn, p.458; Macartney to Michael Lincoln, 19 Dec. 1666 (Macartney 1, p.486); and see 1
   above.
3 Macartney to William Biggar, 7 Nov. 1666, and to William Watt, 3 July 1667 (Macartney 1, pp
   467, 569); Macartney to Charles Chartors, 14 Aug. 1679, and to William Hamilton, 18 May
   1680 (Macartney 2, pp 114, 254); and see 1 above.
4 *Town book*, pp 254, 323; Benn, p.457
5 *Historic memorials*, pp 63, 107.
6 *Town book*, p.323.
7 See 6 above.
8 Williamson, *Trade tokens*, ii, p.1360; abstract of chancery bill, 7 Nov. 1677 (P.R.O.N.I.,
   T808/8179); and see notes 1 and 5 above.
9 It has not been possible to determine the relationships between the older and younger
   generations.
10 Will pedigree (P.R.O.N.I., T559/9, p.186).
11 Registry of Deeds, Dublin, 56 179 37500, and 182 408 121350.
12 Ibid., 64 382 44928, and 113 14 76976.

MACARTNEY of Auchinleck.[13]

brother and sisters: Robert; Anne = James Smith, merchant of Belfast, his will dated 10 May 1699; Mary, unmarried in 1694.[14]

cousin and executor: William Bigger (below)

William Bigger, merchant of Belfast and Dublin, merchant stapler of Belfast 1681, *gratis*; freeman of Dublin 1708; died intestate, administration granted 1 Feb. 1714.

property: Cullentree, County Antrim; Dublin.[15]

wife: Jane

children: George, Anne, Jane and Elizabeth

cousins: Alexander Bigger (above); George MACARTNEY of Auchinleck; James ANDERSON; (possibly) John and Alexander McMunn, merchants of Belfast; also related to Joseph Bigger (below).[16]

Joseph Bigger, aged 24 in 1700, passenger on the *Friendship* of Belfast, when taken by pirates off Virginia,[17] merchant of Belfast.

wife: (? 1705) Lilias, widow of Alderman John GALT the elder of Coleraine, probably daughter of Patrick and Catherine Jordan of Castleroe, County Londonderry, and step-daughter of Dominic Heyland of Castleroe, and if so, sister-in-law of Rev. John Abernethy of Antrim, and William Galland of Vow.[18]

son: Jordan Heyland Bigger, linen-draper of London, will dated 6 Apr. 1768, proved 1771.[19]

relations: Catherine, widow of John Bigger, mariner, 1693; Margaret McMunn.[20]

3

John BLACK, merchant of Belfast

career[1]: born c.1647, apprentice of Thomas POTTINGER; freeman 1675; travelled to Bordeaux to choose wines 1679–80, and to Holland and West Indies; fled to Ayr with family after 'Break of Dromore' in his own ship, March 1689; attainted; buried 17 Apr. 1726.[2]

religion: presbyterian[3]

wife: Jane, daughter of John ECCLES of Malone; she died aged 48, 15 Oct. 1701.[4]

sons: incl: Charles of Cadiz and London; Robert, consul at Cadiz, died 11 Dec. 1759; John, born at Belfast 1682, apprenticed to uncle Alderman John ECCLES of Dublin, settled in Bordeaux 1699 and became eminent merchant there, died at Blamont, County Armagh, 1767, = (1716) Margaret (born Jan. 1692), daughter of Robert Gordon of Hillhead, Aberdeenshire, later of Bordeaux, and his wife Isabel, sister of Robert Byres,

13 Copy will (P.R.O.N.I., Mussenden papers, D354/1); copy will of George Macartney, 1691 (P.R.O.N.I., D1184); will pedigree (P.R.O.N.I., T559/3, p.231).
14 Copy wills (P.R.O.N.I., D354/1, 2), and see 10 above.
15 Conveyance of mortgage, 1698 (P.R.O.N.I., Weir deeds, D298/2); Registry of Deeds, Dublin, 18 84 8442, and 12 457 5843; Donegall minority accounts, pt 1, p.26.
16 Registry of Deeds, Dublin, 29 109 16271, and 32 255 19621; and see notes 13 and 15 above.
17 Deposition of Joseph Biggar (P.R.O., HCA1/26, p.14).
18 Settlement, 15 Jan. 1704/5 (P.R.O.N.I., D298/3); Registry of Deeds, Dublin, 7 25 1541, and 44 113 27862.
19 Belfast leases (P.R.O.N.I., D298/19, 22, 28 etc.).
20 See note 18 above.

1 Journals of John Black of Bordeaux, 1751–64 (P.R.O.N.I., T1073/7–8, 12, 16).
2 Macartney to Henry Lavie, 6 Sept. 1680 (Macartney 2, p.326); King, *State of the protestants*, p.227; claims of protestant refugees, 1689 (T.C.D., MS 847, f.4); baptism of son Samuel, May 1690 (G.R.O.S., Ayr O.P.R.); Agnew, *Funeral register ... Belfast*, p.31.
3 *Gen. synod Ulster rec.*, i, p.144.
4 Notes on Black family (P.R.O.N.I., Clarke MSS, MIC92).

merchant of Dublin, and had 15 children incl. Dr Joseph Banks.[5]
daughters: incl. Priscilla, died Nov. 1746, = (1706) James Arbuckle, merchant of Belfast.[6]

sons: William Arbuckle, buried 25 Oct. 1727,[7] = Anne, daughter of Captain John Craford, grand-daughter and heiress of William CRAFORD.

James Arbuckle the younger, freeman 1728, died 1 May 1739 on Isle of Man, = Mary, daughter of Walter Lutwidge of Whitehaven[8]

father: John Black, born near Ballymena, County Antrim, 'trooper against Cromwell'; had one hearth in Belfast in 1666 and 1669, shipowner; 'lived more than 104 years'; = Miss Martin of Comber, County Down.[9]
brother: David Black, merchant of Cork, prerogative will proved 5 June 1696.[10]
sister [or sister-in-law]: Helen Black, aged 94 in 1752, living at Mr Patton's, near Comber, County Down, lived to ?104.[11]
brothers-in-law: Sir John ECCLES of Dublin, James ECCLES of Waterford.
sisters-in-law: Mary Eccles = William Legg; Margaret Eccles = Israel Coates; x = Moses Jones.
related to: George Boyd, merchant of Bordeaux, born at Coleraine.[12]

4
Colonel **Edward BRICE**, merchant and shipowner, Belfast and Kilroot
career: born c.1659, served apprenticeship in Belfast, freeman 1680, and active as a merchant and shipowner from 1680s; fled to Scotland during Jacobite wars and raised a company there; matriculated his arms in Scotland, 10 July 1693; burgess 1697, elected sovereign 24 June 1707 but declined to qualify himself under test act; removed as burgess 29 Nov. 1707; M.P. for Dungannon, 1703-13; lieutenant colonel, and captain of Upton's Horse, 1715; died 11 Aug. 1742 aged 83, buried at Templecorran, County Antrim; Connor will.[1]
religion: presbyterian, elder of first Rosemary Street congregation; one of the trustees of the Lisburn brief, 1710; gave set of silver communion cups to congregation at Ballycarry, County Antrim, with Dublin hallmark of 1680, and left money to Belfast congregation.[2]
property: land in Dunboe leased by [Arthur] Upton held in trust by Brice c.1696; involved with James ANDERSON and Richard Cadell of Downpatrick in purchase of lands in County Down from forfeiture commissioners, 1703; in 1718 purchased Kilroot, incl. mansion house, and lands in baronies of Dunluce and Cary, County Antrim, and

5 See note 1 above; *U.J.A.*, 1st series, viii (1860), p.176; John Black to Alex. Black, 31 Jan. 1761 (P.R.O.N.I., D719/54); pedigree from will of Robert Byres, 1712 (P.R.O.N.I., T559/14, p.156); for Joseph Black, see entry in *D.N.B.*
6 Extract from journal of William Rainey, 20 Aug. 1706 (L.H.L., Joy MSS, 10); copy of Shankill burial register (P.R.O.N.I., T679/237).
7 Agnew, *Funeral register ... Belfast*, p.33.
8 See note 1 above; notes on Arbuckle family (P.R.O.N.I., D1950/1).
9 See notes 1 and 5 above.
10 Will pedigree (P.R.O.N.I., T559/9, p.259).
11 See note 1 above; Black pedigree (P.R.O.N.I., D1838).
12 See note 1 above.

1 Account book of Edward Brice, c.1686-96 (P.R.O.N.I., Maxwell papers, D1556/16/7); William Stanus to James Hamilton, 8 Apr. 1689 (P.R.O.N.I., Hamilton of Tollymore letters, MIC147/18, vol.16, no.55); *Town book*, p.196; Benn, p.566n; Brice papers (N.L.I., MS 21, 961); *Gravestone inscription series*, County Antrim, ii, p.110; abstract of will (P.R.O.N.I., copy of Stewart Kennedy notebooks, T700, p.18); *Memorials of the Dead*, ix, p.1.
2 *Gen. synod Ulster rec.*, i, p.146; Kirkpatrick, p.448; *Town book*, p.338; abstract of will (P.R.O.N.I., T700, p.18).

in barony of Ards, County Down, for consideration of £325 and annuity of £280, from nephew Randal Brice, to settle on the children of his second marriage.[3]

first wife: Dorothy, born 20 Mar. 1667, fourth daughter of Arthur Upton of Castle Upton and his wife Dorothy Beresford; alive in 1705.[4]

daughter: Dorothy, baptised at Glasgow 28 Oct. 1690, = (1713) Henry Maxwell of Finebroague, County Down; buried 29 June 1725.[5]

brothers-in-law: (brothers of first wife) Captain Arthur Upton, killed at Aughrim, 1691; Clotworthy Upton of Castle Upton, M.P. for County Antrim, died 1725; John Upton, M.P. for County Antrim; Hercules Upton died 1732; Thomas Upton, M.P. for Antrim and City of Londonderry.

brothers-in-law: (husbands of first wife's sisters) Hugh Kennedy of Cultra = Mary Upton who = (2 Dr John Peacock of Belfast; Thomas Dawson of Dawson's Bridge = Olivia Upton; William Conyngham of Springhill = Anne Upton; William Shaw of Ballygally = Margaret Upton; Hercules Rowley of Somerhill = Frances Upton; John LENNOX of Londonderry = Rebecca Upton.

uncle by marriage: Sir Hercules Langford, burgess of Belfast, died 1683, = Mary Upton.

second wife: (1718) Jane, daughter of Richard Dobbs of Castle Dobbs and Mary, daughter of Archibald Stewart of Ballintoy.[6]

children: Mary Elizabeth, died 12 Feb. 1726, aged 2;[7] Edward Brice of Kilroot, born c.1725.[8]

brothers-in-law: (brothers of second wife): Arthur Dobbs of Castle Dobbs, governor of North Carolina;[9] Richard Dobbs.

father: Robert Brice of Castle Chichester, J.P., probably one of the '49 officers, merchant, issued tokens 1671, acquired a fortune and died in Dublin 22 Nov. 1676 aged 63 or 67, funeral 23 Nov. 1676 at St Nicholas Within; administration granted 31 Mar. 1676(/7) to son 'Randolph'.

mother: Elizabeth, possibly a Stewart of Ballintoy, died 14 Jan. 1704 aged 88.[10]

grandfather: Rev. Edward Brice, born Airth, Scotland, 1569, prebendary of Kilroot, deposed by bishop of Down in 1636 and died same year aged 67, buried at Templecorran.[11]

brothers: include Randal Brice of Hillhall and Lisburn, high sheriff of County Antrim 1675, and County Down 1676; freeman of Carrickfergus; claimed loss of £300 from estate, 1689; commissioner of array, 1692; M.P. for Lisburn 1692-3, 1695-7; died in

3 T.W. Moody and J.G. Simms (ed.), *The bishopric of Derry and the Irish Society of London, 1603–1705* (2 vols, Dublin, 1968, 1983), ii, p.174; leases and releases, 1704–05 (P.R.O.N.I., Leslie of Ballybay papers, D3406/D/7/10/1–2); Registry of Deeds, Dublin, 21 442 12076, 23 182 13037, 24 61 13036, and 26 341 15650.

4 *Miscellanea Genealogica et Heraldica*, iv, 2nd series (1892), pp 46–7 (main source of information about Brice's Upton connections); Macartney to Edward Brice, 21 Feb. 1704/5 (Macartney 3, pp 54–5).

5 Baptism, 28 Oct. 1690 (G.R.O.S., Glasgow O.P.R.); draft marriage articles, 1713 (P.R.O.N.I., D1556/16/3); Agnew, *Funeral register ... Belfast*, p.30.

6 M'Skimin, *Carrickfergus*, pp 324–6.

7 *Memorials of the dead*, ix, p.1, xii, p.455; Arthur Dobbs to Michael Ward, 20 Feb.1725/6 (P.R.O.N.I., Ward papers, D2092/1/2/85); Agnew, *Funeral register ... Belfast*, p.32.

8 His descendants changed their name to Bruce.

9 D.H. Rankin and E.C. Nelson (ed.), *Curious in everything, the career of Arthur Dobbs of Carrickfergus, 1689–1765* (Carrickfergus, 1990).

10 *Memorials of the dead*, ix, p.1, xii, no.1 (1926), p.25* [sic]; O'Hart, *Irish landed gentry*, p.376; Williamson, *Trade tokens*, ii, p.1367; extract of letter from Sir William Betham, Jan. 1826, but other information in this letter is inaccurate (P.R.O.N.I., copies of papers at Royal Irish Academy, T3374/1/3).

11 See entry in *D.N.B.*

Dublin, Sept. 1697, aged 51.[12]

> **wife**: (1676) Penelope, daughter of Peter Beaghan of Dublin; her will dated 29 July 1707, proved 16 Aug. 1707.[13]
>
> **son**: Randal, entered T.C.D. 1707 aged 16, admitted to Middle Temple 1710, later of Inner Temple, London.[14]
>
> **daughters**: Penelope = (1699, dowry £1,000) Charles Ryves; Elizabeth = (dowry £600) Joshua Wilkins
>
> **wife's sister**: Margaret Beaghan = (1676) Dr Henry Leslie, archdeacon of Down and dean of Dromore

sisters: Mary = Thomas KNOX and died 21 Oct. 1717 aged 66; Grissell = William Brown, merchant of London, who died Dec. 1712; (possibly) Jane = William Innis of Belfast and Dublin.[15]

uncle (possibly): Captain Edward Brice, active c.1655[16]

aunt (possibly): Elizabeth = Alexander Innis[17]

cousin or nephew: Captain Charles Brice of Castle Chichester, born c.1682, died c.1746, buried Islandmagee; a professional soldier, lieutenant in Colonel Dormer's regiment and served in Spain.[18]

> **wife**: Jane Robinson of Newtownards, County Down, died 28 Aug. 1769, buried in St George's Chapel, Temple St., Dublin
>
> **sons**: Edward, Robert and Arthur[19]
>
> **daughter**: Dorothea = William Innis of Belfast and died 24 Feb. 1785 aged 58.[20]

relations (probably): Edward Bryce, writer to the signet at Edinburgh, and his brother James Bryce of Kilroot;[21] Randle Brice, late captain or master of ship *St George* 1707;[22] William Brice of Lisburn, died 26 Apr. 1696, = Jane Kelso.[23]

executor to: William Brown, merchant of London; Dr Victor Ferguson of Belfast; Helen, widow of Andrew Maxwell, merchant of Belfast, 1722; (possibly) Thomas Dawson of Castle Dawson.[24]

servant: Samuel Mitchell[25]

12 *Memorials of the dead*, ix, p.1; list of freemen of Carrickfergus, c.1683 (P.R.O.N.I., Dobbs papers, D162/1); Benn, p.738.

13 Copy will of Peter Beaghan of Dublin, 19 Feb. 1682/3 (N.A., prerogative will book 1664–84, ff 448–53, and P.R.O.N.I., D3406/D/4/2/1); copy will of Penelope Brice (N.A., prerogative will book 1706–08, f.109).

14 Counsel's opinion for Mr Randall Brice, 1715, containing information about Brice family and property (N.A., M 1325).

15 *Memorials of the dead*, iii, pp 510–11; copy will of William Brown, 4 Dec. 1712 (P.R.O., PROB.11/530); Innis pedigree (P.R.O.N.I., Gelston papers, D3562/16).

16 Extracts from council order books, 1650s (N.A., Betham 10/18).

17 Innis pedigree (P.R.O.N.I., D3562/16).

18 Extract of letter from Sir William Betham, Jan. 1826 (P.R.O.N.I., T3374/1/3) and Brice pedigree (Geneal. Office, MS 169); these two sources contain inaccurate information and no contemporary source suggests that Charles Brice was the son, legitimate or otherwise, of either Edward or Robert Brice; transcripts of state papers (P.R.O.N.I., T448, p.136).

19 *Complete baronetage*, ed. G.E.C. (6 vols, Exeter, 1900–09), v, p.331.

20 Will pedigree (P.R.O.N.I., T559/24, p.245).

21 Copy will of Edward Bryce, 1692 (S.R.O., Register of Deeds, MACK 70 577); list of freemen of Carrickfergus, 1690s (P.R.O.N.I., Dobbs papers, D162/18).

22 Copy will of Penelope Brice (N.A., prerogative will book, 1706–08, f.109).

23 Will pedigree (P.R.O.N.I., T559/12, p.11).

24 Copy will of William Brown, 4 Dec. 1712 (P.R.O., PROB.11/530); copy will of Dr Victor Ferguson, 5 Oct. 1723 (N.A., prerogative will book, 1726–28, ff 260–1); abstract of will of Helen Maxwell, 1722 (P.R.O.N.I., Mussenden papers, D354/45a); Registry of Deeds, Dublin, 64 280 43840.

25 Registry of Deeds, Dublin, 26 341 15650.

5
David BUTLE/BUTTLE, merchant and shipowner of Belfast

career: served apprenticeship in Belfast, freeman 1680; refugee during Jacobite wars; probably collector at Coleraine 1690; freeman of Carrickfergus; merchant in Belfast in 1690s; burgess 1700; sovereign 1702–03, 1703–04; resigned 29 July 1704 after passing of the test act; removed as burgess 29 Nov. 1707; buried 25 Dec. 1714.[1]

religion: presbyterian; petitioned against the test act in 1705.[2]

place of origin: Scottish-origin family, settled in County Antrim since 1615.[3]

property: Ballysillan, Ballymurphy, Ballygarry, and extensive property in barony of Glenarm, County Antrim, some inherited from his brother, and some leased from the commissioners of the forfeited estates of the earl of Antrim.[4]

wife: Anne, daughter of William Conyngham the elder of Springhill, County Londonderry; she was buried 6 Sept. 1712.[5]

sons: George Butle Conyngham of Springhill, attorney, inherited Springhill estate from his uncle, William Conyngham, and died 1765.[6]

> **wife**: (1721) Anne, daughter of Dr John Peacock of Belfast and Mary, daughter of Arthur Upton, and widow of Hugh Kennedy of Cultra.[7]
>
> **cousin**: Francis Clements of Straid, will dated 1718.[8]

Arthur Butle of Toome, will dated 22 Feb. 1739[9]

grandfather: David Buthill of 'Glandrine', letters of naturalization or denization 22 June 1615, died 20 Oct. 1631.[10]

father and uncle: Randal Buthill, aged 22 in 1631, son of David, will dated 1668; David Buttle, presbyterian minister of Ballymena 1645, ejected 1661, died 1665.[11]

brother: George Butle of Tullymore, attainted by James II in 1689, died 1704.[12]

relation: Alexander Butle of Belfast, served apprenticeship in Belfast, freeman 1674, merchant 1679.[13]

wife's brother: William Conyngham of Springhill = (1680) Anna, daughter of Arthur Upton; left estate to nephew George Butle Conyngham; buried 12 June 1721.[14]

wife's sister: Elizabeth = Sir Alexander Staples

1 List of freemen of Carrickfergus, 1690s (P.R.O.N.I., Dobbs papers, D162/18); Benn, p.325; claims of protestant refugees, 1689 (T.C.D., MS 847, f.1); out-letter book of David Butle, 1696–1703 (P.R.O.N.I., Lenox-Conyngham papers, D1449/13/1); *Town book*, pp 194–5; Agnew, *Funeral register ... Belfast*, p.16.

2 *Commons' jn. Ire.*, iii, p.279; *Gen. synod Ulster rec.*, i, p.159.

3 Stewart, *Scots in Ulster*, pp 13–14.

4 Registry of Deeds, Dublin, 12 13 4280, 13 313 5816, and 13 388 6082; abstract of chancery bill, 20 Jan. 1691/2 (P.R.O.N.I., T808/235); collectors' accounts, 1700 (P.R.O.N.I., Annesley papers, D1854/2/34, p.219).

5 Pedigree of the Conynghams and Butle Conynghams (Mina Lenox-Conyngham, *An old Ulster house and the people who lived in it* (Dundalk, 1946), pedigree opposite p.242); Agnew, *Funeral register ... Belfast*, p.16.

6 Copy will of William Conyngham (P.R.O.N.I., D1449/1/33).

7 Copy of agreement, 3 Aug. 1721 (P.R.O.N.I., D1449/1/38).

8 Abstract of will of Francis Clements, 1718 (P.R.O.N.I., copy of Stewart Kennedy notebooks, T700, pp 37–8).

9 Copy of will of Arthur Butle, 1739/40 (P.R.O.N.I., D1449/1/50).

10 *Inquisitionum in officio rotulorum cancellariae hiberniae asseveratum reportorum*, ii (*Ultonia*) (London, 1829), p.40; and see 3 above.

11 It is not clear which was Butle's father; deed, 1636 (P.R.O.N.I., D1449/1/3); J.B. Leslie (ed), *Clergy of Connor from patrician times to the present day* (Belfast, 1993), p.234; and see notes 3 and 10 above.

12 King, *State of the protestants*, p.213; *Town book*, pp 194–5.

13 *Town book*, p.277, Buttell printed as Boccell; Cuthbert Jamison, Nevis, to Alex. Butle, 25 June 1679 (Butle, p.136).

14 Marriage articles, 18 May 1680, and copy will (P.R.O.N.I., D1449/1/11, 33); Agnew, *Funeral register ... Belfast*, p.24.

wife's relations: Andrew Stewart of Castle Stewart; Colonel Josias Campbell = Lettice MARTIN; Patrick Orr of Clough.[15]

6

Henry CHADS the elder, merchant of Belfast

career: freeman of Belfast 1670, paid 13s 6d; burgess in James II charter 1688; active in Belfast militia and supplied them with arms 1689, attainted and fled to Ayr, in Glasgow in June 1689; freeman of Carrickfergus; prerogative will dated 26 Dec. 1710, proved 29 June 1711.[1]

religion: presbyterian, ruling elder at Belfast 1692, 1698, 1704.[2]

place of origin: unknown, probably related to Thomas Chads who issued tokens at Charlemont, County Armagh, and was part-owner of ship *Charlemont* at Belfast from 1660s.[3]

sons: Henry the younger, merchant of Belfast, probably in Bruges c.1696, name and date '1696' were inscribed on bridge at Belfast over river Farset, partner in Belfast pottery; John, merchant, lived on Hanover Quay, Belfast, 1726, Connor will 1633; Thomas, buried 26 Sept. 1734 by William Ringland, goldsmith; James.[4]

relations: Thomas Chads, gent., freeman of Belfast 1670, *gratis*; George Chads, mariner, Connor will 1695; Eleanor Joy, died 1711, whose executors were Henry Chads the younger and John Chads; she and her husband John Joy were also related to the THETFORDS, Garnetts and Richardsons.[5]

executor: son Henry[6]

executor to James Stewart 1693,[7] and Thomas KNOX 1706.

administrator to will of Henry Christian of Belfast, 1707.[8]

overseer, with William Ringland, to will of Moses Richardson, watchmaker, 1710.[9]

7

James CHALMERS/CHAMBERS, merchant and shipowner of Belfast

career: served apprenticeship in Belfast, merchant stapler 1661; had 1 hearth in 1666, 2 in 1669; burgess of Edinburgh 1668; issued tokens in 1670 with coat of arms; signed petition to move customhouse to Belfast, 1673; died 31 Aug. 1680 and left £5 to Belfast poor;[1] prerogative will 27 Aug. 1681, proved 27 Sept. 1681, died worth about £3,000.[2]

15 Abstract of will of Andrew Stewart, 1715 (P.R.O.N.I., T700, p.424); Registry of Deeds, Dublin, 36 135 21811; and see note 14 above.

1 *Reg. privy council of Scotland*, xiii, pp 450, 537; King, *State of the protestants*, p.227; list of freemen of Carrickfergus, 1690s (P.R.O.N.I., Dobbs papers, D162/18); will pedigree (P.R.O.N.I., T559/15, p.133).
2 *Gen. synod Ulster rec.*, i, pp 7, 27, 75.
3 Williamson, *Trade tokens*, ii, p.1368; Benn, pp 310–11.
4 Will pedigree (P.R.O.N.I., T559/15, p.133); account book of Edward Brice, c.1686–96 (P.R.O.N.I., Maxwell papers, D1556/16/7, p.3 in second run of pagination); *Town book*, p.328; Registry of Deeds, Dublin, 26 89 14738, and 84 496 62211; Agnew, *Funeral register ... Belfast*, p.41.
5 Abstracts of wills of John and Eleanor Joy, 1711 (P.R.O.N.I., Mathews papers, T681, pp 311–12).
6 Registry of Deeds, Dublin, 24 287 13822.
7 Abstract of will of James Stewart (P.R.O.N.I., Stewart abstracts, D1759/3B/1, p.71).
8 Donegall minority accounts, pt 2, p.4.
9 Abstract of will of Moses Richardson, 1710 (P.R.O.N.I., T808/12843).

1 C.B. Watson (ed.), *Roll of Edinburgh burgesses and guild-brethren, 1406–1700* (Edinburgh, 1929), p.102; Benn, p.460; petition, 1673 (P.R.O., SP.63/333, no.82); Strain, *Belfast and its Charitable Society*, opp. p.16.
2 Copy will of James Chalmers, 1681 (N.A., prerogative will book, 1664–84, ff 293–4).

religion: presbyterian[3]
place of origin: probably Ayrshire, coat of arms resembles that of Chalmers family of Kildonan.[4]
wife: Ellinor Kennedy of Edinburgh, she = (2 (by 1693) Captain James Shaw of Belfast, overseer to will of Hugh CRAFORD, burgess in James II charter 1688, signatory to Antrim association and attainted 1689, living in Ayr 1689, part of deputation to William III in 1690, possibly alive 1702; she was a widow again in 1704.[5]
son: David, minor and unmarried 1681, inherited £700 under father's will, merchant of Belfast, living in Ayr 1689, buried 3 Oct. 1719; witness to will of James ANDERSON 1706.[6]
daughters: (under age and unmarried in 1681, dowries £500, £400, £300): Jane = Arthur MACARTNEY, Isabel = (1689) Samuel Moor of Ayr, and Margaret = James Hamilton of Lisburn.[7]
relations: uncle David Chalmers; brothers David (? merchant stapler 1669) and John; nephew and godson James Chalmers, niece Jennett McQuilly; William Chalmers of Belfast, gent., who was granted administration for wife, Margaret ANDERSON, 14 Jan. 1698.[8]
wife's parents: David Kennedy, surgeon of Edinburgh, burgess of Edinburgh, 28 Apr. 1641, buried in Greyfriar's burying ground, 23 Oct. 1663, = Janet Henderson, who was buried 20 July 1660.
wife's brother: Robert Kennedy, surgeon, burgess of Edinburgh, 13 Sept. 1664.
wife's sisters: Jeane Kennedy = William Orr, apothecary, burgess of Edinburgh, 6 May 1663; Margaret Kennedy = (5 Feb. 1652) James Inglis/English of Muirhouse, burgess of Edinburgh, 15 Sept. 1686.[9]
apprentices: John Chalmers, merchant stapler 1671, David English
executors: wife, brother David Chalmers, cousin John Chalmers
overseers: John HAMILTON, William Orr, William LOCKART
witnesses to will: Hugh Kennedy,[10] Patrick Adair, Samuel MARTIN and William Orr
overseer to will of Hugh ECCLES but predeceased him
nephew or cousin: John Chalmers, merchant of Belfast, probably served apprenticeship with James Chalmers, merchant stapler 1671; burgess in James II charter 1688; burgess 1693, sovereign 1701–02; removed by 17 Feb. 1708; buried 15 Aug. 1725, prerogative will dated 3 Dec. 1724, proved 1725.[11]

3 See note 2 above; *Historic memorials*, p.108.
4 Benn, p.460; personal communication from the Lord Lyon King of Arms, 6 Nov. 1991.
5 For Ellinor Kennedy see: bond, 1671 (S.R.O., Register of Deeds, DAL 30 319); abstract of chancery bill, 11 Feb. 1692/3 (P.R.O.N.I., T808/8118); Registry of Deeds, Dublin, 28 173 17085; for James Shaw see: Mackenzie, *Memorials*, p.62; King, *State of the protestants*, p.213; baptism of David Macartney, 25 May 1689 (G.R.O.S., Ayr O.P.R.); notes on Dobbin family (P.R.O.N.I., T367, p.9); Benn, p.492.
6 Baptism of David Macartney, see note 5 above; Agnew, *Funeral register ... Belfast*, p.21; Benn, p.581.
7 Registry of Deeds, Dublin, 28 173 17085; marriage of Isabel Chalmers, 13 June 1689 (G.R.O.S., Ayr O.P.R.); James Paterson, *History of the county of Ayr with a genealogical account of the families of Ayrshire* (2 vols, Ayr, 1847, Paisley, 1852), ii, p.362.
8 See note 2 above.
9 For the Kennedys and Inglises, see note 2 above, and Watson, *Edinburgh burgesses*, pp 268, 285–6, 387; Henry Paton (ed.), *Register of interments in Greyfriars' burying-ground, Edinburgh* (Edinburgh, 1902), p.356; Henry Paton (ed), *Register of marriages for the parish of Edinburgh, 1595–1700* (Edinburgh, 1905), p.375.
10 Probably Dr Hugh Kennedy of Cultra, who may have been a cousin of Chalmers's wife, Ellinor Kennedy; abstract of his will (P.R.O.N.I., copy of Stewart Kennedy notebooks, T700, p.278).
11 See note 2 above; transcript of will, 1724 (N.A., Crosslé abstracts, Smith xii, p.28); Agnew, *Funeral register ... Belfast*, p.31.

religion: presbyterian, elder, trustee for the Lisburn brief 1710.[12]
wife: sister of John GALT the younger of Coleraine; probably buried 12 June 1718.[13]
sons: James, John (in Antigua in 1731),[14] William.[15]
daughters: Mary = Patrick Smith, moved to Waterford 1746; Anne/Agnes = (1716) John Mathers/Mathews of Belfast and Portadown; Elizabeth = Dr Andrew Smith of Belfast, son of Andrew Smith of Dublin.[16]
brother: David Chalmers, captain of ship bound for Jamaica, will dated 26 Jan. 1702, proved 30 Oct. 1702.[17]
brothers-in-law: Alderman James LENNOX of Londonderry, Gilbert Hall, Alderman Edward Brooke of Londonderry, John RAINEY of Belfast.
apprentice/servant: John Mathers[18] = Agnes CHALMERS (above)
executors: William RAINEY and son-in-law Patrick Smith
executor of wills of John HAMILTON (probably) and David SMITH

8

John CLUGSTON the elder, merchant of Belfast
career: active as merchant from 1640s, probably shipowner; freeman of Belfast 1643, paid 20s; issued tokens 1656; listed in poll tax return of 1660 as John Clugston, gent.; assessed at £3 in subsidy rolls 1661 and 1666; had 3 hearths in 1666, 1 in 1669; died 6 Aug. 1671 and left £10 to poor of Belfast, administration granted 26 Aug. 1671 to widow.[1]
religion: presbyterian
place of origin: probably Wigtown, Scotland[2]
wife: Grissell Shaw; she = (2 (1674) William SMITH, merchant of Belfast; her will dated 30 May 1700, dead by 1705.[3]
son: Robert, under age in 1671, probably freeman 1678, attainted 1689, died in or by 1711.

> **property**: 34 acres in Malone[4]
> **wife**: Margaret, her will dated 2 Sept. 1727, buried 11 Sept. 1727.[5]
> **son**: John, burgess ?1717 (so member of established church); sovereign 1726 (part), 1727, 1728, 1732, 1733; will dated 21 Jan. 1736, buried 24 Jan. 1736.[6]
> **daughters**: incl. Margaret = (as second wife) Richard Dobbs of Castle Dobbs

daughters: (all minors in 1671) Janet = William CRAFORD, Grizell = David SMITH, x = James YOUNG, x = Aitkins (probably parents of John Aitkins,

12 *Gen. synod Ulster rec.*, i, p.264; Kirkpatrick, p.448.
13 Macartney to John Galt, 21 Feb. 1704/5 (Macartney 3, p.57); Agnew, *Funeral register ... Belfast*, p.20.
14 John Chalmers, Antigua, to Arthur Dobbs, 21 June 1731 (P.R.O.N.I., Dobbs papers, D162/24).
15 Registry of Deeds, Dublin, 54 366 36082.
16 *U.J.A.*, 1st series, iv (1856), p.208; copy marriage settlement of Anne/Agnes Chalmers, 1716 (P.R.O.N.I., Burges papers, T1007/291); and see note 15 above.
17 Abstract of will (N.A., Crosslé abstracts, Smith vii, p.811).
18 Registry of Deeds, Dublin, 16 61 6901.

1 Benn, pp 58, 77, 296, 306, 314–5, 456; Macartney to Henry Browne, 15 Feb. 1661/2 (Macartney 1, pp 49–51); Strain, *Belfast and its Charitable Society*, opp. p.16; transcripts of material relating to Clugston family (N.A., Crosslé abstracts, Clugston).
2 *Kirkcudbright sheriff court deeds 1623–75*, nos 270, 325, 2021.
3 Abstract of will of Grissell Smith als Clugston, 1705 (N.A., Crosslé abstracts, Smith xxii, p.14).
4 See notes 3 and 5 above; rental of Donegall estate, c.1719 (P.R.O.N.I., D2249/61, no.107).
5 King, *State of the protestants*, p.213; Donegall minority accounts, pt 1, pp 10, 18; Agnew, *Funeral register ... Belfast*, p.33; and see notes 1, 2 and 3 above.
6 Agnew, *Funeral register ... Belfast*, p.42; Young, *Historical notices*, pp 166–7.

merchant of Belfast, administration granted 20 Mar. 1706 to sister Hannah[7]).

brothers: Robert Clugston of Belfast, merchant stapler 1645, paid £1, on list of proposed transportees 1653, dead by 12 Feb. 1658;[8] and (possibly) William Clugston of Belfast, free stapler 1637, paid 30s, out of the country in 1639, presumably to avoid the Black Oath; witness to will of Robert Millikine 1643, had 2 hearths 1669.[9]

relations: John Clugston the younger, merchant of Belfast, served apprenticeship in Belfast, merchant stapler 1661, had 1 hearth in 1666, 5 in 1669; as part owner of ship *James* of Belfast petitioned council for plantations, 30 Apr. 1672; in financial difficulties in 1675 with wife and five young children; was possibly the John Clugston who was removed as sergeant in 1691 for his unfitness to serve Belfast corporation in that capacity.[10]

Michael Clugston of Belfast, merchant, freeman of Belfast 1672, having served apprenticeship, trading to Rouen 1679-80;[11]

(probably) William Clugston, provost of Wigtown, 1675.

9

William CRAFORD/CRAWFORD of Belfast, merchant and M.P.

career: freeman of Belfast, elected burgess, when styled 'quarter-master'; shipowner, traded in partnership with Thomas KNOX 1678; burgess in James II charter 1688; attainted 1689; refugee in Glasgow 1689; commissioner of array, County Antrim, 1693; encouraged printers Patrick Neill of Glasgow and James Blow to settle in Belfast, and was in partnership with them; sovereign of Belfast 1692-3, 1693-4; removed as burgess 29 Nov. 1707; M.P. for Belfast 1703-13; signed loyal address against test act 1711; prerogative will dated 4 June 1716, buried 14 July 1716.[1]

place of origin: Scottish origin, but may have been second generation immigrant

religion: presbyterian, founder member of second Belfast congregation.[2]

property: manor of Florida, County Down; advowson of Kilmood which he sold to Nicholas Price in 1711.[3]

wife: Janet, daughter of John CLUGSTON, and step-daughter of William SMITH; Connor will dated 24 June 1726, buried 13 Dec. 1729.[4]

sons: Captain John, predeceased his father, died after 1709.

   son: William, died 1725

   daughter: Anne = William Arbuckle, son of James Arbuckle and Priscilla BLACK

James, baptised 1689 in Glasgow, witnesses William LOCKHART and David SMITH

7 Will pedigree (P.R.O.N.I., T559/5, p.105).

8 Young, *Historical notices*, p.80; and see notes 1 and 2 above.

9 Transcript of exchequer inquisition (N.A., Record Commissioners, RC9/1, pp 39–41); abstract of will of Robert Millikine (P.R.O.N.I., T731/1).

10 Petition of John Clugston and others, 30 Apr. 1672 (P.R.O., CO1/XXVIII, 46); Lewis Thompson to Jacob David, 6 Nov. 1675 (P.R.O., C114/76(2):6); *Town book*, p.170.

11 Macartney to Peter Cossart, 27 Dec. 1679 (Macartney 2, p.210).

1 *Town book*, pp 269, 280, and p.232, where 'Qr. Mar.' is transcribed as '2nd Mar'; he may have been one of the '49 officers (O'Hart, *Irish landed gentry*, p.380); *Cal. treas. bks*, v, p.1036; Benn, p.425; King, *State of the protestants*, p.227; baptism of son, James, 24 Dec. 1689 (G.R.O.S., Glasgow O.P.R.); note of commissioners of array (P.R.O.N.I., T808/15185); loyal address 1711 (P.R.O., SP.63/367, no.157); abstract of will (N.A., Crosslé abstracts, Smith x, p.1238 et seq.); Agnew, *Funeral register ... Belfast*, p.18.

2 *Gen. synod Ulster rec.*, i, pp 15, 159.

3 Deeds, 1692–94 (P.R.O.N.I., Londonderry papers, D654/D1C/5, 6, 8); Registry of Deeds, Dublin, 7 337 2614.

4 Agnew, *Funeral register ... Belfast*, p.35; abstract of will (P.R.O.N.I., Benn papers, D3113/5, p.139).

David, merchant of Belfast, and lord of the manor of Florida, County Down; will dated 19 Jan. 1734, proved 1737, buried 8 May 1734 by Archibald McNeill[5]

　　wife: Mary, sister of William Hamilton of Donamana, County Tyrone, dowry £500; = (2 (2 Oct. 1754), Andrew Dixon of Cavan, barrack-master of Ballyshannon, who died 1757.[6]

　　executor of will of Lieutenant Cornelius Crymble[7]

daughter: Elinor = (1709) Roger HADDOCK of Carnbane, County Down, burgess and sovereign of Belfast.[8]

brothers: Hugh, merchant of Belfast, merchant stapler 1669, prerogative will dated 9 June 1686, proved 28 Sept. 1686 (wife Janet, sons John, Anthony and William of Dublin), overseers James Shaw and Thomas CRAFORD (below); Alexander, will dated 24 Sept. 1706 (daughter Mary = John SMITH).[9]

sisters: Jenat = John McGown; Grisall McCulogh, probably buried 5 Mar. 1733.[10]

brothers-in-law: David SMITH = Grizell CLUGSTON, James YOUNG = x CLUGSTON, [?Thomas] Aitkin = x CLUGSTON

executors: wife, George McCARTNEY of Belfast, Rev. James Kirkpatrick, Robert Donaldson, attorney.

executor of Thomas Aitkin of Belfast 1685,[11] of brother Hugh Craford 1686, of James Smith of Belfast 1699,[12] and of David SMITH of Belfast 1707.

arbitrator under will of George MACARTNEY of Auchinleck

overseer of will of William SMITH 1684

trustee with William LOCKHART for children of William Thompson, merchant[13]

witness to will of James ANDERSON 1706

relations (possibly): Neill McNeill, burgess of Belfast, and his nephew, Archibald McNeill, both physicians.

relation (possibly): Thomas Craford, merchant of Belfast, shipowner,[14] and notary public; attainted 1689, as quarter-master; town clerk, 1690–99; partner in Belfast pottery; will dated 7 Oct. 1707; dead by 1 Sept. 1708.[15]

　　religion: presbyterian, presented a silver communion cup to Belfast congregation, 1698; treasurer for *regium donum* from at least 1699; ruling elder 1707.[16]

　　wife: Janet, daughter of William SMITH, alive 1710[17]

　　sons: two sons poisoned by eating berries of deadly nightshade in the castle gardens in 1701[18]

　　wife's sisters: Margaret SMITH = Archibald WHYTE, Elizabeth SMITH = Matthew King.

5　Abstract of will (P.R.O.N.I., T700, p.55); Agnew, *Funeral register ... Belfast*, p.40.
6　Registry of Deeds, Dublin, 62 90 42015; will pedigree (P.R.O.N.I., T559/16 p.342).
7　Registry of Deeds, Dublin, 65 78 44464.
8　Registry of Deeds, Dublin, 5 48 1268; see also appendix B.2.
9　Abstract of will of Hugh Craford (N.A., Crosslé abstracts, Beatty ii, pp 32–3); Macartney to Peter Cossart, 27 Dec. 1679 (Macartney 2, p.210); abstract of will of William Craford (N.A., Crosslé abstracts, Smith x, p.1238 et seq.); will pedigrees (P.R.O.N.I., T559/16, pp 337, 338a).
10　Registry of Deeds, Dublin, 17 37 8105; Agnew, *Funeral register ... Belfast*, p.38.
11　Copy schedule of debts of James Montgomery, c.1691 (P.R.O.N.I., Montgomery papers, T1030/9a).
12　Copy will of James Smith, 1699 (P.R.O.N.I., Mussenden papers, D354/2).
13　Statement of account from Mr William Crawford to the children of the widow Janet Thompson, n.d. (P.R.O.N.I., D354/1076); Registry of Deeds, Dublin, 7 305 2455.
14　Macartney to Messrs Cairnes, 8 Jan. 1704/5 (Macartney 3, pp 34–5).
15　King, *State of the protestants*, p.227; Registry of Deeds, Dublin, 4 305 976, and 26 89 14738.
16　*Historic memorials*, p.109; *Gen. synod Ulster rec.*, i, pp 40, 124.
17　Exchequer bill, Whyte v. Smith, 20 Nov. 1701 (N.A., Crosslé abstracts, Smith viii, pp 894–9); Donegall minority accounts, pt 1, p.15.
18　Notes on Belfast history (L.H.L., Joy MSS, 12, p.6).

executor of John Mills of Dublin, merchant, 1697, David Kennedy of Cultra 1699, Robert Neilson of Belfast 1704 (but renounced),[19] James ANDERSON 1706.
overseer: to will of Hugh CRAFORD (above)
arbitrator under will of George MACARTNEY of Auchinleck
witness to wills of William SMITH 1684, James Read of Belfast 1690,[20] George MACARTNEY of Auchinleck 1691.

10 Hugh DOAKE, merchant of Belfast
career: in Belfast cess lists from 1639, burgess 1645, sovereign 1647–48; on list of proposed transportees 1653; issued tokens 1656; in poll tax returns of 1660 as Hugh Doake, gent.; assessed at £2 in subsidy roll of 1666; had 2 hearths in 1666; in partnership with son-in-law Thomas POTTINGER in 1660s; died 11 Aug. 1669, left £10 to poor of Belfast, Connor will.[1]
religion: presbyterian
place of origin: possibly Ayr[2]
daughter: Janet = (1663) Thomas POTTINGER, merchant of Belfast; she was 'lately dead' in 1669;[3] he =(?3 Esther ECCLES, and died in 1715.
  son: Hugh Pottinger, alive in 1669.[4]
relations (probably): Robert Doake, in Belfast cess lists in 1640s;[5] John Doake, merchant, freeman 1671, paid 10s; Hugh Doak, merchant of Belfast, freeman 1674, paid 10s; Robert Doake, merchant, freeman 1675, paid 10s; Robert Doock, burgess of Ayr, 1680s.[6]

11
Captain William DOBBIN of Moneyglass, merchant of Belfast
career: born c.1650, served apprenticeship with Hugh ECCLES, merchant stapler 1669; clerk at Belfast customhouse, dismissed 1685; burgess in James II charter 1688; captain in Colonel Robert White's regiment from 1689; advocate of the court martial which sat permanently in Londonderry towards end of siege; collector at Donaghadee and Strangford from 1689; one of a deputation to William III, to draw his attention to difficulties for Irish merchants arising from the navigation acts, 1690; receiver for forfeiture commissioners, 1700–03, at £200 p.a. (Sir Robert Adair of Ballymena stood surety); agent for County Antrim estates of the Hollow Sword Blade Co. of London; died 7 Oct. 1723 aged 73, buried at Duneane.[1]

19 Abstracts of wills: Mills (P.R.O.N.I., T946), Kennedy (P.R.O.N.I., T700, pp 265–7), Neilson (P.R.O.N.I., T808/11690).
20 Abstract of will of James Read of Belfast, 1690 (N.A., Crosslé abstracts, Smith xxii, p.8).

1 *Town book*, p.11; Young, *Historical notices*, p.80; Benn, pp 149, 246–7, 296, 315, 456; Macartney to Moore & Holman, 18 Nov. 1665 (Macartney 1, p.270); Strain, *Belfast and its Charitable Society*, opp. p.16.
2 Letters from Robert Doock of Ayr to Andrew Russell, 1680s (S.R.O., Russell MSS, RH15/106/371, 411–12, 448, 485).
3 Benn, pp 246–7; Macartney to Edward Moore, 25 Sept. 1663 (Macartney 1, p.70).
4 See note 3 above.
5 *Town book*, p.21.
6 See note 2 above.

1 *Memorials of the dead*, vii, pp 515–6; notes on the Dobbin family and copy wills (P.R.O.N.I., T367); *Cal. treas. bks*, vii, pp 1430, 1440–1, 1514, ix, p.252; notes on army officers (Derry Cathedral, Tenison Groves papers, 4/1); Benn, p.325; records of forfeiture commission (P.R.O.N.I., Annesley papers, D1854/2/30 at front of vol., 31, ff 19–20); most of the information about Dobbin's family is from the first two sources.

religion: presbyterian/conformist[2]

place of origin: descended from Old English family of Carrickfergus, armigerous.[3]

property: Moneyglass, County Antrim; family property at Duneane, County Antrim, held by lease from WARING family; inherited leases of land in several townlands under father's will.

wife: (married pre-1680) Mary Eccles, daughter of Hugh ECCLES, merchant and burgess of Belfast; she was alive in 1725.

son: Captain James, of Innisrush, County Londonderry, born c.1682, died 11 Apr. 1714, buried at Duneane,[4] = (1713, portion £450) Olivia, sister of Thomas Kennedy, merchant of Dublin.

daughter: Anne, born c.1695, died 15 Sept. 1735, buried at Duneane, = (1719) William Morris Jones of Moneyglass.

father: Lieutenant James Dobbin of Duneane, County Antrim, born c.1610, royalist officer, on list of Scots proposed for transportation in 1653; will proved 24 Jan. 1683.[5]

mother: Mary Hamilton, possibly daughter of Rev. James Hamilton of Ballywalter.

brothers: Anthony of Golladoe, County Donegal, = Elizabeth Bunbury; Major John, born c.1649, at siege of Londonderry, buried at Duneane 9 Jan 1717, = Dorothy Kennedy; James = Elizabeth Francis; and:

Humphrey, born c.1650, merchant of Belfast, merchant stapler 1666, paid 10s; had 2 hearths in 1669; issued tokens with coat of arms 1670; burgess in James II charter 1688; died 16 Apr. 1721, buried at Duneane, County Antrim.[6]

   wife: Mary Rigby, heiress and possibly daughter of John Rigby or Ridgby, tanner, burgess of Belfast and sovereign 1661.

   son: Rigby Dobbin, mayor of Carrickfergus 1724, died 22 Apr. 1764, aged 88.

   daughter: Mary = Hercules Ellis of Innisrush

sisters: Margaret = Thomas O'Cahan (parents of Brigadier-General Richard O'Kane, who died 19 Dec. 1736); Alice = Philip Morris; Katherine = Hans Grindell of Hamiltons Bawn; Mary = (18 Aug. 1702) Hercules McManus; Sarah = William Savage; Anne = Edward Sharman.

uncle: Alderman William Dobbin of Carrickfergus, freeman of Belfast 1671 *gratis*, merchant and shipowner, will dated 24 Sept. 1675.

   wife: Mary, sister of Samuel Welby of Lincolnshire, alderman of Carrickfergus.[7]

   daughters: Elizabeth, born c.1666, = (1 Captain James Gibbons, = (2 Captain Henry South, = (3 George MACARTNEY, M.P. for Belfast;[8] Hannah, born c.1670, = Edmund Reynells (her cousin).

aunts: Katherine Dobbin = Edward Reynells, burgess of Belfast 1660, sovereign 1665–6, 1666–7, he died 29 Aug. 1682; Margaret Dobbin = Michael Edgar; x = Hugh Montgomery.

aunt: administration granted 24 Aug. 1724 to Elizabeth Shaw of Belfast for nephew William Dobbin of Moneyglass.[9]

cousin: Jane, daughter of Solomon Faith, mayor of Carrickfergus, and Catherine

---

2 William's father and another relation are in the list of Scots to be transplanted from Counties Antrim and Down in 1653 (Young, *Historical notices*, p.81) but neither William nor his brother Humphrey are listed as presbyterian burgesses in Kirkpatrick, p.424.
3 Benn, p.459.
4 Agnew, *Funeral register ... Belfast*, p.15.
5 O'Hart, *Irish landed gentry*, p.382; Young, *Historical notices*, p.81.
6 See note 3 above.
7 Letter from Thomas Welby of Boston, Lincs., to Samuel Welby and William Dobbin, about death of daughter Mary Dobbin, 14 Feb. 1673/4 (P.R.O.N.I., Macartney papers, D572/21/3).
8 M'Skimin, *Carrickfergus*, p.327.
9 If this is Captain William Dobbin, she must have been a sister of his mother, Mary Hamilton.

Dobbin; she married Captain Edward POTTINGER.[10]
executor of will of Hugh ECCLES
overseer of will of uncle Edward Reynells, 1682[11]

12

Hugh ECCLES, merchant and shipowner of Belfast
career: merchant stapler 1656, paid 40s; issued tokens with arms in a shield; assessed at
£6 in subsidy roll 1661; had 3 hearths in 1666, 4 in 1669; built bridge over River Farset
opposite his new house in High Street, 1664; burgess 1667, sovereign 1674–5, high
sheriff of County Down 1678; died 14 Dec. 1680,[1] will dated 6 Aug. 1680, with codicil
12 Dec., proved 4 Jan. 1681, stock etc. valued at £4,500, left £40 to poor of Belfast.[2]
religion: presbyterian, had front seat in old Belfast meeting house[3]
property: house in Lisburn, lands in County Armagh[4]
place of origin: family said to be from Kildonan, Ayrshire[5]
first wife: Janet, widow of Archibald Moore of Lisburn, married soon after 1651.[6]
second wife: Grizell, sister or sister-in-law of Thomas LEATHES of Hillsborough;
fled to England with one son in 1689, = (2 Samuel Adams of London; alive in 1701.[7]
sons: Hugh, under 21 in 1680, inherited £1,000; burgess of Belfast in James II charter
of 1688; captain; high sheriff of County Wicklow 1698; probably freeman of Dublin
1701, described as merchant; M.P. for Carysfort 1698–9, 1703–13–14, 1715–16; will
dated 8 Oct. 1716, proved 15 Nov. 1716, buried St Mary's, Dublin.[8]

    religion: Church of Ireland
    property: Ecclesgrove, County Wicklow, bequeathed to cousin Sir John Eccles.
    wife: (19 Dec. 1693 at St Michan's, Dublin) Mary, daughter of Sir John Temple,
    widow of Abraham Yarner; her will made 18 June 1706, but she is mentioned in her
    husband's will.[9]
    step-daughters: Catherine Yarner = Richard Stone; Jane Yarner = Pierce Bryan;
    Mary Yarner = Benjamin Woolley.
William, under 21 in 1680, inherited £700 and estate in County Armagh, possibly
freeman of Dublin 1707.
daughters: Mary = William DOBBIN; Jane = Michael Hall of Dublin; Elizabeth =
(1700) William Disney of Stabanon, County Louth; Ellinor (born 1680) = Captain
Wiseman.[10]
father: either Gilbert Eccles, active as a merchant in Carrickfergus in 1640s, freeman of

10 M'Skimin, *Carrickfergus*, p.326.
11 Copy will of Edward Reynells (P.R.O.N.I., T315).

1 Benn, pp 314–5, 458; *Town book*, p.99.
2 Abstract of will of Hugh Eccles (P.R.O.N.I., Society of Genealogists, T581/2, p.24).
3 Registry of Deeds, Dublin, 8 308 2810.
4 See note 2 above.
5 *Memorials of the dead*, xi, p.88.
6 Belmore, *Corry family*, pp 10–11; *Town book*, p.72.
7 Claims of protestant refugees, 1689 (T.C.D., MS 847, f.4); transcript of exchequer bill, Adams
   v. Smith, 25 June 1701 (N.A., Crosslé abstracts, Smith viii, p.893); and see note 2 above.
8 Abstract of will of Hugh Eccles, 1716 (P.R.O.N.I., T581/3, p.418); lease and assignment, 1717,
   1724 (P.R.O.N.I., Bangor (Ward), T1128/11, 15); information from History of Irish
   Parliament; and see notes 2 and 3 above.
9 Henry F. Berry (ed.), *The registers of the church of St Michan, Dublin*, (2 vols, Dublin, 1907,
   1909), ii, p.349; abstract of will of Mary Eccles, als Yarner, 1706 (P.R.O.N.I., T808/4312); will
   pedigree (P.R.O.N.I., T559/20, p.135).
10 Letters from John to William Leathes, 20 Aug. 1720, Michael Hall to William Leathes, early
   1700s (Suffolk R.O., Ipswich branch, de Mussenden Leathes papers, T1039/6/34, T1039/7);
   abstract of chancery bill, 1701 (N.A., Tenison Groves abstracts, C I, pp 211, 220); and see note
   2 above.

Belfast 1647, married (?secondly) between 1643 and 1646, Elizabeth, daughter of Robert Ker of Trearne, Ayrshire, soldier in commonwealth period, on list of proposed transportees from Ulster 1653, purchased land in County Fermanagh late 1650s, and was granted 2,000 acres in County Westmeath 1666, died aged 92 in 1694, buried at Donacavey;[11] or Major Hugh Eccles.[12]

brother: John Eccles of Malone, entertained William III in 1690; Connor will dated 15 June 1704, proved 16 Feb. 1705, buried in Drumbeg church.[13]

 sons: Sir John Eccles, born c.1660, settled in Dublin pre-1682, captain, alderman 1701, and mayor of Dublin 1710–11, knighted 1714, collector of Dublin 1715, died 1728.[14]

  religion: conformist, but second wife was a presbyterian.

  property: in Counties Dublin and Wicklow[15]

  first wife: Elizabeth Best of Hornby Castle, Yorks., related to Jane Lane, died in childbirth Mar. 1706 leaving one son and six daughters, buried St Mary's church, Dublin.[16]

  son: Hugh, T.C.D. 1710 aged 18, Middle Temple 1714, of Clonroe, County Wicklow, = Elizabeth, daughter of Isaac Ambrose, clerk of the Irish house of commons.[17]

  second wife: Joyce, sister of Alderman Thomas Stoker of Drogheda, widow of Alderman Andrew Brice, sheriff of Dublin; her will dated 1709, proved 23 Oct. 1709.[18]

  step-daughters: Susanna Brice = Thomas Kirkpatrick; Margaret Brice = Joseph Leeson (father of first earl of Milltown).

  third wife: (1711) Elizabeth Westgarth, will dated 7 Mar. 1725, administration granted 27 Dec. 1728.[19]

  apprentice: John BLACK, his nephew

  servant: Christopher Parsons, buried 1698 at St Michan's[20]

 James Eccles, freeman of Waterford 1693, common councilman and sheriff 1698,

11 Young, *Historical notices*, pp 67, 81; O'Hart, *Irish landed gentry*, p.414; deed, 1651 (S.R.O., Register of Sasines, Ayr, 8, pp 336–7); Paterson, *Ayrshire families*, i, p.292; indenture of fine, 1659 (P.R.O.N.I., D1048/1); copy deeds, 17 Sept. 1663, 30 May 1671, 13 Nov. 1674, 16 Nov. 1678, 2 and 3 May 1681 (N.A., Lodge's records of the rolls, vii, p.114, viii, pp 8, 40, 51, 123); abstract of chancery bill, 1664 (P.R.O.N.I., T808/636); extracts concerning Gilbert Eccles (P.R.O.N.I., T808/4332); *Memorials of the dead*, i, p.499, xi, p.88; evidence suggests a relationship between the Belfast branch and Gilbert Eccles's descendants, see abstract of exchequer bill, 1703/4 (P.R.O.N.I., T498/1, p.167), and journal of John Black, 18 Aug. 1752 (P.R.O.N.I., T1073/7).
12 Notes on Rainey family (L.H.L., Joy MSS, 10); Reid, *History of the presbyterian church*, i, p.69.
13 *U.J.A.*, 1st series, i (1854), p.134; abstract of will (P.R.O.N.I., T581/3, p.59, and copy at Geneal. Office, Dublin).
14 *The genealogical magazine*, i (1897), p.356, but is generally inaccurate; Isaac Macartney to Eccles, 9 Feb. 1705/6 (Macartney 3, p.265); Hayton, 'Ireland and the English ministers', p.63; William A. Shaw, *The Knights of England* (2 vols, London, 1906), ii, p.280.
15 Abstract of will of Hugh Eccles, 1716 (P.R.O.N.I., T581/3, p.418); lease and assignment, 1717, 1724 (P.R.O.N.I., T1128/11, 15); Registry of Deeds, Dublin, 17 191 8509; forfeiture commission, trustees' accounts, 1700–02 (P.R.O.N.I., Annesley MSS, D1854/2/29a, ff 1, 3).
16 Bernard Burke, *Landed gentry of Great Britain and Ireland* (London, 1858), p.333; Hall to Leathes, 6 Mar. 1705/6 (Suffolk R.O., Ipswich branch, T1039/7/19).
17 Other children were buried in St. Michan's (Berry, *Registers of St Michan*, pp 319, 330, 440, 451); copy marriage settlement, 1 Sept. 1735 (P.R.O.N.I., T1128/24).
18 Will pedigrees (P.R.O.N.I., T559/12, p.10, /20, p.136, /36, p.158); abstract of will of Joyce Eccles, 1709 (P.R.O.N.I., T808/4311 and T581/3, p.207).
19 Marriage settlement, 28 Feb. 1710/11 (N.L.I., D18, 711); abstract of will of Lady Eccles, 1725 (P.R.O.N.I., T581/4, p.399).
20 Berry, *Registers of St Michan*, p.443.

mayor of Waterford 1706–07, buried in Christ Church cathedral, Waterford, 24 Dec. 1707.[21]

    religion: conformist

    wife: Mary, sister of Minard Christian of Dublin, her will dated 31 Oct. 1710, proved 20 Dec. 1710.[22]

    daughters: Jane = John BLACK of Belfast, died 15 Oct. 1701 aged 48;[23] Mary = William Legg of Malone, died 28 July 1700 aged 33, buried Drumbeg graveyard; Margaret = (23 July 1691 at Lisburn) Israel Coates; x = Moses Jones.[24]

    executors: Moses Jones, John BLACK

    witnesses to will: Gaven Barr, John Jones, David Black

brother or cousin: William Eccles, of Dundesart, parish of Killead, County Antrim, will dated 23 June 1688; wife: Janet.[25]

    sons: Captain Hugh Eccles, of Dundesart, ruling elder of presbyterian congregation at Killead.[26]

        wife: daughter of Francis Shaen of Cherry Valley[27]

        brother-in-law: John RAINEY = Martha Shaen

John Eccles, merchant of Belfast, possibly freeman 1681 having served apprenticeship, burgess in James II charter of 1688, refugee in 1689; ruling elder of second Belfast congregation 1720, prerogative will dated 7 Feb. 1726, left 40s. to poor of Killead, buried 22 Jan. 1727.[28]

    wife: (1693) Jane, daughter of William RAINEY the elder, born 1675, her will dated 24 Apr. 1738, proved 8 Oct. 1747.[29]

    overseers of will: John Eccles of Belfast and William Nillson of Dundesart.

[?half-]brothers or cousins: Daniel Eccles of Shannock, 1646–88; Charles Eccles of Fintona, high sheriff of County Tyrone, administration granted 1726; Joseph Eccles of Rathmoran, will dated 2 Aug. 1709, proved 17 Sept. 1723.[30]

sisters: incl. x = John RAINEY[31]

brothers-in-law: Thomas LEATHES of Hillsborough, James Cole

servants: Thomas Kirkpatrick and nephew John Eccles

related to: Esther Eccles = Thomas POTTINGER

executors: Thomas LEATHES of Hillsborough, William RAINEY, William DOBBIN

overseers: James Corrie, John HAMILTON, James CHALMERS

apprentices: William DOBBIN, Robert Whiteside, George THEAKER, Hugh Lundie

21 Butle to Eccles, 20 July 1696 (Butle, p.36); Seamus Pender (ed.), *Council books of the corporation of Waterford 1662–1700* (Dublin, 1964), 1925, 1948, 2118, 2125; additional information from Julian Walton.
22 Abstract of will of Mary Eccles, 1710 (P.R.O.N.I., T808/4311).
23 Genealogical notes (P.R.O.N.I., Clarke MSS, MIC92).
24 Abstract of will of John Eccles (P.R.O.N.I., T581/3, p.59, and copy at Geneal. Office); *Gravestone inscriptions series*, County Down, iii, p.17; Blaris (Lisburn) parish register (P.R.O.N.I., T679/112).
25 Abstract of will of William Eccles (P.R.O.N.I., T581/2, p.240).
26 *Gen. synod Ulster rec.*, i, pp 63, 385, 515; Registry of Deeds, Dublin, 44 74 27602.
27 Shaen will pedigree (P.R.O.N.I., T559/34, p.198)
28 Claims of protestant refugees, 1689 (T.C.D., MS 847, f.4); Agnew, *Funeral register ... Belfast*, p.32; copy will of John Eccles, 1726 (N.A., prerogative will book, 1726–28, f.156).
29 Abstract of will of Jane Eccles (P.R.O.N.I., T581/6).
30 *U.J.A.*, 2nd series, ix (1903), p.144; transcript of tablet in porch of parish church of Enniskillen (P.R.O.N.I., D2081/2/1); John Black's journal, 18 Aug. 1752 (P.R.O.N.I., T1073/7); notes on Eccles family (P.R.O.N.I., McWilliams, T1299); these were sons of Gilbert Eccles by his second wife.
31 See note 2 above for information about family, executors, etc., of Hugh Eccles the elder.

13

John HAMILTON, merchant and shipowner of Belfast

career: merchant stapler 1669, having served apprenticeship with [Black George] MACARTNEY; supercargo on the *Swan* of Donaghadee to Cadiz and Malaga, 1667; burgess 1678, sovereign 1683–85, gave information to the government about a presbyterian plot in 1684, and described as 'a very honest man';[1] as sovereign, sent loyal address to James II on his accession, 1685; styled Cornet John Hamilton in 1682; died 20 Mar. 1687;[2] will dated 5 Feb. 1672, administration granted 4 Jan. 1688 to George MACARTNEY, William LOCKHART and John CHALMERS, and Hamilton's children by second marriage; lawsuit, 1687, in prerogative court, between above, together with Hamilton's second wife's sisters and their husbands, versus Hamilton's sisters, which was decided in favour of the former.[3]

religion: Church of Ireland

origin: said to be a Hamilton of Granshaw, County Down, left legacy to poor of Bangor parish.[4]

property: purchased townland of Cotton/Cottown or Ballymenetragh, County Down, from earl of Clanbrassil in 1672.[5]

second wife: (after 1672) Mary Norris (died before 1687), daughter of Tobias Norris of Newcastle, County Down, and his wife Alice, daughter and co-heiress of Sir Claud Hamilton of Cochnoch, Scotland;[6] Norris was commissary at Belfast for victualling the army in Ulster in 1646, and commissioner of revenue at Belfast in 1651.[7]

children (all minors in 1687): George d.s.p. 1702; Elizabeth and Lettice, died unmarried before 1702; Martha (died ?1732) = (13 Oct. 1702, as third wife) Robert LENNOX, merchant of Belfast.[8]

sisters: Margaret = David WHYTE; Elizabeth = Archibald McDoughal; Jane [?Whitehead] = Robert (or Alexander) Hamilton, merchant, of Killyleagh.[9]

brothers-in-law: Patrick Hamilton of Granshaw = Lettice Norris; Robert Ormsby = Alice Norris.

nephew: Hans Hamilton

relation: Alderman Thomas Bell of Dublin;[10] (possibly) Black George MACARTNEY as the Macartney children were beneficiaries under Hamilton's will of 1672.

executors: probably George MACARTNEY, William LOCKHART, John CHALMERS; his executors employed John MOORE of Belfast to receive money due to Hamilton and to pay his debts, and he was responsible for paying for board and lodging of the Hamilton children.[11]

executor to will of James Glasgow, mariner, 1686.[12]

overseer of wills of Hugh ECCLES 1680, James CHALMERS 1681

---

1 Macartney to Hamilton, 16 Oct. 1667 (Macartney 1, p.609); *Ormonde MSS*, (ns), vii, pp 132, 293–4.
2 Benn, p.153; *Town book*, pp 152–3.
3 Abstracts of cause papers and bond, 1687 (P.R.O.N.I., T808/6264, 6900, 7544).
4 Hamilton genealogical notes (P.R.O.N.I., T1116/1–2, but no satisfactory relationship is given).
5 Copy indenture, 23 Nov. 1672 (N.A., Lodge's records of the rolls, vii, p.387).
6 George Hamilton, *A history of the house of Hamilton* (Edinburgh, 1933), pp 252–3; Hamilton pedigree (P.R.O.N.I., T732/47).
7 Dunlop, *Ireland under the commonwealth*, i, p.41n.
8 Abstracts of cause papers, 1687 (P.R.O.N.I., T808/6264); genealogical notes (P.R.O.N.I., T1116/1–2).
9 Abstracts of cause papers, 1687 (P.R.O.N.I., T808/6264, 6900); Hamilton, op.cit., p.993.
10 Macartney to William Cairnes, 30 Oct. 1704 (Macartney 3, p.3).
11 Abstracts of cause papers (P.R.O.N.I., T808/905, 921); and see note 10 above.
12 Abstract of administration bond (P.R.O.N.I., Nicholson extracts, T828/15).

14
Thomas KNOX, merchant of Belfast, and Dungannon
career: active as a merchant and shipowner in Belfast from mid-1660s; merchant stapler
1670, paid £1 10s; burgess of Belfast 1680; burgess of Glasgow 1686; resigned as
burgess of Belfast in 1697, after moving to Dungannon, in favour of brother-in-law
Edward BRICE;[1]
high sheriff for County Antrim 1685, and County Tyrone 1702; burgess in James II
charter 1688; contributed to the northern association; in Glasgow 1689–90; matriculated
his arms in Scotland 1693; commissioner of array, County Antrim, 1693; M.P. for
Newtown 1692–3, and for Dungannon 1695–9, 1703–13, 1714, 1715–27; privy councillor
1715; died 11 May 1728, buried 17 May in church of St Ann, Dungannon; prerogative
will dated 2 Apr. 1725, proved 25 Sept. 1728, left £20 to poor of Belfast.[2]
religion: Church of Ireland[3]
place of origin: Glasgow
property: purchased Dungannon estate from Lord Donegall in 1692, 'worth near
£1,000 per annum'.[4]
wife: Mary, daughter of Robert BRICE of Kilroot and Castle Chichester, County
Antrim; she died 21 Oct. 1717, aged 66.[5]
daughters: Mary = (1701) Oliver St George; Anne = Charles Echlin of Ardquin,
County Down; Penelope, baptised 4 Dec. 1689 in Glasgow, died 12 June 1696;
Dorothea, died young.[6]
parents: Thomas Knox of Glasgow, merchant, burgess of Glasgow, died May 1685, =
(1640) Elizabeth, daughter of Andrew Spang, burgess of Glasgow, and Marion
Buchanan of Drumakill.[7]
brothers: William Knox, burgess of Glasgow, died April 1728 aged 76; John Knox of
Ballycreely and Ringdufferin, County Down, ancestor of earls of Ranfurly, buried
29 Apr. 1718 at Comber, County Down, = Elizabeth, daughter and heiress of Hugh
Keith of Ballycreely, she was buried 27 Feb. 1697 at Comber.[8]
sisters: Helen = Henry Crawford, merchant of Glasgow; Margaret = John Hay of
Inchuoch.
brothers-in-law: Randal BRICE and Colonel Edward BRICE
uncles: Lieut Col Andrew Spang; William Spang, pastor of Scottish church at
Campveere.
trustees under will: Colonel Edward BRICE and Arthur Knox of Gweebeg, County
Mayo.
executor to William ANDERSON
kinsmen: Samuel Morrison of Dublin, gent., will dated 14 Apr. 1690, brother of
Joseph Morrison of Londonderry;[9] and:
Thomas Knox, merchant of Belfast, will dated 27 May 1706, died July 1706, adminis-

1 *Cal. treas. bks*, v, p.1036; *Town book*, p.190; Kirkpatrick, p.422.
2 *Clarendon corr.*, i, p.287; *Cal. treas. bks*, ix, p.1801; *Reg. privy council of Scotland*, xiii, p.391;
deeds 1691–92 (S.R.O., Register of Deeds, DAL 72, 833, 835–6, DUR 77, 465); copy grant of
arms, 1693 (Geneal. Office, MS 103, p.6); names of commissioners of array (P.R.O.N.I.,
T808/15185); E.W. Monteith, *A history of the parish of Drumglass* (Dungannon, 1967), p.5;
copy will (N.A., prerogative will book, 1728–29, ff 59–63).
3 *Clarendon corr.*, i, p.287.
4 Kirkpatrick, p.422; extract from recovery book, 1692 (P.R.O.N.I., T808/8885).
5 *Memorials of the dead*, iii, pp 510–11.
6 Register of baptisms (G.R.O.S., Glasgow O.P.R.); see also notes 2 and 5 above.
7 John McUre, *A view of the city of Glasgow* (Glasgow, 1736), pp 132–4; this is also the main
source of information about Knox's brothers, sisters and uncles.
8 Comber parish register (P.R.O.N.I., T679/415B).
9 Extracts from will of Samuel Morrison (N.A., Betham will extracts); Londonderry minutes,
19 Feb. 1693/4.

tration bond to George [Mc]CARTNEY, junior, 1721.[10]
   religion: presbyterian
   wife: Sarah (dowry £500), daughter of James Stewart, merchant of Belfast;
   she = (2 (1714), as second wife, Richard Hodgkinson, merchant of Belfast; his will
   dated 24 Jan. 1720.[11]
   daughter: Mary (born post 1693) = George McCARTNEY, merchant of Belfast;[12]
   her guardians during her minority were Robert Donaldson and Richard
   Hodgkinson.
   wife's sister: Rose Stewart = (1 (1703) Andrew McMinn, merchant of Belfast, who
   was buried 13 Jan. 1714; she = (2 Abel Hodgkis, nailer of Belfast.[13]
   wife's cousin: Samuel MARTIN, attorney of Dublin
   half-brothers: Francis and Paul Edmonds
   executors on behalf of wife: Henry CHADS senior, Andrew McMinn
   executors on behalf of daughter: Thomas KNOX of Dungannon and John Knox of
   Ballycreely

15
William LEATHES, merchant of Belfast
career: burgess 1642 (having refused office in 1641); quarter-master of Lord
Chichester's regiment, 1642; sovereign 1645–6, 1657–8, 1658–9, 1659–60; died in office
6 May 1660, great lamentation made for the 'Losse of soe honest just and upright man
and eminent in his place being ever a support to ye needy fatherless and widdows',
given an heraldic funeral attended by eight of his surname, paired in brothers; wife
probably survived him.[1]
religion: Church of Ireland
place of origin: family originated in Cumberland, registered arms[2]
sons: Ensign John Leathes, junior, free stapler 1639, burgess 1646, royalist officer;
probably storekeeper at Charlemont 1655; by 1659 acquired land at Rathnugent, County
Westmeath, claimed pardon under declaration of Breda 1660; had 1 hearth in 1666, and
3 in 1669; died at Whitehaven and was buried there, 3 Apr. 1693; wife: Jane.[3]
Captain Robert Leathes of Belfast
   career: royalist captain in 1649; activities during inter-regnum unknown but
   claimed pardon under declaration of Breda, 1660; freeman 1657, town clerk 1657,
   burgess 1669, sovereign 1687–90, 1696–7, 1714–15; comptroller to first earl of
   Donegall; signed petition for customhouse to be moved to Belfast, 1673; responsible,
   with Black George MACARTNEY, for installation of piped water supply in Belfast,
   1678–80; resisted attempt of bishop of Clogher to turn town house or school into
   chapel for officers of Roman catholic garrison, 1688; ousted as sovereign by charter
   of James II 1688, remained in Belfast and signed letter of submission 14 Mar. 1689,
   restored as sovereign after invasion of Schomberg, 1689, and greeted William III on

10 Abstracts of will, 1706, and administration bond, 1721 (P.R.O.N.I., T808/8887); Macartney to
   Daniel Hays, 13 July 1706 (Macartney 3, p.331).
11 Abstract of will of James Stewart, 1693 (P.R.O.N.I., Stewart abstracts, D1759/3B/1, p.71);
   Registry of Deeds, Dublin, 28 309 17713, and 31 222 18830.
12 Acquittance, McCartney to Donaldson and Banks, 31 Dec. 1723 (P.R.O.N.I., Mussenden
   papers, D354/10); see also appendix B.5.
13 Marriage settlement, 8 Feb. 1702/3 (P.R.O.N.I., D354/5–6); Agnew, *Funeral register ... Belfast*,
   p.15; Registry of Deeds, Dublin, 44 462 30120.

1 *Town book*, pp 52, 241; Benn, p.310.
2 Benn, p.243; *Town book*, p.241; Bernard Burke, *The general armory of England, Scotland, Ireland
   and Wales* (London, 1884), p.592.
3 O'Hart, *Irish landed gentry*, p.395; Young, *Historical notices*, p.100; *Town book*, pp 87, 170;
   Pender, *Census Ire.*, p.517, as 'Lease'.

his visit to Belfast, 1690; involved in setting up of pottery, 1698, and described as 'a man of great ingenuity'; visited Dublin to give evidence about disputed parliamentary election, 1713; freeman of Carrickfergus, seneschall of manor of Belfast, J.P. for County Antrim, constable of Belfast Castle 1708 and 1717; resigned as burgess and was replaced 1717; alive May 1718; will dated 1717, proved 1723.[4]

wife: (possibly) Anne Gray[5]

daughter: Mildred = John Byrtt of Carrickfergus; she fled to England with one child in 1689; alive in 1717.[6]

grandson: Robert Byrtt or Le Byrtt, constable of Belfast Castle 1712, burgess 1713, many times sovereign, died 1745.[7]

executors: Mildred and Robert Le Byrtt

witnesses to will: John Carpenter, Thomas Hewetson, George Robertson

witness (probably) to will of Letitia Andrews of Belfast 1679[8]

brothers (orobably): John, senior, of Belfast, burgess, sovereign 1638–39, 1655–56; had 2 hearths 1666; dead by 14 June 1677 when he was replaced as burgess; wife: Katherine, dead by 1686; son: John, born pre-1638, freeman 1656, had 1 hearth in 1666, alive in 1686.[9]

Adam, possibly freeman 1641, dead by 1644; son: Roger Leathes, tanner, merchant stapler 1644, had 1 hearth in 1666, and 2 in 1669, Connor will 1678.

relations incl.: Adam Leythes of Belfast, gent., 1622;[10] Bradshaw Leathes, served apprenticeship in Belfast, merchant stapler 1667, had property at Dunluce, County Antrim;[11] Peter Leyths, mariner of Belfast, aged about 29 in Jan. 1662;[12] Josiah Leathes, master of the *Endeavour* of Belfast, c.1690;[13] Thomas Laythes of Cumberland, quaker;[14] Alexander Leathes, freeman of Carrickfergus, had 6 hearths in Carrickfergus in 1669;[15] Robert Leathes of Liverpool, after of Belfast, bound on a voyage to Barbados, will dated 1703, proved 1724;[16] Robert Leathes, named as cousin in will of Patrick Traill, son-in-law of Thomas POTTINGER, 1723.[17]

cousin or nephew: Thomas Leathes, merchant of Hillsborough, receiver of rents for William Hill of Hillsborough, issued tokens; probably freeman of Belfast 1674; dead by Nov. 1689; died in debt and intestate, administration 25 Sept. 1690 to Patrick

4 O'Hart, *Irish landed gentry*, p.395; *Town book*, pp 88, 149–52, 166–7, 199–200, 213, 234, 242–3; list of freemen of Carrickfergus, c.1683 (P.R.O.N.I., Dobbs papers, D162/1); Benn, p.722; extracts from grants under act of settlement (N.A., Lodge, act of settlement iii, p.246); extracts from Leathes's journal (L.H.L., Joy MSS, 7, which also includes extracts from journal of William Rainey; in one version, Joy combines the two and this has been copied by Young, *Town book*, p.326); petition, 1673 (P.R.O., SP.63/333, no.82); letter of submission, 14 Mar. 1688/9 (N.A., M 2541, f.21); Sacheverell, *Account of the Isle of Man*, p.125; Donegall minority accounts, pt 2, p.45; copy will, 1723 (P.R.O.N.I., Mussenden papers, D354/55).

5 *Appendix to 26th report of Deputy Keeper ... Ire.* (Dublin, 1895), p.517.

6 List of payments to protestant refugees, 1689 (T.C.D., MS 847 (1449), f.12).

7 Registry of Deeds, Dublin, 7 98 1805.

8 Abstract of will of Letitia Andrews, 1679 (P.R.O.N.I., Crosslé abstracts, T283B, p.27).

9 Said by Young (*Town book*, p.326) to be father of William, but dates suggest they belonged to the same generation; *Town book*, p.135; lease, 1686 (P.R.O.N.I., Donegall leases, D509/29).

10 Inquisition as to parishes in Counties Down and Antrim, 1622 (P.R.O.N.I., Reeves MSS, MIC35/5).

11 Lease, 2 Jan. 1667/8 (P.R.O.N.I., Antrim deeds, D265/86).

12 Testimony of Peter Leyths of Belfast, 3 Jan. 1661/2 (P.R.O., HCA13/74, pp 141–2).

13 *Cal. treas. papers*, xlii, p.41.

14 Robert Leathes to Thomas Laythes, 5 Oct. 1670 (Religious Society of Friends' Library, London, Thomas Laythes's book of letters, 1659–1689, p.280).

15 List of freemen of Carrickfergus, c.1683 (P.R.O.N.I., Dobbs papers, D163/1).

16 Will pedigree (P.R.O.N.I., T559/26, p.109).

17 Will of Patrick Traill, 1723 (Orkney Archives, D14/2/6).

McFerran, principal creditor, and son John Leathes.[18]
  religion: Church of Ireland
  property: Aughnatrisk, County Down; house and land in Hillsborough.[19]
  wife: sister of John Johnston of Newforge[20]
  sons: John, born c.1667, T.C.D., vicar of Magheragall c.1691–94, rector of Termonamongan 1699–1702, and of Tamlaghtard 1702–36, died 22 Dec. 1737 aged 70; gave quarter of annual income to poor and left them half his goods.[21]
    first wife: (1711) daughter of a clergymen, she died 1715.[22]
    second wife: (1721) Margaret, daughter of Anthony Black of Dromore; her will dated 10 Jan. 1739, proved 28 Feb. 1739.[23]
  Moses, colonel of Royal Regiment of Foot of Ireland, brigadier, will dated 3 Aug. 1729.[24]
  William, surveyor and receiver for the forfeiture commissioners 1700–03, diplomat, minister at the Hague, lived in London, died 6 May 1727, buried St James's Piccadilly.[25]
  daughters incl.: Jane, baptised 31 July 1671, died 1736, = John Mussenden who died 1700;[26] Penelope, died May 1721, = (1 (1703) Charles Matthews of Listullycurran, County Down, who died Feb. 1712, = (2 (1712) John White of Balloo, son of Hercules White of Oldstone, County Antrim.[27]
  brother-in-law: Hugh ECCLES, burgess of Belfast
  sister-in-law: Isabella Johnston = (1682) Francis Mussenden; (he died 1690 and letters of administration were taken out by John Johnston of Lisburn, Moses Leathes and John Mussenden of Hillsborough, next of kin of Francis Mussenden jun.).[28]
  (?step)-father: [?William] Close, of Lisburn[29]
  relations: Jennet Leathes = (1644 as second wife) William Close of Lisburn;

18 *Cal. S.P. Ire., 1666–69*, p.601; Heslip, 'Lisburn seventeenth-century tokens', pp 8, 10; Blaris (Lisburn) registers, entry for burial of his daughter Elinor, 22 Nov. 1689, refers to him as defunct (P.R.O.N.I., T679/112; chancery bill, 1691 (N.A., Crosslé abstracts: Cole, index to chancery bills 175a).
19 John to William Leathes, 1 Aug. 1712 (Suffolk R.O., Ipswich branch, de Mussenden Leathes papers, T1039/6/8); lease, 16 Apr 1662 (P.R.O.N.I., Downshire papers, D671/LE8/32/2).
20 John to William Leathes, 8 May 1721 (Suffolk R.O., Ipswich Branch, T1039/6/44).
21 J.B. Leslie (ed.), *Derry clergy and parishes* (Enniskillen, 1937), pp 275, 289, 297; J.B. Leslie (ed.), *Clergy of Connor from patrician times to the present day*, p.436; *Gravestone inscription series*, County Down, xviii, p.74; will of Rev. John Leathes, 1737 (Suffolk R.O., Ipswich branch, T1039/6/53).
22 John to William Leathes, 10 July 1711 (Suffolk R.O., Ipswich branch, T1039/6/5).
23 Same, 4 Mar. 1720/1, (ibid., T1039/6/42); abstract of will of Margaret Leathes 1738/9 (P.R.O.N.I., Society of Genealogists will abstracts, T581/5/339).
24 Copy will of Moses Leathes (Suffolk R.O., Ipswich Branch, T1039/5/663).
25 Records of forfeiture commission (P.R.O.N.I., Annesley papers, D1854/2/15, 30, 31, 38); D.B. Horn (ed.), *British diplomatic representatives, 1689–1789* (Camden Society, 3rd series, vol. xlvi, London, 1932), pp 8, 9, 162; copy will of William Leathes (Suffolk R.O., Ipswich branch, HD12:2700/60); Registry of Deeds, Dublin, 54 508 36610.
26 Blaris (Lisburn) parish registers contain many baptisms and funerals of the Leathes family of Lisburn (P.R.O.N.I., T679/112); pedigree, containing inaccuracies (Suffolk R.O., Ipswich branch, T1039/12); copy will of Jane Mussenden als Dean, 1701 (P.R.O.N.I., Downshire papers, D671/D8/8/1).
27 John White to William Leathes, 16 May 1721 (Suffolk R.O., Ipswich branch, T1039/7/92); Antrim burial register, 13 May 1721 (P.R.O.N.I., T679/133/1); marriage settlement and will (P.R.O.N.I., Downshire papers, D671/D8/5/5, D8/6/3, 4).
28 Will pedigree (P.R.O.N.I., T559/3, p.316); prerogative administration, sub 'Meissenden' (P.R.O.N.I., T490/6).
29 *Cal. S.P. Ire., 1666–69*, p.601.

Brigadier Richard WARING, son of William Waring of Clanconnell.[30]
brother: Adam Leathes, merchant of Lisburn, receiver for Lord Conway from 1660s, issued tokens with coat of arms; had 3 hearths in 1666, and 2 in 1669; collector of Lisburn 1678–81; buried 26 Dec. 1702.[31]

    religion: Church of Ireland
    wife: Sidnie, sister of Quartermaster John Olphert of Lisburn, his prerogative will dated 12 Mar. 1664; she was buried 20 Mar. 1694.[32]
    children incl.: Sidney 1670–90 (godparents were Lady Rawdon and bishops of Dromore and Killaloe).[33]
    cousin: Rev. Philip Tandy of Lisburn = Mercy, sister of Sir George Rawdon.[34]
    wife's sisters: Mary, wife of Captain Marino Roma or Romano; Elizabeth Hamilton.

16

Robert LENNOX/LENOX, merchant and shipowner[1] of Belfast
career: with Alderman Alexander Lecky petitioned privy council of Scotland for pass to send ship to take provisions to Londonderry, 26 July 1689; moved from Londonderry to Belfast between 1689 and 1691;[2] died Feb. 1733 aged 71 or 79, prerogative will dated 21 Feb. 1733, proved 22 Mar. 1733.[3]
religion: presbyterian, elder of first Belfast congregation[4]
place of origin: Londonderry, armigerous Scottish family[5]
property: townland of Cotton or Ballymenetragh, County Down, inherited by third wife
first wife: Ann Lecky
second wife: Ann Conyngham
third wife: (13 Oct. 1702) Martha, daughter and heiress of John HAMILTON of Belfast; she died intestate in ?1732.
daughters: Margaret = (probably pre-1726) James BIGGER, merchant of Belfast; daughters of third marriage: Elizabeth = (1726) Alexander YOUNG, merchant of Belfast; Anne (1719–1806) = (1741) Thomas Drennan, presbyterian minister of Belfast.[6]
brother: Alderman James Lennox, merchant and shipowner of Londonderry, born c.1652, captain of one of the eight companies raised for defence of Londonderry, burgess and alderman 1692, mayor of the staple 1694, mayor of Londonderry 1693, 1697, and elected for 1694 but election not approved; J.P. 1697, M.P. for County Londonderry 1697 but election declared invalid; M.P. for Londonderry borough

---

30 Richard Waring to William Leathes, 5 June 1714, (Suffolk R.O., Ipswich branch, T1039/7/65).
31 Heslip, 'Lisburn seventeenth-century tokens', pp 8, 10; *Cal. S.P. Ire., 1669–70*, p.311; list of collectors, 1678 (Bodl., Carte MSS 38, f.391); collectors of revenue in Ireland, 1678 (B.L., Add. MS 15, 899).
32 Copy will of John Olphert (N.A., prerogative will book 1664–84, ff 91–2).
33 Rawdon to Conway, 2 Mar. 1669/70 (P.R.O., SP.63/327, no.38)
34 Leslie, *Clergy of Connor*, p.619; *Cal. S.P. Ire., 1662–65*, p.454.

1 He owned a share in the *Laurel* (Macartney to John Cunningham, 6 Jan. 1704/5 (Macartney 3, pp 33–4)).
2 *Reg. privy council of Scotland*, xiii, pp 555, 589; Victor Ferguson to Hans Sloane, 14 July 1691 (B.L., Sloane MS 4036, f.106).
3 Notes on Lennox and Drennan families (P.R.O.N.I., T468), most of the information about Lennox's family is from this source; same (P.R.O.N.I., Duffin papers, T1116/1); *Gravestone inscriptions series*, Belfast, iv, p.164; will pedigree (P.R.O.N.I., T559/26, p.159).
4 *Gen. synod Ulster rec.*, i, p.146.
5 Genealogical notes (P.R.O.N.I., Lenox-Conyngham papers, T3161/1/16).
6 Registry of Deeds, Dublin, 56 179 37500, and 182 408 121350; see also note 3 above

1703–13; resigned as alderman 1704; died 4 Aug. 1723 aged 71, buried 7 Aug. 1723.[7]
       religion: presbyterian, ruling elder[8]
       wife: Elizabeth, daughter of John GALT the elder of Coleraine, died 30 Aug.
       1731 aged 67.
       sons: John, born 11 May 1684, = (1707) Rebecca Upton of Castle Upton;
       Robert, governor of Bencoolin in Sumatra, died 8 Aug. 1775.[9]
       daughters: Sarah, died 1779, = Mr Pope, merchant of Bristol; Mary =
       (1718, dowry £1,000) James Hillhouse of Bristol, her cousin (below).[10]
       brothers-in-law: John GALT the younger of Coleraine, and Gilbert Hall,
       Alderman Edward Brooke of Londonderry, John CHALMERS of Belfast, and
       John RAINEY of Belfast (husbands of Galt's sisters).
relations: Humphrey Lennox, died 1680, and wife Margaret died 28 Sept. 1698.[11]
nephew: James Hillhouse of Bristol[12] = Mary Lennox (above)
cousin: Richard Cadell, merchant of Downpatrick[13]
brother-in-law: John Cunningham/Conyngham, merchant of Liverpool[14]
relative of third wife: Alderman Thomas Bell of Dublin[15]
apprentice: John Stewart[16]

17
William LOCKHART, merchant and shipowner of Belfast
career: merchant stapler 1670, paid £1 15s; issued tokens jointly with Thomas Aitkin,
merchant of Belfast; burgess 1687; burgess in James II charter 1688; in Glasgow in
1689;[1] sovereign 1692–93; died, and was replaced as burgess on 6 Sept. 1698; intestate,
administration to Elizabeth ANDERSON or Lockhart, daughter, 9 Nov. 1698; another
administration granted 3 Jan. 1709 to Samuel MARTIN, principal creditor of James
ANDERSON of Dublin, father of Elizabeth Anderson, Dublin, grand-daughter.
religion: presbyterian[2]
place of origin: Scotland, but may have been second generation immigrant
wife: daughter of George MACARTNEY of Auchinleck, she was probably dead by
1691.[3]
daughter: Elizabeth, under 25 and unmarried in 1691,[4] alive 1698, = James
ANDERSON of Belfast and Dublin.

  7 Macartney to James Lennox, 19 May, 27 May, 2 July, 30 July 1705 (Macartney 3, pp 108, 134,
     156–7); W.R. Young, *Fighters of Derry* (London, 1932), pp 3, 68; Londonderry minutes, 3 Dec.
     1692, 7 Feb. 1692/3, 2 Nov. 1693, 20 Nov. 1693, 26 Jan. 1693/4, 2 Nov. 1696, 1 May 1697, 6
     Sept. 1697; copy of poll for Londonderry election, 1697 (P.R.O.N.I., T3161/1/4); *Ormonde
     MSS*, (NS), viii, p.104; Lennox gravestone inscription (P.R.O.N.I., MIC1/29); Londonderry
     cathedral registers (P.R.O.N.I., MIC1P/26).
  8 Copy minutes of Laggan meeting, 21 Dec. 1692, 30 Apr. 1695 (P.R.O.N.I., Stewart abstracts,
     D1759/1E/2, pp 167, 275).
  9 Genealogical notes (P.R.O.N.I., Lenox-Conyngham papers, T3161/1/2).
 10 Articles of marriage, 24 May 1718 (P.R.O.N.I., T3161/1/9); and see note 9 above.
 11 Lennox gravestone inscription (P.R.O.N.I., MIC1/29).
 12 Macartney to Hillhouse, 17 Aug. 1706 (Macartney 3, p.342).
 13 Same to Cadell, 28 Jan. 1705/6 (ibid., p.260).
 14 Same to Cunningham, 20 Nov. 1704 (ibid., pp 14–15).
 15 Same to William Cairnes, 30 Oct. 1704 (ibid., p.3).
 16 Registry of Deeds, Dublin, 56 179 37500.

  1 Benn, p.462; was witness at baptism in Glasgow of son of William CRAFORD, 24 Dec. 1689
     (G.R.O.S., Glasgow O.P.R.).
  2 Kirkpatrick, p.421.
  3 Copy will of George Macartney, 1691 (P.R.O.N.I., D1184)
  4 See note 3 above.

grand-daughter: Elizabeth ANDERSON, dead by 1706[5]
brothers-in-law: Justice James MACARTNEY, Arthur MACARTNEY, Chichester MACARTNEY and George MACARTNEY, M.P. for Belfast
relations: (possibly) Alexander Lockard, on list of proposed deportees 1652;[6] various poor relations to whom son-in-law James Anderson left £30 in 1706.[7]
executor: to James CHALMERS, 1681, and probably to John HAMILTON, 1687.
administrator: to Elizabeth BIGGAR, 1694
trustee: with William CRAFORD, for children of William Thompson, merchant[8]
arbitrator: with William and Thomas CRAFORD, appointed 1691 by George MACARTNEY to settle differences between his sons after his death[9]
witness to will of James Read, merchant of Belfast, 1690[10]

18

George MACARTNEY/McCARTNEY, of Auchinleck, merchant and shipowner of Belfast
career: born 1626, merchant burgess of Kirkcudbright 1649; moved to Belfast 1649, freeman 1652, paid £2; appeared in poll tax returns of 1660, as gent.; issued tokens 1656; burgess 1659; assessed at £5 in subsidy roll 1661 and at £3 in 1666; had 2 hearths in 1666, and 6 (and kiln) in 1669; provided premises in High Street to be used as court house 1663; sovereign 1662–64, 1667–69, 1675–80; J.P., high sheriff of County Antrim 1671; burgess in James II charter 1688; died 23 May 1691;[1] will dated 22 Apr. 1691, proved 4 June 1691, left £40 to poor of Belfast;[2]
partner in iron works with William SMITH 1665, leased four corn mills and a tuck mill from Lord Donegall, had licence to import arms 1679, part owner of sugar refinery;[3] registered coat of arms 1680; surveyor-general of customs of Ulster 1683, dismissed 1685; collector at Belfast 1688 and supplied revenue to northern association; captain of troop of horse which he raised, which was first to proclaim William and Mary in Ireland; attainted, fled to Scotland with wife and four children in 1689 when his property was seized by Peter Knowles who succeeded him as collector; cleared of charges of Jacobitism and misuse of revenue.[4]
religion: Church of Ireland, but first wife came of a presbyterian family[5]
place of origin: born at Auchinleck, near Kirkcudbright, Scotland

5 She is not mentioned in the will of James ANDERSON, 14 Sept. 1706 (N.A., prerogative will book, 1706–08, ff 24–5).
6 Young, *Historical notices*, p.80.
7 See note 5 above.
8 Registry of Deeds, Dublin, 7 305 2455.
9 See note 3 above.
10 Abstract of will of James Read of Belfast, 1690 (N.A., Crosslé abstracts, Smith xxii, p.8).

1 Genealogical history of the family of the Rt. Hon. Sir George Macartney ..., 1773 (MS at L.H.L.); Lodge, *Peerage*, vii, pp 87–94; *Kirkcudbright town council records* (2 vols, Edinburgh, 1958), ii, 849, 863; Benn, pp 206, 314–5, 455; *Town book*, pp 101–2, 169, 234; Rawdon to Conway, 12 Nov. 1670 (P.R.O., SP.63/329, no.96); the first two are the main sources of information about Macartney's family.
2 Copy will of George Macartney, 1691 (P.R.O.N.I., D1184)
3 Macartney to Thomas Wakefield, 4 Nov. 1665, and to Elizabeth Brittan, 7 Aug. 1666 (Macartney 1, pp 260–1, 402); *Ormonde MSS*, ii, p.257; and see note 2 above.
4 Confirmation of arms, 1680 (P.R.O.N.I., D3000/109/1); funeral entry for Frances Macartney, 1684 (Geneal. Office, MS 76, p.235); Rawdon to Conway, 14 Feb. 1683 (P.R.O., SP.63/343, no. 94); *Cal. treas. bks*, vii, pp 1514, 1636, ix, p.1801, x, p.901; claims of protestant refugees 1689 (T.C.D., MS 847, f.6); petition of George Macartney, 27 Sept. 1689 (P.R.O., T.1/5, p.105); King, *State of the protestants*, p.213; *Cal. treas. papers, 1556–7–1696*, p.72; Benn, p.259.
5 Young, *Historical notices*, p.80.

property: very large estate, in and around Belfast, yearly value at least £400 in 1689; estate at Auchinleck, said to worth about £100 p.a.[6]

first wife: Jane, daughter of Quintin Calderwood of Belfast, recently dead in 1670; probably cousin of Robert NEVIN of Belfast.[7]

sons: James, born c.1651–3; freeman 1669; burgess, 1676, resigned 1715, sovereign 1691–2; Middle Temple 1671, King's Inns 1677; signatory, Antrim association, contributed to northern association and fled to Scotland, claimed losses of £150; seneschall of manor of Belfast, M.P. for Belfast 1692–3, 1695–9; justice of the king's bench in Ireland 1701–11, 1714–15, and of common pleas 1714–26; died 16 Dec. 1727, will dated 17 Sept. 1727, proved 29 Dec. 1727.[8]

> **religion**: Church of Ireland
>
> **property**: Auchinleck; manor of Hansborough als Corronary, County Cavan.
>
> **first wife**: (15 June 1679) Frances, daughter of Sir Anthony Ireby of Boston, Lincoln, died 3 Mar. 1684, buried Christ Church, Dublin.
>
> **second wife**: Alice, third daughter of Sir James Cuffe of Ballinrobe, County Mayo, and his wife Alice Aungier, and niece of earl of Longford, born 31 July 1663, died 7 Oct. 1725.
>
> **executors**: son James and Hugh Henry of Dublin

Arthur Macartney, merchant of Belfast, freeman 1678, attainted by James II 1689, burgess 1691, died shortly before 21 Dec. 1706 when he was replaced as burgess.[9]

> **religion**: presbyterian
>
> **wife**: Jane, daughter of James CHALMERS of Belfast.
>
> **sons**: George, M.P. for Belfast 1721–24, major, attorney, burgess 1709, sovereign 1724, but died in year of office before 11 Aug.; James, merchant of Dublin; Charles, merchant of Dublin = Margaret McCulloch of Piedmont, County Antrim.
>
> **daughters**: Eleanor = (25 May 1716) Rev. Francis Iredell, presbyterian minister, Dublin, he died 1 Feb. 1738;[10] x = Captain Coleman.

daughters: youngest = William LOCKHART, merchant of Belfast

second wife: Elizabeth Butler, grand-daughter of Henry Butler of Rawcliffe, Lancs.; she was alive in 1694.[11]

sons: Chichester Macartney, godson of first earl of Donegall, will dated 23 July 1693.[12]

George Macartney, born 7 Feb. 1672, T.C.D. 26 Jan. 1688, Christ Church Oxford, Middle Temple, attorney, burgess 1702, sovereign 1704–05, 1705–06, 1706–07, 1707–08, high sheriff of County Antrim, M.P. for Belfast 1692–3, Newtown Limavady 1703–13, Donegal 1713–14, Belfast 1715–57, collector of customs at Belfast, died 17 Oct. 1757.[13]

6 Copy deeds, 24 June 1674, 1 Nov. 1678, 24 May 1679, 1 Jan. 1685/6 (N.A., Lodge's records of the rolls, vii, p.452, viii, pp 207–8, 219); Benn, pp 254, 737; McKerlie, *Galloway*, v, p.100; and see note 2 above.

7 Copy lease, 24 May 1679 (N.A., Lodge's records of the rolls, viii, p.208).

8 *Cal. treas. bks*, ix, 1801; claims of protestant refugees, 1689 (T.C.D., MS 847, f.6); Benn, p.737; funeral entry for Frances Macartney, 1684 (Geneal. Office, MS 76, p.235); *Cal. S.P. dom., 1690–91*, p.221; *Town book*, p.236; Joseph Haydn, *The book of dignities* (London, 1890), pp 579, 581; copy will of James Macartney (P.R.O.N.I., D2225/7/62); Lodge, *Peerage*, iii, p.379.

9 King, *State of the protestants*, p.227; Donegall minority accounts, pt 1, p.6.

10 Registry of Deeds, Dublin, 28 173 17085.

11 Dugdale, *Visitation of Lancashire*, p.64; *Cal. treas. papers, 1556–7–1696*, p.72; Benn, p.259; pedigree of Macartney family down to 1772 (Geneal. Office, MS 76, p.304).

12 Will pedigree (P.R.O.N.I., T559/3, p.321); since family details abstracted from Chichester's will exactly mirror those of his father, Betham may have confused the two.

13 T.C.D. entrance book, 26 Jan. 1687/8, says 'filius Georgii Macartney De Dundalk' and 'natus Dundalk in comitatu Anthrom'; Dundalk was probably substituted in error for Belfast, *passim*, because he was educated there (T.C.D., entrance book 1657–1725, V/23/1); pedigree of Macartney family down to 1772 (Geneal. Office, MS 76, p.304); information from History of Irish Parliament.

religion: Church of Ireland

property: through first wife, Porter estate in County Wexford, King's County, and cities of Dublin and Kilkenny; through second wife, property in and near Carrickfergus; substantial Belfast property; sold the bulk of these to purchase estates at Loughguile (Lisanoure), and Dervock, County Antrim, and Killinchy, County Down.[14]

first wife: (14 Aug. 1700 at St Marie's, Dublin) Letitia, daughter and co-heiress of Sir Charles Porter, lord chancellor of Ireland and lord chief justice (died 1697), she died 1721 (grandparents of Earl Macartney).

second wife: Elizabeth, daughter and co-heiress of William DOBBIN of Carrickfergus and widow of Captain James Gibbons and of Captain Robert South of Ballyeaston; she died in 1754.[15]

sisters-in-law: Elizabeth Porter = (1 Edward Devenish, and = (2 (1708) Rev. John Moore;[16] Hannah DOBBIN = Edmund Reynells.

parents: Bartholomew McCartney of Auchinleck and Catherine, daughter of George Maxwell and Janet Cairnes of Orchardtown; she = (2 Sir William Sinclair.

brother-in-law: Sir Nicholas Butler, merchant and doctor of physic, London, knighted 1682, commissioner of customs 1680–88, privy councillor 1686, will proved 26 June 1700.[17]

cousins: Robert NEVIN, John Nasmyth, William BIGGER and Elizabeth, widow of Alexander BIGGER; distantly related to Alexander, William and Henry Cairnes, bankers of London and Dublin.[18]

apprentice: James Smith[19]

servants: Mary Watson, Jane Hunter, Isabell Deemster, William Ferguson, Thomas Craford

executors: wife and sons James and George

arbitrators between sons, appointed in will: William LOCKHART, William CRAFORD, Thomas CRAFORD

witnesses to will: Robert Dallway, Robert Stewart, Andrew Craford, James Calwell, William Ferguson, Thomas CRAFORD, notary public.

executor to Robert NEVIN, the younger.

19

Black George MACARTNEY/McCARTNEY, merchant and shipowner of Belfast

career: merchant stapler 1656, paying '20s now and 20s when he is better able'; may have issued tokens in 1650s; assessed at £3 in subsidy rolls of 1661 and 1666; burgess 1665, sovereign 1672–3, 1673–4, 1680–1, 1700–01; high sheriff of County Antrim 1681; burgess in James II charter 1688; signed letter of submission, 14 Mar. 1689; fled to England with wife and four children, and was at Preston, Lancs., in June 1689; dead by 18 Oct. 1702 when he was replaced as burgess; Connor will dated 17 July 1702, proved 5 Oct. 1703;[1]

14 Peter Roebuck, *Public service and private fortune, the life of Lord Macartney, 1737–1806* (Belfast, 1983), pp 4–6.
15 M'Skimin, *Carrickfergus*, p.327.
16 Lodge, *Peerage*, ii, p.111.
17 Rawdon to Conway, 14 Feb. 1682/3 (P.R.O., SP.63/343, no.94); copy will of Sir Nicholas Butler (P.R.O., PROB.11/457).
18 Lawlor, *Family of Cairnes*, p.180; see note 2 above.
19 Petition of George Macartney, 27 Sept. 1689 (P.R.O., T.1/5, p.105); and see note 2 above.

1 Out-letter books of George Macartney, 1661–68, 1679–81 (L.H.L.); Benn, pp 314–15, 455; Macartney to Humphrey Jervis, 18 Dec. 1680 (Macartney 2, p.405); letter of submission, 14 Mar. 1688/9 (N.A., M 2541, f.21); claims of protestant refugees, 1689 (T.C.D., MS 847, f.6); Hewitson, *Diary of Thomas Bellingham*, p.70; will pedigree (P.R.O.N.I., T559/27, p.8).

built new house in High Street, 1666, with 9 hearths 1669; responsible, with Robert LEATHES, for piping Belfast water supply, 1678–80; helped to raise money for Christian slaves in Algeria, 1680; supplied salt, brandy and bullets to northern association; with Edmund Harrison of London supplied goods worth £1,000 for Schomberg's artillery train.[2]

religion: Church of Ireland, but became a presbyterian a few years before his death.[3]

property: claimed loss of £300 from estate, 1689.[4]

place of origin: was a cousin of the McCartneys of Blacket in the parish of Urr, Scotland.

wife: Martha, 'of the family of Sir John Davies, attorney general for Ireland', and a connection of John Vesey, archbishop of Tuam;[5] died 21 Nov. 1705; Brown George McCARTNEY and Nicholas THETFORD made a valuation of her goods.[6]

sons: George, c.1660–1730, (probably) freeman of Dublin 1686, general in British army.[7]

    wife: (1694) Anne, widow of General Douglas.[8]

Isaac, born c.1670, merchant and shipowner of Belfast, burgess 1701, resigned Apr. 1707; built George and Hanover Quays, Belfast, at his own expense; ruined by his brother-in-law Haltridge's debts, his own 'inattention to business', and inefficiency of trustees appointed to manage his estates; died Apr. 1738, will dated 30 Jan. 1737, proved 18 Dec. 1738.[9]

    religion: presbyterian, leading elder of first Belfast presbyterian church, 1709, 1716.[10]

    property: income of £400 p.a. from leasehold properties in Belfast; inherited Haltridge estates in Counties Down and Armagh.[11]

    wife: Anne HALTRIDGE, dowry £1,200, died 20 Feb. 1748, buried 26 Feb. 1748.[12]

    sons: George, freeman 1623, burgess 1746, many times sovereign; high sheriff of County Antrim 1743; died ?1776, will dated 30 Nov. 1772, proved 14 Nov. 1778.[13]

        wife: Sarah, daughter of Rev. William Read of Fahan and ?Mary, daughter of Rev. Isaac Collyer, master of the Royal School, Armagh; she was buried 31 Mar. 1754.[14]

2 Macartney to John Rowan, 30 Dec. 1665, and 21 Jan. 1665/6 (Macartney 1, pp 295, 317); *Town book*, pp 138–9, 149–52; Macartney to Joshua Allen, 18 May, 18 Dec. 1680, 23 Apr. 1681 (Macartney 2, pp 256, 404, 453); *Cal. treas. bks*, ix, pp 1322, 1801.

3 Kirkpatrick, p.436.

4 Claims of protestant refugees, 1689 (T.C.D., MS 847, f.6, extracts printed in Benn, p.737).

5 History of the Macartney family by Clotworthy Macartney (P.R.O.N.I., T2970/12, this is the main source of information about family relationships); Macartney to William Cairnes, 17 Mar. 1704/5, to Theodore Maurice, 17 Mar. 1704/5 (Macartney 3, pp 69, 71).

6 Macartney to William Cairnes, 24 Nov. 1705, to General Macartney, 8 Dec. 1705 (ibid., pp 231, 235b–36).

7 See entry for General George Maccartney in *D.N.B.*

8 *Calendar of marriage licences issued by the faculty office 1632–1714*, ed. G.E. Cokayne and E.A. Fry (London, 1905), p.127.

9 Letter book of Isaac Macartney, 1704–06 (Macartney 3); Benn, pp 478–82; case papers (P.R.O.N.I., Ellison-Macartney, D3649/5); notes on Macartney family (P.R.O.N.I., D3513/5); abstract of will of Isaac Macartney (P.R.O.N.I., D1759/3B/1, p.59).

10 *Gen. synod Ulster rec.*, i, pp 159, 167, 384.

11 Case papers (P.R.O.N.I., D3649/21); copy will of John Haltridge, 3 Mar. 1720/1 (N.A., prerogative will book, 1726–28, ff 122–4).

12 Macartney to Charles Campbell, 23 Mar. 1705/6 (Macartney 3, pp 290–1); case papers (P.R.O.N.I., D3649/5); Shankill (Belfast) parish register (P.R.O.N.I., T679/237); and see appendix B.3.

13 Will pedigree (P.R.O.N.I., T559/27, p.8).

14 Shankill (Belfast) parish register (P.R.O.N.I., T679/237).

William, c.1715–93, godson of William SLOANE; agent for Donegall estates; burgess 1745; M.P. for Belfast 1747–60; involved in lawsuits with Donegall, Blackwood, Blundell and Downshire families.[15]

> **wife**: Catherine, daughter of Thomas Banks, merchant of Belfast and agent for Donegall estate, and Elizabeth Montgomery.
>
> **daughters**: Grace, born 10 July, baptised 16 July 1706, = (settlement 3 Oct. 1729, dowry £2,000) Sir Robert Blackwood of Ballyleidy;[16] Anne, died unmarried in 1742.[17]
>
> **cousins**: Theodore Maurice, archdeacon of Tuam;[18] Thomas Milburn of Dublin, vintner;[19] Captain John Montgomery of Donaghadee;[20] William SLOANE (by marriage).
>
> **godchild**: daughter of Nathaniel Hornby, agent of Lord Conway at Lisburn.[21]
>
> **apprentices**: James MACARTNEY (grandson of George MACARTNEY of Auchinleck), Alexander Stewart (father of first marquess of Londonderry).[22]
>
> **servant**: John Sharp[23]
>
> **executors**: Arthur Hill of Belvoir, William Montgomery of Rosemount
>
> **executor** to Thomas Morton of Dunmurry[24] and George ANDERSON (after death of James Anderson).
>
> **overseer** to wills of Dr Victor Ferguson[25] and Rev. Alexander Gordon of Rathfriland.[26]

daughters: Alice, died 1700, administration granted 20 July 1700, = Francis Cromie/Cromey, merchant stapler 1676 having served apprenticeship in Belfast, merchant of Dublin, buried 11 Jan. 1692 at St Michan's, Dublin.[27]

> **children**: George Cromie, T.C.D. 1701, Harderwyck 1708, physician, freeman of Belfast 1723, buried 19 Mar. 1731, witness to wills of John HALTRIDGE and Dr Victor Ferguson.[28]
>
> Henry Cromie, died on board *H.M.S. Grafton*, administration granted, 20 Jan. 1704.[29]
>
> Mary (Molly) Cromie, will proved 1765, buried St Michan's, Dublin, = John Magenis of Shanrod, parish of Garvaghy, County Down.[30]
>
> **brother-in-law**: William Cromie, freeman of Dublin 1692, merchant of Dublin in partnership with James Stevenson, will dated 10 Mar. 1723, proved 15 May 1723, buried St Michan's, = (11 Feb. 1697) Deborah, daughter of Michael Christian of

15 See note 9 above.
16 Pedigree of Blackwood family (L.H.L., Blackwood, li); Stevenson, *Two centuries of life in Down*, p.124.
17 Registry of Deeds, Dublin, 114 312 79065.
18 Macartney to Theodore Maurice, 17 Mar. 1704/5 (Macartney 3, p.69); David Williams, 'The Drelincourts of Berse and Ffynnogion' in *Clwyd Historian*, xxix (1992), pp 2–7; J.B. Leslie (ed.), *Armagh clergy and parishes* (Dundalk, 1911), pp 219, 220, 268.
19 Macartney to Cairnes, 17 Mar. 1704/5, and to Millburn, 21 May 1705 (Macartney 3, pp 71, 109).
20 Macartney to Montgomery, 23 Feb. 1704/5 (ibid., pp 57–8).
21 Macartney to Hornby, 22 June 1706 (ibid., p.327).
22 Registry of Deeds, Dublin, 8 149 2456, and 8 338 2869; draft letter from William Macartney to Arthur Macartney, n.d. (P.R.O.N.I., D3649/11).
23 Copy of lease, 27 Mar. 1722 (P.R.O.N.I., T808/4547).
24 Registry of Deeds, Dublin, 10 446 4106.
25 Copy will of Victor Ferguson, 5 Oct. 1723 (N.A., prerogative will book 1728–29, ff 260–1).
26 Notes on Gordon family (L.H.L., Blackwood, lx, p.127).
27 Berry, *Registers of St Michan*, pp 396, 398.
28 John McBride to Hans Sloane, 15 Jan. 1704/5 (B.L., Sloane MS 4039, f.229); Agnew, *Funeral register ... Belfast*, p.36.
29 Prerogative administration (P.R.O., PROB.6/80/243).
30 Abstract of will of Mary Magenis (P.R.O.N.I., T185, p.14).

Dublin, merchant.[31]
Elizabeth, unmarried, buried 28 Jan. 1736[32]
cousins: George McCartney of Blacket, Scotland, c.1640–1704;[33] John McCartney of Armagh.
relations (? by marriage): Sir Humphrey Jervis of Dublin or his first wife Catherine, daughter of Alderman Robert Walsh of Carrickfergus;[34] Rev. Peter Morris/Maurice, rector of Drumglass, dean of Derry, died 2 July 1690.[35]
apprentices: John HAMILTON, James YOUNG, George ANDERSON, and probably William SLOAN and Francis Cromie
executor to Thomas Stewart,[36] John HAMILTON, and William ANDERSON.
overseer to will of Captain George THEAKER.

20
George MARTIN, merchant of Belfast
career: trading from Lisburn in 1637; free stapler 1638, paid £3; fled from Ulster 'for fear of the High Commission', 1638–39; burgess 1645; sovereign 1649–50; property plundered on refusal to quarter parliamentary troops 1649; on list of proposed deportees 1653; issued tokens, 1657, 1666; in poll tax return of 1660 as George Martin, gent.; dead by 25 July 1678 when he was replaced as burgess; Connor will 1678, left £5 to poor of Belfast.[1]
religion: presbyterian
place of origin: unknown, England or Scotland[2]
property outside Belfast: house in Lisburn, property at Whitehouse, Listilliard and Clough Castle, County Antrim.[3]
sons: eight, including: John, merchant and shipowner; James, freeman in 1677 or 1678 (will dated 1705 mentions son Robert and cousin John WHITE).[4]
Robert, merchant stapler 1661, owned gabart pressed in Jacobite wars; had government debentures for advance of money to Williamite forces which were never paid.[5]
wife: Catherine WHITE
daughters: Sarah = David Tomb, presbyterian minister at Clough, he died 6 Oct. 1726; Ann = John Tomb, presbyterian minister at Magherafelt, brother of David (above), he died 28 Feb. 1718, buried 3 Mar. 1718;[6] Margaret = Francis Joy.

31 Exercise book of Thomas Agnew, 1686 (S.R.O., GD154/935, mentions William Cromey and his brother Francis, at front); letters from Isaac Macartney to Cromie & Stevenson, 1704–06 (Macartney 3, *passim*); Cromie will pedigree (P.R.O.N.I., T559/1, pp 46–7); Cromie pedigree (L.H.L., Blackwood, i, pp.82 et seq.).
32 Agnew, *Funeral register ... Belfast*, p.42.
33 McKerlie, *Galloway*, v, p.301.
34 Macartney to Jervis, 25 July 1666 (Macartney 1, p.394); M'Skimin, *Carrickfergus*, p.323; funeral entry for Catherine Jervis, 1 June 1676 (Geneal. Office, MS 76, p.185).
35 J.B. Leslie (ed.), *Derry clergy and parishes* (Enniskillen, 1937), p.35; Drumglass parish register (P.R.O.N.I., MIC1/36, vol. 1); and see note 18 above.
36 Notes on Stewart family (P.R.O.N.I., Clarke MSS, MIC92).

1 Monck's survey of customs, 1637 (B.L., Harleian MS 2138, f.180); Benn, pp 129, 247, 292n, 296, 457; Strafford, *Letters*, ii, p.227; transcript of exchequer inquisition, 1639 (N.A., RC9/1, pp 39–41); notes on Martin family (L.H.L., Joy MSS, 6, 10, Henry Joy was a descendant of George Martin and although his seventeenth century genealogy is suspect, this is the main source for Martin's family); Young, *Historical notices*, p.80; abstract of will of George Martin (T.C.D., Stewart Kennedy notebooks, MS 2116, p.64).
2 Benn, pp 247–8; notes on Martin family (B.L., Martin of Antigua, Add. MS 41,474, f.80).
3 Lease, 1670 (P.R.O.N.I., Donegall leases, D509/24).
4 Abstract of will of James Martin, 1705 (P.R.O.N.I., T700, p.351); Registry of Deeds, Dublin, 9 40 3182.
5 *Reg. privy council of Scotland*, xvi, pp 309–10; notes on Martin family (L.H.L., Joy MSS, 6).
6 Agnew, *Funeral register ... Belfast*, p.19.

wife's sister: x = James Shannon, (?) parents of Samuel Shannon, presbyterian minister at Portaferry.
Samuel, merchant and attorney in Dublin, protegé of Sir Audley Mervyn; freeman of Dublin 1679; acted for Belfast corporation 1687, and for general synod 1705; attorney in court of common pleas; will dated 20 Feb. 1720, buried 11 May 1720, will proved 24 June 1721.[7]

   religion: presbyterian, member of Capel Street congregation, Dublin
   first wife: Elizabeth, buried 14 Aug. 1671, St Michan's, Dublin; related to Sir Audley Mervyn.[8]
   children: Elizabeth, c.1668–c.1696 = John GALT the younger of Coleraine; Audley, buried at St Michan's, 7 Aug. 1671.
   second wife: Agnes Stewart, widow of Mills or Miller
   sons: Colonel John Martin, will dated 30 Apr. 1760; Dr George Martin, physician of Dublin, born c.1677, Glasgow University 1695, Leyden 1697, will dated 29 July 1746, proved ?1755; Samuel, killed in war in Spain; James Martin of Dublin = (1709) Alice Peters.[9]
   third wife: (14 July 1679) Mary, daughter of Sir Richard Carney, Ulster king of arms; she died 11 July 1685, buried 13 July, St Warburgh, Dublin.[10]
   daughter: Letitia, baptised St Michan's, 29 Dec. 1682, = (1700) Colonel Josias Campbell of Dublin.[11]
   brothers-in-law: Richard Carney, Ulster king of arms 1692–98; George Wallis, Ulster king of arms 1684–95, = Anne Carney; Hugh Ridgate = Lettice Carney.[12]
   cousin: Archibald WHITE, senior
   executor to James Stewart, merchant of Belfast (who named him as cousin, possibly related through second wife, Agnes Stewart);[13] James ANDERSON of Belfast; John GALT the younger of Coleraine (but predeceased him).
   overseer to will of James CHALMERS 1681
   witness (probably) to will of John Clarke of Maghera, 1708[14]
daughter: Elizabeth = (1 William ANDERSON, merchant of Belfast, (died 1676), and = (2 Patrick Adair, presbyterian minister of Belfast (died 1694).[15]
nephew or cousin: James Martin, merchant of Dublin, a leading presbyterian, will proved 9 May 1727, related to the SMITHS and WHITES of Belfast and Dublin.[16]
grandson: Captain Samuel Martin of Greencastle, Antigua, died 27 Dec. 1701.[17]
apprentice: George Hardie, merchant stapler 1667
(?executor): John WHITE, merchant of Belfast

7 Martin to Sir G. Rawdon, n.d. [1678] (P.R.O.N.I., copies of Granard papers, T3765/L/1/5/11); bundle incl. letters from Martin to Captain Robert Stewart of Eary, 1666–93 (P.R.O.N.I., Castle Stewart papers, D1618/5/42/1–8); letters from G. Macartney 1679–81 (Macartney 2, pp 59, 87, 449, 481); copy schedule of debts of James Montgomery, c.1691 (P.R.O.N.I., T1030/9A); letters from David Butle, 1698 (Butle, pp 56–8); *Town book*, p.158; *Gen. synod Ulster rec.*, i, pp 3, 101; Donegall financial papers (P.R.O., C106/95/15); abstract of will of Samuel Martin (T.C.D., MS 2116, p.120).
8 Berry, *Registers of St Michan*, p.188.
9 Copy wills of George Martin, 1746, and John Martin, 1760, and pedigree (B.L., Add. MS 41, 474, ff 4–7, 77–8).
10 Funeral entry for Mary Martin, 1685 (Geneal. Office, MS 76, p.252).
11 Berry, *Registers of St Michan*, p.144; Registry of Deeds, Dublin, 36 135 21811.
12 McCarthy, 'Ulster Office', p.279.
13 Abstract of will of James Stewart, 1693 (P.R.O.N.I., D1759/3B/1, p.71).
14 Abstract of will of John Clarke of Maghera, 1708 (P.R.O.N.I., T808/9167).
15 Benn, p.403.
16 Irwin, *Presbyterianism in Dublin*, pp 34–5; Kilroy, *Protestant dissent*, p.123; copy will of James Martin of Dublin (N.A., prerogative will book 1726–28, ff 192–7); the relations named suggest several Martin/White marriages
17 Notes on Martin family of Antigua (B.L., Add. MS 41, 474, ff 73–4).

21

William MOORE, merchant and shipowner of Belfast
career: merchant stapler 1656, paid £1; issued tokens; assessed at £3 in subsidy roll, 1661; had 4 hearths in 1669; signed letter of submission, 14 Mar. 1689;[1] alive in 1694.[2]
religion: presbyterian[3]
place of origin: Scotland
great-nephew: John Moore, merchant of Belfast; armigerous; appointed by executors of John HAMILTON to receive money due to him and to pay his debts; will dated 25 Dec. 1694, proved 5 Feb. 1695; left 40s to poor of Belfast meeting house, and 10 guineas towards relief of John Whitehead (below) from his captivity in Algiers.[4]
　　wife: Jean Whitehead, sister of Archibald Whitehead; she = (2 John Baird, merchant of Dublin, will dated 17 June, proved 1 July 1710.[5]
　　father: John, will dated 13 Feb. 1688.[6]
　　grandfather: Lieutenant John Moor, royalist officer; administration granted 19 June 1659 to John Whitehead and Jane his wife, als Moor, the relict, and John Moor the son.[7]
　　half-brother of father, and also half-brother of wife: Archibald Whitehead
　　half-brother of father: John Whitehead (the younger), captive in Algiers, dead by 1702.[8]
　　beneficiaries: Archibald Whitehead, Hugh Moor of Bangor, Hugh Rae
　　executors: John YOUNG and Brice Blair
relations: James Moor of Bangor, issued tokens 1657;[9] Hugh Moor of Bangor, alive 1694; (probably) Robert and William Moore of Barbados.[10]
apprentice: William Ramsey

22

Robert NEVIN the elder, merchant of Belfast
career: in Belfast from c.1633; fled to Scotland in 1638 'for fear of the High Commission';[1] free stapler 1642, will dated 19 Jan. 1643, left £10 to poor of Belfast
religion: presbyterian[2]
place of origin: probably from Ayr[3]
wife: Janet Ritchie = (2 John Stewart, merchant of Belfast[4]
son: Robert Nevin, the younger, merchant of Belfast, free stapler 1658; Connor will dated 13 March 1661, in which he valued total estate at £1,599, incl. £1,000 owing to him, and his own debts at £1,092 3s 8d.[5]

1　Benn, pp 314, 460; letter of submission, 14 Mar. 1688/9 (N.A., M 2541, f.21).
2　Abstract of will of John Moore (P.R.O.N.I., Stewart abstracts, D1749/3B/1, p.85).
3　*Historic memorials*, pp 107–8.
4　See note 2 above; brief abstract of will of John Moore with note of arms (N.A., Betham will abstracts); abstract of exchequer bill, 13 Nov. 1707, etc. (P.R.O.N.I., T808/905, 921); abstract of prerogative cause papers, 1687 (P.R.O.N.I., T808/6264); Macartney to William Cairnes, 30 Oct. 1704 (Macartney 3, p.3).
5　Abstracts of cause papers, 1701, 1707, etc. (P.R.O.N.I., T808/905, 921, 925).
6　Abstracts of legal papers, 1701 (P.R.O.N.I., T808/925, 963).
7　O'Hart, *Irish landed gentry*, p.399; transcript of administration (N.A., Crosslé abstracts, Moore i, p.3).
8　*Gen. synod Ulster rec.*, i, pp 11, 60, 109.
9　Williamson, *Trade tokens*, ii, p.1360.
10　Macartney to William Moore, 18 Jan. 1704/5 (Macartney 3, p.43).

1　Strafford, *Letters*, ii, p.227.
2　Benn, p.292n
3　Abstract of part of will of Robert Nevin, the elder, 1643 (P.R.O.N.I., T761/8).
4　*Town book*, p.77.
5　Abstract of will of Robert Nevin, the younger, 1661 (P.R.O.N.I., T761/10).

property: land in County Armagh worth £80
wife: Elizabeth
son: Robert, under 16 in 1661, merchant, freeman 1674.
half-brother and sister: Robert and Elizabeth Stewart
cousins: George MACARTNEY of Auchinleck (husband of Janet Calderwood), James King.
executors: George MACARTNEY of Auchinleck, Michael BIGGER, James King[6]
witnesses: Samuel Agnew, Alexander Spottswood, Will Johnston
daughter: Eliza = (possibly) Alexander BIGGER
nieces or cousins: (probably) Janet and Helen Calderwood
executors: Gilbert Ritchart, 'bailzie' of Ayr, and John Ferguson of Ayr.
overseer: Captain Hugh Kennedy of Ayr.[7]

23
Thomas POTTINGER, merchant and shipowner of Belfast
career: supercargo for Black George MACARTNEY on the *Angel Gabriel* 1661–2; merchant stapler 1664, paid £1; had 4 hearths in 1669; never burgess, but was sovereign under charter of James II, 1688–89; petitioned queen for recompense for expenses incurred in safeguarding merchants' property and in helping Schomberg, 1691; commissioner for prizes at Belfast 1691–97; at the Hague in 1703, living in London 1709, returned to Belfast and lived in reduced circumstances; about 80 in 1713; buried 6 April 1715.[1]
religion: presbyterian
place of origin: probably Kirkwall, Orkney[2]
property: in 1672 bought townland of Ballymacarrett, County Down, from Lord Clanbrassil for £300 plus £30 p.a[3]
first wife: (1663) Janet, daughter of Hugh DOAKE, merchant and burgess of Belfast; dead by 1669.[4]
son: Hugh, alive in 1669 but died young
second (or third) wife: (post-nuptial settlement 18 May 1682) Esther ECCLES, buried 29 Aug. 1729.[5]
son: Joseph, merchant of Belfast, = Mary Dunlop
daughter: Esther = (1709, marriage bigamous under Scottish law) Patrick Traill, mariner, of Elsness in the Orkneys, later of Ballymahon, born 1679, his will was dated 22 Feb. 1723 and proved 13 Jan. 1724; died 21 Mar. and buried 23 Mar. 1723; his executors were Joseph Pottinger and cousin Robert LEATHES.[6]

6 Macartney to Thomas Moore, 3–4 Dec. 1661, to Richard Chandler, 30 Dec. 1663, and to John Chandler, 9 Nov. 1664 (Macartney 1, pp 32–3, 94, 134); and see note 5 above.
7 See notes 2 and 3 above.

1 Macartney to Pottinger, 17 Dec. 1661, to Thomas Lewis, 29 Nov. 1662 (Macartney 1, pp 35–8, 60); Leslie, *Answer to King*, p.148 et seq.; *Town book*, p.242; Benn, pp 165–8, 730–33; *Cal. S.P. dom., 1690–91*, p.434; *Cal. treas. papers, 1656–7–1696*, p.260; *Cal. treas. bks*, ix, p.1248, x, pp 321, 875; copies of petition from Pottinger to Godolphin, c.1695 (B.L., Add. MS 28,904, ff 297–8); Pottinger to John Ellis, 31 July 1697, 28 Aug. 1703, 19 Oct. 1703 (B.L., Ellis MSS, Add. MSS 28,881, f.375,28, 890, f.397, 28,891, f.145); Hugh Marwick, *Merchant lairds of long ago* (Kirkwall, 1936–39), pp 32, 51–2; Kirkpatrick, pp 423–5; Agnew, *Funeral register ... Belfast*, p.16.
2 Marwick, *Merchant lairds*, p.33; Pottinger pedigree (Orkney Archives, D20/3/10).
3 Copy entry book of tenancies, Clanbrassil estate, 1615–78 (P.R.O.N.I., T671/3, p.74).
4 Macartney to Edward Moore, 25 Sept. 1663 (Macartney 1, p.70); Benn, pp 246–7.
5 Tombstone inscription suggests another wife (Benn, p.264); Pottinger pedigree (L.H.L., Blackwood, iii, p.134); Agnew, *Funeral register ... Belfast*, p.35.
6 Marwick, *Merchant lairds*, pp 33, 103; James Fergusson, *The white hind and other discoveries* (London, 1963), pp 114–25; copy will of Patrick Traill (Orkney Archives, D14/2/6).

father (probably): Edward, of Hobbister, skipper of Kirkwall, died between 1641 and
1643.[7]
apprentice: John BLACK
brother: Captain Edward Pottinger, merchant, ship's captain and shipowner of Belfast
    career: active in trade from 1660s; freeman of Belfast 1680, master of the *Insiquin*
    1670s, and the *Donegall* 1680s; burgess in James II charter 1688; in March 1689
    raised a company at his own expense in Coleraine and, by his skill with artillery,
    beat off attack by the Jacobites; went to London, made captain of yacht *Fanfan*
    which he brought to the walls of Carrickfergus when beseiged by Schomberg; in list
    of refugees, with wife and 3 children, 1689; naval captain 19 March 1690,
    commanded the *Dartmouth*, and had 'under orders the *Lark*, and *Mary* and another
    and has orders to cruise about the Isle of Mull or wherever he shall find any rebels;
    great things are expected from him for he understands all those places to perfection
    and is a man brave, true and industrious'; was part of a deputation to William III at
    Belfast; lost with ship and most of crew in the Sound of Mull, 9 Oct. 1690;
    intestate, administration 18 Dec. 1691 to widow; brother Thomas petitioned
    government on behalf of his widow and children 1691.[8]
    property: in Carrickfergus, and Lisnalinshee, Rathshee, Ballyclare, County Antrim
    (wife's inheritance); claimed losses of £100 real and £115 personal property in list
    of refugees, 1689.[9]
wife: (by 1677) Jane, daughter of Solomon Faith, captain in Colonel Venables's
    regiment, mayor of Carrickfergus in 1677, by wife Catherine DOBBIN; was left £10
    for a ring or piece of plate in will of dowager countess of Donegall, 1691; she died
    4 Nov. and was buried 8 Nov. 1721.[10]
daughters: Jane = (1 (1695) John Reynolds of Loughscur, County Leitrim (son,
    John Reynolds, minor, administration granted 1699), = (2 (July 1700) Sir Thomas
    Butler of Garryhunden who died 1703, = (3 Agmondisham Vesey.[11]
    Letitia, born c.1685, died 17 Nov. 1740 aged 55, = (1 (30 May 1704) Alexander
    Hamilton, who died intestate, administration 21 Jan. 1716?, (children William and
    James) = (2 (pre-1721), James Hamilton Maxwell of the Drum, County Down.[12]
    Mary, died 28 Sept. 1763, = (18 Mar. 1721 at St Marie's Dublin) Sir Walter Dixon
    Burrowes, who died 9 June 1741.[13]
    executor of will of Jane Tooley, widow of John Tooley, chirurgeon and burgess of
    Belfast, in 1690.[14]

---

7 Pottinger pedigree (Orkney Archives, D20/3/10).
8 Benn, pp 310–11, 737; list of Belfast shipping, 1680s (*B.N.L.*, 24 May 1793); claims of
    protestant refugees, 1689 (T.C.D., MS 847, f.7); *Reg. privy council of Scotland*, xv, pp 384, 590,
    607, xvi, pp 179–80; William Stannus to James Hamilton, 8 Apr. 1689 (P.R.O.N.I., MIC147/8,
    vol. 16); notes on Dobbin family (P.R.O.N.I., T367, p.9); copy account of landing of William
    III at Carrickfergus, 22 Mar. 1690 (P.R.O.N.I., copy papers from Society of Friends (Dublin),
    T1062/4/12); 'Commissioned sea officers of the Royal Navy, 1660–1815', iii, p.737 (L.H.L.,
    typescript); *Cal. S.P. dom., 1690–91*, p.314; *Cal. treas. bks*, ix, p.1198.
9 Donegall estate rental, 1719 (P.R.O.N.I., D2249/61, nos 188, 221, 237, 242, 245); letters to
    Agmondisham Vesey from James Kirk and James Hamilton Maxwell, 1720s (N.A., Sarsfield-
    Vesey letters, 140–75).
10 O'Hart, *Irish landed gentry*, p.414; M'Skimin, *Carrickfergus*, p.326; Jane to Edward Pottinger,
    1677 (N.A., Sarsfield-Vesey letters, 42–3); Benn, p.260; Agnew, *Funeral register ... Belfast*, p.24.
11 *56th Report of Deputy Keeper ... Ireland*, p.354; *Memorials of the dead*, iii, p.442.
12 Maxwell was the inventor of the beetling mill in 1725 (Hugh McCall, *Ireland and her staple
    manufactures* (Belfast, 1865), p.58); *Gravestone inscription series*, County Down, iii, p.23.
13 Lodge, *Peerage*, i, p.103n.
14 Benn, p.260, should read Tooley, not Pooley.

24

William RAINEY the elder, merchant and shipowner of Belfast

career: born 1639 or 1640 at Whitehouse, County Antrim; merchant stapler 1669, paid 15s; fled to Scotland with family, 11 Dec. 1688; merchant of Belfast; buried 9 May 1722.[1]

religion: presbyterian, ruling elder 1697, 1711: member of second Belfast congregation.[2]

place of origin: third generation immigrant, family from Ayrshire.

wife: Jane McCormick or McConville of Portaferry, buried 13 July 1716.[3]

sons: John, born 8 Oct. 1669, merchant of Belfast, buried 25 Nov. 1717.[4]

    religion: presbyterian

    wives: (1 Martha Shaen of Cherry Valley, and (2 (1704) Eleanor, daughter of Alderman John GALT of Coleraine.[5]

    brothers-in-law: sister of first wife = Hugh ECCLES of Dundesart; sisters of second wife = Gilbert Hall, Alderman James LENNOX and Alderman Edward Brooke of Londonderry, and John CHALMERS of Belfast.

William Rainey the younger, merchant of Belfast, born 1671 in North Street, Belfast, sailed as supercargo to Dieppe 1698, freeman of Londonderry 1703, died of a fever 6 Nov., buried 8 Nov. 1725, will dated 5 Nov., proved 12 Dec. 1725.[6]

    religion: presbyterian, purchased half a seat in the meeting house in 1703.

    first wife: (1701)[7] Jane, daughter of Alderman Edward Brooke of Londonderry, grand-daughter of Alderman John GALT of Coleraine; she died in 1710.

    daughter: Jane = Andrews

    second wife: Katherine Shaw, niece of Arthur Maxwell of the Drum, County Down.[8]

    sons: Arthur, inherited the Drum estate, took the name Rainey-Maxwell; John, of Greenville, died 1793 aged 76; Patrick, army captain, 1720–68.[9]

    uncles by marriage: Alderman James LENNOX, Alderman Robert Shannon and 'uncle Gordon'.

    sisters-in-law: Mary Brooke = (1704) William Ewing; Betty Brooke = (1706) Alexander Vance.

    executor to will of John CHALMERS

    executors: widow Katherine and Patrick Smith[10]

Robert, presbyterian minister at Newry, died 1736, = Martha Shaw.

Daniel, born 1682, minister of English Church at Amsterdam, will dated 1744, proved 1746, buried 7 July 1746, = Cornelia Russell.[11]

daughters: Margaret, born 1673, = Joseph Morrison, merchant of Londonderry; Jane,

1 Notes on Rainey family by Henry Joy, who was a descendant, including extracts from journal of William Rainey the younger (L.H.L., Joy MSS, 10), this is the main source of information about the family; Agnew, *Funeral register ... Belfast*, p.77.

2 *Gen. synod Ulster rec.*, i, pp 16, 159.

3 Rainey pedigree (L.H.L., Blackwood, xxii, p.7); Agnew, *Funeral register ... Belfast*, p.18.

4 Ibid., p.19.

5 Shaen will pedigree (P.R.O.N.I., T559/34, p.198).

6 Account book of Edward Brice (P.R.O.N.I., D1556/16/7, p.4); Patrick Smith to Michael Ward, 6 Nov. 1725 (P.R.O.N.I., D2092/1/2/101); will pedigrees (P.R.O.N.I., T559/32, pp 101–105) containing details from Rainey wills, but the tables produced are very confused; Agnew, *Funeral register ... Belfast*, p.31.

7 Dean Bolton to William King, 21 Nov. 1701 (T.C.D., King correspondence, MS 1995–2008, f.846).

8 Copy will of Arthur Maxwell of the Drum, 2 Nov. 1720 – 19 Jan. 1721 (P.R.O.N.I., D1255/3/3).

9 *Gravestone inscriptions series*, County Down, ii, p.90.

10 Registry of Deeds, Dublin, 51 326 33864.

11 Shankill parish register (P.R.O.N.I., T679/237); Burke, *Landed gentry of Ireland* (1912), p.598.

born 1675, will dated 24 Apr. 1738, proved 8 Oct. 1747, = (1693) John ECCLES of Belfast; Grizell, born 1678, unmarried, buried 29 Dec. 1724; Elizabeth = (1702) Robert Millikin; Anne = Robert Hutchinson of Newry, merchant; Mary, born 1687, = Adam McKibbin.[12]

grandfather: William Rainey, said to have been a militia officer from Ayrshire who settled in Belfast in 1605.

father: John Rainey of Killybegs, County Antrim, 1602–82.

mother: a sister of Hugh ECCLES of Belfast

brothers: Robert Rainey of Killybegs, will dated 25 Feb. 1722, proved 17 July 1725.

   sons: incl. John, buried 25 Jan. 1739 at Magherafelt, County Londonderry, = Mary Shannon[13]

Captain Hugh Rainey of Magherafelt, merchant and ironfounder, issued tokens 1671; attainted by James II 1689; ascribed escape from death by shipwreck to divine providence and endowed a charity school at Magherafelt; prerogative will dated 11 Apr. 1707, proved 9 May 1709.[14]

   daughter: Elizabeth = (1692) Thomas Ash, active at siege of Londonderry, high sheriff of County Londonderry 1694, alderman of Londonderry; she died aged 57 and was buried 11 Nov. 1728 at Magherafelt.[15]

executor of wills of uncle Hugh ECCLES, 1681, and James Stewart, merchant of Belfast, 1693.[16]

25

William SLOANE, merchant of Belfast and London

career: born 1658, served apprenticeship in Belfast, probably with Black George MACARTNEY who later employed him; freeman 1678; was in Portsmouth 1704–06, staying out of Ireland because of debts which were settled in 1708; said to have died worth 'upwards of £100,000'; grant of arms, 9 April 1726, died 1728.[1]

religion: uncertain

place of origin: born near Killyleagh, County Down, of Scottish family

property: held mortage and annuity on part of Donegall estate, and property in County Down.[2]

wife: (1682) Jane Hamilton, daughter of Alexander Hamilton of Killyleagh and probably niece of John HAMILTON of Belfast; they had marital problems in 1705–06,

12 Abstract of will of Jane Eccles (P.R.O.N.I., T581/6); Registry of Deeds, Dublin, 41 294 25978; Agnew, *Funeral register ... Belfast*, p.29.

13 Magherafelt parish register (P.R.O.N.I., MIC1/1); they were grandparents of Henry Joy, see note 1 above.

14 McCracken, *Irish woods*, p.92; Williamson, *Trade tokens*, ii, p.1406; King, *State of the protestants*, p.215, as 'Reamy'; copy will of Hugh Rainey (N.A., prerogative will book 1706–08, ff 212–4).

15 W.R. Young, *Fighters of Derry* (London, 1932), p.23; account of the Ash family by Thomas Ash (P.R.O.N.I., T989/1); his descendants attended Rainey's charity school.

16 Abstract of will of James Stewart, merchant of Belfast, 1693 (P.R.O.N.I., D1759/3B/1, p.71).

1 Sloane pedigree (P.R.O.N.I., T2974/3); Sloane pedigree (L.H.L., Blackwood, v, p.194); Macartney to Edmund Harrison, 22 Mar. 1678/9 (Macartney 2, p.38); Mountalexander to Hans Sloane, 4 Dec. 1706 (B.L., Sloane MS 4040, f.266); Macartney to Sloane, 17 Oct. 1705, (Macartney 3, pp 211–12); E. St. John Brooks, *Sir Hans Sloane, the great collector and his circle* (London, 1954), pp 31, 215; all subsequent information about Sloane's family is from the first two sources.

2 Papers concerning debts of third earl of Donegall (P.R.O., C106/95/15); Macartney to William Sloane, 19 Aug. 1706 (Macartney 3, pp 346–8); Donegall rental, 1719 (P.R.O.N.I., D2249/61, nos 249–54); Donegall minority accounts, pt 1, pp 5, 7.

and were living apart in 1708.[3]
children: William; Sarah, died 14 Sept. 1743, = (1 (19 Sept. 1706 at St Paul's, London) Sir Richard Fowler, died c.1731, = (2 Francis Annesley of the Inner Temple, M.P. for Westbury and Downpatrick.
father: Alexander Sloane, agent for the Hamiltons of Clanbrassil, probably royalist officer, died Nov. 1666.[4]
mother: Sarah, daughter of Rev. Dr Hicks, said to be chaplain to Archbishop Laud; she = (2 Captain John Bailie of Inishargy, County Down, as his second wife, he died 11 May 1687, she died 24 Feb. 1692.
brothers: James Sloane, barrister of Inner Temple, London, M.P. for Thetford, c.1655–1704, = Mary Rumbold, son Joseph; Sir Hans Sloane, 1660–1753.[5]
half-sister: Alice Bailie = (c.1700) John Elsmere/Elsmore, collector of customs at Belfast, died 1752.
step-brother: James Bailie of Inishargy
cousins: related to the Hamiltons of Killyleagh
wife's cousin: Anne HALTRIDGE = Isaac MACARTNEY
godsons: William Annesley, Lord Glerawley, son of Francis Annesley who became third husband of Sloane's daughter Sarah (above); William, son of Isaac MACARTNEY.

26

William SMITH, merchant and shipowner of Belfast
career: merchant stapler 1656, paid 40s; issued tokens 1657; assessed at £4 in subsidy roll of 1661, and £2 in 1666; had 2 hearths in 1666 and 9 in 1669; partner in iron works with George MACARTNEY of Auchinleck 1665; burgess of Glasgow 1673; prerogative will dated 12 May 1684, proved 24 July 1684, died worth at least £3,800, left £3 to poor of Belfast.[1]
religion: presbyterian
place of origin: Glasgow
first wife: Margaret WHYTE, died before 1674.
sons: Captain David Smith, merchant of Belfast, supercargo on *Olive Branch* to Danzig, 1680; probably master of the *Thomas*, 1680s; burgess in James II charter 1688; fled to Glasgow, attainted by James II, 1689; burgess 1690; sovereign 1698–99, and 1699–1700 (as deputy for Charles Chichester); he and his sons ran the sugar refinery in Belfast; partner in Belfast pottery from 1700, with brother Patrick, Thomas CRAFORD and Henry CHADS the younger; dead by 6 Aug. 1705.[2]
  religion: presbyterian, gave psalm book to Belfast meeting house 1705.[3]
  wife: Grissell CLUGSTON, his step-sister, her will dated 24 July 1721, buried

3 Copy marriage articles, 1682 (P.R.O.N.I., T1030/7–9); Macartney to Sloane, 17 Oct. 1705, 11 Feb. 1705/6, (Macartney 3, pp 211–12, 267–8); Brooks, op cit., p.31.
4 O'Hart, *Irish landed gentry*, p.406.
5 Macartney to Sloane, 27 Nov. 1704 (Macartney 3, pp 20–1); for Sir Hans Sloane's career, see entry in *D.N.B.*

1 Benn, pp 314–15, 458–9; letters from Macartney to Thomas Lewis, 25 Nov. 1661, to Thomas Wakefield, 4 Nov. 1665, to William Watt, 18 Apr. 1666, to John Moore, 23 July 1666, and to William Smith, 23 July 1666 (Macartney 1, pp 26–7, 260–1, 345, 393); J.R. Anderson (ed.), *The burgesses and guild-brethren of Glasgow, 1573–1750* (Edinburgh, 1925), p.196; abstract of will (N.A., Thrift 1544).
2 Macartney to John Paul, 15 May 1679 (Macartney 2, p.68); list of Belfast shipping, 1680s (*B.N.L.*, 24 May 1793); King, *State of the protestants*, p.227; Donegall minority accounts, pt 1, pp 3, 15, 18, 20, 26; Registry of Deeds, Dublin, 26 89 14738; *Town book*, p.195.
3 *Gen. synod Ulster rec.*, i, p.15; Benn, pp 458–59.

10 Jan. 1722.[4]

sons: John, merchant of Belfast, = (probably) Mary CRAFORD.

William, baptised 13 Oct. 1689 in Glasgow (witnesses, uncle Patrick Smith and John WHYTE), merchant of Belfast, buried 13 Oct. 1725.[5]

daughters incl.: Grissell = (1 William Magee, merchant of Dublin, and = (2 John WHITE of Whitehill, who was granted administration 20 Feb. 1731.

executors: wife, William CRAFORD and John CHALMERS[6]

executor, with brother, to will of uncle, Hugh WHYTE of London.[7]

Patrick Smith, merchant of Belfast, = Margaret Bennet; was in Glasgow 1689, partner in Belfast pottery 1700, dead by 1727.[8]

daughters: Janet = Thomas CRAFORD, Margaret = Archibald WHYTE of Dublin, Elizabeth = Matthew King.

second wife: (1674) Grissell Shaw, widow of John CLUGSTON, her will dated 30 May 1700, died c.1705.[9]

step-children: Robert CLUGSTON, and his sisters, Janet = William CRAFORD, Grissell = David SMITH (above); x = James YOUNG, x = Aitkin.

father: Robert Smith, burgess of Glasgow, dead by 1673.[10]

brothers: Robert, burgess of Glasgow 1654, merchant stapler of Belfast 1659, 3 hearths in 1666, 4 in 1669, Connor will dated 12 June 1671; (possibly) David, burgess of Glasgow 1645; Patrick, burgess of Glasgow 1655, = Jonet Shaw.[11]

brother-in-law: Hugh WHYTE, merchant and banker of London

apprentices: William Arthur and Ninian Hill

executors: wife Grissell, sons David and Patrick, John WHYTE of Belfast, merchant.

overseers: William CRAFORD and William Arthur, merchants of Belfast

witnesses to will: John Shaw, James Gemmill, Thomas CRAFORD

27

Thomas THEAKER, merchant of Belfast,

career: captain of foot, burgess, confirmation of arms 1644, sovereign 1643–44 when attempt was made by covenanting freemen to change constitution of Belfast; royalist officer; entrusted with money for use of Belfast poor 1647–54; sovereign 1654–55; was one of the jurors who assembled at Antrim in 1657 to enquire into the state of the churches in the county; died 12 March 1660, buried 14 March at St Audoen's, Dublin.

religion: Church of Ireland

place of origin: family presumably of English origin, armigerous.

property: Cullentree, Country Antrim[1]

4 Abstract of will of Grissell Smith (N.A., Crosslé abstracts, Smith viii, pp 978–79); Agnew, *Funeral register ... Belfast*, p.24.
5 Baptism, 13 Oct. 1689 (G.R.O.S., Glasgow O.P.R.); Agnew, *Funeral register ... Belfast*, p.31.
6 Registry of Deeds, Dublin, 14 56 5163.
7 Will of Hugh Whyte, 21 Feb. 1692 (P.R.O., PROB.11/409); abstracts of exchequer bills, 1701 (N.A., Crosslé abstracts, Smith viii, pp 893–9).
8 Baptism of son, 24 Sept. 1689 (G.R.O.S., Glasgow O.P.R.); copy will of James Martin (N.A., prerogative will book 1726–28, ff 192–7).
9 Abstract of will of William Smith (N.A., Thrift 1544); abstract of will of Grissell Clugston als Smith (N.A., Crosslé abstracts, Smith xxii, pp 14–15).
10 Anderson, op. cit., p.196.
11 Ibid., pp 117, 141, 143; abstract of will of Robert Smith (N.A., Crosslé abstracts, Smith x, p.1246); testament-dative of Patrick Smith (S.R.O., CC9/7/32); administration, 5 Nov. 1657, to William Smith, brother (N.A., Crosslé abstracts, Smith vii, p.761).

1 Assignment of mortgage, 1698 (P.R.O.N.I., Weir deeds, D298/2); notes (P.R.O.N.I., Brett deeds, D271/1); copy fee farm grant, 1619 (P.R.O.N.I., D1769/66/1B).

wife: Elizabeth, as widow was granted prerogative administration, 27 Feb. 1661.[2]
son: Sampson Theaker of Belfast and Armagh
  career: listed in poll tax returns in Armagh borough, 1660; with others, leased tolls and customs of markets and fairs at Armagh for 10 years at £5 p.a. with obligation to build market house at own expense before Michaelmas 1666;[3] merchant stapler of Belfast 1666; assessed at £2 on land at Belfast in subsidy roll, 1666; burgess 1681; dead by 7 Mar. 1692 when he was replaced as burgess; Connor administration bond, 26 Oct. 1695.[4]
  sons: Captain George Theaker, merchant of Belfast and Dublin, served apprenticeship with Hugh ECCLES, freeman 1674; in unspecified government service, fled to England, 1689, and claimed losses of £80 personal estate and £40 by office; will dated 7 Sept. 1690, proved 24 Nov. 1691, left £5 to poor of Belfast; buried 11 Nov. 1691 at St Audoen's, Dublin.[5]
    wife: Mary
    cousin: Rev. Thomas Theaker, son of Thomas Theaker (? brother of Sampson), born at Belfast c.1653, T.C.D. 1667, vicar of Rathmore, County Kildare, = (1 (1679) Hannah, daughter of Alderman Robert Arundell of Dublin, = (2 Elizabeth, who survived him; his will dated 7 July 1713.[6]
    overseers: Black George MACARTNEY, James Buller, tanner, and Rev. Thomas Theaker.
  Rev. Shelston Theaker, born c.1657 in County Armagh, T.C.D., freeman 1680, *gratis*; curate at Kilsallaghan from 1687; assigned property in Belfast and Cullentree to William BIGGER of Dublin, 1698.[7]
  Clements Theaker, alive in 1690.
father: George Theaker of Cullentree, and of Belfast, sovereign 1619–20.

28

Francis THETFORD, merchant of Belfast
career: freeman 1649; lands assessed at £3 in subsidy roll 1661, and £2 in 1666; had 2 hearths in 1666 and 1669; burgess 1665, sovereign 1681–82, died 23 May 1690.[1]
religion: Church of Ireland
place of origin: family presumably of English origin
property: Old Park, parish of Belfast[2]
(?) first wife: Anne, widow of Robert Forster (probably Robert Foster, sovereign of Belfast 1632–33, 1644–45, 1648–49, alive 1651), mother of Richard Forster.[3]

---

2 Draft ratification of arms, 2 Apr. 1644 (Geneal. Office, MS 85, f.146); examination of Thomas Theaker, 16 July 1644 (T.C.D., MS 838, ff 7–8); Benn, pp 108–10; notes by Benn (P.R.O.N.I., D3113/4/5); O'Hart, *Irish landed gentry*, p. 408; abstract of chancery bill, Theaker v. Chichester, 4 Nov. 1658 (P.R.O.N.I., T808/15018); *Town book*, pp 55, 67, 73; funeral entry (Geneal. Office, MS 76, f.34).
3 Copy rent roll of archbishopric of Armagh (P.R.O.N.I., T727, ii, p.107).
4 Benn, pp 147, 296, 315; Pender, *Census Ire.*, p.25; *Town book*, p.169 (date given, unamended, as 1691).
5 Claims of protestant refugees, 1689 (T.C.D., MS 847, f.8); Benn, pp 244–5; St Audoen's burial register (*Memorials of the dead*, xii, no.1 (1926), p.82* [sic]).
6 Benn, pp 244–5; Registry of Deeds, Dublin, 16 422 7876; marriage licence extract (P.R.O.N.I., Steele abstracts, T277, p.142).
7 Biographical succession lists for diocese of Dublin (P.R.O.N.I., Leslie papers, T1075/1, p.202).

1 Benn, pp 314–5; *Town book*, p.168.
2 Mentioned in lease, Lord Donegall to Sir Audley Mervyn, 19 July 1670 (P.R.O.N.I., Donegall leases, D509/24).
3 Abstract of chancery bill, 1677 (P.R.O.N.I., Society of Genealogists, T581/1, p.424).

(?) **second wife**: Ellen, buried 11 May 1667, at Lisburn.[4]
(?) **third wife**: Dorcas, buried ?4 Nov. 1750, = (2 (c.1693) James Gurner, born Belfast 1657, burgess 1707, sovereign 1713, 1716; their daughter, Dorcas Gurner, was born 1694, = (1721) Charles Lewis of Radnorshire.[5]
sons (of last marriage): Francis Thetford, merchant of Belfast, will dated 9 Nov. 1720.[6]
    wife: (1709) Jane, daughter of John Brown of Carrickfergus, merchant, and widow of John Buller, son of James Buller, tanner and burgess of Belfast.[7]
    sons: Francis, John, Edward, Nicholas
    executors: Thomas Banks, Joseph Innes, Robert Magee, Captain Edward Thetford.
Captain Edward Thetford, alive in 1720
father: Francis Thetford, the elder, dead by 1649;[8] intestate, administration to sons, 18 Nov. 1650.
brothers: John, merchant stapler 1644
Henry, joiner, freeman 1654, had 1 hearth in 1666, 5 in 1669, burgess 1677, died, and was replaced as burgess on 25 July 1678.
    wife: Ellinor, alive 1693, daughter of Nicholas Garnett of Belfast, chandler and churchwarden, his will dated 14 May 1668, proved 8 Aug. 1668.[9]
    sons: William, merchant, will dated 27 Aug. 1693, proved 1 Apr. 1701.[10]
Francis, farmer of Drumcree, County Armagh, alive 1713.[11]
Nicholas, merchant and tallow chandler, freeman of Carrickfergus, burgess of Belfast 1708, having refused election 29 Nov. 1707; died intestate 21 Feb. and was buried 23 Feb. 1722.[12]
    religion: Church of Ireland
    wife: Elinor, alive 1723
    sons: Rev. Nicholas, born c.1690, freeman 1723, Connor administration bond 1731; William, merchant, freeman 1723; Anthony, merchant, Connor administration bond 1733; Arthur, merchant and chandler, freeman 1723, burgess 1729, died, and was replaced as burgess 17 May 1733, Connor will 1730, = (1726) Esther, daughter of William Rogers, merchant of Belfast, her will dated 1 Jan. 1731, she was buried 3 Jan. 1731.[13]
    daughters: Anne = (1 Richard Robinson of Monaghan (his will dated 7 Sept. 1715), = (2 Rev. William Dowdall; Sarah = Henry Negans, (?) sugar baker of Belfast.[14]
    relations incl.: Rev. Nicholas Garnett; Rev. Matthew Garnett, curate of Belfast and vicar of Carnmoney; John and Ellinor Joy, died 1711.[15]
    witness to will of John HALTRIDGE
    (?) **administrator** to Martha, widow of Black George MACARTNEY

4 Blaris (Lisburn) parish register (P.R.O.N.I., T679/112).
5 Burial in Shankill (Belfast) parish register (P.R.O.N.I., T679/23); extracts from Lewis family bible (P.R.O.N.I., T937).
6 Macartney to Andrew Skeen, 15 Jan. 1704/5 (Macartney 3, p.38); abstract of will (P.R.O.N.I., Innis papers, T1514/10).
7 Copy marriage settlement, 28 May 1709 (P.R.O.N.I., T1514/4); Registry of Deeds, Dublin, 3 210 843.
8 *Town book*, p.253.
9 Will pedigrees, Garnett and Thetford (P.R.O.N.I., T559/3, p.85, T559/37, pp 247–8).
10 Will pedigrees (P.R.O.N.I., T559/37, pp 247–8).
11 Registry of Deeds, Dublin, 12 162 4693.
12 List of Carrickfergus freemen, late 1690s (P.R.O.N.I., Dobbs papers, D162/18); *Town book*, p.236; Registry of Deeds, Dublin, 34 116 20819; Agnew, *Funeral register ... Belfast*, p.25.
13 Will pedigrees (P.R.O.N.I., T559/37, pp 247–8); Registry of Deeds, Dublin, 41 39 24379, 44 463 30124 and 63 137 42968; Agnew, *Funeral register ... Belfast*, p.36.
14 Registry of Deeds, Dublin, 18 58 8336, 44 463 30124, and 49 528 33048.
15 Abstract of will of Eleanor Joy (P.R.O.N.I., T681, pp 311–12).

29
Lewis/Ludovick THOMPSON, merchant of Belfast
career: trading with Holland from Belfast in 1620s; factor at Belfast for Sir Christopher Lowther in 1630s; burgess of Belfast, sovereign 1631–2 and 1634–5; removed as burgess in 1642 for having been out of the kingdom for six years.[1]
religion: Church of Ireland
place of origin: Lower Germany, naturalized 1624[2]
son: Leonard Thompson, merchant, in Dublin in early 1630s, free stapler 1640, dead by 1655.
> **wife**: Margaret Foster (married 29 Aug. 1631 at St John's, Dublin).
> **son**: Lewis Thompson, merchant and shipowner of Belfast
>> **career**: baptised 25 Sept. 1632 at St John's, Dublin; (probably) freeman 1655, having served apprenticeship as saddler; assessed at £2 in subsidy roll of 1666, had 2 hearths in 1666, and 3 in 1669; in partnership with Thomas Owen(s), late 1670s, and involved in lawsuits against him; burgess 1678, sovereign 1682–3, 1696–7; petitioned Scottish privy council for return of gabarts pressed in Jacobite wars; died 11 Feb. 1708; intestate, administration granted to widow, 8 Mar. 1708.[3]
>> **property**: 48 acres in Ballysillan, County Antrim.[4]
>> **wife**: Anne, married by 1672, alive in 1709.[5]
> **daughter**: Margaret, baptised 24 Apr. 1635, at St John's, Dublin.
> **relation**: Lewis Thompson, master of the ship *Friends' Adventure*, in 1680s.[6]

30
Thomas WARING, merchant, tanner and shipowner of Belfast
career: probably settled in Belfast in early 1640s, free stapler 1643, burgess 1652, sovereign 1652–3, 1653–4, 1656–7, 1664–5, re-elected for 1665–6 but died in office; in poll tax returns of 1660; high sheriff of County Antrim 1663; died 23 Nov. 1665, buried in church of Belfast; prerogative will dated 2 Nov. 1665, proved 2 Jan. 1666, left £40 to poor.[1]
religion: Church of Ireland
place of origin: armigerous family from Lancashire, settled in County Antrim in early seventeenth century.[2]
property: he and son William acquired substantial leasehold property in Belfast including tan pits and plantation; leasehold property at Ballymena, County Antrim, and on Brownlow estate, near Lurgan, County Armagh.[3]

1 Scottish admiralty decreets, 13 Sept. 1628 (S.R.O., AC.7/1); statement by Cornelius Pietersz Werden about trade with Louijs Tomas of Belfast in 1629 (Municipal Archives, Amsterdam, Not. Arch. 842, notaris J.C. Hoogeboom; I am indebted to Rolf Loeber for this reference); Hainsworth, *Commercial papers of Sir Christopher Lowther*, pp 2–3, 42, 116, 137, 163; *Town book*, p.24.
2 Shaw, *Letters of denization*, p.330
3 James Mills (ed.), *The registers of St John the Evangelist, Dublin, 1619–99* (Dublin 1906), pp 20, 21, 25; Benn, p.315; *Town book*, pp 196, 254; Macartney to Cossart, 8 Mar., 5 May, 27 Dec. 1679, 2 June, 7 Aug. 1680 (Macartney 2, pp 34, 59, 210, 266, 303); letters from Thompson to Mme Marescoe and Jacob David, 1675–76 (P.R.O., C114/72(2):5, C114/73(1):6, C114/76(1):5, C114/76(2):6, C114/77(1):9); *Reg. privy council of Scotland*, xvi, pp 309–10.
4 Donegall rental, 1719 (P.R.O.N.I., D2249/61, no.182).
5 Registry of Deeds, Dublin, 13 445 6225; Donegall minority accounts, pt 1, pp 9, 11.
6 List of Belfast shipping, 1680s (*B.N.L.*, 24 May 1793).

1 Waring to Ormond, 14 Aug. 1663 (N.L.I., Ormond MS 2331, no.1740), this suggests he was sovereign in 1663 but see *Town book*, pp 35, 93, 241; Waring to Sir Richard Kennedy, 20 Sept. 1665 (Bodl., Carte MSS 34, f.397); copy will of Thomas Waring (N.A., prerogative will book 1664–84, ff 59–60); Benn, pp 206, 250–2.
2 Benn, p.249; Atkinson, *An Ulster parish*, p.153.
3 Copy leases, 1659, 1666, 1670 (N.A., Lodge's records of the rolls, vii, pp 429, 555); Benn, pp 283–4; lease for 21 years, Adair to Waring, 7 Oct. 1637 (P.R.O.N.I., Adair papers,

wife: Janet, alive 1665

sons: William, tanner and merchant of Belfast, in poll tax returns of 1660; assessed at £8 in subsidy roll 1661 and £5 in 1666 (both highest); had 4 hearths in 1666, 2 in 1669; freeman 1660 (as 'Warren'), burgess 1660, sovereign 1669–70, 1670–1; will dated 15 Apr. 1676, dead by 19 Oct. 1676 when he was replaced as burgess.[4]

    religion: Church of Ireland

    wife: Anne, alive 1670,[5] referred to his 'pretended wife' in will.

Roger, born at Belfast c.1643, educ. Lisnegarvey (Lisburn), entered T.C.D. 1658, B.A. 1664, D.D. 1684; received £500 under father's will and inherited brother's property; freeman of Belfast 1680; rector of Donaghcloney, archdeacon of Dromore; fled to England with family and was attainted by James II, 1699; will proved 23 July 1692, buried in Belfast church.[6]

    wife : (?1667[7]) Isabella, daughter of Peter Westenra, merchant of Dublin;

    she = (2 Robert Green, merchant of Belfast and agent for Donegall estate; his will dated 1 Oct. 1726, proved 5 Apr. 1727.

    children incl.: Jane, born 8 Oct. 1674, died 1720, (Swift's 'Varina').[8]

    Westenra, born 6 Oct. 1677, educ. Dulwich, T.C.D. 1692, arms confirmed 1706; active against presbyterians and non-jurors, high sheriff of County Antrim 1706, 1712, and of County Down 1713, M.P. for Randalstown 1713.[9]

    brother-in-law: Peter Westenra, M.P. for Athaboy

parents: John, tanner, of Toome and Derriaghy, = Mary, daughter of Thomas Peers, vicar of Derriaghy from 1634.[10]

brothers: John, tanner of Derriaghy, probably freeman of Belfast 1644.

William of Clanconnell, County Down, 1619–1703, high sheriff of County Down 1669, = (1 (1656) Elizabeth, daughter of William Gardiner of Londonderry, = (2 Jane Close of Lisburn; father, by second wife, of Brigadier Richard Waring, cousin of William and John LEATHES.[11]

apprentices: James Buller, John MOORE, John Roads, Richard Workeman

servant: Daniel Christian

witnesses to will: Edward Breres, Roger Waring

31

John WHITE/WHYTE, the younger, merchant of Belfast

career: merchant and shipowner of Belfast, refugee in Glasgow in 1689, Connor will dated Feb. 1712, died 1712.[1]

place of origin: family tradition is that Fulke White (below) came from Yorkshire

---

D929/HA12/F4/1/20); details of lease, 1652 (P.R.O.N.I., Brownlow lease book, T970, p.39).

4 Benn, pp 206, 250–1, 314–15.

5 Named as life in lease of 1670, see note 3 above.

6 J.B. Leslie and H.B. Swanzy (ed.), *Succession lists of the diocese of Dromore* (Belfast, 1933), pp 42–3; King, *State of the protestants*, p.227; claims of protestant refugees, 1689 (T.C.D., MS 847, f.9).

7 Macartney to Luke Hoare, 12 Mar. 1666/7 (Macartney 1, p.505).

8 Leslie and Swanzy, op. cit., p.43 ; Waring pedigree (L.H.L., Blackwood, vol. lxxviii).

9 Kirkpatrick, pp 472–4, 527; *Commons' jn. Ire.*, iii, p.114; Bernard Burke, *The general armory of England, Scotland, Ireland and Wales* (London, 1884), p.592; *Historic memorials*, p.55; and see note 8 above.

10 Benn, p.249; Atkinson, *An Ulster parish*, p.153; Leslie, *Clergy of Connor*, p.456; and see note 2 above.

11 Waring pedigree, containing some inaccurate information (P.R.O.N.I., Graham notes, T1289/14), and see note 10 above.

1 Baptism of son Hugh, 6 Aug. 1689 (G.R.O.S., Glasgow O.P.R.); abstract of will (T.C.D., Stewart Kennedy notebooks MS 2110, p.60); Donegall minority accounts, pt 1, p.20.

c.1650 and settled in County Antrim; however the careers and education in Scotland of Fulke and his son suggest the family was of Scottish origin, and the will of Margaret Kennedy (below) suggests a large family group in County Antrim by 1669.
religion: presbyterian
wife: (probably) Margaret MARTIN, but his widow was named Jennet.[2]
sons: Archibald, the younger, merchant of Dublin, will dated 25 Feb. 1734, proved 25 Nov 1735.[3]

> **wife**: Jane Smith, daughter of Andrew Smith of Dublin and niece of Alderman Thomas Bell of Dublin.[4]
> **brothers-in-law**: James Smith; John Smith, bookseller of Dublin; Dr Andrew Smith of Belfast = Elizabeth, daughter of John CHALMERS, merchant of Belfast; Charles Smith, merchant of Cork.[5]
> **uncle**: James MARTIN of Dublin[6]
> **relatives**: Timothy White, Hugh White of Dublin
> **administrator**: to Alderman Thomas Bell of Dublin[7]

Patrick, died 1727, father of Margaret = Carmichael.
David, of London, dead by 1726, father of David.
brothers: incl. Archibald, the elder, refugee in Glasgow 1689, settled in Dublin, freeman 1697, attended Capel Street meeting house but children buried at St Michan's.[8]

> **wife**: Margaret, daughter of William SMITH of Belfast
> **brothers-in-law**: David and Patrick SMITH; Thomas CRAFORD = Janet Smith; Matthew King = Elizabeth Smith.

Fulke, of Whitehall in County Antrim, presbyterian minister of Broughshane 1687–1716, buried 20 Aug. 1716, = (Feb. 1680) M. Hodson.[9]

> **son**: James, of Whitehall, presbyterian minister of Broughshane from 1716, died 24 Apr. 1761, = (?1 Jane McCullum, and = (2 Grissell Magee als SMITH.

sister: Jane = (1 (18 Oct. 1690) John Clarke of Maghera, County Londonderry, = (2 Alexander McCracken of Maghera, = (3 Andrew Ballagh.[10]
brother-in-law (probably): James MARTIN of Dublin.
cousin: James MARTIN of Belfast, will dated 1705.
overseer to will of John Clarke of Maghera, 1708.[11]
relations: Margaret Kennedy, Connor will 1669;[12] Catherine White = Robert MARTIN; David Whyte = Margaret, sister of John HAMILTON.
relation: John White the elder, merchant and shipowner of Belfast, probably merchant stapler 1670, paid £1; alive in 1678 when mentioned in will of George MARTIN.[13]

> **wife**: (probably) Janet Whyte

2 See note 1 above.
3 Abstract of will (N.A., Betham, B1/71).
4 Registry of Deeds, Dublin, 60 112 40113; and see note 3 above.
5 Will pedigree (P.R.O.N.I., T559/35, p.2); and see note 4 above.
6 Copy will, 4 Apr. 1726 (N.A., prerogative will book 1726–28, ff 192–7).
7 Registry of Deeds, Dublin, 22 384 12336.
8 Baptism of daughter Margaret, 20 Oct. 1689 (G.R.O.S., Glasgow O.P.R.); copy power of attorney, 1701 (P.R.O.N.I., T808/15306); Berry, *Registers of St Michan*, pp 452, 466; abstract of exchequer bill, White v. Smith, 1701 (N.A., Crosslé abstracts, Smith viii, pp 894–9).
9 Notes on White family (P.R.O.N.I., D2861/E/1); *Fasti*, p.83; Agnew, *Funeral register ... Belfast*, p.18; First Antrim presbyterian church, marriage register (P.R.O.N.I., MIC1P/3/1).
10 First Antrim presbyterian church, marriage registers (P.R.O.N.I., MIC1P/3/1); Young, *Fighters of Derry*, p.67; abstracts of wills and legal papers relating to Clarke family (PRONI, T808/9166–7).
11 See note 10 above.
12 Abstract of will, 1669 (P.R.O.N.I., Stewart Kennedy transcripts, T700, p.296).
13 Probably not the father of John White the younger; since no date of death has been found for this John White, it is impossible to distinguish their separate careers.

brother-in-law (and probably cousin): Hugh Whyte/White of London, merchant and banker, will dated 21 Feb. 1692, proved 22 July 1692; executors were nephews David and Patrick SMITH, Abraham Cary and David Strong of London.[14]

sisters-in-law: Margaret = William SMITH, merchant of Belfast; Anne = John Jones.

32
John YOUNG, merchant of Belfast

career: possibly freeman 1671; creditor of third earl of Donegall; prerogative will dated 29 Aug. 1722, proved 4 June 1724, buried 8 Dec. 1723.[1]

religion: presbyterian

place of origin: unknown, probably Scottish, family not in Belfast in hearth money roll of 1669.

property: townlands of Listooder, Ballydian, etc., County Down, purchased 1706–09 from trustees for sale of estates of Sir Hans Hamilton.[2]

wife: Mary, younger daughter of Rev. Andrew Hutcheson, presbyterian minister; she was buried 1 Sept. 1726.[3]

sons: incl. Alexander, intestate 1754, = (1726) Elizabeth, daughter of Robert LENNOX; Hugh, buried 16 Feb. 1734, intestate, administration granted 1735 to widow Anna; James = Jane Milliken.[4]

daughters: incl. Abigail = Robert Milliken

wife's brother: Rev. John Hutcheson, presbyterian minister at Downpatrick 1690–7, and at Armagh 1697–1729, will dated 26 Mar. 1728, proved 26 Apr. 1729.[5]

wife's sister: Beatrix = (24 May 1687) Hugh Wallace of Balliobikin and Ravara; she and her husband both died June 1716.[6]

relations (probably): James Young, merchant and shipowner, 1660s–70s; James Young, merchant of Belfast, freeman 1672 having served apprenticeship with George MACARTNEY, = daughter of John CLUGSTON the elder; Robert Young, merchant, probably freeman 1681, armigerous, prerogative will dated 16 Dec. 1693;[7] Thomas Young, merchant and shipowner of Belfast, freeman 1674, having served apprenticeship in Belfast, = Elizabeth Stewart of Antrim, 11 Feb. 1679;[8] David Young, freeman 1677, trading to Rouen in late 1670s, buried 3 Sept. 1715 by John Young.[9]

executors: son Alexander, Daniel Mussenden, William Stevenson of Ballymacarret.

witnesses to will: James Park, Thomas Sturgeon, both of Belfast

executor (possibly) to will of John MOORE

14 *Cal. S.P. dom., 1677–78*, p.4; will of Hugh Whyte (P.R.O., PROB.11/409); abstract of exchequer bill, Whyte v. Smith, 1701 (N.A., Crosslé abstracts, Smith viii, pp 893–9).

1 Papers relating to debts of third earl of Donegall (P.R.O., C106/95/15); Donegall minority accounts, pt 1, p.16; Registry of Deeds, Dublin, 39 433 26213; Agnew, *Funeral register ... Belfast*, p.28.
2 Conveyances, 1706, 1708 (P.R.O.N.I., Trevor estate papers, D778/32, 39, 42).
3 Hutcheson pedigree (L.H.L., Blackwood, i, p.196 et seq.); Agnew, *Funeral register ... Belfast*, p.32.
4 Registry of Deeds, Dublin, 58 191 39155–6 and 182 408 121350; Agnew, *Funeral register ... Belfast*, p.40.
5 Abstracts of Hutcheson wills (P.R.O.N.I., Stewart abstracts, D1759/3B/1, pp 36–40).
6 Agnew, *Funeral register ... Belfast*, p.18.
7 Will pedigree (P.R.O.N.I., T559/4, p.351).
8 First Antrim presbyterian church, marriage register (P.R.O.N.I., MIC1P/3/1).
9 Macartney to Peter Cossart, 27 Dec. 1679 (Macartney 2, p.210); Agnew, *Funeral register ... Belfast*, p.17.

Appendix B

PROFILES OF RELATED FAMILIES

I

John GALT, the elder, merchant of Coleraine
career: elected burgess of Coleraine, 22 Dec. 1676, but refused to take oath of supremacy, and again on 15 Apr. and 3 Aug. 1680; fine imposed for refusal; was burgess by 13 Sept. 1681; refused office of alderman, 28 Mar. 1684; alderman of Coleraine by 1691;[1] will dated 5 Feb. 1700, proved 2 Oct. 1700.[2]
place of origin: probably Irvine, Ayrshire[3]
religion: presbyterian[4]
first wife: Mary Hazlett, died 27 June 1697.[5]
son: John Galt the younger, born 1660 or 1666,[6] merchant of Coleraine, will dated 17 June 1715, proved 11 Dec. 1733.[7]

    religion: presbyterian
    first wife: Eliza, daughter of Samuel MARTIN, attorney of Dublin; born c.1666, died 13 Oct. 1696.[8]
    son: John, 'disobedient and extravagant' in 1717, 'married into a sober family' 1721.
    second wife: Sarah, daughter of William Moore of Garvey, married by 1702.[9]
    sons: William of Coleraine, merchant, will dated 10 Nov. 1759 proved 4 Jan. 1776; Richardson, dead by June 1727.
    daughters (dowries £300-£200): Mary = Hercules Heyland, Elizabeth = Hugh Bankhead, Lydia, Nancy = (probably) Samuel Smith the younger of Belfast.[10]
    cousins: Jane Patterson, John Hall, Nancy Hall als Vance, Adam Galt, Andrew Stewart.
    brothers-in-law: Colonel Robert McCausland of Fruit Hill = Hannah Moore; Robert Wilson = Elizabeth Moore; Matthew Cummine of Glasgow = Mary Moore; William Cairnes of Killyfaddy = Lydia Moore; Dominic Heyland.
    [11]executors: Samuel MARTIN, attorney of Dublin; Alderman James LENNOX of

1 Coleraine minutes, 1676-91.
2 Copy will of John Galt the elder (P.R.O.N.I., Given abstracts, D2096/1/15C).
3 *Muniments of the royal burgh of Irvine* (2 vols, Edinburgh, 1890-1), ii, p.88; Mullin, *Coleraine*, p.64.
4 See note 1 above.
5 Burke, *Landed gentry of Ireland* (1912), p.255.
6 Abstract of will of George Martin, 1678, and notes (T.C.D., Stewart Kennedy notebooks, MS 2116, p.64); and see note 5 above.
7 Copy will of John Galt the younger (P.R.O.N.I., D2096/1/15D); this is the main source of information about Galt's family and connections.
8 See notes 5 and 6 above.
9 Copy release, 29 June 1702 (P.R.O.N.I., Gaussen papers, D2315/1/8).
10 Smith pedigree (P.R.O.N.I., T2366/23).
11 Burke, op.cit., p.433; copy releases, 11 Oct. 1700, 1 May 1702 (P.R.O.N.I., D2315/1/5,7);

Londonderry; John Thompson, merchant of Coleraine; Robert McCausland of Fruit Hill; Patrick Smith and John RAINEY, merchants of Belfast.

overseers: John CHALMERS, merchant of Belfast; John Patterson, merchant of Coleraine; Dominick Heyland of Castleroe; Alderman Edward Brooke and Alexander Vance, merchants of Londonderry; Rev. Robert Higginbotham.

daughters: Mary = Gilbert Hall; Elizabeth = Alderman James LENNOX of Londonderry; x = John CHALMERS of Belfast; x = Alderman Edward Brooke of Londonderry; Eleanor = John RAINEY of Belfast.[12]

second wife: (settlement 15 Oct. 1697)[13] Lilias, probably daughter of Patrick Jordan of Castleroe, burgess of Coleraine (died July 1690), and his wife Catherine who (possibly) = (2 Dominic Heyland of Castleroe; Lilias = (2 Joseph BIGGER of Belfast.[14]

daughter (probably): Isabella

father: John Galt of Coleraine, called 'the elder' in Coleraine corporation minutes when he refused to take oath of supremacy, 24 Apr. 1673, admitted freeman 22 Jan. 1677.[15]

brother: William Galt, merchant of Coleraine, prerogative will dated 5 June 1678.[16]

brothers-in-law: [?Benjamin] Hill;[17] Rev. John Abernethy of Antrim, husband of Susanna Jordan, probably sister of second wife Lilias.[18]

executor of Rev. Thomas Fulton of Newtownlimavady, 1688.[19]

2

John HADDOCK of Belfast, merchant

career: sovereign 1640, Connor will 1643, who was presumably John Haddok, merchant and master of the *Neythgaill* of Belfast, trading to Glasgow in 1627.[1]

religion: descendants were members of the Church of Ireland

place of origin: possibly Glasgow where the name Haddock or Haddo is common.

son: Lieutenant James Haddock of Malone, freeman of Belfast 1641, royalist officer, died 18 Dec. 1657 and was buried at Drumbeg, prerogative will dated 18 Dec. 1657, proved 11 May 1658, overseers John Coslet and John Walsh; his ghost is said to have returned to protect his son's interests against his widow's second husband.[2]

> **wife**: Arminella (possibly Walsh), died 23 Mar. 1690/1?, = (2 (by 1662) ?Francis Davis.[3]

> **son**: John Haddock, gentleman of Carnbane, County Down

>> **career**: born post 1636 (a minor in 1657); merchant stapler of Belfast 1670, *gratis*; agent or receiver of rents for William Hill of Hillsborough; attainted by James II and fled to England in 1689; had personal estate to value of £6,000 in 'long and beneficial leases'; 'unperfected' will dated April 1706, led to exchequer

Memorials of the dead, xii, p.299.

12 Extracts from journal of William Rainey (L.H.L., Joy MSS, 10); Macartney to John Galt, 21 Feb. 1704/5 (Macartney 3, p.57); see also note 2 above.
13 See note 2 above.
14 Deed, 15 Jan. 1705 (P.R.O.N.I., Weir deeds, D298/3); Registry of Deeds, Dublin, 7 25 1571.
15 See note 1 above.
16 Abstract of will (P.R.O.N.I., D2096/1/15B).
17 Macartney to William Galt, 8 Oct. 1667 (Macartney 1, p.606); and see note 16 above.
18 Registry of Deeds, Dublin, 7 25 1571; Duchal, *Sermons of Rev. John Abernethy*, p.vi; see also note 2 above.
19 Will abstract (P.R.O.N.I., T808/4776).

1 J. D. Marwick and Robert Renwick (ed.), *Charters and other documents relating to the city of Glasgow*, ii, 1649-1707 (Glasgow, 1906), p.587.
2 Abstract of will, 1657 (P.R.O.N.I., T732/1); O'Hart, *Irish landed gentry*, p.390; *Gravestone inscription series*, County Down, iii, p.13; narrative of the Haddock ghost story (L.H.L., Joy MSS, 7, p.39); *U.J.A.*, 1st series, iii (1855), p.325 et seq.
3 *Gravestone inscription series*, County Down, iii, p.13.

lawsuit; buried in Blaris churchyard, 22 Jan. 1707.[4]
property: in Carnbane, Culcavy, Ballyardayne, Cloncavy, Ravernan etc. near
Hillsborough, County Down; Malone, Ballynafy, Ballydownfyne, Ballyogorman,
County Antrim.[5]
wife: Letitia, probably daughter of Francis Davis; she = (2 (as second wife,
settlement 20 Oct. 1713) Robert McMullan of Ballyrony, County Down.[6]
sons: incl. Roger Haddock of Carnbane and Belfast, baptised 2 Feb. 1683;
burgess 1708, sovereign 1710, 1711, 1712, resigned as burgess 14 Nov. 1713;
agent for Downshire estates; died intestate, Connor bond dated 1745.[7]
    wife: Elinor, daughter of William CRAFORD, merchant of Belfast
daughters: Arminella, baptised 20 Feb. 1685, = (11 Aug. 1703, at Lisburn)
John McMullan of Dublin, his prerogative will dated 1716, buried 10 Nov.
1716.
Penelope, baptised 21 June 1688, = (1713) John Vere, lieutenant in Lord
Orkney's regiment, both alive 1722.
Alice (dead by 1722) = Edward Studdard.[8]
brothers-in-law: William Redman of Blerismore, County Down; Michael
Jackson of Lisburn.
?uncle and trustee: John Coslet or Costlett
relations: Arminella, died 14 Nov. 1740 aged 68, = (1 St John Turnley of
Ballydollaghan, = (2 James Willson, clerk to John Haddock in 1706, later of
Purdysburn, died 21 Dec. 1741 aged 68;[9]
'Miss Haddock of Garnerabane' = Faustus Cuppage.[10]

3
William HALTRIDGE, merchant of Dromore
career: born c.1642; issued tokens at Dromore in 1668; made substantial loans
to gentry in 1680s; attainted 1689; died 18 April 1694 aged 52, buried inside
Dromore cathedral; will dated 4 Nov. 1691, proved 11 June 1694, left £5 to poor of
Dromore.[1]
place of origin: Scotland
religion: presbyterian
property: estates in Scotland, Counties Down and Armagh.[2]

4 Abstracts of Haddock wills, copy exchequer bill, copy legal papers (P.R.O.N.I., T732/1, 11, 14,
    23, 32); King, *State of the protestants*, p.214; claims of protestant refugees, 1689 (T.C.D., MS
    847, f.4); copy will of John Haddock (N.A., prerogative will book, 1706-08, ff 161-4); Blaris
    (Lisburn) parish register, 1666-1739 (P.R.O.N.I., T679/112).
5 Registry of Deeds, Dublin, 5 130 1430, 7 192 3496, 9 278 3633, 68 99 47179; Donegall
    minority accounts, pt 1, p.12.
6 Copy legal papers (P.R.O.N.I., T732/23); Registry of Deeds, Dublin, 68 99 47179.
7 John Haddock's children were baptised in Blaris (Lisburn) parish church (P.R.O.N.I.,
    T679/112); *Town book*, pp 210-11.
8 See note 4 above; Agnew, *Funeral register ... Belfast*, p.18.
9 *Gravestone inscription series*, County Down, iii, p.33; abstract of will of Joshua Turnley, 6 Nov.
    1704 (P.R.O.N.I., T732/12).
10 Burke, *Landed gentry of Ireland* (1912), p.156.

1 Gravestone inscription, at foot of chancel steps in Dromore cathedral; Williamson, *Trade tokens*,
    ii, p.1375; copy deed, 3 May 1692 (N.A., Lodge's records of the rolls, ix, pp 9-10); records of
    forfeiture commissioners (P.R.O.N.I., D1854/2/18, ff 125-6); Macartney to William Sloane,
    19 Aug. 1706 (Macartney 3, pp 346-8); King, *State of the protestants*, p.214; abstract of will
    (N.A., Crosslé abstracts, Haltridge, and P.R.O.N.I., D1759/3B/1, p.34).
2 Copy conveyance, 2 Nov. 1681 (N.A., Lodge's records of the rolls, viii, p.115, and P.R.O.N.I.,

wife: Elizabeth Hamilton, daughter of Hugh Hamilton of Lisbane, died 8 Oct. 1707, buried in Dromore cathedral.[3]

son: John, born c.1670, T.C.D. 1687, M.P. for Killyleagh 1703-25, high sheriff of County Down 1699, burgess of Belfast 1707, involved in expensive lawsuits for the recovery of his wife's dowry, died 4 Feb. 1725, buried 6 Feb. 1725; prerogative will dated 3 Mar. 1721, proved 30 Dec. 1726.[4]

    religion: Church of Ireland

    wife: (16 May 1699 at St Marie's, Dublin) Grace Sands; she = (2 Captain Russell, and = (3 Captain James Forrester of Dublin, and died 2 Jan. 1728.

    wife's parents: Sir William Sands of County Kildare (died 14 Aug. 1687) and Grace Thwaites who = (1 William Hawkins of Dublin, died 1680, and = (3 David Clarkson.[5]

    wife's half-brother: William Hawkins 1670-1736, Ulster king of arms, = Lettice, daughter of Hugh Ridgate and his wife Lettice Carney.

    executor: Isaac MACARTNEY

    witnesses to will: Nicholas THETFORD, Dr George Cromie[6]

daughters: Margaret (dowry £1,000) = John McDowell;[7] Anne (dowry £750) = Isaac MACARTNEY.

brothers: Alexander, merchant of Newry, County Down, will dated 18 Dec. 1679, proved 10 Mar 1680; John, born Scotland, M.A. Glasgow 1654, presbyterian minister at Ballycarry from 1672, died 1697; Matthew, M.A. Glasgow 1669, presbyterian minister at Ahoghill from 1676, died 20 Oct. 1705.[8]

executors: wife and son

overseers: Nicholas Atcheson of Market Hill, Matthew Studdert and Alexander Williamson

witnesses: Hugh Campbell and Robert Murdoch

4

Captain Edward HARRISON, gentleman, of Magheralave, Lisburn

career: born c.1644, T.C.D., member of Irish bar; merchant stapler 1669, *gratis*; high sheriff of County Armagh 1671, of County Antrim 1678; burgess of Belfast 1680; freeman of Carrickfergus; signatory to Antrim association, attainted and fled to England, lost £5,000 by Williamite wars; M.P. for Lisburn 1692-3, 1695-99; sovereign 1694-5; deputy governor of County Antrim 1699; died 12 Oct. and buried 13 Oct. 1700 at Lisburn; will dated 12 Sept. 1700, proved 24 Oct. 1700.[1]

religion: Church of Ireland

property: leasehold property at 'Marlea' (Magheralave), County Antrim, and Belfast;

T808/14939); see also note 1 above.

3 George Hamilton, *House of Hamilton* (Edinburgh, 1933), p.994.

4 Legal case papers (P.R.O.N.I., Ellison-Macartney papers, D3649/4); *Lords' jn. Ire.*, ii, pp 395-6; *Commons' jn. Ire.*, iv, pp 851-2; Agnew, *Funeral register ... Belfast*, p.30; copy will, 3 Mar. 1720/1 (N.A., prerogative will book 1726-28, ff 122-24).

5 Burke, *Landed gentry of Ireland* (1912), p.304.

6 See appendix A.19.

7 McKerlie, *Galloway*, i, p.67.

8 Macartney to William Cairnes, 22 Oct. 1705 (Macartney 3, p.217); Haltridge will abstracts and notes (N.A., Crosslé abstracts, Haltridge).

1 *Cal. S.P. dom., 1699-1700*, pp lix-lxi, 232, 393, *1700-02*, p.133; *Cal. S.P. Ire., 1669-70*, p.300; list of freemen of Carrickfergus, late 1690s (P.R.O.N.I., Dobbs papers, D162/18); Mackenzie, *Memorials*, p.62; King, *State of the protestants*, p.213; Blaris (Lisburn) parish register, which also contains baptisms of his children (P.R.O.N.I., T679/112); will pedigree (P.R.O.N.I., T559/23, p.55).

freehold property in Counties Armagh, Donegal, Tyrone and Down.[2]

wife: (1669, dowry £800) Johanna, daughter of Jeremy Taylor, bishop of Down and Connor; she was alive in 1706.[3]

sons incl.: Michael, baptised 15 July 1671, T.C.D., Middle Temple 1688, captain, probably high sheriff of County Antrim 1697, commissary general of Ireland, muster master general and clerk of the cheques 1700-09, freeman of Dublin 1702, M.P. for Lisburn 1703-09, burgess of Belfast 1705, died Apr. 1709, will dated 9 Dec. 1708, proved 1709.[4]

>**wife**: (1700) Mary daughter of James Vernon, secretary of state; her will dated 27 Sept 1728, proved 6 Nov. 1728.[5]

Francis, baptised 19 Apr. 1676, banker of Dublin in partnership with Benjamin Burton; M.P. for Knocktopher 1703-13, Lisburn 1713-14, County Carlow 1715-25; sheriff of County Dublin 1715, died 27 June 1725, had estate at Castlemartin, County Kildare.[6]

daughters: Ann, baptised 26 July 1677, = John Pacey, M.P.; Mary, baptised 15 July 1679, = (1 Benjamin Collumbine, = (2 (1721), Sir Cecil Wray.[7]

father: Michael Harrison of Marlea, aged c.45 in 1652, seneschal to Lord Conway; constable of Belfast castle 1664; had 4 hearths in Belfast in 1666, and 13 at Derriaghy, County Antrim, in 1669; freeman of Dublin 1665, water bailiff of Belfast 1674, will dated 16 Sept. 1681, buried at Lisburn, 6 Sept. 1683.[8]

mother: daughter of Theophilus Sandford of Moyclare, County Meath.

sisters: x = Thomas Conway, Alice = Roger Jackson.

uncles: Matthew Harrison, will dated 2 Aug. 1660, died 1667; John Parry of Devinagh, County Armagh (father's brother-in-law).[9]

father's cousin: Thomas Chambers of Armagh, will dated 6 Feb. 1663.[10]

brother-in-law: Francis Marsh, archbishop of Dublin, = Mary Taylor, half-sister of Johanna Taylor.

5

Brown George McCARTNEY, merchant and shipowner of Belfast

career: served apprenticeship in Belfast, freeman 1681; lived in Ayr 1689-90; merchant and shipowner; buried 13 July 1722.[1]

religion: presbyterian[2]

wife and executor: Jennet McCulloch, buried 4 Oct. 1730.[3]

sons: James, physician of Belfast, burgess 1715 (so member of Church of Ireland),

2 *Cal. S.P. dom., 1699-1700*, p.185.

3 Copy of marriage articles, 8 May 1669 (P.R.O.N.I., Clarke MSS, MIC92); Macartney to Johanna Harrison, 22 June 1706 (Macartney 3, p.325).

4 *Report on the MSS of the earl of Egmont* (2 vols, London, 1905, 1909), ii, p.235; and see note 1 above.

5 See note 1 above, and entry for Vernon in *D.N.B.*

6 Tenison, 'Old Dublin bankers', pp 36-8; copy will (N.A., prerogative will book, 1726-28, ff 61-2).

7 Pedigrees (P.R.O.N.I, Clarke papers, D1430/E/19, Falkiner papers, D3000/27/1).

8 O'Hart, *Irish landed gentry*, p.391; *Town book*, pp 120, 241; copy will (N.A., prerogative will book 1664-84, ff 446-47); and see note 1 above.

9 *Cal. S.P. Ire., 1666-69*, pp 425, 456.

10 Will pedigree (P.R.O.N.I., T559/15, p.145).

1 Marriage of servant, 10 Jan. 1690, (G.R.O.S., Ayr O.P.R.); Macartney to John Cunningham, 24 Feb. 1704/5, and to John Oneile, 18 Apr. 1706 (Macartney 3, pp 60-1, 298-9); Agnew, *Funeral register ... Belfast*, p.26.

2 *Gen. synod Ulster rec.*, i, p.159.

3 Agnew, *Funeral register ... Belfast*, p.36.

sovereign 1725-26, died in office, buried 15 Apr. 1726.[4]
George, merchant of Belfast and Dublin, alive 1728.[5]
    wife: (probably) Mary, daughter of Thomas KNOX of Belfast.
John, merchant of Belfast, buried 4 Jan. 1729, prerogative will dated 2 Jan. 1729, proved 19 Feb. 1729.[6]
    wife and executor: (1723) Elizabeth, daughter of Alexander Dallway, M.P. for Carrickfergus, and Anna Helena, daughter of Archibald Edmonston of Red Hall; alive in 1760.[7]
    wife's brothers: Robert Dallway, M.P. for Newry; Archibald Dallway, merchant of Dublin, died intestate, administration granted 17 Jan. 1725 to sister Elizabeth Mccartney.
    wife's sister: Lettice Dallway = John Hamilton of Ballyboy
    wife's aunts: Eleanor Dallway = Andrew Stewart of Castle Stewart; Anne Dallway = (1 Lieutenant Colonel Thomas Travers, = (2 (1715) Arthur Maxwell of the Drum, County Down, = (3 (1721) Rev. Samuel Halliday, presbyterian minister of Belfast.[8]
    overseers: John Gordon, merchant of Belfast, Francis Clements of Straid
    witnesses: Samuel Halliday, Conway Courtenay, John Cobham
David, born 20 May 1689 at Ayr; witnesses to baptism, Captain James Shaw and David CHALMERS.[9]
father: (possibly) James McCartney, merchant, freeman of Belfast 1674.
brother: (probably) James, lieutenant in Colonel St John's Regiment of Foot, prerogative will dated 22 May 1696, sisters: Mary and Margaret.[10]
executor (probably) to William CRAFORD, 1716, and David CHALMERS, 1719, and made inventory of goods of Martha MACARTNEY, 1705.

4 John McBride to Hans Sloane, 16 Jan. 1701/2 (B.L., Sloane MS 4038, f.288); Young, *Historical notices*, p.165; Agnew, *Funeral register ... Belfast*, p.31.
5 Copy will of John McCartney (N.A., prerogative will book 1728-29, f.157).
6 See note 5 above; Agnew, *Funeral register ... Belfast*, p.34.
7 M'Skimin, *Carrickfergus*, pp 395-7; abstracts of Dallway and Edmonston wills (P.R.O.N.I., T700, pp 111-13, 164).
8 Registry of Deeds, Dublin, 22 184 11739; James Hamilton Maxwell to Agmondisham Vesey, 18 Nov. 1721 (N.A., Sarsfield Vesey letters, 158); see also note 7 above.
9 Baptism, 25 May 1689 (G.R.O.S., Ayr O.P.R.).
10 Will pedigree (P.R.O.N.I., T559/3, p.319).

Appendix C

The fact that the first two Macartney letter books were written by Black George Macartney rather than George Macartney of Auchinleck is of little importance to the economic historian and does not, in any way, affect previous research using this source. However, for a study of the Belfast merchant community, it has been necessary to dismantle the composite figure created by George Benn in his *History of Belfast* and to distinguish the separate careers of the two Macartneys. Benn did not, himself, use the letter books but he contributed to the confusion between the two men which led to the letter books being wrongly attributed to George Macartney of Auchinleck.

The Macartneys themselves attempted to deal with this confusion by adopting a standard form of address to be used by their correspondents. Macartney of Auchinleck was invariably called 'George Macartney esquire' and Black George styled himself 'George Macartney merchant'. A passage in the second letter book, in a letter from Macartney to Humphrey Jervis of Dublin dated 18 December 1680[1] is the key to its authorship. Jervis, who was a business partner and friend of Black George had addressed his previous letter to him as 'George Macartney esquire'. Macartney replied: 'I pray you write me nothing but George Macartney merchant, for the sovereign's place or sheriff's is but for a year and then the esquire is gone, so I intend to continue as I was and will be after'.

The lists of sovereigns and burgesses in the town book are compilations written after the dates covered. The list of sovereigns says that George Macartney esquire was elected for the year ending Michaelmas 1676 and was then re-elected from year to year successively until the end of 1681. The list of burgesses says that he was sovereign in the years 1676, 77, 78, 79, 80 and that Francis Thetford was sovereign in 1681.[2] However, the

1 Macartney to Jervis, 18 December 1680 (Macartney 2, p.405).
2 *Town book*, pp 234, 242.

only reasonable explanation of the passage above is that the writer had just become sovereign and sheriff and did not intend to adopt the courtesy title of esquire for his year of office. A study of the actual signed transactions of the corporation makes it clear that George Macartney esquire was sovereign until Michaelmas 1680, that he was then succeeded by Black George, who was in turn succeeded by Francis Thetford at Michaelmas 1681. An independent confirmation that Black George became sovereign at Michaelmas 1680 occurs in a letter of 3 November 1680 from Sir George Rawdon to Lord Conway, commenting on the dear exchange on Conway's last bill: 'these Irish merchants being more needy than Black George, now Sovereign of Belfast'.[3] Black George was also high sheriff for County Antrim in the year 1681 but never assumed the style of esquire. George Macartney of Auchinleck on the other hand registered his coat of arms in February 1680[4] and would certainly not have entreated his correspondents not to address him as esquire.

The two letter books have been assumed, correctly, to be by the same man. The earlier letter book also contains proof that this man was Black George. In a letter of 28 June 1665 to Daniel Arthur of London he refers to 'one of my name who is a justice of the peace', a clear reference to Macartney of Auchinleck.[5]

The mistake in the list of sovereigns was spotted by Sir William Ellison-Macartney who proved that Black George Macartney (his own ancestor) rather than George Macartney esquire was responsible for the piping of Belfast's water supply in 1678-80.[6] Although Ellison-Macartney did not used the original town book he was able to deduce from the printed version that Benn had confused the two George Macartneys. Strain also distinguished correctly between the two men.[7] Neither, however, used the letter books of George Macartney so the wider implications of the identity of the sovereign from 1680-81 did not occur to them.

3 *Cal. S.P. dom, 1680-81*, p.76.
4 Confirmation of arms (P.R.O.N.I., D3000/109/1).
5 Macartney to Daniel Arthur, 28 June 1665 (Macartney 1, p.192)
6 Millin, *Additional sidelights*, p.85 et seq.
7 Strain, *Belfast and its Charitable Society*, p.9.

Appendix D

The town book includes lists of burgesses and sovereigns. These were probably written towards the end of the seventeenth century and contain some errors, particularly of sovereign years. The sovereign was elected on 24 June and held office for a year from the following Michaelmas. This has led to confusion as the lists sometimes give the year of appointment, and sometimes the year in which the greater part of the sovereign's term fell. The information in the lists has been compared with the freemen's roll, which names the sovereign for most years, and, where they differ, the latter has been followed in the table below. Matters are further confused by the fact that although old style dating was used in the town book, R. M. Young assumed that the town clerks started the year on 1 January, as was the practice in Scotland at that date, and has occasionally re-arranged items which were, as he thought, out of chronological order.

The list overleaf shows the name and occupation of each burgess, his family's place of origin, and his religion. It gives the year in which he was elected burgess, with the name of the burgess whom he replaced, and also the year in which he ceased to be burgess, with the name of his replacement. Since burgess-ships were for life, most burgesses died in the latter year. A few resigned and they have been distinguished by an asterisk * for those who resigned voluntarily, and a dagger † for those who were forced to resign.

BURGESSES AND SOVEREIGNS 1660–1790

name and occupation	origin	religion	replaced	years as burgess	replaced by	terms as sovereign
Edward BRICE, merchant	Scottish	presbyn	Thomas Knox, 1697	10	1707† Edward Wilson	
James BULLER, tanner	unknown	presbyn	Thomas Walcot, 1690	13	1793 Neil McNeill	
David BUTLE, merchant	Scottish	presbyn	Edward Harrison, 1700	14	1707† George Portis	1702–3, 1702–4
John CHALMERS, merchant	Scottish	presbyn	John Leathes jun, 1693	14	1707/8† Roger Haddock	1701–2
Charles CHICHESTER, gentleman	English	CI	Lord Donegall, 1697	4	1701 Isaac McCartney	1699–1700
John I. CHICHESTER, gentleman	English	CI	William Lockhart, 1698	?23	?1721 John Clugston	1711–2
John CHICHESTER jun., child of 6	English	CI	Arthur Macartney, 1706	1	1707† James Gurner	
William CRAFORD, merchant	Scottish	presbyn	John Hamilton, 1687	20	1707† Nathaniel Byrtt	1692–3, 1693–4
John DAVIES, merchant	English	CI	Lewis Thompson sen. 1642	25	1667 Hugh Eccles	
Hugh DOAKE, merchant	Scottish	presbyn	John Haddock, 1645	24	1669 Robert Leathes	1647–8
third earl of DONEGALL	English	CI	Sampson Theaker, 1692	5	1697* Charles Chichester	1697–8
Hugh ECCLES, merchant	Scottish	presbyn	John Davis, 1667	14	1681 Sampson Theaker	1674–5
John HAMILTON, merchant	Scottish	CI	George Martin, 1678	9	1687 William Craford	1683–4, 1684–5
Edward HARRISON, gentleman	English	CI	Sir Hercules Langford, 1680	20	1700 David Butle	1694–5
Michael HARRISON, gentleman	English	CI	David Smith, 1705	4	1709 Major George Macartney	
Thomas KNOX, merchant	Scottish	CI	Gilbert Wye, 1680	17	1697* Edward Brice	1685–6
Sir Hercules LANGFORD, gentleman	Scottish	presbyn	John Ridgby, 1669	11	1680* Edward Harrison	
John LEATHES sen., merchant	English	CI	elected in or before 1634	33	1667 Henry Thetford	1638–9, 1655–6
John LEATHES jun., merchant	English	CI	Thomas Stephenson, 1646	47	1693 John Chalmers	1686–7, 1688–9, 1689–90, 1696–7,1713–4
Robert LEATHES, Donegall agent	English	CI	Hugh Doake, 1669	48	1717 John Carpenter	1645–6, 1657–60
William LEATHES, merchant	English	CI	John Wassher, 1642	18	1660 Thomas Walcot	
William LOCKHART, merchant	Scottish	presbyn	John Tooley, 1687	11	1698 John I. Chichester	1690–1
Arthur MACARTNEY, merchant	Scottish	presbyn	George Macartney, 1691	15	1706 John Chichester jun.	
George MACARTNEY, merchant	Scottish	CI	John Ash, 1659	32	1691 Arthur Macartney	1662–3, 1663–4, 1675–6, 1676–7, 1677–8, 1678–9, 1679–80
Black George MACARTNEY, merchant	Scottish	CI/presbyn	Francis Meeke, 1665	37	1702 George Macartney	1672–3, 1673–4, 1680–1, 1700–1
George MACARTNEY, gentleman	Scottish	CI	Black George Macartney, 1702	55	1757 John Ludford	1704–5, 1705–6, 1706–7, 1707–8
Isaac MACARTNEY, merchant	Scottish	presbyn	Charles Chichester, 1701	6	1707* John Haltridge	1691–2
James MACARTNEY, lawyer	Scottish	CI	William Waring, 1676	39	1715* Edward Clements	
Neil McNEILL, doctor	Scottish	presbyn	James Buller, 1793	4	1707† Henry Ellis	
George MARTIN, merchant	unknown	presbyn	Henry Le Squyre, 1645	33	1678† John Hamilton	1649–50

name and occupation	origin	religion	replaced	years as burgess	replaced by	terms as sovereign
Francis MEEKE, Donegall agent	unknown	unknown	Richard Gately, 1657	8	1665 Black George Macartney	1660–1
Edward REYNELLS, gentleman	English	CI	? John Mitchell, 1660	22	1682 John Tooley	1665–6, 1666–7
John RIDGBY, tanner	English	CI	Thomas Hannington, 1655	14	1669 Sir Hercules Langford	1661–2
David SMITH, merchant	Scottish	presbyn	Francis Thetford, 1690	15	1705 Michael Harrison	1698–9
Sampson THEAKER, gentleman	English	CI	Hugh Eccles, 1681	11	1692 Lord Donegall	
Francis THETFORD, merchant	English	CI	Thomas Waring, 1665	25	1690, David Smith	1681–2
Henry THETFORD, joiner	English	CI	John Leather sen, 1677	1	1678 Lewis Thompson	
Lewis THOMPSON, merchant	Dutch/Flemish	CI	Henry Thetford, 1678	30	1708 Nicholas Thetford	1682–3, 1695–6
John TOOLEY, apothecary	English	CI	Edward Reynells, 1682	5	1687 William Lockhart	
Thomas WALCOT, gentleman	English	CI	William Leathes, 1660	30	1690 James Buller	1671–2
Thomas WARING, tanner/merchant 1664–5, 1665–(6)	English	CI	Robert Foster, 1652	13	1665 Francis Thetford	1652–3, 1656–7,
William WARING, tanner/merchant	English	CI	Thomas Theaker, 1660	16	1677 James Macartney	1669–70, 1670–1
Gilbert WYE, Donegall agent	English	CI	Walterhouse Crymble, 1662	18	1686* Thomas Knox	

Index